# VARRO THE AGRONOMIST

# VARRO THE AGRONOMIST

Political Philosophy, Satire,
and Agriculture in the Late Republic

## GRANT A. NELSESTUEN

THE OHIO STATE UNIVERSITY PRESS • COLUMBUS

Library of Congress Cataloging-in-Publication Data
Nelsestuen, Grant A., 1979– author.
 Varro the agronomist : political philosophy, satire, and agriculture in the late Republic / Grant A. Nelsestuen.
       pages cm
 Includes bibliographical references and index.
 ISBN 978-0-8142-1291-2 (cloth : alk. paper)
 1. Varro, Marcus Terentius. Rerum rusticarum libri tres. 2. Political science—Rome—Philosophy. 3. Satire, Latin—History and criticism. 4. Agriculture, Ancient—Rome. I. Title.
 PA6792.A4N45 2015
 630.937—dc23
                              2015017403

Cover design by Laurence J. Nozik
Text design by Juliet Williams
Type set in Adobe Minion Pro
Printed by Thomson-Shore, Inc.

9  8  7  6  5  4  3  2  1

# CONTENTS

# ABBREVIATIONS

## REFERENCE WORKS

*EAH*    R. S. Bagnall, K. Brodersen, C. B. Champion, A. Erskine, and S. R. Huebner (Eds.). (2013). *The Encyclopedia of Ancient History*. Malden, MA: Wiley-Blackwell.

*IGRom.*    (1906–). *Inscriptiones Graecae ad res Romanas pertinentes*. Paris: E. Leroux.

*LSJ*    Liddell, H. G., R. Scott, and H. S. Jones. (1940). *Greek-English Lexicon*. Ninth Edition. Oxford: Clarendon Press.

*MRR*    Broughton, T. R. S. (1952). *The Magistrates of the Roman Republic*. New York: American Philological Association.

*OCD3*    S. Hornblower and A. Spawforth (Eds.). (1996). *The Oxford Classical Dictionary*. 3rd Edition. Oxford: Oxford University Press.

*OCD4*    S. Hornblower, A. Spawforth, and E. Eidinow (Eds.). (2012). *The Oxford Classical Dictionary*. 4th Edition. Oxford: Oxford University Press.

*OLD*    Glare, P. G. W. (Ed.). (1982). *Oxford Latin Dictionary*. Oxford: Oxford University Press.

*L&S*    Lewis, C. T. and C. Short. (1879). *A Latin Dictionary*. Oxford: Clarendon Press.

*SIG*    Dittenberger, W. (1915–24). *Sylloge Inscriptionum Graecarum*. 3rd Edition. Lipsiae: S. Hirzelius.

*TLL*    (1900–). *Thesaurus Linguae Latinae*. Lipsiae: Teubner.

# ANCIENT AUTHORS

| | |
|---|---|
| *Anth. Pal.* | *Anthologia Palatina* |
| App. | Appian |
| *B. Civ.* | *Bella Civilia* |
| *Mith.* | *Mithradateios* |
| Arist. | Aristotle |
| *Pol.* | *Politica* |
| Augustus | Augustus |
| *RG* | *Res Gestae* (or *Monumentum Ancyranum*) |
| August. | Augustine |
| *De Civ. D.* | *De Civitate Dei* |
| Aul. Gell. | Aulus Gellius |
| *NA* | *Noctes Atticae* |
| Caes. | Caesar |
| *BCiv.* | *Bellum Civile* |
| *BGall.* | *Bellum Gallicum* |
| Cato | Cato |
| *Agr.* | *De Agri Cultura* or *De Re Rustica* |
| *Orig.* | *Origines* |
| Charisius | Charisius |
| *Gramm.* | *Ars Grammatica* |
| Cic. | Cicero (M. Tullius) |
| *Acad.* | *Academicae Quaestiones* |
| *Att.* | *Epistulae ad Atticum* |
| *Balb.* | *Pro Balbo* |
| *Brut.* | *Brutus* or *De Claris Oratoribus* |
| *Caecin.* | *Pro Caecina* |
| *Cat.* | *In Catilinam* |
| *Clu.* | *Pro Cluentio* |
| *De Or.* | *De Oratore* |
| *Div.* | *De Divinatione* |
| *Dom.* | *De Domo Sua* |
| *Fam.* | *Epistulae ad Familiares* |
| *Fin.* | *De Finibus* |
| *Leg.* | *De Legibus* |
| *Leg. Agr.* | *De Lege Agraria* |
| *Leg. Man.* | *Pro Lege Manilia* or *De Imperio Cn. Pompeii* |
| *Nat. D.* | *De Natura Deorum* |
| *Off.* | *De Officiis* |

| | |
|---|---|
| *Phil.* | *Orationes Philippicae* |
| *Q. Fr.* | *Epistulae ad Quintum Fratrem* |
| *Rep.* | *De Re Publica* |
| *Rosc. Am.* | *Pro Sexto Roscio Amerino* |
| *Sen.* | *De Senectute* |
| *Sest.* | *Pro Sestio* |
| *Tusc.* | *Tusculanae Disputationes* |
| *Verr.* | *In Verrem* |
| Columella, *Rust.* | Columella, *Res Rusticae* |
| *Dig.* | *Digesta* |
| Dio Cass. | Dio Cassius |
| Diog. Laert. | Diogenes Laertius |
| Diom. | Diomedes Grammaticus |
| Dion. Hal. | Dionysius Halicarnassensis |
| *Ant. Rom.* | *Antiquitates Romanae* |
| Eutr. | Eutropius |
| Flor. | L. Annaeus Florus |
| Frontin. | Frontinus |
| *Str.* | *Strategemata* |
| Hom. | Homer |
| *Il.* | *Iliad* |
| *Od.* | *Odyssey* |
| Hor. | Horace |
| *Ars P.* | *Ars Poetica* |
| *Carm.* | *Carmina* or *Odes* |
| *Sat.* | *Satirae* or *Sermones* |
| Hdt. | Herodotus |
| Isid. | Isidorus |
| *Etym.* | *Etymologiae* |
| Juv. | Juvenal |
| Livy, *Per.* | Livy, *Periochae* |
| Macrob. | Macrobius |
| *Sat.* | *Saturnalia* |

| | |
|---|---|
| Non. | Nonius |
| Oros. | Orosius |
| Ov. | Ovid |
| *Fast.* | *Fasti* |
| Pers. | Persius |
| Pl. | Plato |
| *Resp.* | *Respublica* |
| Plaut. | Plautus |
| *Asin.* | *Asinaria* |
| *Rud.* | *Rudens* |
| Plin. | Pliny (the Elder) |
| *HN* | *Naturalis Historia* |
| Plut. | Plutarch |
| *Mor.* | *Moralia* |
| *De Alex. Fort.* | *De Fortuna Alexandri* |
| *Vit.* | *Vitae Parallelae* |
| *Caes.* | *Caesar* |
| *Cic.* | *Cicero* |
| *Crass.* | *Crassus* |
| *Flam.* | *Flamininus* |
| *Pomp.* | *Pompeius* |
| Polyb. | Polybius |
| Prop. | Propertius |
| Ptol. | Ptolemaeus Mathematicus |
| *Geog.* | *Geographia* |
| Quint. | Quintilian |
| *Inst.* | *Institutio Oratoria* |
| *Rhet. Her.* | *Rhetorica ad Herennium* |
| Sall. | Sallust |
| *Cat.* | *Bellum Catilinae* or *De Catilinae Coniuratione* |
| Sen. | Seneca |
| *Ben.* | *De Beneficiis* |
| *Ep.* | *Epistulae* |

| Serv. | Servius |
|---|---|
| *ad Aen.* | *In Vergilii Aeneidem Commentarii* |
| *ad Georg.* | *In Vergilii Georgica Commentarii* |
| | |
| Suet. | Suetonius |
| *Aug.* | *Divus Augustus* |
| *Iul.* | *Divus Iulius* |
| | |
| Tac. | Tacitus |
| *Ann.* | *Annales* |
| | |
| Ter. | Terence |
| *Phorm.* | *Phormio* |
| | |
| Theoc. | Theocritus |
| *Id.* | *Idylls* |
| | |
| Theophr. | Theophrastus |
| *Caus. Pl.* | *De Causis Plantarum* |
| *Hist. Pl.* | *Historia Plantarum* |
| | |
| Thuc. | Thucydides |
| | |
| Tib. | Tibullus |
| | |
| Val. Max. | Valerius Maximus |
| | |
| Varro | Varro (M. Terentius) |
| *ARD* | *Antiquitates Rerum Divinarum* |
| *ARH* | *Antiquitates Rerum Humanarum* |
| *Ling.* | *De Lingua Latina* |
| *RR* | *De Re Rustica* |
| *Sat. Men.* | *Saturae Menippeae* |
| | |
| Vell. Pat. | Velleius Paterculus |
| | |
| Verg. | Vergil |
| *Aen.* | *Aeneid* |
| *Ecl.* | *Eclogues* |
| *G.* | *Georgica* |
| | |
| Vitr. | Vitruvius |
| *De Arch.* | *De Architectura* |
| | |
| Xen. | Xenophon |
| *Mem.* | *Memorabilia* |
| *Oec.* | *Oeconomicus* |

# ACKNOWLEDGMENTS

THE SEEDS of this book were sown in the doctoral dissertation I completed at the University of Texas at Austin in 2008. Various conversations with Jen Ebbeler, Larry Kim, Gwyn Morgan, Steve White, and Emma Dench (who served as an external reader) all benefited that work and helped to shape its future direction, but special thanks must go to Andrew Riggsby for his quiet ability to prod his students into looking at the familiar in new and productive ways as well as for his moral support. Austin is a city known for its conviviality, and it would be remiss of me to omit mention of the time spent in a variety of venues—academic or otherwise—with Marquis Berrey, Shrita Gajendragadkar, Keith Kitchen, Steve Lundy, Jess Miner, Wolfgang Polleichtner, and Luis Salas.

Outside that time in Austin, a prior stint at the University of Michigan–Ann Arbor played a formative role in my approach to classical literature and the ancient world, and particular thanks go to Ben Acosta-Hughes, Sarah Ahbel-Rappe, Don Cameron, Basil Dufallo, Ray Van Dam, and the late Traianos Gagos. A brief, post-Austin gig at Trinity University in San Antonio served as fertile ground for the germinating book and my colleagues there—especially Erwin Cook, Tom Jenkins, and Tim O'Sullivan—deserve special mention as well.

Over the past five years, I have been blessed to enjoy the support of wonderful colleagues at the University of Wisconsin–Madison, and I am especially indebted to the guidance of William Aylward, Jeff Beneker, Dan Kapust, Laura McClure, and Patricia Rosenmeyer. Will Brockliss provided valuable comments on a couple of chapters at a crucial moment, while conversations with Mustafa Emirbayer and Larry Nesper were important in a number of subtle ways. Alex Dressler read drafts of several chapters, but it is undoubtedly his uncanny knack for stimulating conversation that was most helpful and kept me invigorated throughout the process of writing this book.

For better or for worse, material considerations necessarily factor into the production of any project, and well-timed funding from the University of Wisconsin's Graduate School and, above all, a Loeb Classical Library Foundation Fellowship in 2013–14 afforded me the necessary *otium* for putting the finishing touches on the book.

Portions of chapters were delivered to gracious audiences at the American Philological Association, Durham University, the Midwestern Political Science Association, and the Universities of Iowa and Wisconsin.

I am also particularly indebted to Phil Horky for his inestimable friendship and guidance over the years. In addition to reading various drafts of the entire manuscript, he has provided more encouragement than any friend could reasonably ask for.

I would also like to thank Eugene O'Connor of the Ohio State University Press for his invaluable help and impeccable support throughout the publication process. The Press's readers, Robert Rodgers and Thomas Habinek, provided detailed and immeasurably helpful comments on the manuscript. Answering their criticisms has made the book much stronger.

On a personal level, I have been blessed with the support of my parents, Rod and Diane, and siblings, Erik and Kathryn. Numerous friends also played various roles as sounding boards for ideas and as occasional outlets for the venting of those anxieties inevitably attendant to the composition of a first book; particularly deserving of thanks are Andy Benson, Brent Berger, Eric Buras, Jon Crawford, Jacob Gullick, Leif Olsen, Andrew Riskin, Jim Schaaf, and Greg White.

Above all, however, it is my wife, Nina, whose love, patience, and support have meant more to me than she could imagine and who shepherded me through the completion of this project. I dedicate this book to her.

# INTRODUCTION

# From One Country House to Another

Οὐάρρων δὲ ἦν φιλόσοφός τε καὶ ἱστορίας συγγραφεύς, ἐστρατευμένος τε καλῶς καὶ ἐστρατηγηκώς, καὶ ἴσως διὰ ταῦτα ὡς ἐχθρὸς μοναρχίας προυγράφη. φιλοτιμουμένων δὲ αὐτὸν ὑποδέξασθαι τῶν γνωρίμων καὶ διεριζόντων ἐς ἀλλήλους, Καληνὸς ἐξενίκησε καὶ εἶχεν ἐν ἐπαύλει, ἔνθα Ἀντώνιος, ὅτε διοδεύοι, κατήγετο· καὶ τὸν Οὐάρρωνα οὐδεὶς ἔνδον ὄντα ἐνέφηνε θεράπων, οὔτε αὐτοῦ Οὐάρρωνος οὔτε Καληνοῦ.

Varro was a philosopher and a historian, a fine soldier and a fine general, and perhaps for these reasons was proscribed as an enemy to monarchy. His intimates were ambitiously seeking to take him in and contending with one another to do so, [but Q. Fufius] Calenus won out and kept him in a country house, where Antony used to stop when he would travel. Yet no slave of Varro himself or of Calenus revealed his presence.

—Appian, *Bella Civilia* 4.6.47

THE LONG and remarkable life of Marcus Terentius Varro (b. 116 BC, d. 27) nearly came to an untimely end in 43 BC when the Roman statesman and intellectual became another one of those proscribed by the Triumvirate of Octavian, Lepidus, and Mark Antony. Amidst all that civil carnage, in which prior domestic and social relations often ceased to matter, Varro found salvation in the form of refuge at the "country house" (ἔπαυλις) of his friend, Q.

Fufius Calenus.[1] To be sure, Varro was not alone in his escape from death, and his survival in what was probably a villa or, less likely, one of its actual work buildings, was not unique.[2] Yet, Appian's brief vignette of the man from Reate, who was both a "philosopher and historian" (φιλόσοφός τε καὶ ἱστορίας συγγραφεύς) and "a fine soldier and fine general" (ἐστρατευμένος τε καλῶς καὶ ἐστρατηγηκώς), is rife with irony and paradox: the "ambitious strivings" (φιλοτιμουμένων) of his friends were directed towards *not* the personal gain from the bounty placed on the head of this doubly distinguished individual, but the honor of housing him in his time of need and at their own peril; not one of the slaves of either Varro or Calenus ended up revealing the subter-fuge; and, unlike so many other competitions (cf. διεριζόντων) in Roman Italy of 43 BC, the victor who "prevailed" (ἐξενίκησε) won the privilege of hiding him in a "country house" that Antony apparently liked to frequent.

The present book is about another "country house" that mattered to Varro: the Roman agricultural estate (*praedium*). What exactly transpired for the man in the six years between his brush with death and the composition of *De Re Rustica* (*RR*), an agricultural treatise written in the form of a philosophical and satirical dialogue, is largely lost to the travails of history.[3]

1. For Q. Fufius Calenus, who (among other things) defended Clodius in the *Bona Dea* Scandal in 61, was a partisan of Caesar and Antony, and died in Gaul in 40 at the head of eleven legions that were soon transferred to Octavian, see Syme (1939) s.v. *Q. Fufius Calenus*. On the basis of this passage from Appian, Osgood (2006) 208–9 suggests that Calenus actually had Antony's permission to shelter Varro. For Varro's works, *Calenus* and *Epistola ad Fufium*, which may corroborate their friendship, see *idem* n. 32.

2. Originally denoting a "steading" for animals and/or their keepers (e.g., Hdt. 1.111, Polyb. 5.35.13), ἔπαυλις appears to have come to denote a "farm building" or a "country house" by the late Hellenistic and imperial periods per its lemma in LSJ, which cites Diodorus Siculus 12.43 and Plutarch's *Life of Pompey* 24 as examples. The context of the latter example makes clear that it is "villas" that are being denoted, while the former probably denotes spaces intended for work (and not necessarily habitation). Perhaps the potential slippage stems in part from the "problems" with the terminology of the Roman "villa"; see n. 8 in chapter 6. In any case, that the voluptuary Antony liked to stay there strongly suggests that it is a "villa" to which Appian refers. For the proscriptions, see App. *B. Civ.* 4.1–51 and Dio Cass. 47.1–17; and for scholarly discussions, see Syme (1939) 187–201; Hinard (1985); Gowing (1992); and Osgood (2006) 64–81.

3. On the basis of scant evidence and often by way of inference, this period is usually seen as a period of intense scholarly activity, in which Varro composed (among other works) *De Gente Populi Romani, De Familiis Troianis,* and *De Vita Populi Romani,* all in 43; possibly the *Logistorici* in 40; and the *Hebdomades* in 39. Those dates are the ones given by Dahlmann (1935) 1172–77, who frequently follows the magisterial work of Cichorius (1922) 189–241. See also Cardauns (2001) 9–13 and Morgan (1974) 117–28. As for other activities, Osgood (2006) 252 intriguingly speculates that Varro may have helped Asinius Pollio establish Rome's first public library in the latter's manubial renovation of the Atrium Libertatis. Unfortunately, the sources (especially Suet. *Aug.* 29.5 and Pliny *HN* 7.115) do not provide concrete dates; the project's *terminus post quem* is 39 on the basis of his triumph, but the state of its progress

But what Varro tells us in 37 BC is that his wife, Fundania, has recently purchased an estate for which she will surely need agronomical instruction once the now-elderly 80-year-old has passed from this life (*RR* 1.1.1–2): hence, the *RR*. Those are (apparently) the personal circumstances, yet this book argues that there are intellectual, sociocultural, economic, and, above all, political threads to Varro's rustic ruminations as well. The original motivating question for this book stemmed from the oft-noted dissonance perceived between the technical material and its formal presentation; starkly put, why convey dry agronomical precepts with intricate schemes of systematization in the form of three highly stylized philosophical dialogues? Dissatisfaction with answers that stressed the "charm" added to the text, or the rustic "escapism" offered its author, or even that author's antiquarian and apolitical pedantry, led in turn to consideration of the text's historical and political backdrop of 37 BC. On a cursory reading, there seemed to be little in the way of reference to the ongoing civil strife formally commenced with the hostilities between Caesar and Pompey and propagated by their partisan successors; closer attention reveals that the text is profoundly interested, and implicated, in those events and in the broader historical trends that engendered them. Like the praise of *res rusticae* put into the mouth of Cicero's octogenarian Cato (*Sen.* 51–60; cf. 32[4]), composition of the *RR* may have provided Varro with a productive and pleasurable way to spend his old age, but this book will show that it also gave him the opportunity to contemplate the condition of the Roman state. In particular, it argues that Varro uses the *RR* to provide a new theoretical account of *res rusticae*, which attempts to rationalize the changed realities of Roman farming in the context of its Mediterranean empire. In turn, through its formal and generic affiliations as well as a whole host of literary devices, this account provides an agronomical allegory of Roman *imperium* in 37 BC, which stands as an early conceptualization and theory of empire in the Roman world.

My approach is primarily literary or philological in the sense that I pursue close readings of the three books of the *RR* (as well as other contemporary texts), but I do so against the cultural and historical backdrop of the late Republican and Triumviral periods and, thus, my reading is also strongly historicized. At times, biographical elements come into consideration, for

---

over the next several years remains unclear. For the possible identification of Asinius Pollio with "Pinnius," the dedicatee of *RR* 3, see Green (1997) 46–47.

4. I have preferred to cite ancient sources in the body of the text and have generally adopted the conventions for abbreviation as specified in the *Oxford Classical Dictionary* (4th ed.). The primary exception to this latter practice is the abbreviation of Varro's *De Re Rustica* as *RR*. See the list of abbreviations on pp. vii–xi. Modern sources are cited primarily in the notes and by name, year, and page number(s).

Varro's dialogues (like many of Cicero's) contain a substantial authorial presence in the preface and, to a lesser degree, in the staged conversations as an interlocutor. Material evidence occasionally factors into my account as well, as Varro's dialogues intimately engage the urban and provincial locations in which they are set. Those interested in Roman agriculture as it was actually practiced on the ground may not find as much material as they might like, though my discussion will undoubtedly be of interest for gaining insight into the mentality of an intellectually and politically engaged Roman farm*owner*. For the view of *res rusticae* that the *RR* espouses is one that comes primarily from the praxis of ownership and is keyed to the concerns of other elite owners of productive estates. Perhaps more importantly, it is also deeply imbued with an understanding of Rome's history, its customs and traditions, and the precarious position of the individual citizen within the larger civil and social contexts of its Mediterranean empire. It is my hope that investigation into these aspects of the *RR* will reveal much of interest to intellectual and cultural historians of the late Republic and scholars of Latin literature in general.

Part I, which comprises the first two chapters, is devoted to examination of the text's literary form, genre, and intellectual scope. While the *RR* may appear to be a simple work of agronomy adorned with the trappings of the dialogue form and the occasional literary conceit, close reading reveals the work's generic affinities and intellectual agenda. On the one hand, the *RR* revises the terminology and taxonomy of farming so as to create a new theoretical field of *res rusticae,* which supports the text's broader goal of rendering the multifarious activities of the field (*RR* 1), pastures (*RR* 2), and villa (*RR* 3) as objects worthy of philosophical inquiry. In this respect, the text represents a marked intellectual development in the history of Roman agronomy. On the other hand, the various literary aspects—including the use of the dialogue form as well as tropes found in philosophy and satire—generate a productive tension with the *RR*'s technical material so as to proffer a text that encourages interpretation on a number of levels: not only agronomical, but also philosophical, satirical, and, above all, political.

On the basis of this approach, Part II offers individual readings of the work's three books: *RR* 1 (chapter 3), *RR* 2 (chapters 4 and 5), and *RR* 3 (chapter 6). Each book of the *RR* comprises a separate dialogue that treats one part of the total study of *res rusticae*: field cultivation (*agri cultura*) in *RR* 1, animal husbandry (*pastio*) in *RR* 2, and husbandry of the villa (*pastio villatica*) in *RR* 3. These three disciplines are differentiated from one another, and the objects of their study are also assigned respectively to fields, pastures, and the villa. Taken collectively, they comprise the total economy of the ideal Roman estate (*praedium*). In turn, through a variety of literary devices, the *RR*'s three individual dialogues analogize the three parts of the estate to their respective parts of the Roman state: the farmland as Italy, the pastures as provinces, and the villa as the city of Rome. The result, explored in chapter 7, is that the Varronian *praedium* provides a model *of*, and *for*, the contemporary Roman *imperium*, which not only delineates the relationships between its various parts but also offers a theory of Roman empire. In so doing, the *RR* provides an early, perhaps even the earliest, vision of Roman *imperium* as a coherent territorial empire.

That the *RR* functions as a work of rudimentary political philosophy may not be so surprising when we consider Varro's extensive service in various capacities to the Roman state and over a broad range of its geographical expanse.[5] His political career was distinguished, for he had served as tribune of the plebs, quaestor, praetor, and proconsul by 67 BC.[6] He was a *triumvir capitalis* (likely in the 90s BC), a member of Caesar's twenty-man commission for assigning Campanian lands in 59 BC, and probably a member of the priestly college of the *quindecimviri sacris faciundis* as well.[7] As Appian reminds us, his military career was perhaps even more prestigious. He served in campaigns in Dalmatia (under either L. Sulla in 85 BC or C. Cosconius in 78/7 BC) and, as legate under Pompey, against Sertorius in Spain in the 70s BC and pirates in the area from Sicily to Delos in 67 BC.[8] For this last stint of service, he even received the prestigious *corona rostrata*.[9] While his reprisal of that role for Pompey, a lifelong friend, at the head of two outmatched legions in Spain ultimately ended in surrender to Caesar in 49 BC, the confrontation neither deterred him from appearing in Dyrrhacium shortly before Pompey's own ignominious defeat at Pharsalus in 48 BC nor precluded the dictator

---

5. For biographies of Varro, see Cichorius (1922) 189–207, Dahlmann (1935) 1172–1277, and Della Corte (1965). Cf. Cardauns (2001). In English, good accounts of his life are hard to come by, but Rawson (1985) offers a sort of (indispensable) running commentary on Varro and his voluminous oeuvre, and Wiseman (2009) 107–51 contains much that is new and invaluable. See also the entries in the *OCD4* and *EAH*.

6. The ancient evidence comes from Varro himself: *ARH* F 21.1 Mirsch [= Aul. Gell. *NA* 13.12.6] and *Ling.* 7.109. Cf. the previous note's bibliography, especially Wiseman (2009) 113–15, who offers 86–84 for his tribuneship and 70–68 for his praetorship and proconsulship.

7. See, respectively, *ARH* F 21.1 Mirsch [= Aul. Gell. *NA* 13.12.6]; *RR* 1.2.10 and Pliny *HN* 7.176 (cf. Roselaar [2010] 286–87 for discussion); and Varro *De Vita Sua* F 1 Peter [= Charisius, *Gramm.* 1.89 Keil].

8. The primary piece of evidence for the campaign in Dalmatia is *RR* 2.10.8, which is then connected with either App. *B. Civ.* 1.77 or Eutr. 6.4 and Oros. 5.23.23. Again, the parsing and commentary of Wiseman (2009) 113–15 is invaluable. For Varro's service in Spain and in the pirate campaign, see, respectively, *RR* 3.12.7 and 2.pref.6; cf. *ARH* F 2.12 Mirsch [= Serv. *ad Aen.* 3.349].

9. See Pliny *HN* 3.101; 7.115; and 16.3–4. Cf. p. 154 in chapter 5.

from honoring the pardoned Reatinian with the (unrealized) opportunity to establish a public library at Rome.[10] He was proscribed in 43 BC but survived in the "country house" of Calenus and lived to hear of Antony's defeat at Actium in 31 BC and, possibly, of Octavian's rebirth as Augustus in 27 BC.

Yet, in the midst of all that public service and civil chaos, he still managed to find time to produce the wide-ranging and voluminous oeuvre for which he is best known today.[11] In his earlier years, he had studied under the Roman intellectual L. Aelius Stilo and the Greek philosopher Antiochus of Ascalon in Athens.[12] Up to 67 BC, he wrote some 150 satires in the "Menippean" mode and turned to his massively influential works on the history, customs, laws, and language of the Roman people thereafter.[13] Little of this output is extant, and what does survive tends not to impress modern scholars to the degree that it did his contemporaries. But in a Sibyl-like fashion (cf. *RR* 1.1.3), Varro himself would almost seem to be prescient of his future reception when he states in the *RR*'s opening line: "*Otium*—if I had pursued it, Fundania, I would write these things to you in a more agreeable form" (*Otium si essem consecutus, Fundania, commodius tibi haec scriberem*; 1.1.1).[14] It would help to know something about the man's exact activities post-proscription, but *otium* was apparently something Varro lacked, which in turn led to a less than

---

10. For Varro's failed campaign, see Caes. *BCiv.* 1.38 and 2.17–21. For his time in Dyrrhacium, see Cic. *Div.* 1.68 and 2.114; Plut. *Caes.* 36; and *RR* 1.4.5 (cf. appendix 6). For the offer of building the first public library, see Suet. *Iul.* 44. Cf. n. 3.

11. To be sure, Varro's apparent absence from the political scene from 59 BC onwards aided in the production of, among other works, the *Antiquitates*; for Dahlmann (1935) 1175–76, this period represents the natural culmination of his inherently "apolitical nature" (*unpolitische Natur*).

12. For the importance of L. Aelius Stilo on Varro's formative years, see *idem* 1173–74. Cf. Cic. *Brut.* 205. For a good overview of the influence of Antiochus on Varro, see Blank (2012) 250–89.

13. For the *Saturae Menippeae*, see especially Wiseman (2009) 132–51. Cf. pp. 19–23 in chapter 1.

14. The reference to the Sybil and her prophecies is intriguing, especially in the light of Varro's possible priesthood (cf. p. 5), for the *quindecimviri sacris faciundis* were charged with consulting the Sybilline Books at times of crisis: be it "natural," "religious," or "political." Varro thus suggests that his *RR* responds to a similar crisis (cf. *portentum*) and offers advice that requires close interpretation. Furthermore, in foregrounding *otium* in a work that is composed in the form of a philosophical dialogue, Varro may be alluding in some way to Cicero and/or his work; see Kronenberg (2009) 108 n. 2, who follows the estimation of Diederich (2007) 180 n. 1033 that the passage is an "ironic sideswipe" (*einen ironischen Seitenhieb*) at Cicero's *De Oratore*. On the difficult relationship between Varro and Cicero, Rösche-Binde (1998) and Wiseman (2009) 108–9 are essential, but much work remains to be done. In addition to his apparent lack of *otium*, Varro proceeds to stress the brevity of his life due to his age, but this statement also anticipates his program of "excising" extraneous material from *res rusticae*. For conciseness as a programmatic element to the *RR*'s approach to agronomy, see pp. 41–43 in chapter 2, pp. 142–43 in chapter 4, and pp. 150–51 in chapter 5.

"agreeable" (*commodius*) presentation of *res rusticae*. His political and military service and the disruption that proscription brought would suggest that this claim is not entirely self-deprecatory, ironic, or unfounded. But, if Cicero's famous formulation of the man as the one who repatriated "the peregrine Romans wandering as strangers within [their] own city" (*nos in nostra urbe peregrinantis errantisque tamquam hospites*; *Acad.* 1.8) is anything to go by, perhaps Varro considered his scholarly endeavors as political acts of *negotium*; after all, this is a man who claimed that the restoration of the gods from the "neglect of the citizens" (*neglegentia civium*) through his books was an act of "more useful care" (*utilior cura*) than Metellus's snatching of the Palladium from the burning Temple of Vesta in 241 BC or Aeneas's rescue of *penates* from the destruction of Troy.[15]

Like the *RR,* Varro is something of an enigma. He is a man whose work can appear to be ludicrous at times, yet commands the respect of his contemporaries in all spheres political and intellectual. He was older than most of his more famous contemporaries but would outlive them all.[16] Cicero was wary of him and may even have found him intimidating.[17] Pompey frequently relied on him in military and political matters.[18] Antony repeatedly begrudged him of his lavish properties.[19] Asinius Pollio appears to have been so impressed with the former *Pompeianus* that he placed Varro's bust, the only one of a living writer, in the newly renovated Atrium Libertatis.[20] He could—and still does—elicit such varied characterizations as a crabbed antiquarian, a lively poet, and "the most learned" (*doctissimus*) of the Romans.[21] His works seem

---

15. See *ARD* F 2a Cardauns. For discussion, see Moatti (1991) 31–46 and the valuable new perspective of Van Nuffelen (2010), which shows that a Stoicizing agenda in recovering philosophical truth works in conjunction with his avowed rescue of Roman tradition for tradition's sake.

16. To reframe the sum of his nearly ninety years in comparative terms, Varro (b. 116, d. 27) was some ten to fifteen years older than Pompey (b. 106, d. 48) and Caesar (b. 100, d. 44), Cicero (b. 106, d. 43) and Sallust (b. 100, d. ca. 35), and would survive them all by a similar amount of time.

17. See, for example, *Att.* 331.3 [= 13.23.3], where Cicero calls Varro a "clever man" (*deinos aner*) in slippery Greek. Cf. n. 14.

18. In addition to his military service, Pompey requested Varro to prep him on senatorial procedure (i.e., the *Eisagogikos*; Aul. Gell. *NA* 14.7.2).

19. See Cic. *Phil.* 2.103–4 and Varro *Hebdomades* F 1 Chappuis [= Aul. Gell. *NA* 3.10.17]. For discussion, see Osgood (2006) 208–10.

20. Cf. n. 3.

21. The latter two points are brought out quite clearly by Wiseman (2009) 131. For an extensive (though not exhaustive) list of ancient estimations of him as *doctissimus* and as poet, see *idem* nn. 2–3. Perhaps most famous is Quintilian's (backhanded) appraisal as the "most expert Roman in the Latin language and Greco-Roman antiquities" (*peritissimus linguae Latinae et omnis antiquitatis et rerum Graecarum nostrarumque*), whose "most learned books" (*libri*

to lurk everywhere in Augustan literature, but remain woefully fragmentary.[22] For better or for worse, the *RR* becomes a sort of litmus test for the man and his work. This book hopes to explain how a deceptively simple account of a country house is as intellectually complex and politically engaged as its author, a man whose salvation once lay in a country house of just this sort.

---

*doctissimi*) contain "more knowledge than eloquence" (*plus tamen scientiae conlaturus quam eloquentiae*; *Inst.* 10.1.95).

22. See, for example, Conte (1994a) 213, 218–20 or the Servian scholiasts on Vergil's work, in which there are over one hundred references to Varro alone.

# CHAPTER 1

# The Form and Genre of Varronian *res rusticae*

~

IN TERMS of its content, Varro's *De Re Rustica* (hereafter, the *RR*) initially appears to be a work of agronomy in the mold of other manuals such as Cato's *De Agri Cultura* (mid-second century BC), Columella's *Res Rusticae* (mid-first century AD), and Palladius's *Opus Agri Culturae* (ca. third to fourth century AD). Yet, to refer to it merely as a "technical treatise" does not do justice to the sophisticated form of this complex, even enigmatic, work. For one thing, unlike the other agricultural texts with which it was transmitted down through antiquity,[1] the *RR* stands alone in its use of the dialogue form—including artfully arranged settings and colorful characters—to convey its agronomical precepts. In these respects, the *RR* might compare more fruitfully with the philosophical dialogues of Plato, Xenophon, and, especially, Varro's contemporary Cicero. Moreover, other elements—for example, the prevalent use of puns, intermittent irony and moralizing, and chance encounters between freewheeling friends and dinner-bound acquaintances—imbue the text with a distinctly satirical hue as well. What are we to make of the *RR*'s variegated nature? How does the text's form matter for our understanding of its genre, and what are the implications for how we read it?

---

1. Cato's and Varro's agricultural works were paired together in the lost Marcianus codex, the readings of which Politian preserved in his collation; thereafter, these two works were generally grouped together, sometimes with Columella and/or Palladius. For a fuller discussion, see Reynolds (1983) 40–42 and Von Albrecht (1997) 1.401–2.

This chapter explores the formal aspects of *De Re Rustica*'s dialogues with a view to demonstrating the text's generic affinities with philosophy and satire. By virtue of paying attention to the text's form and genre, it breaks with the majority of twentieth-century scholarship on the *RR*—which tended to ignore or, perhaps worse, discount such questions[2]—and, instead, builds on more recent work that has begun to reconsider these mostly neglected aspects.[3] In part, this shift in critical approach has stemmed from the late twentieth century's increasing emphasis on the importance of genre—that is, that ever-modulating nexus of formal features, content, and context or occasion[4]—as a sort of lens that focalizes our reading of texts as well as an analyti-

---

2. For example, in opening his 1968 monograph on *RR* 1, Skydsgaard simultaneously invoked and dismissed the *RR*'s employment of the dialogue form as "having in itself no direct bearing on the structuralization of the material" (10). In part, Skydsgaard justified his denial of formal (and generic) significance by appeal to Heisterhagen's 1952 dissertation, which—on Skydsgaard's estimation—had demonstrated that Varro's choice of form served as pleasant, entertaining "variation" for what might otherwise be a thoroughly dull technical discussion. To be sure, Heisterhagen's evaluation went far beyond this minimalistic estimation, which was more indicative of Skydsgaard's certitude (as well as that of the scholarly *communis opinio*; cf. White [1973] 488–94 and Conte [1994a] 219) in the straightforwardly simple nature of the *RR* as an "agricultural treatise." Ably discussing the features that the *RR* shares in common with "peripatetic dialogues" (by way of association with Aristotle and Heraclides) and Varro's own output of "Cynic-Menippean satires," Heisterhagen (1952) 102–5 claimed that the *RR* represented a "unification" (*Vereinigung*) of the two genres. See p. 21 for further discussion. As will become clear, my bipartite approach takes its inspiration from Heisterhagen, though I focus less on merely delineating formal similarities, correspondences, and differences between the *RR* and its literary progenitors and more on extracting the attendant implications of its generic invocations (or deviations).

3. Silke Diederich's *Römische Agrarhandbücher zwischen Fachwissenschaft, Literatur und Ideologie* (2007) and Leah Kronenberg's *Allegories of Farming from Greece and Rome* (2009) represent the first substantial monographs on the literary and ideological aspects of Varro's *RR* since Heisterhagen. Cf. the important articles on *RR* 3 by Green (1997) 427–48 and Purcell (1995) 151–79. See pp. 172–75 in chapter 6 for further discussion.

4. I am indebted to Riggsby (2006) 4 for his concise articulation of genre as a "pattern of associations between features of form, content, and context/occasion of verbal production." Within classical studies, the most famous attempt at a systematic, though overly prescriptive, classification of genres remains Cairns (1972). For good discussions of the problems with generic classification in antiquity, see Conte (1994b) 104–28, and by modern scholars, see Perkins (1992) 61–84. Given the manifold problems in posing generic identifications in rigidly fixed terms, I believe that genre should *not* be considered as an entirely discrete category within a nexus of various substantive and formal possibilities, for the process of generic identification inevitably depends on the historical setting and intellectual perspective of both the author and the reader. In other words, historical considerations (authorial intention, context of production, reception, etc.) inevitably do—and should—play a role in guiding our taxonomic classifications. Thus, this notion of genre, when filtered through the screens of these contextual and empirical considerations, is ultimately a useful one for approaching texts and, moreover, allows for them to be indicative of multiple genres at once and, potentially, to evince multiple representations of the world (*pace* Conte [1994b] 117–25, for whom a text has one and only one genre that in turn filters the model of reality presented

cal tool for interpreting them. And in the case of *De Re Rustica*—a mundane technical treatise, according to older accounts[5]—any approach must not only be informed by the understanding that all verbal production is inherently "generic" and "complex,"[6] but also be sufficiently robust to account for Varro's careful construction of a text that simultaneously articulates and ironizes its own generic status.

My analysis of the *RR* in terms of philosophy and satire thus entails several related claims. First, I maintain that Varro's text employs formal features evocative of philosophical and satirical texts for substantive purposes that go beyond mere literary adornment. While sporadic in appearance and varied in purpose, these elements both enhance the *RR*'s treatment of technical content and facilitate additional—especially metaphorical or allegorical—ways in which to read the *RR* above and beyond its agronomical precepts. Furthermore, by deploying these philosophical and satirical elements within an otherwise genuinely technical treatment of farming, the *RR* in fact constitutes itself as *sui generis,* resembling its generic models, yet concurrently being different enough to warrant its recognition within a novel generic category. The sum result is that *De Re Rustica* cultivates an irresolvable, but ultimately *constructive,* tension between and among its three literary progenitors, so as to create a multivalent and novel admixture: one that might be termed (albeit, ponderously) a "philosophico-satirico-technical dialogue."

## PHILOSOPHICAL DIALOGUE AND THE FORM OF THE *RR*

The defining characteristic of the *RR*'s form—as well as its most conspicuous point of affinity with philosophy—is its use of the "dialogue," by which I

---

in the text). Finally, my allowance for the reader's role in assigning generic identification is generally influenced by the reader-oriented theories of Jauss (1982) and Fish (1980).

5. So White (1973) 488–94, who views the dialogue form as Varro's humble attempt to add a modicum of literary polish and charm to a potentially dry technical discussion.

6. In Bakhtinian terms (1986) 60–104, the *RR* would be a single "utterance" that draws upon various speech genres so as to communicate with its audience in an inherently "responsive" fashion. Because speech genres—particularly "secondary" or "complex" ones (e.g., the novel), which are either predatory or parasitic on "primary" or "simple" ones (e.g., a greeting)—are "relatively stable types" of utterances, potentially infinite in number, and characterized by their "extreme heterogeneity," all communication is inherently "generic" and "complex." My analysis in this chapter, then, examines Varro's use of two preexisting, "secondary" (i.e., complex) speech genres—philosophical dialogue and satire—to impart his own utterance (i.e., the *RR*). And by virtue of engaging in this complex, generic communicative process over the course of three distinct books in a roughly consistent manner, the *RR* as a whole merits identification within its own genre, which I deem "philosophico-satirico-technical."

am referring generally to the prose representation of a spoken conversation and, more specifically, to those formal features (e.g., stylized settings, historical or quasi-historical interlocutors, etc.) that this mimetic, traditional, and venerable mode of philosophical discourse entails.[7] However murky the origins (or advent) of the dialogue form at Rome may be,[8] the works of M. Tullius Cicero, Varro's contemporary and the most famous Roman practitioner of the dialogue, predate the *RR*'s composition and, consequently, serve as a relevant and useful set of generic comparanda for Varro's work.[9] Given the sheer volume of Cicero's massive philosophical oeuvre, any comparison must necessarily be selective and, moreover, runs the risks of overshadowing the relevance of other models for the *RR* (especially Xenophon's *Oeconomicus*[10]) and of undervaluing the fact that a number of Varro's satires in the so-called Menippean mode had already employed the dialogue form.[11] Nonetheless, not only did the *novus homo* from Arpinum leave a lasting imprint on the Roman rhetorical and philosophical landscape of literary production, but Cicero also actively conversed with Varro about the compo-

---

7. The two-volume study of Hirzel (1895) remains the most thorough overview of the dialogue tradition in antiquity.

8. The earliest-attested Latin dialogues would appear to be the second-century BC juristic works of M. Junius Brutus; see *idem* 1.431–32. For Cicero's youthful translation of Xenophon's *Oeconomicus*, see Pomeroy (1995) 70.

9. Whereas Varro tells us that he composed the *RR* in 37 BC, the latest of Cicero's dialogues, which were seminal contributions to the landscape of Latin literature (cf. Mayer [1991] 27–31), is securely dated to the year of his death in 43 BC. Throughout my analysis of the formal elements of each, I will have recourse to appendix 1.

10. An unquestionably important precursor to the *RR*, Xenophon's *Oeconomicus* appears to have enjoyed some popularity at Rome and, more clearly, overlaps substantially in terms of general subject matter. Scholars (esp. Green [1997] 428–29) have viewed Xenophon's thirdhand reporting of the conversation between Ischomachus and his wife as the probable inspiration for Varro's dedication of the *RR* to his wife, Fundania. Note also Varro's opening claim (1.1.7), like Xenophon (*Oec.* 1), that he is relating conversations he once heard. Cf. the opening of Plato's *Symposium* (172a1–174a2). Most recently, Kronenberg (2009) 32 n. 110 has raised the intriguing possibility that Varro consciously modeled his *RR* on an ironic reading of the *Oeconomicus*, but she prudently observes that the state of the evidence does not allow for this claim to be established definitively.

11. So Zetzel (1995) 5 observes. Traditionally dated to 80–67 BC, these works predate the earliest of Cicero's dialogues, *De Oratore*, by at least ten years. Thus, any discussion of Cicero's dialogues and Varro's *RR* runs the risk of circular logic: overemphasizing the former's influence upon the latter and at the expense of formal features possibly developed in Varro's satirical output, but which may in fact have influenced Cicero. If we possessed Varro's satires, one could imagine that the terms of my discussion might be substantially different. For these reasons, I have chosen to proceed with my analysis on a broadly intertextual level. For a tentative discussion of one possible instance of Varronian allusion to Cic. *Fin.* 3.4, see Nelsestuen (2011) 330–33. For possible allusions to *De Oratore*, see Martin (1995) 80–91 and Diederich (2007) 180 n. 1033, and for parodic echoes of *De Re Publica*, see Kronenberg (2009) 108–11.

sition of some of these dialogues and even cast the Reatinian as an interlocutor in the revised version of the *Academica*.[12] For these reasons, the two sets
of dialogues virtually demand to be read in tandem. Two additional cave-
ats are in order. First, I am presently not attempting to posit any definitive
causal relationship between the authors—if only because such an approach
remains inherently fraught with a whole host of problems.[13] Second, evaluating Varro's dialogues vis-à-vis Cicero's is by no means a novel endeavor, but
unlike previous treatments, my approach does not merely acknowledge the
parodic spirit in which Varro *may* emulate the practices of his predecessor,
but emphasizes that deviation, inversion, and even subversion constitute a
sort of dialogue with the Ciceronian dialogic practice and inherently contribute to the *RR*'s unique program. Thus, in addition to adding to the burgeoning scholarly interest in the formal and ideological aspects of ancient
dialogues,[14] comparison of the two dialogicians' general practices will help to
contextualize the Varronian dialogue and to identify and explicate its principal and distinctive features.

I begin with an obvious (and uncontroversial) feature common to Cicero's
and Varro's dialogues: the representation of both major and minor interlocutors, who vocalize the treatise's content and drive its argumentation, and
whose crafted, quasi-historical *personae* not infrequently reflect the themes
and arguments expressed thereby.[15] Cicero's dialogues can vary greatly in

---

12. Cf. n. 30.

13. Not the least of which might include the intractable ravages of time and transmission as well as the very real possibility that each simply worked from a similar intellectual
background and critical stance towards the Hellenistic world and its learning. This is not
to say that a consideration of the specifically allusive relationship between Varro's and Cicero's dialogues is out of the question; indeed, future work by Sarah Culpepper Stroup and
by Susan Drummond promises to shed some light on this tantalizing question. See also p.
178 in chapter 6 and pp. 227–28 in chapter 7, which will suggest some specifically allusive
interactions between *De Re Publica* and the *RR*.

14. There is an emerging scholarly consensus that the dialogue form matters for reasons
*beyond* simplistic literary ornamentation or historical plausibility. In the case of Cicero's
works, instead of merely reflecting historical veracity or verisimilitude (e.g., R. E. Jones [1939]
307–25), the dialogue form may serve as a vehicle for "self-fashioning" (e.g., Dugan 2005,
Fantham 2004); an "open-ended kind of skepticism which denies [the] certainty" of any one
absolute position (Fox 2007); or implicit critique of the prevailing regime (Gildenhard 2007).
In what follows, I adhere in spirit to the approaches of Fox and Gildenhard in that I maintain, respectively, that (a) the dramatization of the multiple interlocutors and their at-times
competing views contribute to a project larger than the individual parts and (b) the form,
by virtue of its mimetic nature and dramatic components, facilitates oblique, potentially
symbolic or ironic, utterances (e.g., puns, metaphors, allegory, etc.) that intermittently signify
something other than the signifier.

15. In addition to serving as an introduction to Cicero's "dramaturgical" practices (so
Dyck [1998a] 151–64 aptly calls Cicero's construction of characters in his dialogues), *Att.*
89.2 [= 4.16.2] implicitly distinguishes between major and minor *personae* of *De Re Publica*:

terms of the number of these *personae,* but most of them generally have two
or more major characters and at least one or two minor ones (see appendix 1). As for the *RR*'s dramatic casts, all three dialogues also evince this
twofold typology. Thus, Book 1 has two primary interlocutors (Scrofa and
Stolo), Book 2 has seven (Scrofa, Varro, Atticus, Cossinius, Murrius, Lucienus, and Vaccius), and Book 3 has four (Q. Axius, Varro, Appius Claudius
Pulcher, and Cornelius Merula). In these respects, the number of main interlocutors employed by Varro generally resembles the practice of Cicero, especially in the latter's earlier, more literarily ambitious, texts: *De Oratore* and
*De Re Publica.* On the other hand, the number of minor interlocutors in the
*RR* tends to be greater than the number found in Cicero's oeuvre. Thus, in
addition to the brief appearances of a freedman (1.69.2), a couple of servile
messengers (2.8.1; 2.11.12), and a successful candidate (3.17.10), Book 1 contains five minor characters (Varro, C. Fundanius, P. Agrasius, C. Agrius, L.
Fundilius), Book 2 has possibly one (Menates), and Book 3 includes four others (Fircellius Pavo, Minucius Pica, M. Petronius Passer, Pantuleius Parra).
Still, insofar as their contributions are sporadic and generally inconsequential, Varro's minor characters play a role comparable (once again) to those
found in *De Oratore* or *De Re Publica,*[16] that is, as merely conversational entities, whose contributions tend to add color to the dialogue but do not really
enrich its substance.

   The degree of participation relates to another twofold, Ciceronian typology: the distinction between so-called "Aristotelian" and "Heraclideian"
types of dialogues.[17] Little evidence exists to suggest that this classification

---

"major" characters are those characters who occupy a significant portion of the text articulating or facilitating the discussion, or otherwise have such an impact that their absence
would somehow fundamentally disrupt the conversation, while minor characters intervene
only occasionally or contribute little or even are merely present at the discussion. To use
*De Re Publica* as an example of this analysis, Scipio Africanus and Laelius would clearly be
major characters, while Rufus and Scaevola are minor ones. It is worth acknowledging that
the line between major and minor characters remains inherently hazy and, moreover, not all
of Cicero's dialogues contain minor *personae.*

   16. Generally speaking, minor characters in later Ciceronian dialogues tend to be mute
and, for all intents and purposes, shadow participants. The ancient technical term for a character who did not speak was *kophon prosopon.*

   17. See *Att.* 326.4 [= 13.19.4]; cf. 89.2 [= 4.16.2]. Using these letters as well as rather late,
often suspect, and sometimes contradictory sources, Heisterhagen (1952) 4–13 attempts to
summarize the formal features of each type: "Aristotelian" dialogues have (1) lengthy and
uninterrupted lectures, (2) the author as the main character, (3) proems, and (4) a minimal
amount of setting; whereas "Heraclideian" dialogues have (1) well-developed and dramatic
settings, (2) lengthy (but probably alternating) lectures, and (3) proems (like Aristotle). Given
the inherent difficulties with reconstructing no-longer-extant types of dialogues, I follow the
testimony of Cicero, which, however accurate or not it may be, nonetheless speaks to the

was widely recognized outside Cicero and his correspondents, yet the terminology remains a convenient way to distinguish dialogues that represent the author conversing with contemporary figures (i.e., "Aristotelian") from those that present a discussion among deceased ones (i.e., "Heraclideian"). Apparently turning on chronological proximity to the author, this distinction actually conflates two separate, but closely related, dramaturgical choices: (a) the author's choice to include himself (or not) as a primary character and (b) the employment of living or deceased characters. Thus, Cicero's *De Senectute* and *De Amicitia* may admit characterization as "Heraclideian" dialogues by virtue of the fact that they represent figures of the past conversing with one another; *De Legibus, Brutus,* and the first four books of *De Finibus* might fall under the heading of "Aristotelian" because they depict their author conversing with his contemporaries;[18] and *De Oratore* and *De Re Publica* could represent an amalgamation of the two modes in the combination of a past setting (i.e., "Heraclideian")[19] with Cicero's substantial authorial presence in the lengthy prefaces (i.e., "Aristotelian").

In the case of the *RR*, it is difficult to assign Varro's dialogues to the "Heraclideian," "Aristotelian," or "mixed" types. On the one hand, Varro speaks (*qua* authorial persona) in the prefaces to each of the three books and, moreover, participates in the discussions (*qua* interlocutor), which might render them "Aristotelian" except that he neither presides over the discussion as the *magister*-like figure of the others nor even contributes substantially.[20] On the other hand, calling the dialogues "Heraclideian" entails its own set of problems as well. Ignoring for now the problematic dating of Book 1's setting (almost certainly 45–37 BC; possibly 58–54), Books 2 and 3 both take place at periods earlier (67 and 50 BC, respectively) than their date of composition,[21] yet those

state of literary-critical reception of dialogues in Rome. For an overview of Heraclides Ponticus, the mid-fourth-century BC philosopher of the Academy, see Gottschalk's 1980 monograph. Cf. Schütrumpf (2008) and Fortenbaugh and Pender (2009).

18. Note that *De Natura Deorum* represents a conversation at which Cicero was present, but in which he did not take part due to his status as a man younger than the primary interlocutors. Book 5 of *De Finibus* stages a similar scenario, although Cicero does assume a more substantial role for a short period (5.76–86).

19. Cf. the analysis of Zetzel (1995) 3–4, who rightly acknowledges another implicit benefit from setting *De Re Publica* in the past: it also enabled Cicero "to evoke the model uppermost in [his] mind," namely, Plato.

20. Varro's participation in Book 1 is quite minimal, rendering him little more than a minor character, whereas he delivers preliminary comments on the "origin" and "dignity" of animal husbandry (2.1.3–10) in Book 2 and describes (by way of interlude) his lavish aviary (3.5.9–17) in Book 3. For these reasons, Varro's status as a major, though still not dominant, interlocutor would appear to fly in the face of what Cicero means by "Aristotelian."

21. In fact, Book 2 is the only the one that provides a concrete timeframe for the discussion (2.Pref.6): "at that time when I presided over the fleets of Greece between Delos

periods can be said to be of a previous generation only with great difficulty and, at least in the cases of Varro and Atticus, dramatize characters who in fact live well past the actual date of composition.[22] From an analytical stand-point, then, the dialogues of the *RR* would thus appear to represent a unique mélange of Cicero's "Aristotelian" and "Heraclideian" modes:[23] incorporating aspects of both, yet adhering fully to neither one nor quite even the Cicero-nian amalgam.

Another issue at play in Cicero's and Varro's dialogues is the nature of the characters and, in particular, the degree of plausibility (or verisimili-tude) in their characterization. That Cicero *aims* for historical plausibility in his dialogues is demonstrable,[24] but it has become commonplace and, indeed, largely uncontroversial, to assert that the representation of char-acters in Cicero's dialogues can also serve an ideological or partisan pur-pose.[25] The plausibility or verisimilitude of the *RR*'s characterization is also fraught with interpretative cruces, albeit different ones. With the exception of Appius Claudius Pulcher, the augur, consul (54 BC), and censor (50 BC),

---

and Sicilia in the war with the pirates," that is, the spring of 67 BC. See p. 119 in chapter 4 for further discussion. While Books 1 and 3 do not specify any such span of time, their focus on the motivating occasions for each discussion would have presumably allowed for ready recognition by the ancient reader. In the case of *RR* 3, Linderski (1985) 248–54 (*pace* J. S. Richardson [1983] 456–63) has plausibly identified the date of Book 3 as the aedilician election of 50 BC, which puts it shortly before the onset of the civil war between Caesar and Pompey (cf. the settings of *De Oratore* and *De Re Publica*). The date of *RR* 1 has also elicited scholarly debate, but, as Flach has shown (see n. 11 on p. 77 in chapter 3), the dialogue takes place sometime between 45 and 37 BC.

22. As we know from Cornelius Nepos's biographical sketch, Atticus, the friend and erst-while correspondent of Cicero, lived well into the mid-to-late 30s BC, while Varro's death is usually dated to 27 BC. Aside from those two, the most famous and well-attested figures in the *RR* are the agronomist Cn. Tremelius Scrofa (Brunt [1972] 304–8; [1973] 195; Kronenberg [2009] 77–93; Martin [1971] 237–55; Nelsestuen [2011] 315–51; and Perl [1980] 97–109), whose date of death is unknown, and Appius Claudius Pulcher (e.g., Tatum [1992]), the augur, con-sul, and censor, who died abroad in 49 or 48 BC.

23. Cf. the discussion of Heisterhagen (1952) 19–20, who reaches a similar conclusion.

24. See esp. *Att.* 89.2 [= 4.16.2]. Cf. *Att.* 303 [= 13.30] and *Fam.* 113 [= 8.32]. Even the inclusion of archaisms in dialogues such as the *De Re Publica* and *De Senectute* should be considered to be part of Cicero's project of creating dialogues that are more or less histori-cally plausible (for discussion of which, J. G. F. Powell [1988] 22–23 and Zetzel [1995] 30–31 are instructive). Until the early 1970s, scholars generally accepted Cicero's characterizations at face value (e.g., R. E. Jones [1939] 307–25). More recent scholarship has increasingly em-phasized the differences between modern and ancient conceptions of "history" and "verac-ity"; for Cicero's understanding of these two concepts—and their rather wide divergence from a more modern one—see Woodman (1988) 70–116.

25. The debunking of the so-called Scipionic circle by Zetzel (1972) 173–79 shifted schol-arly approaches to the characters of Cicero's dialogues and prefigured more recent approaches that consider the text as an ideological creation of an author with his own goals and objec-tives (cf. n. 14). Cf. Dyck (1998a) 151–64.

Varro's characters frequently include men less dignified and prominent than Cicero's consular-studded cast or, at the very least, are ones about whom we simply do not know enough even to begin to evaluate their historicity.[26] Further complicating the problem is that the rustic etymological origins of some interlocutors' names would appear to have motivated their inclusions.[27] My point here is *not* that Cicero's dialogues are necessarily more historically grounded than Varro's (though, as we shall see, the latter do incorporate a fantastic element typically not found in Cicero's works), but rather that the inhabitants of the worlds created by both authors can vastly differ in *kind*. Whereas Cicero prefers to use characters personally known to or, in the case of the "Heraclideian" dialogues, esteemed by and ideologically palatable to the author himself, Varro employs a wider variety of interlocutors from a broader swath of Roman society:[28] not only personal *familiares* and venerable *nobiles,* but also equestrians, Italian *municipales,* and Roman expatriates. In this respect, the social world of Varro's dialogues ranges well beyond the tidy bounds and rarefied atmosphere of his younger predecessor.

Not inconsequential differences in setting abound as well. Almost without exception, Ciceronian dialogues take place at an interlocutor's private Italian villa.[29] The motivating occasion may vary slightly, but generally either a religious holiday or a planned social visit of one (or more) Roman aristocrat(s) to another prompts the meeting.[30] In either scenario, however, Cicero is careful to stage the meeting in a *private* (i.e., not public) space and at a time of

26. The treatment of Linderski (1989) 105–28 brings out these points very clearly, although, as Green (1997) 428 n. 6 points out, a full prosopographical study of the *RR* remains to be undertaken. Discussion of each character will be left to the appropriate places in chapters 3 through 6.

27. Linderski (1989) 114–16.

28. Linderski (*ibid.*) rightly notes this difference between the two dialogicians, though his explanation of Varro's inclusion of characters of lower social rank as a result of the humble status of *res rusticae* both overstates the rigidity of the distinction and obscures the ideological dimensions of all three dialogues' careful staging.

29. For example, *De Oratore* (1.24–27) and *De Re Publica* (1.14), the earliest dialogues, take place at the respective villas of L. Licinius Crassus and Scipio Aemilianus. Moreover, various of Cicero's own abodes serve as the backdrop of the conversations in *De Legibus* (2.3), *Brutus* (10), and the first two books of *De Finibus* (1.14), while the villas of others host the other dialogues (e.g., Lucullus's villa, *Fin.* 3.7). In fact, the only Ciceronian dialogue that does not take place at a villa is the fifth book of the *De Finibus,* where the garden of the Academy in Athens entertains the supposed discussion of the author's youth (5.1).

30. For examples of religious holidays, see *De Re Publica* (*Feriae Latinae,* 1.14), *De Oratore* (*ludi,* 1.24), and *De Natura Deorum* (*Feriae Latinae,* 1.15). For examples of aristocratic social visits, see *De Finibus* (L. Manlius Torquatus at Cicero's villa at Cumae, 1.14) and *Academica* (Cicero and Atticus at Varro's villa at Puteoli, 1.1–2). The sole exception to this scenario is found in *De Finibus*'s (3.7) representation of Cicero's unforeseen encounter with Cato the Younger as each peruses Lucullus's library.

culturally sanctioned *otium* (i.e., not *negotium*). Of course, for those leisurely discussants of matters directly related to the state—particularly rhetoric (e.g., *De Oratore*) and the ideal *res publica* (e.g., *De Re Publica*)—the pleasure of *otium* brought to bear on the utility of *negotium* proves particularly felicitous for the discussants and dialogician, thereby underscoring the need for, as well as obligation of, the Roman elite and their diligent attention to Roman *res publica*.

The *RR*'s dialogues, on the other hand, carefully eschew the place-occasion matrix of Ciceronian *otium*. In Book 1, the occasion for the discussion of *agri cultura* is a promised dinner party in the Temple of Tellus on the Feriae Sementivae, a sowing festival (1.2.1). The conversation of Book 2 is also motivated by a dinner party, or rather, dinner parties, as the various interlocutors appear to have met only by chance and on their way to attend two different gatherings (2.11.12; cf. 2.8.1; 2.1.1), while the motivating holiday is no longer the Feriae Sementivae, but the Parilia.[31] As for a precise location, it is impossible to say (except that it is *not* the villas of either host, as implied by 2.11.12), but the interlocutors' seemingly random encounter points to a well-frequented area of Epirus: perhaps some kind of public space in Bouthrotos, where Atticus had an estate.[32] Finally, Book 3 makes a great deal out of its explicit setting in the Villa Publica (3.2.4), which is located in the Campus Martius at Rome. The aedilician elections prompt the appearance of each group of interlocutors, yet their collective gathering is, once again, unplanned (3.2.2), and the successful election of Varro's candidate (3.17.10) marks the dialogue's conclusion. Thus, unlike Cicero's works, which are nominally divorced from public life and ensconced so deeply in the space and time of private *otium,* the dialogues of the *RR* are circumstantially and spatially located in intervening spaces: the meetings are neither planned nor completely random, the occasions between *otium* and *negotium,* and the locations entwined in private and public life. In these respects, the *RR*'s dialogues offer a marked contrast to the scenery of staged Ciceronian *otium.*

In limited ways, then, the *RR*'s dialogues are akin to those of Cicero. Yet, the "deviation" from some of Cicero's practices and the nearly wholesale "reversal" of still others suggests that something else is going on here. Aside from the fact that a number of these elements are, as we shall see shortly,

---

31. While earlier editions commonly held that there is a lacuna between the preface and the beginning of the dialogue proper (e.g., Hooper and Ash [1934]), Flach (1996) persuasively argues that the dialogue simply begins rather abruptly and with little development of scenery. See pp. 118–24 in chapter 4 for further discussion.

32. Atticus bought his estate in 68 and spent much time there; see Shackleton-Bailey (1965) 4. For further discussion of Atticus and other Italians in Bouthrotos, see Sakellariou (1997) 118; 124–25.

characteristic of satire as well, the *RR*'s dialogues are explicitly incorporated into the "everyday life" of the city in ways that Cicero's idealized holidays clearly are not.[33] These differences may stem from—or, perhaps better, calculatedly reflect—the fact that the *RR*'s subject of *res rusticae* is categorically different than Cicero's explicitly philosophical, rhetorical, and political topics. In other words, by creating a backdrop that directly engages the events of quotidian experience, Varro crafts a setting more appropriate to the mundane world of agriculture.[34] Yet, by relocating its rustic conversations from country villas to urban landscapes, the *RR* simultaneously inscribes *agri cultura* into the city and imparts the sense that agronomy is somehow connected with its political life. In this way, Varro's urban locations for matters of the countryside may be understood as the flipside to Cicero's setting of political philosophy in rural villas, as particularly found in (yet again![35]) *De Oratore* and *De Re Publica*. Even so, Varro's conversations *de re rustica* still come off as more directly related to, integrated within, and, in fact, integral to, the city of Rome and its political, social, and cultural life, than any of Cicero's elite excursions into the leisurely villas of the countryside.

## PHILOSOPHICAL SATIRE IN THE *RR*

So far, we have considered the *RR*'s form from the vantage of philosophical dialogues—particularly those of Cicero—yet some of its same features also admit analysis as satirical. Given that Varro composed (on a conservative estimate) some 150 satires in the Menippean mode from 80 to 67,[36] it is perhaps unsurprising that satirical features have found their way into the *RR*. Yet, the satirical side of the *RR*'s form is not merely due to Varro's previous literary endeavors, for it also reflects the fact that satire is a parasitic genre—one that often involves the antagonistic appropriation and ironized redeployment of other genres and generic features—and especially so when it comes to phi-

33. In this respect, Varro's dramaturgical practices may have more in common with Plato's and, admittedly, it is tempting—though highly speculative—to understand these practices to constitute Varro's correction of his contemporary counterpart's dialogues.

34. Cf. Linderski (1989) 118–20, although I disagree with his conclusion that the differences between villa and urban settings reflect a lower social status attached to *res rusticae* than to philosophy and rhetoric.

35. On pp. 227–28 in chapter 7, I speculate on the relationship between the *RR* and Cicero's *De Re Publica*.

36. For a survey of this phase of Varro's literary biography, see Knoche (1975) 53–69. Wiseman (2009) 131–51 rightly stresses the poetic and theatrical qualities to these writings and offers intriguing biographical connections. All citations of Varro's *Menippeans* come from the Bücheler edition.

losophy.[37] Moreover, the relationship between satire and philosophy actually goes much deeper than what the predatory pose often struck by the former might suggest.[38] As an inherently seriocomic (*spoudogeloios*) enterprise, satire generally combines ridicule (or the ridiculous) with the serious in its critical, often aggressive, investigations into the sorts of topics, figures, and modes frequently associated with philosophy. Thus, Lucilius, the second-century BC Roman satirist and, for his countrymen, the most important originator of this putatively homegrown genre, intermingled seemingly serious philosophical (and philological) aspects into his satirical output, thereby paving the way for the substantial presence of philosophy in later Roman satire and satirical works.[39] Conversely, philosophy—and especially its practice in the form of the Socratic dialogue—not infrequently uses humor and ridicule in its relentless pursuit of wisdom and truth. Thus, when Socrates' Delphi-inspired mission to examine all those in the city with pretensions to wisdom (Plat. *Apol.* 21a4–23b9) publically reduces pretenders to a laughable state, it is perhaps not unreasonable to consider this early practitioner of moral philosophy also as an "inventor of a form of satire . . . devoted to unmasking in public all those considered wise for the amusement and edification of their fellow citizens."[40] Or in the case of the Romans, Lucretius famously does not rise above the satirical diatribe in his poetic account of Epicureanism,[41] while the philosophical "badinage" so characteristic of Cicero's letters attests to the way that humor and irony facilitated genuine philosophical learning, argumentation,

---

37. For good treatments of the parasitic relationship between philosophy and satire, see Keane (2004), Gowers (2005) 48–61, and R. Mayer (2005) 146–59. For the potential hybridity of all satire, see Fowler (1982) 188–90.

38. I am particularly indebted to Branham (2009) 139–61 for the following discussion.

39. For examples of philosophy in Lucilian satire, F 35, 200–7, 507–8, 805–11, 815–23, 835–43, 1022–23, 1189–90, 1196–1208, and 1234; and of philology, see F 401–18. Note also that Ennius, who (strictly speaking) was the earliest of the Roman satirists, composed philosophical works (e.g., *Epicharmus*). For some particularly good examples of philosophy in later Roman satirists, see Hor. *Sat.* 2.3; Pers. 5; and Juv. 10. Cf. Rudd (1989) 64–88; Cucchiarelli (2006) 62–80; and Highet (1949) 254–70. For an intriguing analysis of Horace's *Ars Poetica* as an example of "the mixed genre of *sermo*—an *Aufhebung* of the simple forms of technical handbook, didactic poem, and letter," see Frischer (1991) 87–100. If his contention—as well as his dating of the work to the mid-to-late 20s BC —is correct, could *De Re Rustica* have served as an important spiritual predecessor to Horace's work?

40. Branham (2009) 144. Most famously, Bakhtin (1981) 21–27 and Frye (1957) 308–12 both see the "Menippean" form of satire as an outgrowth (or, in Bakhtin's formulation, "product of the disintegration") of Plato's dialogues. For tentative arguments for the "genetic relationship" of Xenophon's Socratic dialogues with Menippean satire by way of the Cynics, Antisthenes, and Menippus himself, see Kronenberg (2009) 4.

41. See Kenney (1971) 17–20.

and positions amongst the elite.[42] Even Varro's own *Menippeans* apparently contained weighty philosophical content within its compositions of *hilaritas*.[43] Given the way that philosophy and satire are actually "the kind of opposites that converge," it is perhaps more prudent to conceive of their relationship as one of "fratricidal siblings" locked in a sort of "dialogic dance."[44] And in the case of the *RR*, this "dialogic dance" pervades both the dialogue's form and its content.

The *RR*'s affinities with satire—especially of the Menippean strand—first received serious attention in Heisterhagen's 1952 dissertation, which argued on the basis of form and content that Varro's work has a distinctly Menippean "complexion" (*Kolorit*) that empowers this conservative, yet putatively Cynic-leaning, Roman to indulge his penchant for moralistic critique of the contemporary decay in traditional Roman values.[45] Nonetheless, it was not

---

42. For this concept of "philosophical badinage" in Cicero's correspondence, see Griffin (1995) 325–46.

43. Cicero has Varro (*qua* interlocutor) in *Academica* characterize the works as follows (1.8): "And yet in those old works of ours, which we interspersed with a certain humor, in imitation (not translation) of Menippus, there are many things mixed in from profound philosophy and many things said dialectically (*et tamen in illis veteribus nostris, quae Menippum imitati non interpretati quadam hilaritate conspersimus, multa admixta ex intima philosophia, multa dicta dialectice*; transl. by Kronenberg [2009] 6 n. 22).

44. So Branham (2009) 140–41 aptly describes the relationship.

45. In particular, Heisterhagen considered five formal elements—names of interlocutors (63–70), parody of literary forms (70–79), representation of speech and its exchange (79–89), use of proverbs (89), and wordplays and alliteration (89–92)—and two substantive ones: criticism of his own day and age (92–99) and criticism of general human weakness (99–101). Perhaps Heisterhagen's most intriguing claim (103; cf. 66) was his almost paradoxical conclusion that this Cynic-inspired mode of satire enabled Varro both to indulge his penchant for moralizing and to give a particularly Roman "imprint" (*Gepräge*) to his work; on this view, the unforced style and acerbic wit of Cynicism is congruent with the mentality of earlier, pre-Hellenicized Romans and thus allowed Varro to add levity to an otherwise potentially dry topic as well as to criticize the decayed mores of his contemporary Romans. In other words, Heisterhagen's Varro was both a traditional Roman and a Cynic at heart and he rendered Cynicism a peculiarly Roman worldview. Aside from the problems with approaching Cynicism as a "philosophical system," Roman attitudes to the Cynics were incredibly variegated; see Griffin (1998) 190–204. Two other problems plague Heisterhagen's estimation. First, the question of Varro's philosophical affinities is anything but straightforward; in addition to Cynicism (cf. Knoche [1975] 57), Pythagoreanism (e.g., Skydsgaard [1968] 92–96, Cardauns [2001] 10) and Stoicism (e.g., Conte [1994a] 215) can be shown to have played varying roles in various parts of his life and his oeuvre—not to mention his apparent devotion to Antiochus and the Old Academy (cf. p. 6 and n. 12 in the introduction). Second, any putative sympathy between Cynicism and traditional Roman respect for the *mos maiorum* dissolves in the face of the former's rejection of tradition for simple tradition's sake and the latter's valorization of "the customs of the ancestors." For, as Relihan (1993) 65–71 rightly points out, "a Roman Cynic is a contradiction in terms; certainly pure Cynicism, mendicant and anti-institutional, ought not be espoused by a lover of Roman traditions" (66); thus, when aspects of Cynicism in the *Menippeans* can be detected, their presence is generally undercut in some way and

until a pair of roughly contemporaneous articles on the *RR*'s third dialogue by Carin Green (1997: 427–48) and Nicholas Purcell (1995: 151–79) that the text's satirical side received further scholarly attention. I will return to the specific arguments of each in chapter 6, but it should presently suffice to say that their readings of *RR* 3's technical matter in conjunction with its formal aspects represented a salutary approach to Varro's work, which I have also adopted in spirit herein. Furthermore, Green was the first to propose reading the *RR* as an implicitly political tract: one that articulates a view of "farming as a Xenophontic, or Cincinnatan, metaphor for wise government."[46] Building on Green's symbolic approach, Leah Kronenberg has since read the *RR* within a tradition of "agricultural allegory" directed towards the critique of moral and political turpitude in Greco-Roman societies. Rather than bemoaning the loss of Rome's traditional agrarian society (*a la* Heisterhagen) or using agriculture as a symbolic model for political restoration and stability (*a la* Green), Kronenberg's *RR* subverts the traditional valorization of the farmer as a virtuous citizen by exposing the "materialistic value system," which he, as an ideological figuration thereof, embodies and instantiates within normative Roman society. Insofar as Varro's work ironizes, parodies, and satirizes the farmer and farming in a fundamentally devastating fashion, the *RR* thus represents a spiritual (though perhaps not formal) "Menippean satire": one that is "destructive of conventional politics, morality, and learning" (13). The merits of Kronenberg's reading of the *RR* are many,[47] yet its emphasis on the destructiveness of the *RR*'s satire minimizes the work's agronomical/technical side, thereby effectively denying its utility and offering up an unflinchingly pessimistic reading of the work.[48] Whereas the majority of twentieth-

---

Varro, in this respect, is actually "follow[ing] the lead of Menippus in making the trappings of preaching undercut the things preached." For self-parody in the *RR*—especially of its potentially over-intellectualized approach to agronomy—see Kronenberg (2009) 12–13, 85–87 and Nelsestuen (2011) 333–37. That moralizing criticism was common to *all* philosophical traditions only further complicates the viability of Heisterhagen's contention.

46. As she explains (n. 9), Boissier (1861) 354–57 is perhaps the first to associate the *RR* with political life, but he saw little more than occasional reflections of "the violence of the civil wars."

47. In general, Kronenberg's work constitutes a salutary alternative to the Skydsgaardian estimation of the *RR* as a simple technical treatise (cf. n. 2), provides a provocative and productive framework for approaching the work as a whole, and breathes life into the study of ancient Menippean satire. Moreover, her tendency to read Varro's work in conjunction with Cicero's dialogues—particularly as the former's parodic critique of the latter's methods and program—reaps a number of intriguing intertexts between the two oeuvres, adumbrates an intriguingly fraught relationship between the pair of scholastically minded statesmen, and contributes to our understanding of the often polemical context of late Republican intellectual life.

48. In part, Kronenberg's ultimately reductive approach may stem from the teleological thrust of her narrative to situate Varro midway within a tradition that begins with Xenophon's

century scholarship understood the *RR* simply as a work of agronomy with the occasional literary conceit, Kronenberg's reading has completely reversed the terms of its interpretation: the *RR* as pure—and purely destructive—satire.

By reading the satirical aspects of the *RR* in conjunction with its philosophical and technical qualities, and by understanding that satire and philosophy can actually constitute two sides of the same coin, I hope to yield a more nuanced approach to this complex text. To this end, I also reframe the scholarly terms of *RR*'s generic affinity from specifically "Menippean satire"—the ancient, pre-*Apocolocyntosis* tradition of which remains almost hopelessly irrecoverable[49]—to the more general category of "satire," or perhaps better, the "satirical." By "satire" (itself a notoriously slippery and much-discussed generic concept[50]), I do not simply mean that literary category under which the verse works of Lucilius, Horace, Persius, and Juvenal are universally thought to fall and into which Petronius's *Satyrikon* and Seneca's *Apocolocyntosis* are sometimes thrown.[51] Instead, I am referring *also* to that mode

---

"ironic," but still "serious" and "protreptic," dialogue and that culminates in Vergil's poem on farming; unlike the latter's masterwork, which functions as a "meta-Menippean satire" that fundamentally questions the human desire and capability to order and explain the cosmos, Varro's work merely travesties multiple and competing worldviews in an ultimately aporetic fashion.

49. Knowledge of Menippus, the third-century BC Cynic and Syrian slave generally held to be the genre's originator, almost entirely hinges on much-later testimonia, while Varro's *Menippeans* survive mostly in the form of random fragments preserved by later grammarians whose interests lie in grammatical oddities. Even the handful of substantial fragments preserved by Aulus Gellius (e.g., *NA* 1.17.1–5 [= F 83]) allows us to draw few (if any) concrete conclusions regarding the corpus (further exacerbated by the inherently multifarious nature of satire). Considerable speculation about the content of specific satires and tenuous generalizations regarding the corpus as a whole are thus the norm for any study of ancient Menippean satire; see Relihan (1993) 49–53, whose eight "guiding principles" remain the best approach to these issues. Further complicating the issue is the ontological status of "Menippean satire" in the first-century BC. On the one hand, a number of Varro's satires feature the figure of Menippus, and both Cicero (*Acad.* 1.8) and Varro himself (Aul. Gell. *NA* 2.18.7) apparently referred to the collection as "Menippean satires." On the other hand, Quintilian seems to consider Varro's work a variation of Ennian satire, which casts doubt on the recognition of a specific genre of "Menippean satire"; see Relihan (1984) 226–29. It should also be observed that perhaps the most commonly cited characteristic of Menippean satire—prosimetric form (e.g., Conte [1994a] 217)—is simply not present in the *RR*.

50. Freudenburg (2005) 1–30 provides an excellent overview of the ancient and modern endeavors to define, describe, etymologize, revise, and theorize the nature of satire. It may be safe to say that one of the inherent characteristics of ancient Roman satire is the countervailing tension between identification with and differentiation from previous generic incarnations, a self-referential and parasitic aspect that may stem from its originally ludic origins; see Habinek (2005) 177–91.

51. Perhaps a result of an increased emphasis on the intertextual relations between and among Lucilius, Horace, Persius, and Juvenal (as well as the powerful, but tendentious, testimonia of Quint. *Inst.* 10.1.93–95), recent scholarship (e.g., Freudenburg 2001, Keane 2004) has tended to partition the so-called verse satirists from their prosimetric (i.e., Menippean)

of discourse that encompasses and deploys a consistently diverse collocation of farraginous literary elements (e.g., parody, irony, moralizing, puns,
humor, etc.) so as to perform the social functions of interrogating, evaluating,
and critiquing one's actions, attitudes, and/or beliefs against the backdrop of
established social conventions.[52] Of course, nothing prevents those very conventions—the hallowed and much-vaunted *mos maiorum* in the Roman context—as well as the putative satirist himself from occasionally coming under
the satirical lens as well. To give just one example (which I will return to in
chapter 5), *RR* 2 opens with a moralizing prologue (2.pref.1–3), in which Varro
deplores the declined state of contemporary agriculture vis-à-vis the ancestors. While his condemnation is serious, strong, and, on a superficial reading,
unequivocal, Varro inflects his critique with irony and puns in such a way
that *both* wryly subverts his hackneyed rhetoric of decline and its attendant
veneration of the past *and* prepares the reader for his renovation of traditional agrarian ideology: in that case, pastoralism *in,* and *of,* the provinces. In
these respects, Varro's words stand as both critique and corrective, simultaneously appealing to and refashioning Roman mores. Thus, I understand satire
as a complex discursive and social practice that is moral (or, at least, moralizing) in its character, evaluative in its mode, and normative (sometimes nor-
malizing) in its ideology. This discursive mode in turn relates to the genre of
satire by virtue of the former's persistent (though neither exclusive nor necessarily constant) presence in that set of texts which ancient and modern critics
alike claim to share other formal features (e.g., dactylic hexameter, the moral
diatribe, etc.) and, consequently, to merit grouping under the same category
(i.e., genre) of "satire." By employing some of the elements common to the
genre of satire, the *RR* also draws upon its sociodiscursive function, which
enables Varro to invest his work with meaning beyond the agronomy. And
in lieu of cataloguing the satirical (Menippean or otherwise) aspects found
in the *RR,* I focus on some common features and a few specific examples,
which not only illustrate the general connection but also foreshadow the sorts
of satirical (and technical) play in which Varro engages in each of his three
philosophical dialogues.

---

counterparts more rigidly than previous scholars (e.g., Knoche 1975). For the inherently "po-
liticized" nature of generic lists of satirists, see the astute, salutary, and self-aware comments
of Freudenburg (2005) 17–19. Cf. n. 4. Unlike the (largely) secure identification of the *Apocolocyntosis* as a Menippean satire, the generic affinity of the *Satyrikon* remains a recurring point
of scholarly debate, revolving largely around the extent to which one wishes to emphasize the
preeminence of the prosimetric form (i.e., Menippean satire) or its (often perverse) affinities
with the Greek novel; see Conte (1994b) 459–62.

    52. The increasing scholarly tendency to approach satire as a social phenomenon is neatly
illustrated by a recent collection's devotion of nearly a quarter of its contents to "satire as social
discourse" (Freudenburg 2005).

Perhaps the most evident point of connection between the *RR* and satire lies in its rampant use of puns, most prominently in the names of characters.[53] The names of Book 1's minor interlocutors—Fundanius, Fundilius, Agrius, and Agrasius—all derive from *fundus* or *ager,* which is more than fitting for a discussion that will center on activities of the farm and field. In *RR* 2, "the Cow" (i.e., Vaccius) is the character prodded to discuss cattle (2.5.2) and "the Sow" (i.e., Scrofa) examines swine (2.4.1), while *RR* 3's dedicatee, "Pinnius," or "Feathered One," initiates a series of puns on the names of the various birdhouse interlocutors, thereby engaging intertextually with Aristophanes' *Birds* as well as anticipating the dialogue's ensuing account of aviaries.[54] In these respects, the characters populating the *RR*'s world not only hail from a variety of sociocultural backgrounds, but are either talking embodiments of each *sermo*'s topic or, at least, surrounded by them. Thus, far from discussing one aspect or another of rustic practice in a decidedly detached fashion, the interlocutors act as physical incarnations of land, farms, livestock, and game, thereby rendering visible—if only momentarily so—the sorts of implicit literary play underlying the *RR*'s technical discussion.

As we saw earlier, the *RR*'s settings differ from those of Cicero's dialogues in that they straddle the private and public spheres, the latter of which also frequently features as the backdrop to satire's staged encounters.[55] Two additional elements also contribute specifically to the satiric tincture of the dialogues' settings. First, all three occasions are random and subject to chance (Lat. *casus*; Gk. *tuche*).[56] In *RR* 1, Varro himself unexpectedly encounters (*offendere*) Fundanius, Agrasius, and Agrius in the Temple of Tellus (1.2.1) and the group as a whole is pleasantly surprised thereafter by the arrival of the

---

53. See Heisterhagen (1952) 63–70 for a more comprehensive list. Of Varro's *Menippeans,* we possess fragments of *Manius,* an actual Roman name and, in the context of its contrast between pristine virtue and contemporary moral decay, apparently playing off its literal meaning (F 247–68): "Mr. Early-to-Rise." For further discussion, see Relihan (1993) 61. Cf. F 432. In the *Satyrikon* (89), Eumolpus or, "Mr. Good-Singer," composes a none-too-pretty epic.

54. See Green (1997) 434–35, who rightly notes that the Romans also had gods named after animals (e.g., Picus, i.e., "Woodpecker").

55. For example, Horace's *Satires* 1.8 takes place in a public garden and 1.9 during a trek through the city (*via Sacra,* 1; Temple of Vesta, 35), while Juvenal's satire on the perils of urban life in Rome recounts a conversation at the Porta Capena (3.11). For the frequently urban and public settings of satire due to its ludic performance and contestation of elite masculinity, see Habinek (2005) 181.

56. Compare the similar setup in *Satires* 1.9, where "Horace" is unfortunate enough to run into a boor who simply will not leave him alone. In the case of the *Satyrikon,* it is possible to read the text as a series of essentially random encounters; see, for example, chapters 7 (*occurrit*) and 83 (*ecce . . . intravit*). Note also that the conclusion to *RR* 1 has the departing participants explicitly pondering "human chance/misfortune" (*casus humanus,* 1.69.3).

two primary interlocutors, Scrofa and Stolo (1.2.9); the dialogue of the second book commences *in medias res*, but as their separate departures (2.11.12) imply, the two groups of interlocutors randomly encountered one another on their respective ways; and Book 3 also depicts Varro and Q. Axius alighting upon (*invenire*) Appius Claudius Pulcher presiding over his aviary (3.2.2). Thus, each dialogue dramatizes a chance encounter, which is prompted by an opportune moment and facilitated by fortuitous interlocutors.

Second, the *RR*'s settings always entail dinner parties and a concomitant obsession with food, both of which are characteristic of Varro's *Menippeans* as well as earlier and later satire.[57] Thus, *RR* 1 has Varro specifically coming to the Temple of Tellus at the invitation of the sacristan (1.2.2), whose absence prompts the ensuing discussion, but not without the complaints of hungry participants (1.2.11; cf. 1.56). Of course, his assassination (1.69.3) renders the dinner party a disaster and generically evocative of the infelicitous *cenae* of Nasidienus and Trimalchio.[58] Book 2's promised *cenae* transpire more amiably, with both groups going their respective ways (2.11.12) and, presumably, enjoying their impending dinners.[59] In Book 3, the dinner party does not factor directly into the dialogue's staging, but the motif does still find its way onto the scene when Appius refers to a dinner at which Axius had apparently entertained him a few days before and frames the ensuing discussion as an act of reciprocation (*RR* 3.2.2).[60] Moreover, Appius's reference to "burping

---

57. For the culinary and hosting arts in the fragments of Varro's *Menippeans* (as preserved by Aulus Gellius), see *Peri Edesmaton* ("On Gourmet Food"; F 403) and *Nescis Quid Vesper Serus Vehat* ("You Know Not What Late Evening May Bring"; F 333–41). For further discussion—including the connections with the *Satyrikon*'s *Cena*—see Relihan (1993) 54–59. For examples of the interconnections between food, philosophy, and moralizing in Lucilius, see F 200–7, 815–23, 1022–23, and 1234; and of the dinner-party, see F 595–604. Perhaps the most famous examples of dinner parties in Roman satire, however, are those of Nasidienus (Hor. *Sat.* 2.8) and Trimalchio (the so-called *Cena Trimalchionis* [26ff.] of the *Satyrikon*), both of which boast grotesquely extravagant meals. As Gowers (1993b) 109–219 has extensively documented, food is intimately connected in various ways with Roman satire, often functioning as a literary metaphor for the genre and even perhaps the source of its etymological origin (for which, see Diom. 1.485 Keil).

58. As M. S. Smith (1975) xix–xx notes, both Trimalchio's and Nasidienus's dinner parties are interrupted by mishaps from above: the fall of the curtain at Hor. *Sat.* 2.8.54 roughly resembles the acrobat's fatal fall in *Satyrikon* 54. Perhaps the comparisons with the *RR* can be pushed even further, as both occasions elicit trite reflections on human susceptibility to Fortuna, which may find some parallel in the interlocutors' departing laments "over human misfortune" (*de casu humano*; 1.69.3). Of course, Trimalchio's *cena* ends in complete disarray and concludes (like *RR* 1) with the host's "death."

59. Note that a certain amount of irony may attend this successful conclusion with the realization that Romans can enjoy dinner parties in times of external conflicts (in this case, with pirates) but are unable to do so when the conflict is a civil one. Cf. pp. 168–69 in chapter 5.

60. For the full quote and discussion—especially of its cannibalistic connotations—see pp. 181–82 in chapter 6.

up" (*ructor*) the "hospitable birds" (*aves hospitales*) he consumed at Axius's is entirely in keeping with satire's emphasis on the bodily aspects of entertainment.[61] In this respect, Appius's emphasis on the gastronomical delights of their *cena* underscores the differences between the *RR*'s satiricizing dialogues and the Ciceronian dialogues' emphasis on the culture and urbanity of aristocratic *otium,* the delights of which lie in intellectual reflection and *not* gourmandizing. Furthermore, instead of meals capping philosophical discussions, all three dialogues of the *RR* philosophize the meals' components in the forms of grains, olives and figs, and wine (i.e., *agri cultura, RR* 1); animal meat and milk (i.e., *pastio, RR* 2); and luxury game, fowl, and fish (i.e., *pastio villatica, RR* 3). This wryly appropriate intellectualization of the *convivium* perhaps echoes Plato's *Symposium,* which both transformed erotics and drinking into a philosophical discussion of love and provided the paradigm for subsequent literary *cenae*: philosophical, satirical, and otherwise. Yet, by interrogating the origins of gustatory produce, the *RR* may be understood to go one step further, or rather, lower, than its Platonic progenitor to serve as the meta-sympotic *cena* of philosophico-satirical traditions.

## A CASE STUDY OF PARODY AND IRONY IN THE *RR*

So far, we have seen how two aspects evocative of philosophical dialogues—characterization and setting—also evince a distinctly satirical hue. In chapters 3 through 6, we will have further occasion to consider how these urban settings, walking puns, chance meetings, and lurking dinner parties—as well as other philosophico-satirical features like the presence of moralizing discourse, parody,[62] and use of irony in general—not only color the presentation of the technical content, but even facilitate metaphorical and, more specifically, political levels on which to read the three dialogues. Before turning to the *RR*'s agronomical content in chapter 2, however, I would like to conclude with a brief case study, which will illustrate how the philosophical and satirical features can enrich the technical account. As we shall see, this episode involves a dialogic exchange between two characters with some degree of ironic utterance by, and possible parody of, one or more of them. While the exchange is brief and there remains ambiguity as to precisely how we ought to interpret it, the episode nonetheless raises an important preconsideration

---

61. Cf. the comments of Gowers (1993b) 162–63 on the subversion of Plato's *Symposium* in Horatian satire.

62. By "parody," I mean the sense employed by Relihan (1993) 25–26 in his discussion of Menippean satire: the poking fun at "the idea of deriving *auctoritas* from an *auctor.*"

for understanding the *RR*'s account of *agri cultura* and, consequently, contributes positively to the text's ultimately useful technical discussion of farming. Insofar as this humorous and irony-laden passage thus constructively enhances the *RR*'s project of articulating *res rusticae*, it also exemplifies the potential for Varro's work to walk both a sincere and an ironic line: one that simultaneously cultivates and critiques its own intellectual project.

In the exposition of the first dialogue (1.2.11–28), the major (Scrofa and Stolo) and minor interlocutors (Varro, Fundanius, Agrius, and Agrasius) preliminarily mull over what subjects and practices ought to be included under *agri cultura*. The conversation careens from one consideration to another, eventually grappling with previous agronomists' inclusion of nonagronomical material in their agricultural treatises. After reviewing, quoting, and criticizing the work of the Sasernae, a father-son duo,[63] in ways that are both serious and humorous, Stolo[64] and Agrius turn to the most venerable Cato and his treatise, *De Agri Cultura* (1.2.28):

> "An non in magni illius Catonis libro, qui de agri cultura est editus, scripta sunt permulta similia, ut haec, quem ad modum placentam facere oporteat, quo pacto libum, qua ratione pernas sallere?" "Illud non dicis," inquit Agrius, "quod scribit, 'si velis in convivio multum bibere cenareque libenter, ante esse oportet brassicam crudam ex aceto aliqua folia quinque.'"

> [Stolo]: "Or weren't there quite a few similar things written in the book of that great Cato, which was published on *agri cultura*, like the following: how one ought to prepare placenta, the manner of preparing *libum*, the method for salting hams." "Not to mention *that* rule of his," says Agrius, "'If you want to drink a whole lot and to eat freely at a dinner party, you ought to eat some five leaves of raw cabbage with vinegar beforehand.'"

Matching Stolo's initial observation that Cato (like the Sasernae) included a number of country recipes in his treatise, Agrius seemingly ups the ante by actually quoting part of Cato's infamous discussion of the salutary merits of

---

63. For the Sasernae, see Martin (1971) 81–93.

64. Throughout, I have adopted the text of Flach's 2006 edition and unless otherwise noted, all translations are mine. In the present case, however, I follow the understanding of Ash and Hooper (1934) 182, which assigns this speaking part to Stolo per the more conservative texts of Keil (1889) and Goetz (1929). Flach (2006) 54 (cf. 1996: 99, 245), on the other hand, assigns the first part to Varro the interlocutor. For the difficulties in determining whether *inquam* denotes that Varro (*qua* interlocutor) is now speaking (e.g., I say, "*agri cultura* is good") or indicates emphasis by the presently speaking interlocutor (e.g., "*agri cultura* is, I say, good"), see Flach (1996) 40.

cabbage.[65] Insofar as the *RR*'s interlocutors will eventually delineate the subject of *agri cultura* (1.3–1.4.2), a discussion of the medicinal properties of cabbage simply does not belong in an agronomical work. In this respect, the passage rightly adduces Cato's praise of cabbage as the crowning exemplum of previous agronomists' penchants for including impertinent material and thus serves (as we shall see in chapter 2) a serious purpose in the service of Varro's reframing of the field of *agri cultura* from the broader category of "the life of a farmer" to an abstract, more analytical, and "scientific" conception.

Yet, depending on how we understand the valence of each character's part, a certain amount of irony and parody appears to underlie the discussion. On the one hand, Stolo's invocation of Cato actually seems to be meant to defend the Sasernae from the criticism previously directed at them; if Cato included such stuff, then it is no wonder that the Sasernae did as well. In his defense of the Sasernae (cf. 1.2.24), then, Stolo comes off as the thoroughly traditional agronomist of the bunch (cf. 1.2.12), yet his interjection—as wry as it may be (cf. *subridens,* 1.2.27)—only underscores the shortcomings of his predecessors, thereby undercutting his own intentions and perhaps rendering him susceptible to further agronomical attack. Or perhaps it is merely capitulatory banter, which concedes the ill-fated endeavor of defending the old agronomy in the presence of those about to espouse a new one. On the other hand, the precise valence of Agrius's rejoinder remains opaque as well. Is he sincerely, if overenthusiastically, quoting "that famous" passage so as to support a beleaguered Stolo, thereby becoming an object of humor himself and potentially undermining his own critical authority as well? Or is it a self-aware response of irony to Stolo's floundering appeal to Cato's recipes, which trenchantly hammers home the failure of the former's defense? Or is it simply a way for Agrius to humorously invoke the absent *cena,* underscoring his own hunger and intimating yet again the *RR*'s satiric affinities to the reader? Or perhaps Cato's recommendation of cabbage as a hangover preventative—despite its lack of strict relevance to *agri cultura*—actually pertains more to the *cena* of *RR* 1 than any of the interlocutors realize and the joke turns out to be on all of them? Any answer to this sort of inquiry clearly depends on the particular admixture of the humorous and the serious the reader is willing to ascribe to this exchange between Stolo and Agrius, but the fact that these questions arise speaks to yet another philosophico-satirical aspect of

---

65. Aside from the preface, Cato's *laus brassicae* (*Agr.* 157ff.) actually represents the most literarily and intellectually cogent passage of the treatise, and its content suggests the author's familiarity with Hellenistic philosophy and medicine; see Rawson (1985) 135 and Boscherini (1993) 730–40.

the *RR*: the problem of mimetic representation, quotation, and authority.[66] Regardless of its intended force, that Agrius's response concludes the interlocutors' preliminary discussion by problematizing the pertinence of dinner party remedies for agricultural treatises *within* a dinner party that is about to become an agricultural treatise adds a layer of irony to the *RR*'s project and is perhaps a self-effacing wink at the reader in the know.

The following chapter examines Varro's approach to *res rusticae*, focusing on the ways in which the text contextualizes, defines, and structures its subject matter. Instead of assuming the codified existence of *agri cultura* and *pastio* as static conceptual categories inherited by Varro, I argue that many of the *RR*'s recurring verbal and taxonomic features are indicative of Varro's discursive reorganization of *res rusticae* in general, which in its own right represents a positive intellectual contribution in addition to—and in conjunction with—its philosophico-satirical aims.

---

66. For these issues in the *Apocolocyntosis* and *Satyrikon*, see the respective treatments of O'Gorman (2005) 95–108 and Conte (1996) *passim*. In philosophy, this problem particularly preoccupied mid-twentieth-century scholarship on the relationship between the historical Socrates and the one represented in Plato's and Xenophon's dialogues; for two very different approaches, see Vlastos (1991) and Strauss (1972).

# CHAPTER 2

# Creating the Agronomical Field of *res rusticae*

Atque ut omittam has artes elegantes et ingenuas, ne opifices quidem tueri sua artificia possent, nisi vocabulis uterentur nobis incognitis, usitatis sibi. Quin etiam agri cultura, quae abhorret ab omni politiore elegantia, tamen eas res, in quibus versatur, nominibus notavit novis. Quo magis hoc philosopho faciendum est.

And leaving out these refined and liberal arts, not even craftsmen could observe their professions if they did not use words unknown to us, but familiar to them. But indeed even *agri cultura,* which recoils from every kind of more polished refinement/systematic treatment (*politior elegantia*), nevertheless has coined new words for the matters that it treats. For this reason, the philosopher must do this all the more so.

—Cicero, *De Finibus* 3.4

Et ut agricolationem Romana tandem civitate donemus (nam adhuc istis auctoribus Graecae gentis fuit), iam nunc M. Catonem Censorium illum memoremus, qui eam latine loqui primus instituit, post hunc duos Sasernas, patrem et filium, qui eam diligentius erudiverunt, ac deinde Scrofam Tremelium qui etiam eloquentem reddidit et M. Terentium qui expolivit, mox Vergilium, qui carminum quoque potentem fecit.

And that we may at last grant Roman citizenship to *agricolatio* (for it still belonged to those authors of the Greek race), let us now at last recall that famous Cato the Censor, who was the first to train her to speak in Latin; thereafter, the

two Sasernae—father and son—who refined her more carefully; and then [Cn.]
Tremelius Scrofa, who even rendered her eloquent (*eloquens*); and M. Terentius
[Varro], who thoroughly polished her (*expolivit*); and soon thereafter Vergil,
who gave also the power of song.

—Columella, *Res Rusticae* 1.1.12

Some seven years before the *RR*'s composition, Cicero wrote about the Roman
philosopher's need to invent new words, observing that such coinages could
even be found in a subject like *agri cultura,* which "recoils from" every form
of "more polished refinement" (*politior elegantia*): a phrase that encompasses
senses both aesthetic (i.e., "literary polish") and structural (i.e., "systematic
treatment").[1] Less than a century later, Columella will claim that Varro "thoroughly polished" (*expolivit*) the subject.[2] What exactly does Varro do to overcome the discursive shortcomings Cicero imputed to *agri cultura* so as to
merit Columella's praise?

On the basis of the previous chapter, Varronian *politia* and *elegantia* might
reasonably be understood as the recasting of the principles and precepts of *res
rusticae* into a dialogue form so as to create a text of unique generic admixture. But to limit Varro's efforts to philosophico-satirical "literary polish" is
also to overlook the actual agronomical content that makes up the bulk of
the *RR,* thereby ignoring its decidedly "systematic treatment" of *res rusticae*
and propagating the tendency to construe the literary features as somehow
independent of or ornamental to the technical material. In order to avoid
this reductive approach, this chapter explores how Varro intervenes within

---

1. For the meaning of *elegans,* its derivatives, and near-synonyms in the late Republic,
see Krostenko (2001) 114–23.

2. For speculative explorations of the potentially polemical and allusive dynamics between these two passages, see Rawson (1985) 136–37 and Nelsestuen (2011) 320–26 and
330–33. Note also that Varro's project may not be wholly innovative, for the testimony of
Columella may imply that Varro's contribution to *agricolatio* (cf. *expolivit*) relied on the
work of Cn. Tremelius Scrofa, who rendered it *eloquens* and is a staged interlocutor (!) in
the *RR,* no less. As I have argued elsewhere, the *RR* probably both adopts the systematic and
scientific approach espoused by Scrofa (cf. *eloquentia,* Columella, *Rust.* 1.1.12) and adapts
it in a mélange of historical verisimilitude and praise, parody and polemic; see Nelsestuen
(2011) 315–51, but note the quite different estimation of Kronenberg (2009) 76–93, who prefers to see the Varronian Scrofa as a fantastic and incompetent amalgam of the historical
figure and a putative contemporary of Varro. Unfortunately, the complete loss of Scrofa's
treatise fundamentally impairs any decisive disentanglement of Scrofian contributions from
Varronian agronomy. Nonetheless, while the precise extent of Varro's original contributions
to the field of *res rusticae* may be open to question, the processes inscribed within the
*RR*—be they reproduced, inaugurated, or (most likely) some mixture thereof—admit the
same analysis.

the existing "discourse"[3] of farming at Rome in order to articulate, historicize, and rationalize *res rusticae* as a new, abstract, and "scientific" field by
means of the dialogue form as well as a whole host of other analytical and
verbal strategies. My investigation into the *RR*'s technical content thus proceeds from the understanding that the way of talking about practices of the
fields, pastures, and villas—things that modern scholars easily denominate
as "agriculture" and "animal husbandry"—is not self-evident, *a priori,* and
ahistorical;[4] rather than being conceptually uniform within the ancient and
modern worlds, those practices that Varro will come to designate as *agri cultura, pastio,* and *pastio villatica* and that collectively comprise *res rusticae*
need to be approached with an alien eye. Jettisoning our own presuppositions will in turn allow us to approach anew the *RR* as a theoretical account
of *res rusticae* and to see that, far from taking for granted the concepts treated
therein, the text actively constitutes, delineates, and rationalizes its subject
matter; that it does so by winnowing *agri cultura* from the chaff of diverse,
sometimes conflicting, opinions through a process of staged disagreement
and emergent consensus should be understood as Varro's attempt to negotiate
actual ambiguity, uncertainty, or contestation over the subject.

But what prompts Varro's intervention within the apparently muddled
state of agronomy? As we shall see, Varro frames the *RR* as a response to the
intellectual failings of the previous agronomical tradition (e.g., *RR* 1.2.12–13) as
well as to the present ignorance of his fellow Romans (e.g., 2.pref.1–3).[5] Thus
looking both backwards and forwards, the *RR* attempts to walk a fine line
between, on the one hand, critically revaluating and synthesizing its Greek,
Carthaginian, and Roman predecessors and, on the other, redressing the contemporary loss of knowledge traditionally ascribed to the *maiores.* By virtue

---

3. By "discourse," I mean (a) the "way of talking about" a circumscribed subject (such
as a specific field of inquiry, a set of objects or practices, and so on), which (b) is conditioned
by its particular historical, intellectual, linguistic, social, and cultural circumstances. For the
notion of "discourse" as a "way of talking about some subject matter," see Riggsby (2006) 4,
who follows to a degree the approach of Foucault (1972) 21–39. Cf. 193. Note also that the
conditioning circumstances I explicitly add to Riggsby's definition of "discourse" (though
his discussion would already seem to acknowledge them implicitly) are generally informed
by what Foucault refers to as "the rules of [discursive] formation" (e.g., 38).

4. So Skydsgaard (1968) 7–37, who rightly emphasized the prevalence of Varro's analytic
methods in arranging and structuring *RR* 1, but whose implicit subscription to the notion of
a static and universal discourse of *agri cultura* leads him both to overlook the extent to which
Varro's text articulates *agri cultura,* its variables, and its parameters. Cf. his view of the *RR*'s
generic status as a simple technical treatise on p. 10 n. 2.

5. Cf. Varro's famous claim to be performing a superlatively Metellus- or Aeneas-like
service in preserving knowledge of the gods from *neglegentia civium* in *ARD* F 2a Cardauns
[= August. *De Civ. D.* 6.2.48].

of the fact that it views present rustic enterprise in a state of decline from the idealized time of the *maiores* and fundamentally changed in its contemporary form, the *RR* participates in larger Roman debates surrounding the *mos maiorum* and, more specifically, the perceived crisis therein.[6] At the same time, this period of cultural/moral crisis also formed the backdrop—sometimes even the impetus—for profound and often disruptive changes in the ways in which the ancient Romans conceptualized and categorized their world, including the flowering of Hellenistic modes of thought at Rome.[7] The result is that farming as a sociocultural concept and intellectual field was—much like divination, sexuality, and architecture, among others[8]—ripe for reconsideration. This chapter thus argues that the *RR* responds to this ideological crisis by attempting to rationalize a *new* Roman field of *res rusticae,* one that is relatively coherent and markedly disembedded[9] from the more general Roman politico-cultural discourse concerning the salient individual who engages in rustic enterprise: the *agricola.* Instead of presenting a disorganized and wide-ranging account of various things that somehow (and to varying degrees) pertain to farmers, the *RR*'s systematic treatment of *res rusticae* constitutes both an abstraction from the agent (i.e., *agricola*) to the art (i.e., *agri cultura*) and a significant development in Roman intellectual history.

In what follows, I examine three distinct, but concurrent and collaborative, threads to the *RR*'s discursive project. First, I argue that Varro's prefatory

---

6. For important discussions of the crisis in late Republican culture and *mores* attendant to what modern historians typically used to describe primarily in political terms, see Habinek (1998) 34–68; Moatti (1997) 23–54; Wallace-Hadrill (1997) 3–22 and (2005) 55–84. Cf. the important study of Edwards (1993), which laid some of the groundwork for these later studies.

7. See Rawson (1985) 3–114 and Moatti (1997) 55–95, the latter of whom more generally argues for a monumental paradigm shift in ways of knowing during the late Republic by way of occasional analogy to the Enlightenment.

8. For the critical extrication of divination from Roman daily life and its reconstitution into a scientific discourse in Cicero's *De Divinatione,* see Beard (1986) 33–46. Habinek (1997) 23–43 charts a similar development for "sexuality" from Catullus to Ovid. For Vitruvius's creation of *architectura* as an ordered body of knowledge, see McEwen (2003) 15–88.

9. Polanyi (1957) originally applied the terms *embedded* and *disembedded* to distinguish precapitalist and capitalist economies; whereas the former was embedded in a network of social structures, the latter is not. Here, I apply the terms *embedded* and *disembedded* so as to distinguish between a discourse that is, on the one hand, interconnected with and dependent upon other discursive categories for its undifferentiated identity and, on the other hand, a putatively isolated, abstract, and self-sufficient system. Various strands of modern critical thought (esp. the post-structuralists; cf. Bakhtin [1986] 60–102) would rightly object that, because any one particular discourse is always partially entwined with others (if only by means of the whole of shared language), no verbal discourse can truly be wholly "disembedded." Despite its ontological shortcomings, the term *disembedded* retains its usefulness by virtue of its ability to denote a degree of perceived (hence, "putative") discursive autonomy not found in embedded linguistic contexts.

list of sources constructs an agronomical tradition grounded in philosophy, inaugurated by the Carthaginian Mago, and critically elaborated in the course of the *RR* itself. Second, I turn to the issues of definition, systematization, and organization, all of which are constitutive of the *RR*'s disposition of *res rusticae* into a technical field. Third, I trace the emergence of *agri cultura* as a newly established scientific field from the broader and less precise set of activities practiced by an *agricola,* which will allow me to historicize the *RR*'s signature contributions to *res rusticae.* On the final analysis, then, we shall see that Varro's work crafts an *ars* and *scientia* of *res rusticae,* and renders rustic enterprise an object amenable to—perhaps even worthy of—philosophical inquiry.

## SOURCES AND THE CREATION OF A ROMAN AGRONOMICAL TRADITION

Prompted by the prevailing methodology of *Quellenforschung* and bedazzled by the extensive list of sources found in the preface, nineteenth- and early twentieth-century scholars of the *RR* focused on the work's potential for reconstructing a highly speculative history of Greek and Roman agronomy.[10] Casting Varro as a learned antiquarian, whose work represents a valuable compendium of agricultural thought, or even as a mere copyist, whose failures or distortions render his work of questionable value, such approaches generally fail to acknowledge the substance and merits of the *RR*'s seemingly unprecedented, systematic, and occasionally impressive approach to *res rusticae.* I am thus less concerned with the largely irrecoverable historical origins of agronomical thought and Varro's putative debt to these sources than with the terms of engagement he sets with this tradition; in particular, I explore how the *RR* constructs the very tradition within which it locates itself and its professed contributions and innovations. The basic questions I am asking are as follows: who does Varro cite and to what end? As we shall see, by actively creating a history of agronomy, wherein the *RR* stands as the consummation of the tradition, Varro's text also lays the intellectual foundation for its recasting of *res rusticae* into a more theoretical, even "philosophical," form.

All three books of the *RR* sporadically invoke a number of previous authorities,[11] yet nowhere are these sources so extensively discussed as in the

---

10. For a useful and rightly skeptical survey of previous reconstructions, see Skydsgaard (1968) 66–70. Cf. McAlhany (2003) 63–76, who notes Skydsgaard's occasional inability to escape fully from the old *Quellenforschung.*

11. See appendix 2.

formal list provided in the preface to *RR* 1. Dedicating this first book to his wife, Fundania,[12] Varro thereafter provides her with a list of sources—Greek, Punic, and Latin—she could consult should his treatise fall short in one area or another (1.1.7–9):

> As for those things which are left out and you seek, I will point out from what writers—both Greek and our own (*et Graecis et nostris*)—these things are to be found. Those who have written in Greek in a scattered fashion (*dispersim*)—each on separate topics (*alius de alia re*)—are more than 50.
>
> [A.]  These are the ones whom you can consult (*habere in consilio*), if you wish to solicit consultation (*consulere*) on something: Hieron of Sicily and Attalus Philometor;
>
> [B.]  of the philosophers (*de philosophis*), Democritus the natural scientist, Xenophon the Socratic, Aristotle and Theophrastus, the Peripatetics, Archytas the Pythagorean;
>
> [C.]  likewise (*item*), Amphilochus of Athens, Anaxipolis of Thasos, Apollodorus of Lemnos, Aristophanes of Mallos, Antigonus of Cyme, Agathocles of Chios, Apollonius of Pergamum, Aristandrus of Athens, Bacchius of Miletus, Bion of Soli, Chaeresteus and Chaereas of Athens, Diodorus of Priene, Dion of Colophon, Diophanes of Nicaea, Epigenes of Rhodes, Euagon of Thasos, the two Euphronii—the Athenian and the Amphipoliteian—Hegesias of Maronea, the two Menanders—the first of Priene and the second of Heraclea—Nicesius of Maronea, and Pythion of Rhodes;
>
> [D.]  of the rest, whose *patria* I have not received: Androtion, Aeschrion, Aristomenes, Athenagoras, Crates, Dadis, Dionysius, Euphiton, Euphorion, Eubulus, Lysimachus, Mnaseas, Menestratus, Plentiphanes, Persis, and Theophilus.
>
> [E.]  All of these men whom I have mentioned wrote in prose; certain men have treated these same subjects in poetry: Hesiod of Ascra and Menecrates of Ephesus.

When one includes the three subsequent authorities—Mago and his two abridgers, Cassius Dionysius of Utica and Diophanes—Varro's sources in fact total fifty-two, all of whom (with the exception of Mago) are ethnically or linguistically Greek, encompass a number of different professions and statuses

---

12. For Fundanius, the father of Fundania, see p. 77 in chapter 3.

(e.g., kings, philosophers, and poets), and span a wide temporal range, from the archaic (e.g., Hesiod) to the late Hellenistic periods (e.g., Pythion).

More than a haphazard compendium of "agricultural" writers, though, the list in fact evinces rational organization into six distinct categories. Likely stemming from their status as kings and suggestively intimating at the connection between farming and politics,[13] the first group (A) consists of Hiero of Sicily and Attalus Philometor, who were the respective rulers of Syracuse (270–215) and Pergamum (138–133), renowned for their pro-Roman sympathies, and (in)famous for their interest in *res rusticae*.[14] The second group (B) comprises five philosophers: Democritus the physicist, Xenophon the Socratic, the Peripatetics Aristotle and Theophrastus, and the Pythagorean Archytas of Tarentum.[15] To varying degrees, each of these figures composed works that treated matters, if not expressly concerned with, then at least tangentially related to, *res rusticae*.[16] Perhaps more importantly, they also embody four major traditions of classical philosophy: the Atomists (Democritus), Socratics (Xenophon), Peripatetics (Aristotle and Theophrastus), and Pythagoreans (Archytas). The otherwise ill-attested third (C) and

---

13. Cf. Flach (1996) 226.

14. Note that both kings proved a boon to the safety and status of the *res publica*; whereas Hiero switched allegiance from the Carthaginians to the Romans in 263 BC, maintained good relations with them until his death in 215, and, in these respects, facilitated the security of a burgeoning Mediterranean empire (Scullard [1989] 546; cf. 564), Attalus famously bequeathed his kingdom to the Romans upon his death in 133, which marked a significant development in the history of Roman involvement in Asia Minor and was to provide the financial basis for Tiberius Gracchus's controversial agrarian measures (Habicht [1989] 377–78). Might we make something of their contributions to Roman *imperium*—as well as the potential downsides? Regarding their agricultural inclinations, Attalus notoriously cultivated interest in poisonous plants and herbs (Columella, *Rust.* 1.1.8; Plin. *HN* 18.22), while Hiero introduced a new system of taxation on land and appears to have placed a premium on agricultural profitability (Cic. *Verr.* 2.32, 147; 3.28; Columella, *Rust.* 1.1.8). Cf. D. J. Thompson (1984) 364–66, who observes that "interest in agriculture, that is in the economic basis of their kingdoms, is a widely-documented feature of Hellenistic kings."

15. The rationale for the ordering of the philosophers appears to be less chronological and more geographical, moving from east to west: Democritus of Abdera (b. ca. 460 BC); Xenophon (ca. 430–355), Aristotle (384–322), and Theophrastus (ca. 371–287), all three of whom are (presumably) being associated with Athens; and Archytas of Tarentum (fl. ca. 400–350).

16. Democritus was generally concerned with the constitutional makeup of the natural world, while Aristotle certainly touched upon agricultural matters in a number of his treatises; cf. Flach (1996) 227. The inclusion of Archytas may be more problematic as the existence of such a work has recently come under challenge; see Huffman (2005) 27–31. Finally, Theophrastus's botanical treatises are still extant and Xenophon's *Oeconomicus* rates as the surviving Greek work that is most closely related to the Roman agricultural treatises.

fourth (D) groups[17] appear to underscore further the philosophical pedigree of farming[18]—its lineage, breadth, and longevity—while the fifth (E) imparts a closing poetic tincture.[19]

Despite the list's prominent placement, however, the Greek sources remain relatively invisible throughout the course of the dialogues' conversations. In fact, of these forty-nine sources, only the members of group two receive *any* mention in the course of the *RR* and, among them, it is only Theophrastus who attracts any significant attention.[20] Of course, if we possessed the other forty-four sources, the picture regarding the *RR*'s engagement with them might very well be different. Yet, the true value of the list's first five sections would seem to lie not so much with its utility as a compendium of sources—indeed, how is Fundania to know which source to consult for what question?—as with its construction of an agronomical tradition that has political, poetic, and, above all, philosophical roots.

Furthermore, the placement of an almost impossibly long and implausibly collated list of sources in such a prominent position may point to a certain amount of irony attending this opening and suggests that we might read it as a parody of the sorts of lists and other authoritative claims to knowledge that preface comparable expert treatises.[21] Even so, parody itself constitutes

---

17. Of the former two groups—differentiated by *patria* (twenty-four known, sixteen unknown) and ordered alphabetically (cf. Daly [1967])—nearly all of the members are attested only here or in Columella's work as well. As Flach (1996) 227–28 discusses, essentially nothing is known about them aside from what Varro *may* tell us though his use of *item,* which likely speaks to their identification as "philosophers." It is perhaps not unreasonable to surmise that the forty members of C and D postdate the second group, which accords with what we know about the proliferation of technical literature in the Hellenistic period; see Lloyd (1984) 321–52 and D. J. Thompson (1984) 363. Note also that the list cannot be regarded as comprehensive. For example, it does not include Dicaearchus, who appears to underlie the history of agriculture and pastoralism Varro gives at *RR* 2.1.3–5 (cf. 1.2.16). Also noteworthy is the potential omission of Posidonius, whose output on a wide variety of subjects pertinent to farming (e.g., climatology [F 49 = F 28 Jacoby] and production of crops in various lands [e.g., F 55A = F 3 Jac., F 70 = F 19A Jac.]) could have merited his inclusion and whose close connections to elite Romans (especially Pompey) would have likely rendered him familiar to Varro.

18. Note that the *RR*'s implicit posturing as a work of philosophy in fact anticipates a standard topos of later "technical" writers (e.g., Vitr., *De Arch.* 1.1.7). Cf. Quintilian's claim that, because the "perfect" orator is a "good man," oratory supplants philosophy as the master discourse (*Inst.* 1.Pref.9–20).

19. Hesiod disappears from the *RR* hereafter, while Menecrates recurs once at 3.16.18 in the discussion of bees.

20. 1.5.1, 1.7.6, 1.7.7, 1.37.5, 1.40.1, 1.40.3, 1.44.2, 1.44.3, and 1.45.3. Cf. the explicit citation of Aristotle at 2.1.3.

21. For my approach to parody, see p. 27 in chapter 1. As Phillip Horky has pointed out to me, parody often relies on decontextualization, which accordingly requires that the reader be cognizant of the original context; otherwise, the parody loses its force. For the reader who

a parallel process to the theorizing of philosophy, for both involve the act of removing the object of inquiry from its original context so as to be subjected to detached contemplation.[22] To be sure, the ensuing attitude to the object may ultimately differentiate philosophy from parody—a greater degree of earnest criticality in the case of the former, thoroughly multivalent ridicule in the latter—yet their functional similarity is what allows this list to situate the *RR* within the sort of agronomical tradition it constructs while poking fun at its intellectual pretensions at the same time.

The sixth and final group is where the list at last ceases to be a "list" (1.1.10–11):

> Hos nobilitate Mago Carthaginiensis praeteriit, Poenica lingua quod res dispersas comprendit libris XXIIX. Quos Cassius Dionysius Uticensis vertit libris XX ac Graeca lingua Sextilio praetori misit; in quae volumina de Graecis libris eorum, quos dixi, adiecit non pauca et de Magonis dempsit instar librorum VIII. Hosce ipsos utiliter ad VI libros redegit Diophanes in Bithynia et misit Deiotaro regi. Quo brevius de ea re conor tribus libris exponere, uno de agri cultura, altero de re pecuaria, tertio de villaticis pastionibus, hoc libro circumcisis rebus, quae non arbitror pertinere ad agri culturam.

> Mago the Carthaginian outstripped these writers in *nobilitas,* because he put together in the Phoenician language 28 books of diverse subject matter (*res dispersas*), which Cassius Dionysius of Utica translated in 20 books and, in the Greek language, dedicated to Sextilius, the praetor. From the volumes of the Greek books of those I mentioned earlier, he added not a few things and he took away the equivalent of eight books from Mago. It was those books that Diophanes in Bithynia usefully (*utiliter*) redacted to six and dedicated to king Deiotarus. I am trying to explain this subject more briefly than he does in three books: one on *agri cultura,* another on animal husbandry, and a third on husbandry of the villa, with all things cut out in this book [i.e., *RR* 1], which I do not deem to pertain to *agri cultura.*

As the only non-Greek source of the list, Mago represents the pinnacle of all agricultural writing heretofore, an appraisal underscored both by his appar-

---

expects an agronomical work of the Catonian variety, but instead finds one of a Ciceronian ilk, this ironized decontextualization would be all the more acute.

22. As Nightingale (2004) 63–71 discusses, early philosophical *theoria* took the form of a journey abroad, in which the spatially displaced individual came into contact with the foreign/other and thereby attained knowledge and truth.

ently greater *nobilitas* and by his place as the fiftieth source.[23] His contribution to the agronomical tradition, so Varro maintains, resides in his synthesis (*comprendit*) of various and diverse topics (*res dispersae*) into twenty-eight books. Varro does not explicitly articulate the substance of these *res dispersae*, but an earlier comment helps to shed further light on the question. As we saw, Varro emphatically prefaces the list of Greek sources as "those who have written in Greek in a scattered fashion, each on separate topics" (*qui Graece scripserunt dispersim alius de alia re*). If the Carthaginian ranks as the first compiler of these diverse topics, what, then, were those pre-Magonian writers writing on? One reasonable inference is that they were treating individual, highly specific, or overly delimited subjects, as opposed to Mago's more inclusive and comprehensive approach.[24] As an example, let us use Theophrastus, the only Greek source whose extant writings are cited at any length in the *RR*. Assuming that the works Varro had in mind were Theophrastus's botanical works, *De Causis Plantarum* and *Historia Plantarum* clearly treat some matters of interest to a farmer: plant growth (e.g., *Hist. Pl.* 7.2.1.ff.), soil quality (e.g., 8.7.6–7), and so on. Yet, Theophrastus's scope (i.e., the physical characteristics of plants) does not address many other aspects that would naturally appeal to the practical and profit-minded farmer (e.g., harvesting, storage, selling, etc.) and that appear in Roman agricultural treatises.[25] It would seem that the Carthaginian, on the other hand, collected these various subjects and incorporated them into one work (of twenty-eight books).[26] In these respects, the Varronian Mago stands as an innovator of

---

23. Notwithstanding the respect accorded to him here and in Columella (as the *parens rusticationis, Rust.* 1.1.13), remarkably little is known about Mago—indeed, why is he said to surpass the Greeks in *nobilitas* here?—leading some scholars to question his existence, still others to accord him the status as the Hippocrates of ancient agronomy; see Mahaffy (1890) 29–35 and Skydsgaard (1968) 66–69. As White (1970) 18 discusses, extant citations mostly deal with arboriculture and animal husbandry. After the sack of Carthage in 146 BC, the Roman Senate apparently ordered his work to be translated into Latin (Plin. *HN* 18.22; cf. Cicero *De Or.* 1.249)—an instance of senatorial intervention that remains to be explained. Note also that, by locating the foundations of agronomy in Greek and Carthaginian sources, Varro's history may be indicative of the ancient penchant for "orientalizing" the origins of technical knowledge (e.g., Numa and his supposed religious tutelage under Pythagoras in e.g., Livy 40.29.3–14; cf. Burkert [1961] 237 nn. 3–4).

24. Another possibility would be that they treated what Martin (1971) 95–98 (by way of Cic. *De Or.* 1.249) referred to as *communis intelligentia*: "common knowledge," or unsystematic farming lore (cf. 37–52).

25. Cf. pp. 52–54 below.

26. To put it another way, Varro may be suggesting that Mago's synthesis (cf. *comprendit*) of multifarious works and topics rendered him the originator of a dedicated *ars* of *res rusticae*. Compare Cic. *De Or.* 1.108, where Cicero's Crassus observes that an *ars* partially consists of "those things examined closely and clearly understood, and also disjoined from subjective belief and comprehended by *scientia*" (*ex rebus penitus perspectis planeque cognitis atque*

agronomy through his compilation of various subjects to create a dedicated, holistic, and perhaps even comprehensive approach to farming: *res dispersae* reconfigured into *res rusticae*.

Yet, Varro's praise of Mago is also not without its share of criticism, particularly of his predecessor's length and lack of focus. As he goes on to say, Cassius Dionysius and Diophanes translated, condensed, and supplemented these foundational twenty-eight books of Mago into, respectively, twenty and six books—contributions that Varro sees as no small ones given his use of *utiliter*.[27] The rationale behind this praise of Cassius Dionysius's and Diophanes' redactions is presumably that of the traditional Roman partiality for practicality and brevity,[28] and in keeping with this ideal, Varro represents himself as the continuator of this tradition: from six to three books and, in the case of Book 1, "with all things cut out . . . [that] I do not deem to pertain to *agri cultura*." Hence, the implied teleology of the list is unmistakable: while the scattered approaches of the Greeks are compiled and redacted in Mago's work, which in turn undergoes two subsequent abridgments and revisions, the *RR*'s treatment of *res rusticae* attempts to be even "briefer" (*brevius*) and more germane than the Magonian tradition:[29] in only three books and "excised" of all superfluities.

---

*ab opinionis arbitrio seiunctis scientiaque comprehensis*). Explicitly marked by its objective knowledge, *scientia* is necessarily preliminary to the *ars* and enables the "comprehending" of its material. Cf. 1.186: "nothing . . . can be reduced to an *ars*, unless the one who wishes to create an *ars* of the material (*res*) in question already possesses the *scientia* required to produce an *ars* from those things that are not yet an *ars*" (*nihil . . . quod ad artem redigi possit, nisi ille prius, qui illa tenet, quorum artem instituere vult, habet illam scientiam, ut ex eis rebus, quarum ars nondum sit, artem efficere possit*).

27. *Utiliter* is used specifically of Diophanes' redaction. The exact mechanics of transmission are as follows: Dionsyius Cassius cut eight books' worth of material from Mago's original twenty-eight, which he then translated and supplemented with contributions from other Greek writers for a new total of twenty books. In turn, Diophanes abridged these twenty books into six.

28. Note that this typically Roman prejudice also lurks behind the upcoming critique of Theophrastus *ad* p. 70.

29. One may wish to compare the express efforts of Vitruvius (ca. 25 BC)—who praises Varro as a spiritual forebear (9.pref.17), no less!—to perform the "honorable and most useful endeavor" (*dignam et utilissimam rem*) of collecting, ordering, and explicating the "disorderly" (*non inordinata*) and "unfinished" (*incepta*) "precepts and volumes" (*praecepta voluminaque*) of previous writers *de architectura*; cf. Gros (1992) xiii and McEwen (2003) 6–10. In the case of the jurists, whose increasing specialization and focus on internal jurisprudence in the late Republic eventually led to their "rise" as a professional class largely divorced from political life (of which Frier's 1985 monograph remains the classic exposition), Harries (2006) 27–50, esp. 49–50, has intriguingly argued that these experts created a tradition of *ius civile* that extended back to the fourth century BC and was rooted in the regal period so as to buttress their own identity and authority.

Finally, in the course of constituting an agronomical tradition, the list further evinces a *cultural* ordering, with Greeks giving way to Mago the Carthaginian, whom Varro the Roman intends to supersede. To the extent that Roman agronomy is about to supplant its Mediterranean precursors, Varro's construction of an agronomical tradition replicates the gradual extension of Rome's *imperium*—intellectual, in this case—as the Romans themselves understood it.[30] There is but one hitch: fifty-one Greeks and one Carthaginian later, neither Cato the Elder's well-known treatise nor the lost works of lesser-known Romans—the Sasernae and Scrofa (and, possibly, Stolo)[31]— have received any recognition, despite Varro's earlier pledge to review writers "both Greek and our own (*nostris*)" (1.1.7). But instead of either explaining away Varro's omission as an editorial oversight[32] or attributing it to "embarrassment" over the comparatively small number of Roman sources,[33] making sense of this hiatus requires that we contextualize it within the entire *RR*. In the first place, a review of all known citations shows that the three books of the *RR*—individually and collectively—cite Roman sources over Greek and Punic ones at a rate of nearly three to one.[34] The *RR*'s partiality for Roman authorities is also qualitative, for the previous Roman agronomical tradition figures prominently into the first part of *RR* 1's dialogue, where Varro's characters—particularly Scrofa and Stolo—themselves cite and critique both Cato and the Sasernae. In this respect, the opening conversation (1.2.1–28) not only delivers on the preface's promise to discuss Roman predecessors, but even stages that review as a dramatized debate between (living) Roman agronomists over (deceased) ones. Furthermore, this dramatic exchange also has the interlocutors themselves enact the work's synthetic and redactive approach to *res rusticae*. Just as the literary history of the preface places a premium

---

30. For similar arguments in the cases of Cicero's philosophical prefaces, see Habinek (1994) 55–67; and of Vitruvius's *De Architectura*, see McEwen (2003) 12–13, 130–34, 275–80, and 303. Cf. Columella, *Rust.* 1.1.12 on pp. 31–32.

31. Of these, we possess Cato's *De Agri Cultura*, while the other two—one by the Sasernae, a father-son duo, and the other by Scrofa—are no longer extant and known only through quotations or attributions in Varro, Columella, and Pliny the Elder. For the Sasernae, see *RR* 1.2.22 and Columella, *Rust.* 1.7.4. Martin (1971) 81–93 speculates on the tract(s) of the Sasernae, considering their work slightly more advanced than Cato's *De Agri Cultura*. A fourth work may have been produced by Stolo, although the evidence in Columella, *Rust.* 1.Pref.32 is ambiguous at best.

32. This lack of reference has been taken as evidence for an imperfect "double redaction" of the *RR*, the main proponents of which are Martin (1971) and Heurgon (1978); for the fallacy of this theory, see Flach (1996) 7–15.

33. So White (1973) 468, who is beholden to the outdated view of Roman shame over a putative cultural inferiority.

34. See appendix 2.

on more concise and focused treatments of farming, so the opening dialogic exchange narrows the scope of *agri cultura* and, perhaps more crucially, reconstitutes its properties.

## DEFINITION THROUGH THE DIALECTICAL
## EXCHANGE IN *RR* 1

By far the longest opening of the three books, the introductory discussion of *RR* 1 (1.2.1–28) has been characterized as an example of Varro's humor, his penchant for displaying his vast, antiquarian learning, and his efforts to adorn what would otherwise be an excessively dry topic.[35] All of these estimations, however, fail to capture that 1.2.1–28 not only serves as a prologue to the proper discussion of *agri cultura,* but also acts as a programmatic exposition of the *RR*'s agronomical agenda in general: hence, a proem of sorts to all three dialogues. As we shall see, much of this opening exchange interrogates the concept of *agri cultura,* which is defined positively (i.e., what it is), negatively (i.e., what it is not), and relationally (i.e., as one subset, or *genus,* of the overarching domain of *res rusticae*). Moreover, by using conversational exchanges between interlocutors to explore and to refine claims and to advance the overall argument, Varro employs an essentially dialectical form of argumentation—albeit, one that is less rigorous than what we might expect from a philosophical work and which the characters' often dry, sometimes absurdist, humor can overshadow at times. While the conversation is wideranging and verges on the cacophonous, the discussion is, as we shall see, never completely superfluous and, indeed, contributes substantively to Varro's approach to *agri cultura.*

After the initial exchange of pleasantries between Varro, Fundanius, Agrius, and Agrasius (1.2.1–11),[36] the entrance of the two main speakers—C. Licinius Stolo and Cn. Tremelius Scrofa—at last initiates the discussion of *agri cultura* (1.2.12). Agrius inquires about its purpose (*summa*): "whether it is utility (*utilitas*) or pleasure (*voluptas*) or both."[37] Scrofa will eventually opt for

---

35. In Flach's 2006 edition, compare *RR* 1's seven pages to a little over three for *RR* 2 (2.1.1–11) and the four and a half of *RR* 3 (3.2.1–18). For each respective estimation, see White (1973) 479; Tarver (1997) 133 (but cf. McAlhany [2003] 18–20); and White (1973) 491–94.

36. For the exposition of the setting—including the dual *laudes Italiae*—in *RR* 1, see chapter 3, pp. 76–92.

37. Already, we can see the *RR*'s grafting of philosophical concepts onto *res rusticae* at work. As noted by Heurgon (1978) *ad loc.*, this question resembles the one posed in Cic. *Fin.* 1.72. Cf. Hor. *Ars P.* 333ff. for similar statements regarding the aims of poetry. Adducing *De Rep.* 1.38 (as well as *De Or.* 1.209–18), Kronenberg (2009) 82 sees Varro employing, though

both (1.4.1), but he states that the group must first come to define the scope of *agri cultura* (1.2.12–13):

> Scrofa, "Prius," inquit, "discernendum, utrum quae serantur in agro, ea sola sint in cultura, an etiam quae inducantur in rura, ut oves et armenta. Video enim, qui de agri cultura scripserunt et Poenice et Graece et Latine, latius vagatos, quam oportuerit." "Ego vero," inquit Stolo, "eos non in omni re imitandos arbitror et eo melius fecisse quosdam, qui minore pomerio finie-runt, exclusis partibus, quae non pertinent ad hanc rem."

> "First," Scrofa says, "we must determine whether only that which is planted (*serantur*) in the field (*ager*) falls under the heading of *cultura*, or does it also include what is led into the country-side (*rus*), such as sheep and cat-tle. For I see that those who have written on *agri cultura* in Punic, Greek, and Latin have wandered more widely than was fitting." "For my part," says Stolo, "I think that they must not be imitated in every way and that, in this respect, certain ones have done well in having defined the subject with a smaller boundary (*pomerium*), having cut out those parts that do not per-tain to this subject."

Scrofa follows his request for a definition of *agri cultura* with the observa-tion that previous writers—Punic, Greek, *and* Latin—"wandered more widely than was fitting," which is subsequently met by Stolo's response that "certain ones"[38] did indeed circumscribe the subject with a smaller "boundary" (*pome-rium*). By turning first to a critique of previous agronomists' accounts, the two interlocutors who will be responsible for articulating *RR* 1's account of *agri cultura* immediately reenact the two objectives articulated in the preface: the adoption of a critical stance vis-à-vis previous agronomists and the need for demarcating the bounds of the subject.

Thereafter, Stolo distinguishes between *agri cultura* and animal hus-bandry (*pastio*), which then leads into, first, a discussion of the differences between the farm's overseer (*vilicus*) and the head herdsman (*magister peco-ris*) and, second, the supposed etymological affinities between *vilicus*, *villa*, and *veha* (1.2.14). This discussion in turn prompts Fundanius's musical anal-

---

ultimately traducing, the "good Ciceronian practice of starting an investigation by defining the topic under debate."

38. Could Stolo's praise be directed towards Scrofa, an agronomical writer in his own right, or is it an ironic jab at his counterpart? The loss of Scrofa's treatise inherently precludes any definitive answer, but either interpretation is not out of the realm of impossibility; see Nelsestuen (2011) 328–33.

ogy of the upper and lower octaves of a tibia (1.2.15); Varro's subsequent cita-tion of Dicaearchus (1.2.16) is met with Agrius's citation of a homesteader's law (1.2.17), which Fundanius subsequently corrects and, by way of a par-allel with Athenian precedent, expounds upon (1.2.18–20); and the attempt of Varro[39] to direct the conversation back to its original point (1.2.20)—the exclusion of animal husbandry from field cultivation—is then challenged by Agrasius's assertion that cattle (1.2.21), by virtue of their manure, are an essen-tial component of *agri cultura*. Agrius, however, defends the division with a *reductio ad absurdum* (1.2.21), observing that spinners, weavers, and other artisans would be a part of *agri cultura* by that logic, for they, like cattle, can be kept on land (*ager*) and be a source of profit (*fructus*) on it as well.

Scrofa now confirms the detachment of *pastio* from *agri cultura,* and the interlocutors at last seem to be ready to discuss cultivation, but this short-lived concord quickly gives way to more definitional quibbling: fur-ther postponing actual discussion of *agri cultura*, but nevertheless provid-ing important distinctions for the *RR*'s definitional project. The Sasernae, the father-son duo, and more importantly, the first-mentioned Latin writ-ers, apparently included a discussion of clay pits (*figilinae*) in their treatise; what do we, Varro's character asks, make of this (1.2.22)? Apparently tak-ing his cue from Agrius, Varro likewise extends the principle of profitabil-ity to mines and even taverns, which (like *figilinae*) can be located on land (*ager*) but should certainly not be considered a part of *agri cultura* (1.2.23). At this point, Stolo has had enough and jumps in to accuse Varro of denounc-ing the Sasernae's inclusion of *figilinae* merely "for the sake of impeding" (*obstrigillandi causa*)[40]—despite their substantial (*vehementer*) contribution to *agri cultura* (1.2.24). With Scrofa now smirking, Agrasius, motivated at the thought that "he alone knew [the work]" (1.2.25), bids Stolo to back up his statement. To this challenge, Stolo steps up with two quotes, which turn out to be recipes for bedbug repellents: cucumber soaked in water and ox-gall with vinegar. Fundanius's approval of the *dicta* (1.2.26) is met, first, by Scro-fa's sarcastic praise of the Sasernae's recipe for a depilatory from a yellow frog

---

39. Here, I follow Ash and Hooper (1934) in their attribution of the speaker at 1.2.20 and 1.2.22 to Varro rather than Flach (2006), who interprets both uses of *inquam* as emphatic particles of, respectively, Fundanius and Scrofa (i.e., rather than a change in speaker to Varro). Cf. n. 64 in chapter 1. For my present purposes, the precise attribution of speaker ultimately matters less than what one might think, for the consensus that emerges at the end remains the same.

40. *Obstrigillo* is an extremely rare word (cf. *TLL* s.v. *obstrigillo*). It may not be insignifi-cant that, outside a single occurrence in Seneca (*Ep.* 115.6) and mention in later grammarians (Non. 147.16, Isid. *Etym.* 10.199), the word appears only in Ennius's *Satires* (F 5) and in Varro's *Menippeans* (F 264).

and, second, by Varro's reference to a remedy for foot pain (subsequently quoted wryly [*subridens*] by Stolo, 1.2.27). At this point, we finally come to the portion discussed in chapter 1: the sundry recipes found in the manuals of the Sasernae and Cato the Elder and the ultimate irrelevance of these *miracula* to *agri cultura* (1.2.28). After these concluding censures, Agrasius claims that *agri cultura* has received sufficient negative definition (1.3) and the technical discussion properly begins.

Ironically traversing as wide a swath as the sources it critiques,[41] the interchange between Varro and company nonetheless accomplishes several positive and meaningful ends. First, it fulfills the preface's promise to treat the Roman agronomical tradition, extending the critique of the scattered (*dispersae*) approach of the Greeks and the irrelevant and excessively protracted treatment of Mago and his redactors to their countrymen as well. Lest we simply lump in Cato and the Sasernae with the Greek and Punic agronomists, however, we might note that the interlocutors' winnowing of the scope of *agri cultura* from the chaff of mines and taverns, country remedies and cattle, directly engages Roman sources and *not* Greek *nor* Punic ones—despite their decisive numerical advantage. Bestowing a distinctly patriotic color to the work's definitional project, this preference for Roman authorities contributes to its staging of *sermones* amongst Romans who, much like their juristic counterparts' approach to the formation of Roman law,[42] privilege Latin sources and treat Italian agriculture.

More generally, this opening exchange dramatizes the *RR*'s analytical stance towards its subject matter. As we saw, the initial inquiry into the end (*summa*) of *agri cultura* prompted an investigation of "whether only that which is planted (*serantur*) in the field (*ager*) falls under the heading of *cultura,* or does it also include what is led into the country-side (*rus*), such as sheep and cattle" (1.2.12–13). Implied therein is a distinction between two kinds of rustic space—*ager* and *rus*—which necessarily (though not sufficiently) distinguishes *agri cultura* from *res rusticae* and which will receive further elaboration shortly (cf. pp. 47–48). Also cropping up amidst all of the talk of the tibia, Athenian goats, and depilatory frogs are two different, but complementary, claims: the first—endorsed implicitly by Stolo (1.2.13) and explicitly by Scrofa (1.2.21)—reiterates the preface's claim that *agri cultura* and animal husbandry (*pastio*) are two distinct kinds of rustic enterprise (1.1.11), and the second further explicates the way in which land use might be construed as "agricultural" (1.2.23). All three of these claims will, as we shall see, lay the groundwork for Scrofa's ensuing definition of *agri cultura* (1.3).

---

41. As noted also by McAlhany (2003) 263.

42. For the Republican and imperial jurists' self-imposed isolation from Greek law, see Watson (1995) 111–16.

By repeatedly invoking the definitional relevance of *ager* and *rus, pastio* and *agri cultura,* the opening to *RR* 1 is not simply symptomatic of Varro's analytic approach to *res rusticae* and, in particular, his proclivity for seemingly pedantic systematization.[43] Instead, once we abandon our own presuppositions regarding *agri cultura,* the belief that Romans of the late Republic also had a similar and fixed conception, and the corollary assumption that there was a coherent and static discourse existent at Rome, the opening debate suggests that Varro's text genuinely does not take the concept of *agri cultura* for granted. In other words, the preliminary conversation of *RR* 1 attests to a certain amount of disagreement—if not outright uncertainty—concerning the subject, which the *RR*'s definitional agenda will seek to redress.[44]

In the following sections, I sketch the ways in which the *RR* attempts to improve upon previous treatments of rustic matters by reconstituting the terminology and taxonomic structures of *res rusticae.* My argument proceeds on two levels. First, I will trace how each of the three dialogues individually defines, explicates, and systematizes its respective subject of *agri cultura* (*RR* 1), *pastio* (*RR* 2), and husbandry of the villa (*RR* 3). Second, by delineating the activities of the farm and constructing a technical vision for its spaces, these separate treatments in turn collectively formulate the field of *res rusticae* and disembed it from the broader category of the *agricola.* The result is that the *RR*'s theoretical exposition of Roman farming should be viewed as a bold attempt to construct a newly discrete and coherent field of *res rusticae.*

## Defining the Three Subfields of *res rusticae*

At the end of Book 1's prelude, Scrofa at last formally defines *agri cultura* as an *ars* and *scientia* (1.3) that teaches "what things must be planted (*serenda*) and done (*facienda*) on each field *(in quoque agro)* in order that the earth *(terra)* may always return the greatest produce (*maximos . . . fructus*)."

---

43. So Skydsgaard (1968) 36, who interprets 1.2.11–28 as an example of "definitional division," which "seem[s]—as the contemporary [i.e., ancient] reader must also have felt them to be—superfluous, in the sense that they do not clarify something unknown or difficult, but appear rather as pedantic elaboration of something obvious. It is, so to say, definition for definition's sake." Cf. Furhmann (1960) 69ff. Rawson (1985) 137 is more charitable, acknowledging the text's project of definition, but regarding it as simply a narrowing of the scope of *agri cultura.*

44. Alex Dressler has suggested to me the possibility that Varro might be viewed as a sort of consensus builder, who demonstrates the possibility of disagreement resolving in unity through philosophy and irony. In this respect, might we view Varro as an agrarian counterpart to the Cicero magisterially presented by Connolly (2007)? Cf. *De Lingua Latina* 8 and 9, which may mediate between *anomalia* and *analogia* as respectively championed by Cicero and Caesar.

Echoing an earlier sentiment by Varro (*qua* character),[45] Scrofa's formulation of *agri cultura* involves three crucial elements: activity (*satio*), space (*ager*), and *telos* (*fructus*, i.e., "produce" or "profit" per the Latin term's semantic range).[46] As the previous interchange turns out to have explored (1.2.13–28), the removal of even one element renders the practice nonagricultural. Thus, procuring *fructus* on an *ager* from mines, taverns, and cattle does not constitute *agri cultura* on the grounds that the improper activity is being practiced, while husbanding animals in the countryside (*rus*) fails to fulfill the criteria of activity and space. Even in the case where an appropriate activity is being undertaken in the requisite spatial setting, the interlocutors maintain that the enterprise is no longer agricultural if the possibility for *fructus* is nonexistent (e.g., 1.4.3–4). In these respects, the dialogue's exchanges explore how all three criteria are necessary and sufficient for the *RR*'s definition of *agri cultura* and, by virtue of being orderly, systematic, and conceptually nuanced, Varro's account thus represents a marked advance on that of Cato, whose approach to agronomy can perhaps be best encapsulated in the *dictum* that "planting is a thing not to be thought about, but done (*conserere cogitare non oportet, sed facere oportet*; *Agr.* 3.1).

The use of the threefold criteria of activity, space, and end is not limited to *agri cultura* and, in fact, defines the other two spheres of *res rusticae* as well. In the preface to Book 2 (2.pref. 4–5), Varro (*qua* author) begins by sharpening Book 1's distinction between *agri cultura* and *pastio*. Focalizing the distinction through the agents rather than the activity, the *colonus* has regard for "those things that are made to grow from the earth (*terra*) through *agri cultura*," while the *pastor* is concerned with "those things that arise from the herd (*ea quae nata ex pecore*)." Later, Scrofa fleshes out this notion of *pastio* (or, as he formulates it there, *res pecuariae*): the "*scientia* of procuring and maintaining a *pecus* so as to seize the greatest possible profits (*fructus*) from it" (*scientia pecoris parandi ac pascendi, ut fructus quam possint maximi capiantur ex eo*; 2.1.11). Providing a distinct activity ("procuring and maintaining

---

45. Cf. 1.2.23: "For not just any profit that accrues to the owner on account of the field (*agrum*) or even on the field ought to be put down to *agri cultura*, but only that which is born from the earth (*terra*) by planting (*satio*) for our profit" (*Non enim, siquid propter agrum aut etiam in agro profectus domino, agri culturae acceptum referre debet, sed id modo, quod satione terra sit natum ad fruendum*). Flach's emendation of this passage (. . . *quod nec<esse est> satione*)—as well as of 1.3 (where he reads *quae* for *quo*)—is intriguing, but difficult, so I have followed Keil's 1889 text here. In the case of both passages, the sense is largely the same on either reading.

46. In rhetorical terms (cf. Quint. *Inst.* 5.10.55–62; Lausberg [1998] 52–54), the *finitio* of *agri cultura* would seem to fulfill the four requirements of comprehending in terms of *genus* (*scientia*), *species* ("[of] what things must be planted and done on each *ager*"), *proprium* ("in order that *terra* may return") and *differentia* ("always . . . the greatest produce").

a *pecus*") and reiterating the same profit-oriented *telos* as that of *agri cultura*, Scrofa's definition of *pastio* lacks only a spatial location, which the authorial Varro articulated earlier in the preface: *pastio* takes place on pastures (*prata*) and not in grainfields (*segetes*) (2.pref.4).[47]

Affixed to this spatial distinction, moreover, is a temporal one not found in *RR* 1. Perhaps following Dicaearchus,[48] both Varros—authorial (2.pref.4) and interlocutor (2.1.2–5)—maintain that the practitioners of early Roman *pastio* (i.e., *pastores*) taught *agri cultura* to their offspring, who "founded the city" and subsequently passed the practice along to their progeny. In grafting a temporal dimension onto *RR* 1's definitional criteria, *RR* 2 thus also begins to historicize the distinction between *agri cultura* and *pastio*. Varro (*qua* interlocutor) will later invoke the tradition that regarded Romulus, Remus, and Faustulus, their surrogate father, as shepherds (2.1.9), but this historicization of *res rusticae* raises the question of the precise mode of living for these (proto-)Romans—especially given Varro's otherwise rigorous distinction between *agri cultura* and *pastio*. Were the teachers of Rome's earliest inhabitants herdsmen *and* farmers? Or did the *pastores* just happen to have additional, but unused, knowledge of the earth's cultivation? In fact, the answer appears to be the former, as the preface of *RR* 3 makes clear (3.1.7–9):

> Agri culturam primo propter paupertatem maxime indiscretam habebant, quod a pastoribus qui erant orti in eodem agro et serebant et pascebant; quae postea creverunt pecunia, diviserunt, ac factum, ut dicerentur alii agricolae, alii pastores. Quae ipsa pars duplex est (tametsi ab nullo satis discreta), quod altera est villatica pastio, altera agrestis. Haec nota et nobilis, quod et pecuaria appellatur et multum homines locupletes ob eam rem aut conductos aut emptos habent saltus; altera, villatica, quod humilis videtur, a quibusdam adiecta ad agri culturam, cum esset pastio, neque explicata tota separatim, quod sciam, ab ullo. Itaque cum putarem esse rerum rusticarum, quae constituta sunt fructus causa, tria genera, unum de agri cultura, alterum de re pecuaria, tertium de villaticis pastionibus. . . .

> At first, because of their poverty, people treated *agri cultura* indiscriminately (*indiscretam*), because the descendants of shepherds (*pastoribus*) used to sow (*serebant*) and graze (*pascebant*) on the same land (*agro*). Thereafter their wealth increased, and they made a distinction (*diviserunt*), and it was

---

47. Gabba (1988) 134–42 reads this passage as evidence for the inordinate rise of large-scale animal husbandry in post-Hannibalic, Roman-controlled Italy. Cf. Flach (1997) 182.

48. Cf. Nelsestuen (2011) 340–42. For the reception of Dicaearchus in late Republican Rome, see Huby (2001) 315 and Purcell (2003) 329–58, esp. 343–52.

done so that some were called "farmers" (*agricolae*), others "shepherds" (*pastores*). Husbandry (*pastio*) is a twofold matter, although it has been distinguished sufficiently (*satis discreta*) by no one, with the husbandry of the villa (*pastio villatica*) one thing, and that in the countryside ([*pastio*] *agrestis*) another. The latter is well-known and noble, and it is also called [*res*] *pecuaria,* and wealthy men often have pastures (*saltus*)—leased or bought—for this purpose. The other is husbandry of the villa and, because it is seen as lowly, has been added to *agri cultura* by certain men, although it is husbandry (*pastio*), and it as a whole has not been distinguished separately (*neque explicata tota separatim*) by anyone so far as I know. And so, since I thought that there were three kinds of *res rusticae*—*agri cultura, res pecuaria, pastiones villaticae*—which have been established for the sake of *fructus*. . . .

Rationalizing the previous lack of distinction between *agri cultura* and *res pecuaria* as a result of the poverty of early *pastores,* who used to engage in *satio* and *pastio* on the same field (*ager*) as a matter of necessity,[49] Varro claims that it is only *after* these early practitioners of both enterprises attained economic viability that they properly distinguished between the professions of the *agricola* and the *pastor.* Thus, Varro attributes the emergence of this distinction—which is tantamount to "specialization" in modern economic terms—to the increase in wealth, which would presumably enable the holding of lands specifically devoted to each enterprise.[50] Whatever the merits of this claim, it is nevertheless clear that Varro views increased economic prosperity as the catalyst for *both* the dedicated employment of land for a specific activity *and* an attendant linguistic specification, that is, between *agri cultura* and *res pecuaria.* Thus, the preface to *RR* 3 not only adheres to the previous books' definitional and temporal distinction

---

49. In modern terminology, such use is called "mixed intensive farming"; see White (1970) 50–52.

50. Three further points merit observation. First, this account minimizes or even ignores the historically fraught relationship between shepherds and farmers in late Republican Italy (and earlier); see pp. 159–60 in chapter 5 for further discussion. Second, there is a certain tension between Varro's historicizing claim that *pastio villatica* was traditionally considered *humilis* and the dialogue's representation of husbandry at the late Republican villa, which turns out to be an enterprise of—and a source of delectation for—the wealthy. Third, Varro's chronological prioritization of economic growth as a precondition for specialization (and *not* vice versa) runs, to the best of my knowledge, counter to the position maintained elsewhere in classical antiquity. See, for example, the arguments made in Plato's *Rep.* 369B5ff. that the specialization of labor facilitates greater wealth in the case of a city. The implications of Varro's text for Greco-Roman economic thought are outside the current project's scope but certainly merit their own study.

between *agri cultura* and *pastio* but even provides historical and material rationales for it.

This passage further contributes to the *RR*'s discursive project by defining what was (according to Varro) a hitherto undifferentiated type of *res rusticae*: *pastio villatica,* or "husbandry of the villa." Consisting of the raising of the sorts of animals to which the setting of the villa is particularly conducive—especially birds, bees, and fish—this practice, like the husbandry of large herd animals in the countryside (*pastio agrestis*), was once considered to be part of *agri cultura,* thereby reinforcing the last field's chronological priority and conceptual hegemony. Unlike *pastio agrestis,* however, husbandry of the villa apparently remained largely unexamined and, indeed, entirely unidentified as a discrete object of inquiry: "[*pastio villatica*] as a whole has not been distinguished separately by anyone, so far as I know" (*neque explicata tota separatim, quod sciam, ab ullo*). In this respect, Varro tentatively purports to be the first agronomist to identify, define, and articulate these practices as a discrete category of farming.

A formal definition of *pastio villatica* is, however, not provided until the dialogue proper and only then after a lengthy debate over the nature of a villa (3.2.3–18). There, Axius's request for an account of *pastio villatica* is met by Merula's response that it consists of a *scientia* of "how animals can be nour-ished or reared in or around the villa (*in villa circumve eam*) in such a way that they be a source of profit (*fructus*) and delight (*delectatio*) for the mas-ter" (3.3.1). By defining *pastio villatica* in terms of an activity (the rearing of animals) within a space ("in or around the villa") and oriented towards a goal ("profit" and, in this case, "delight" as well),[51] *RR* 3 has at last com-pleted the tripartite articulation of *res rusticae* promised at the treatise's outset (1.1.11). Furthermore, by historicizing *res rusticae* as presently three distinct branches of farming originally rooted in a primeval and undifferentiated state of human existence, the *RR* presents an essentially anthropological account of farming, which is intrinsically intertwined with Varro's view of the changing material circumstances of the Roman state.

For however much the individual definitions of *agri cultura, res pecuaria,* and *pastio villatica* contribute to the understanding of each particular object of inquiry, the broader implication of these analytical and definitional excur-suses should also be clear: the collective distillation of a field of *res rusti-cae.* And by tying this theoretical and systematic account of *res rusticae* to his understanding of the changing material conditions of human—specifi-

---

51. For the importance of delight (*delectatio*) and pleasure (*voluptas*) in all three *genera* of *res rusticae,* see pp. 61–62 and chapter 6.

cally Roman[52]—existence, Varro also historicizes the intellectual discipline of agronomy. Almost paradoxically, then, Varro seems to be acknowledging that with the development and primacy of *res urbanae* comes a concomitant need for the articulation of *res rusticae*.

## The Taxonomies of *res rusticae*

In opening the fourth *Tusculan Disputations'* treatment of the disturbances of the mind, Cicero has his main interlocutor, M.,[53] ask A. whether he should follow the Peripatetics full-sail in their expansive and fluid, yet inadequately defined and partitioned (cf. *spinas partiendi et definiendi praetermittunt*), account of psychological therapies, or carefully labor at it through the slow, but steady, oars of Stoic *dialektike* (*Tusc.* 4.9). To be sure, A. will (predictably) pick both methods of conveyance for the ensuing Ciceronian dialogue, yet the same twofold approach could be said to apply to the *RR*'s account of *res rusticae*,[54] for in addition to defining the three fields of *agri cultura, pastio,* and *pastio villatica,* the text also partitions their individual taxonomies, which in turn govern both the structures and the content of the three books. In what follows, my approach is primarily descriptive (and *not* evaluative), though I will offer some general suggestions as to the rationale(s) behind the mode, number, and function of divisions. As we shall see, sketching the frame of the *RR*'s analyses will elucidate how the structure of each book contributes to the systematic and comprehensive presentation of each particular field as well as to the more general articulation of *res rusticae*.

Divided into two distinct sections of roughly equal length, *RR* 1 has the most theoretical and complex structure of the three dialogues. The first half

---

52. Hints of the muddled, problematic, and declined state of farming of Varro's day as a result of Rome's urbanization sporadically emerge in the *RR*: readers require notice that the farmer's pantheon is not the same as the twelve "urban" ones (1.1.4), *patresfamiliae* forego the manual labor of the farm for theaters "within the walls" of Rome (2.1.1), and villa owners are appraised of the vast differences between their lavish pleasure estates and the austere ones of their forefathers (3.2.6). See pp. 33–34 and chapter 7 for further consideration.

53. For the form, genre, setting, and interlocutors of the enigmatic *Tusculan Disputations,* see Gildenhard (2007) 5–88.

54. This is not to say that Varro is necessarily following the Stoics in the organization and partition of *res rusticae,* though their influence on the organization of technical disciplines—including possibly Roman law—is demonstrable and Varro did study with the Stoicizing Academic Antiochus of Ascalon. For important treatments of *dialectica* in the late Republic, see Moatti (1997) 215–54 and Rawson (1985) 132–42, for whom Varro—more than any other Roman—stars as the *exemplum par excellence*. For the possible influence of Stoicism on Roman law, see *idem* 206–10, and for a counterargument, see Watson (1995) 158–65.

consists of four general parts (*partes,* 1.5.3; cf. 1.5.4)—the *fundus* and its soil, agricultural equipment, operations, and seasons—each of which has at least two subsections. The second half offers an account of the six steps (*gradus*) involved in farming production: preparations, sowing/planting, nurturing, harvesting, storage, and selling. In schematic form, the structure is as follows:[55]

I. "Quadripartite *forma*"
   A. Knowledge of the farm (*cognitio fundi*)
      1. Soil-related matters (*quae ad solum pertinent*)
      2. Building-related matters (*quae ad villas et stabula pertinent*)
   B. Necessary equipment (*quae in fundo opus sunt*)
      1. Humans (*de hominibus*)
      2. The other instruments (*de reliquo instrumento*)
   C. Operations (*quae facienda sunt*)
      1. Preparations (*quae preparanda sunt*)
      2. Locations (*ubi facienda sunt*)
   D. Proper seasons (*quo quicque tempore fieri convenit*)
      1. Yearly schedule (*quae ad solis circumitum annuum sunt referenda*)
      2. Monthly schedule (*quae ad lunae menstruum cursum sunt referenda*)
II. "Sexpartite *forma*"
   A. Preparations (*praeparando*)
   B. Sowing/planting (*serendo*)
   C. Nurturing (*nutricando*)
   D. Harvesting (*legendo*)
   E. Storage (*condendo*)
   F. Selling (*promendo*)

Aside from a handful of minor deviations,[56] the *sermo* adheres to this bipartite

---

55. Unlike the other books' practices of disclosing their organizational structures up front, Book 1 provides an outline of only the first half via the preliminary discussion (1.5.3–4), with the second half being announced upon the completion of the first (1.37.4). Interestingly enough, the two main interlocutors explicitly acknowledge the transition in their exchange; Scrofa's announcement that he has spoken "about the quadripartite form in *agri cultura*" is met by Stolo's claim that "there is another . . . sexpartite form," which he proceeds to discuss (1.37.3–4).

56. So Skydsgaard (1968) 7–37 confirms (though grudgingly) in his thorough overview of *RR* 1. As he notes, minor problems do crop up in the course of Scrofa's sexpartite discussion. For example, Scrofa conflates his initial subdivision of the first *pars* (I. A.1 and I. A.2) into one category and creates a new second subdivision that briefly treats matters "outside the farm" (*extra fundum*; 1.16.1). The emendation by Ross (1979) 52–56 of Scrofa's initial outline (1.5.4)

structure, thereby assisting *RR* 1's analysis of *agri cultura* as a discrete field and contributing to the work's overall discursive project.

Yet, the bipartite structure goes beyond strictly taxonomical issues to provide a systematically collaborative overview of the farm and *agri cultura* as well: the first half focusing on the *fundus*—its objects and its resources (e.g., tools, soils, time, etc.)—and the second treating its practices (e.g., sowing, harvesting, storing, etc.). Implied herein is a difference in temporal perspective, with the first half providing an account of *agri cultura* from a synchronic (or "top-down") perspective, which articulates the necessary preconditions for owning a successful farm by informing readers of various environmental conditions and essential equipment (I. A.1–I. B.2), the preparations that are to be undertaken (I. C.1–2), and the general workings of the farm's calendar (I. D.1–2). In these respects, the first half essentially reads like an introductory manual for potential elite *domini,* providing an overview for those who are looking to purchase a farm and to procure a basic understanding of its equipment, operations, and enterprise. The second half, on the other hand, approaches *agri cultura* from a diachronic (or "horizontal") perspective, tracing the operations of the field in the order that they occur: from preparations (II. A) to growing (II. B–C) and harvesting (II. D–E) to selling (II. F), thereby articulating the actual practices of farming in a process-oriented fashion.[57] Thus, whereas the first half offers an image of the farm at any one given time, the second traces its procedural routine through time.

Scholars wishing to emphasize Varro's "pedantic" or "absurd" proclivity for systematization usually look no further than Book 2's infamous eighty-one-fold division of animal husbandry.[58] For whatever tongue-in-cheek quality it may have, this scheme nevertheless forms the structural basis of Book 2's treatment of *res pecuariae.* Using the type of animal as the principle of his ordering, Scrofa divides *pastio* into three *genera*: smaller, larger, and "other"

---

"solves" this problem but is not textually convincing. Kronenberg (2009) 84, on the other hand, views this as part of Scrofa's intellectual "bungl[ing]."

57. This distinction in temporal framing even applies to the portion of the first half that deals with time: the agricultural calendars (1.27.1–37.3). Recall that the first calendar is an annual one based on the movement of the sun and stars, while the second one is organized according to lunar phenomena (see Skydsgaard [1968] 43–63 for discussion). Whereas these calendars provide an overview of *agri cultura* organized strictly according to the units of solar (and lunar) time, the stages of the agricultural process itself structure the second half. In this respect, the second half adopts, reorganizes, and develops the synopsis provided by the first into a process-oriented account of *agri cultura*'s various operations. Cf. Spencer (2010) 59, who sees Stolo's calendar as "based around human know-how and contingency" and "complementary" to Scrofa's solar and lunar calendars.

58. As noted by Skydsgaard (1968) 35, the best exemplar of this attitude is Fehling (1957) 50, n.2.

animals. The criterion for the first pair of categories is size, while instrumental functionality underlies the third grouping. In turn, each *genus* is subdivided into three *species* (2.1.12):[59]

    A. Smaller animals (*minores pecudes*)
       1. Sheep (*oves*)
       2. Goats (*capra*)
       3. Pigs (*sus*)
    B. Larger animals (*maiores pecudes*)
       4. Bovines (*boves*)
       5. Donkeys (*asini*)
       6. Horses (*equi*)
    C. "Other" animals (*pecudes [quae parantur] propter [fructum] aut ex ea*)
       7. Mules (*muli*)
       8. Dogs (*canes*)
       9. Herdsmen (*pastores*)

Thereafter, Scrofa announces that each of the nine animals admits analysis in nine respects: four pertaining to the purchase of the animals (age, physical condition, breed, and pertinent legal formula[e] for ownership); four on the care of the animals (pasturing, breeding and rearing, feeding, and health); and one that applies to both the pasturing and care of the animals (proper or ideal number). These nine categories structure the order of discussion within each animal's treatment (2.1.13–24):

    E.g., B. Larger animals
       5. Donkeys
          a. Age (*aetas*)
          b. Build (*forma*)
          c. Breed (*seminium*)
          d. Legal formula (*de iure*)
          e. Maintenance (*pastio*)
          f. Breeding and rearing (*fetura*)
          g. Feeding (*nutricatus*)
          h. Health (*sanitas*)
          i. Number (*de numero*)

As another interlocutor points out, not all of these nine categories uniformly apply to each animal (e.g., mules cannot breed). In such cases, Scrofa allows

---

59. Cf. Skydsgaard (1968) 34–36, who follows Fuhrmann (1960).

for a substitution in topic,[60] thereby preserving the book's eighty-one-fold architecture. While it is certainly the case that Varro's or Scrofa's apparent preference for threes and nines creates an artificial discussion at times, the rationale for the arrangement is intelligible from a pragmatic standpoint. In particular, the first grouping of "obtaining" (*parandi*) certainly accounts for the simple fact that the animals' procurement necessarily precedes their care-taking (*pascendi*). Moreover, within the first fourfold grouping (*parandi*), the recitation of the requisite legal formula for purchase (d.) obviously comes after the evaluation of an animal according to the first three criteria (i.e., age [a.], physical condition [b.], and quality [c.]). Similarly, the second grouping (*pascendi*) is organized roughly according to the chronology of a herd's existence; successfully pasturing existing animals (e.) allows for the breeding of new ones (f.), which require feeding (g.) and so forth.[61] In addition, a nine-by-nine structure provides a methodical and quasi-mnemonic approach to *pastio*,[62] thereby possibly offering convenient utility for the practitioner, but certainly facilitating consistent coverage for the agronomist.[63]

A similar scheme of *genus* and *species* undergirds *RR* 3's treatment of husbandry of the villa (*pastio villatica*). Each of the three *genera*—aviaries (*ornithones*), animal hutches (*leporaria*), and fishponds (*piscinae*)—is found in a different location of the villa (3.3.1): "within its walls" (*intra parietes villae*), in "enclosures affixed to the villa," (*saepta afficta villae*), and "near the villa" (*ad villam*). Each *genus* subsequently admits subdivision into two *species* (3.3.2–4[64]):

A. Aviaries (*ornithones*)
   1. Only land

---

60. In place of *fetura* and *nutricatus* of mules, Scrofa suggests that they include the shearing (*tonsura*) of sheep and goats and the use of milk and cheese (*tyropoiia*) (2.1.28) at the end of the dialogue (2.11.1–12). See p. 168 in chapter 5.

61. The only potentially superfluous category is the final one: ideal number (i.). While the number of animals certainly pertains to the decision of how many animals to buy at once (i.e., *parandi*) as well as to how many animals to maintain in a group (i.e., *pascendi*), it does not appear particularly useful to separate out this consideration from either discussion; why not, for example, simply incorporate the ideal number in either the discussion of legal purchase (d.) or the maintenance of health (h.), or in both sections? In this respect, it is no stretch to regard the isolation of this ninth category as Varro's attempt to eke out a ninth point of discussion to parallel his nine types of animals.

62. One might wish to compare the use of *loci* as quasi-mnemonic devices in rhetorical training (e.g., *Rhet. Her.* 3.30–32); see Vasaly (1993) 88–102.

63. As Goody (1977) 52–73 seminally explored, the use of tables is a fundamentally literate phenomenon, and its application to oral cultures entails a whole host of problems. Given Varro's literacy, however, it is no stretch to imagine him as working from such a basis.

64. In practice, other animals end up receiving consideration in the course of *RR* 3; see chapter 6.

      a.  Peacocks (*pavones*)

      b.  Turtle-doves (*turtures*)

      c.  Thrushes (*turdi*)

   2.  Land and water

      a.  Geese (*anseres*)

      b.  Water-fowls (*querquedulae*)

      c.  Ducks (*anates*)

B.  Animal hutches (*leporaria*)

   1.  One kind (*una*)

      a.  Boars (*apri*)

      b.  Roe-deer (*capreae*)

      c.  Hares (*lepores*)

   2.  The other kind (*altera*)

      a.  Bees (*apes*)

      b.  Snails (*cochleae*)

      c.  Dormice (*glires*)

C.  Fishponds (*piscinae*)

   1.  Fresh water (*in aqua dulci*)

   2.  Salt water (*in marina*)

Perhaps a consequence of the variegated and potentially inchoate nature of the subject, Book 3's systematization is neither as elegant nor as symmetrical as that of Book 2. For example, while the *species* of the first two *genera* (i.e., *ornithones* and *leporaria*) receive further subdivision, there is no comparable articulation of the types of fish found in each *species* of *piscina* (3.17.1–9). Moreover, the subcategories of *leporaria* are described simply as "the one kind" (*una*) and "the other kind" (*altera*), but in fact seem to be distinguished by size. Finally, this taxonomy does not order the discussion *within* each topic, operating instead only at a *skeletal* level—perhaps because the differences between maintaining fishponds and beehives are simply too great to allow for the kind of detailed and methodical structure found in Book 2. Notwithstanding these quibbles, Varro's analysis of *pastio villatica*—like those of *agri cultura* and *pastio*—still facilitates a systematic and orderly structure for the subject.

## Fields, Soils, and the Other Spaces of *agri cultura*

At the heart of the *RR*'s analytical and anthropological account of *res rusticae* lie the correct recognition and use of agricultural space for the farming estate (*praedium*): *res rusticae* takes place in the countryside and *not* the urban landscape of the city;[65] fields are not to be misused as lands for grazing; and one kind of husbandry occurs on pastureland, the other at the villa. By delineating the spaces of rustic enterprise in a methodical and prescriptive manner, Varro would almost seem to be playing the part of *agrimensor* for agronomy or perhaps even of its quasi-legislator, similar to the sort behind the lex Agraria of 111, which sought to rationalize the various kinds of lands— as well as to resolve the conditions of their use and ownership—for Italians of disparate juridical statuses.[66] Lurking within the very metaphors used to describe its definitional project (e.g., *pomerium*, 1.2.13; *limitata*, 2.2.1), the *RR*'s obsession with the appropriate construal of the agricultural landscape permeates its deployment of spatial terminology. As we shall see, four terms play a particularly formative and substantive role in the *RR*'s theory of *agri cultura*: *ager* as the conceptually and linguistically central element, and *fundus, locus,* and *terra* as secondarily crucial concepts.

As an entry point into these issues, let me begin with the terms *fundus* and *ager*. As the lexica readily indicate, a *fundus* usually denotes a unit of ownership that includes the land and the buildings (i.e., a "farm"),[67] whereas an *ager* generally indicates a place of activity (i.e., a "field").[68] Perhaps exem-

---

65. As a review of all uses of *rus* in *RR* shows, this term occurs frequently in contexts in which a contrast is being made with the city: 1.2.12; 1.10.1; 1.22.6 [twice]; 1.37.3; 1.59.2; 2.pref.1 [thrice]; 3.1.1; 3.3.5; 3.4.2; 3.7.11; and 3.9.2.

66. For the *agrimensores* in general, see Dilke (1971) and Campbell (2000). The earliest writer of the *ars gromatica* is commonly held to be Frontinus, who lived about two generations after Varro (40–103 AD) and part of whose writings survive in the so-called Corpus Agrimensorum. It may not be insignificant that the "surveyor," L. Decidius Saxa, had risen to the status of tribune of the plebs (appointed by Caesar in 44), general (fighting under the auspices of M. Antony in 42), and governor of Syria (41); see the disparaging references in Cic. *Phil.* 11.12, 13.37, and 14.10 as well as Syme (1937) 127–37 for discussion. For the lex Agraria of 111, the *auctor* of which is unknown, see Lintott (1992) and Williamson (2005) 170–74. Among other things, this fragmentary, complex, and historically invaluable document sought to resolve conflicts over the use, possession, and ownership of private holdings of *ager publicus* in Italia (as well as in parts of Greece and North Africa).

67. *TLL* s.v. *fundus* II.A: . . . *significatur et agri solum cum aedificiis et omnibus, quae ad culturam pertinent* (1), *et solum ipsum* (2).

68. *TLL* s.v. *ager* I. A. *proprie: de agro usui humano subiecto.* To be sure, there is potential for semantic overlap—in some contexts, *ager* may refer to a "farm" (*TLL* s.v. *ager* I.C), while *fundus* rarely refers to the soil alone (s.v. *fundus* II. A.2)—but the vast majority of instances adhere to the above distinction. For the most part, this distinction is consistently made throughout *RR* 1. See appendix 3, to which I will have recourse throughout this section's discussion. There are eight instances where *ager* seems to be used in the sense of "farm" (compared to sixty-three cases of *ager* in the sense of "land"), but all occur either in a context that pertains to the post-harvest operations of an *ager*-based activity or in quotations of Cato's *De Agri Cultura*. For these exceptions, see 1.4.5, 1.7.1, 1.11.2, 1.16.4, 1.18.6, 1.23.4, 1.51.1. Interestingly enough, the distinction between *ager* and *fundus* found in *RR* 1 is not strictly observed in Roman law, which not infrequently uses the two terms interchangeably and, in

plified best in that rejoining *reductio ad absurdum* of Mr. Field (i.e., "Agrius") to Mr. Fielder (i.e., "Agrasius") (1.2.21),[69] *ager* refers to an area of specifically agricultural activity within the ambit of a *fundus,* while *fundus* is that broader entity both incorporative of the *ager* (or *agri*) and potentially inclusive of nonagricultural pursuits: mining, textile-based, or otherwise. To put it another way, the spatial distinction between the two terms is partly quantitative—*ager* being one part of the *fundus's* whole—and partly qualitative in that the *fundus* may accommodate any and all work, which may (or may not) occur on an *ager* and, consequently, may (or may not) be part of *agri cultura.*[70] The owner of a *fundus* could reap *fructus* from the grazing of cattle on an *ager,* yet that use violates the one prescribed for the *ager* (i.e., *satio*; cf. 1.3); that land is consequently rendered pastureland (i.e., *pratum*; cf. 2.pref.4) and, hence, that activity does not constitute *agri cultura.*[71] Thus, a parcel of land accommodative of any work other than sowing or planting ceases to be (or never was) an *ager,* whereas the *fundus* appears to have no such restrictions[72] attached to it due to its qualitatively different status.

This understanding of *ager* receives explicit consideration in the critique of the Sasernae, where "Varro" claims that neither placement (*in aliquo agro*) alone nor suitability (*idonea*) nor profitability (*fructuosa*) renders the use of land "agricultural" (1.2.22–23). Likewise, the land's *locus,* that is, its relational aspect(s), plays no intrinsic role in the conception of an *ager* (or, for that

this respect, would seem to more closely approximate the usage of Cato; see, for example, the variation between the two terms in *Dig.* 6.1.38–49. In other cases, however, the *fundus* is clearly a larger quantitative unit incorporative of *agri* (e.g., 6.1.44, 6.1.53, 7.1.9.7, and esp. 50.16.115; cf. Harries [2006] 181–82). For the Republican jurists' deliberate avoidance of strict definitions so as to preserve legal flexibility and prioritize interpretation, see Watson (1995) 146–57. Rawson (1985) 208–10, on the other hand, would seem to allow for more definition.

69. The full quote is as follows: "But the mistake comes from this, the idea that cattle can be kept on a field (*in agro*) and be a source of profit (*fructus*) on it (*in eo agro*), an idea that must not be followed. For in this way other things distinct (*diversae*) from the field (*ab agro*) will also have to be included, such as if [someone] keeps employed on their farm (*fundus*) many spinners and weavers, and so on with other artisans."

70. For an analysis of the spatial dimensions of Pliny's letters in terms of quantity and quality, see Riggsby (2003) 166–86, who demonstrates that the qualitative aspect of space is the driving force behind Pliny's description of the villa. For the distinction between the quantitatively marked "space" and qualitatively marked "place" in humankind's cosmological worldview, see Tuan (1977).

71. Again (cf. n. 68), the pasturing of cattle on an *ager* is simply not a definitional concern for the Roman jurist (e.g., *Dig.* 8.3.3.1).

72. This formulation raises the question as to whether a *fundus* can be a *fundus* without at least one *ager.* While the *RR* does not explicitly entertain this possibility, I suspect that pastureland might suffice as an acceptable substitute for arable fields in this understanding of a *fundus* (cf. *RR* 2.10.6 and, esp., 3.2.5, where Axius's ruminations on the nature of a villa might be taken to imply that a *fundus* contains either farmland or animals intended for husbandry).

matter, *agri cultura*).[73] To be sure, both *ager* and *locus* may functionally refer to the same piece of land, but *ager* is (or, at least, should be) the location of a specific activity (i.e., *cultura*), while *locus* is that same land viewed in its geographical or topographical guise(s). In this respect, the distinction between these two terms turns *not* on their abilities to connote spatial quantity, but rather, on their qualitative significations. Still, *locus* remains an important (albeit extrinsic) consideration for the would-be farmer, for, as we shall see, it plays an *instrumental* role within the *RR*'s theory of *agri cultura*.

   *Terra* also plays a crucial role in the *RR*'s critical deployment of rustic spatial terminology, but unlike *fundus* and *locus*, it shares a much closer and potentially synonymous semantic affinity with *ager*.[74] In Varro's *RR*, however, the two terms are consistently and rigorously deployed in substantively different manners, as evinced by three particularly significant and programmatic passages,[75] all of which mark *ager* as the "field" (in which sowing or planting occurs) and *terra* as the "earth" (or "soil") that brings forth the produce. Thus, the crucial distinction between *terra* and *ager* is not fundamentally one of quantity (e.g., *ager* in place of *terra*), but rather, of quality: *ager* referring to the arable location composed of *terra*, and *terra* denoting that same land viewed primarily in its generative (and not merely material[76]) aspect, that is, the land as possessed of the quality that produces crops on the *ager*.

---

   73. Cf. *RR* 1.2.23: "Just as it is also the case that, if there is a field (*ager*) lying along a road and the position (*locus*) is suitable for travelers, taverns should be built; still, although they may be profitable (*fructuosae*), they are not any more a part of *agri cultura*." See also appendix 3.

   74. Cf. *OLD* s.v. *ager* 5 and s.v. *terra* 4.a. As synonyms for *terra*, L&S s.v. *terra* gives *solum* and *Tellus*, but not *ager*.

   75. The passages are as follows: (1) 1.2.23: "For not whatever profit accrues to the owner on account of the field (*propter agrum*) or on the field (*in agro*) ought to be put down to *agri cultura*, but only that which is born from the earth (*terra*) by planting for our profit (*fructus*)"; (2) 1.3: [Scrofa] untroubled says, "First it is not only an *ars*, but even a great and necessary one; it is also a *scientia* of what is to be planted and done in each field (*ager*), in order that the earth (*terra*) produces the greatest return (*fructus*) always"; and (3) 1.7.5: "Then there's the second division, in what kind of earth (*quali terra*) the soil (*solum*) of the *fundus* is situated. It is from this part especially that a *fundus* is deemed good or bad. For it matters as to what things and of what kind can be planted in the soil, given that not all the same things can be sown and can grow well in a single field (*in eodem agro*)." See also appendix 3.

   76. The third passage in the previous note also introduces another spatial term for land, *solum*. While Varro is not explicit here about the substantive difference between *solum* and *terra*, it seems relatively clear that *solum* is strictly the material substance of the soil (i.e., "dirt") and not the generative or creative aspect that *terra* also denotes. In any case, the term appears in only three other instances in *RR* 1 (1.5.3; 1.5.4; and 1.6.1.) and, consequently, does not hold much weight in the Varronian agricultural landscape. Cf. the similar distinction between *terra*, *ager*, and *solum* (as well as *fundus*) in *Dig.* 7.4.24.2.1.

According to this analysis, then, a *fundus* is defined quantitatively and qualitatively, serving as both the basic and incorporative space of, and place for, a variety of rustic activities (including *agri cultura* and *pastio*). *Ager,* on the other hand, appropriately denotes a qualitatively defined place that—generally irrespective of (though not completely unresponsive to[77]) quantitative criteria—is devoted specifically to proper *agri cultura*. Finally, while *locus* and *terra* admit potential reference to the quantitatively same parcel of land as *ager,* each term does so with a view to one quality or another: relational position in the case of the former, generative aspect in the case of the latter.

To what end, then, does the *RR* formulate its terminological landscape of *res rusticae*? On a programmatic level, this rigorous and careful construal of space might function as one part of the work's corrective stance vis-à-vis its predecessor's meanderings outside the bounds of *agri cultura*. The exiguous state of evidence may preclude us from establishing unequivocally this intellectual contribution, but it is certainly suggestive that Cato the Elder, the only extant Roman precursor of Varro, openly eschews analytical methodology and deploys spatial terminology markedly more loosely in his account of *res rusticae*.[78] Moreover, the staged process of dialectical exchange—including the seemingly pedantic squabbling, citation of previous agronomists, and emergent consensus—with a view to exploring the bounds of *agri cultura* smacks of the sort of conceptualizing characteristic of the late Republican juristic tradition.[79] In this respect, the interlocutors also emerge as the jurists—albeit highly jovial ones—of *agri cultura*. But beyond any potential correction or revision of the previous agronomical tradition, these terms and their rigorous applications also enable Varro to rationalize what *agri cultura,* the central stake of his new vision for Roman agronomy, may accomplish within the landscape of *res rusticae*.

Shortly after the group's consensus on the definition of *agri cultura*, Scrofa posits that the two goals of the *agricola* are "utility" (*utilitas*) and "pleasure" (*voluptas*), the aim of which is, respectively, profit (*fructus*) and "delight"

---

77. *RR* 1 only minimally treats the size of *agri* (and *fundi*) (e.g., 1.10.1–11.2; cf. 1.18.1–19.3), but refuses to prescribe strict guidelines and, instead, prefers to stress flexible proportionality as the prevailing guideline. Cf. the principle for land division in Plato's *Laws* 745c–d, where the land is evaluated quantitatively and qualitatively, thus being divided into roughly equitable portions per that estimation.

78. Cf. p. 48, n. 68, and appendix 3. All of this is not meant to say that Cato is misguided or "wrong," for language can—and routinely does—allow for some semantic overlap in terminology as well as idiolectic variation. Instead, my point is that verbal precision simply does not matter for Cato, whereas it does for Varro.

79. See Watson (1995) 90–97, although the ultimately explicit and straightforward definition of *agri cultura* given at the end of the discussion is not so characteristic of the jurists' methodology (cf. n. 68).

(*delectatio*).[80] As Scrofa proceeds to develop, *fructus* outranks *delectatio,* yet the two goals often accord with one another (1.4.2):

> Nec non ea, quae faciunt cultura honestiorem agrum, pleraque non solum fructuosiorem eadem faciunt, ut cum in ordinem sunt consita arbusta atque oliveta, sed etiam vendibiliorem atque adiciunt ad fundi pretium; nemo enim eadem utilitati non formosius quod est emere mavult pluris, quam si est fructuosus turpis.

> And yet, those things that make a field (*ager*) more becoming (*honestior*) by *cultura,* most of these same things not only make the land more productive (*fructuosior*), such as when orchards and olive-groves are planted in rows (*in ordinem*), but they also make it more saleable (*vendibilior*) and add to the price of the farm (*fundi pretium*). For given the same utility (*utilitas*), everyone prefers to pay more for land that is beautiful (*formosius*) than unsightly (*turpis*) land, although it is profitable (*fructuosus*).

Illustrating the notion that *agri cultura* can increase an *ager*'s productivity (*fructuosus*) and, consequently, value (*vendibilior . . . pretium),* Scrofa the interlocutor adduces the orderly (*in ordinem*) arrangement of orchards in support of his claim that people are willing to pay more for "beautiful" (*formosius*) land than "unsightly" (*turpis*) provided that the same *utilitas* applies to either parcel. The implication is not merely that the more aesthetically pleasing arrangement produces a more gratifying effect (i.e., *delectatio*)—which renders the land more desirable and thereby boosts the potential value—but also that orderly *agri cultura* can enhance the *ager* in a way that augments its productivity. The question now becomes whether *agri cultura* can affect the generative quality of the *ager,* that is, its *terra* (1.4.3–4):

> Utilissimus autem is ager, qui salubrior est quam alii, quod ibi fructus certus. . . . Quare ubi salubritas non est, cultura non aliud est atque alea domini vitae ac rei familiaris. Nec haec non deminuitur scientia. Ita enim salubritas, quae ducitur e caelo ac terra, non est in nostra potestate, sed in naturae, ut tamen multum sit in nobis, quo, graviora quae sunt, ea diligentia leviora facere possimus.

> But the most useful land (*utilissimus ager*) is that which is healthier (*salubrior*) than others, because profit (*fructus*) is secure there. . . . For which

---

80. Cf. pp. 189–96 in chapter 6.

reason, where there is no healthiness (*salubritas*), *cultura* is nothing other than a crapshoot for the life of the owner and his estate. And yet, these problems are lessened by knowledge (*scientia*). For although *salubritas*, which comes from the climate (*caelum*) and earth (*terra*), is such that it is not in our power (*potestas*), but in that of nature (*natura*), there is still much we can do with the result that we can alleviate very serious things by careful attention (*diligentia*).

As it turns out, *salubritas* comes from *terra*—as well as the climate (*caelum*)—both of which stem from *natura* and are consequently outside the farmer's control (*potestas*).[81] Unlike an *ager*, then, which admits human intervention, *terra* and *caelum* are fixed by nature. But the farmer is not *completely* impotent in the face of these natural circumstances, as he can mitigate any such problems by the careful application (*diligentia*) of agronomical *scientia*. In other words, *agri cultura* can act as a corrective for *terra* and *caelum* much in the same way as spectacles mitigate, but do not permanently fix, poor eyesight. Thus, by grounding *terra* and *caelum* in *natura* but acknowledging the ameliorative efficacy of *agri cultura*, Varro ascribes the essential difference between *ager* and *terra* to a matter of *natura*, maps both terms onto his landscape of *res rusticae*, and carves out an efficacious role for *agri cultura* therein.

In its treatments of field topography (*forma agrorum*; 1.6.1–7.4) and types of earth (*quo in genere terrae*; 1.9.1–7; cf. 1.7.5–10) thereafter, the *RR* provides viable coping strategies for the natural travails of *caelum* and *terra*. In respect to *forma*, Scrofa characteristically distinguishes between two basic types: those due to *natura* (i.e., larger-scale, natural landforms) and those due to *sationes* (i.e., smaller-scale, manual arrangements). Of the *formae* determined by *natura*, three basic kinds are distinguished: flatland, hilly, and mountainous (1.6.2). Providing a descriptive spectrum of the various conditions typical of each landform, Scrofa locates plains at one end, mountains at the other, and hills as a sort of mean between the two. Plains, for example, tend to be too hot in the summer, require earlier planting and harvesting, and are much more temperate in the winter in comparison to mountainous places. Crucially determinative of the particular kind of agricultural praxis to be employed in each topographical situation, these factors stem not from the quality of the soil, but rather, the various environmental factors, that is, the *caelum*.[82] In this respect, Scrofa now formally ties an *ager*'s location—that is,

---

81. Cf. the opening invocation of the first two of the twelve farming gods, Jupiter and Tellus (*RR* 1.1.4–5): "those who comprise all the fruits (*fructos*) of *agri cultura* by means of the heavens (*caelum*) and earth (*terra*)."

82. No use of *terra* occurs here. On the whole, Scrofa uses either nouns that identify

its *locus*—to a particular *caelum* and reinforces the need for adjustments in *agri cultura* to mitigate these environmental factors.

The other kind of *forma*—that "due to *cultura*" (*forma culturae*)—also connects *caelum* with *locus,* but one that *agri cultura* can actively manipulate through proper crop arrangement. Thus, seeds planted in rows (*ordines*) and at proportionately appropriate lengths (*modica intervalla*)—specifically by means of the *quincunx*[83]—attain their requisite share of solar, lunar, and elemental resources (1.7.2) and accordingly sprout greater returns of higher-quality produce (1.7.3).[84] In other words, the farmer's task *qua forma* in general involves not only passively appraising the *caelum* attendant to the broader topographical setting of the *ager,* but also actively managing those environmental conditions by means of the tractable arrangement of the plot. Thus, a complete *scientia* of *agri cultura* entails a knowledge of *caelum,* which attends the natural *locus* of an *ager;* which accepts mitigation by an organizational *locus* imposed on it; and which, when properly negotiated, returns superior harvests.

Even more crucial to Varronian *agri cultura* is *terra,* for its quality (*quali terra solum sit*) determines whether a *fundus* "is deemed especially good or bad" and, consequently, what "can be sown and can grow well in the *ager.*" At 1.9.1,[85] Scrofa introduces the discussion of *terra* by way of a threefold linguistic distinction: *communis, propria,* and *mixta.* In chapter 3, I will deal with the *communis* usage, which approaches English's usage of "land" in the romanticized sense of "country"[86] and which lies outside the present discussion's

---

a specific topographical setting (i.e., *campus, collis,* and *montanus*), adjectives with similar semantic sense (e.g., *infimus, summus, susus, deorsus, altus*), or, more globally, *locus* (1.6.2; 5; 6).

83. This crop formation is easily conceptualized as the pattern of dots on the five-face of a six-sided die. Cf. White (1970) 397 and n. *ad loc.*

84. The full quote is as follows (1.7.2): "plants that are placed each in its own *locus* take up less space and each one blocks (*officit*) the other less from the sun, the moon, and the wind" (*quae suo quicque loco sunt posita, ea minus loci occupant, et minus officit aliud alii ab sole ac luna et vento*). Note the suggestive resemblance of the vocabulary to two of the four sources of the *honestum* identified by Cicero in *Off.* 1.15: the "rendering of each his own" (*tribuendo suum cuique*) and the "order and moderation of all things" (*in omnium . . . ordine et modo*). For discussion of the potential moralistic connotations of Scrofa's account, its possible echo of the resolution of *utilitas* and *honestas* by Cicero in *De Officiis,* and its ironic failure to comprehend the moral lessons of the latter text (as well as a similar discussion in Xenophon's *Oeconomicus* [4.21–25]), see Kronenberg (2009) 97–99.

85. This treatment of types of *terra* has prompted derision or dismissal from modern critics. Heurgon (1978) *ad loc.,* for example, cites this as a typical example of Varronian "rigamarole," while Skydsgaard (1968) 14 estimates it more generously as an example of the Varronian Scrofa's penchant for "linguistic starting-points."

86. Cf. the sense of "land" as expressed (albeit ironically) in Woody Guthrie's folk song, "This Land Is My Land." See further discussion on pp. 104–7 in chapter 3.

scope. The *propria* usage, Scrofa maintains, is employed when it is simply called *terra*, that is, "with no other word (*vocabulum*) or epithet (*cognomen*) attached" (1.9.1). In this respect, it is apparently the one employed in Varro's foundational definition of *agri cultura*: *terra* as that elemental aspect of land construed as possessed of life-producing force. The third kind, *terra mixta*, refers to the actual material itself and prompts a syntactically labored enumeration of the eleven kinds of physical substances (e.g., stone, sand, clay) that may combine with *terra propria* to form it (1.9.2–3). Scrofa further complicates matters by adding three grades (*gradus*) of mixture and three additional degrees (*species*) of moisture to each type, for a grand total of ninety-nine different kinds of *terra* (1.9.3–4). But then he proceeds to identify three major distinctions—*macra*, *pinguis*, and *mediocris*—which serve as the primary qualities that the Varronian interlocutors ascribe or deny to land throughout the rest of the book.[87] This does not mean, however, that we should simply write off this complex and contrived scheme for *terra*, since it explains the role that *agri cultura* can play in managing *terra*. As we have seen, *terra propria* is the sense that Varro employs in his definition of *agri cultura*, that is, the elemental aspect of the land that *agri cultura* cannot change. We have also seen that a *scientia* of *agri cultura* enables the farmer to adjust to the environmental factors (*caelum*) attendant to the *locus* of the *ager* or even simply to alter that *locus*.[88] Now, with knowledge of the types of *terra mixta*, the farmer can adjust his operations to account not for *terra propria*—for that kind of *terra* is not within our power to change (cf. 1.4.4)—but for *terra mixta*, that is, the "other" elements that are contained within the *ager* and combine with the given *terra*. In this way, Varro creates a semantic place for *terra* within the world of *agri cultura*, which bridges both the elemental sense of *terra* (i.e., *propria*) and its usage as a referent to the soil as actual physical substance (i.e., *mixta*) of an *ager*.

With this theoretical articulation of *terra* within the spatial landscape of *agri cultura*, then, Scrofa completes the task he set for himself at the outset (1.3): the exposition of *agri cultura* as an *ars* and *scientia* that teaches "what must be planted and done in each field (*ager*) so that the earth (*terra*) always returns the greatest profits (*fructus*)."

---

87. This recourse to practicality in the end is echoed in the initial quotation of Theophrastus (1.5.1–2), although Scrofa may merit censure here for temporarily indulging the philosopher's penchant for innumerable divisions. For Columella's possible criticism of this passage, see Nelsestuen (2011) 345.

88. Scrofa's gradation of moisture is relevant here, for he shifts into the usage of *locus* when speaking about the humid, dry, or temperate types of *terra* (1.9.4).

## FARMING AND FARMERS, *CULTURA* AND *COLO*

The sheer amount of space devoted to the definition of *agri cultura,* the articulation of its principles and parameters, and the theoretical explication of its efficacy renders *RR* 1 distinct from the other two books, which are invested more in description and less in theorization. While this difference may reflect the inherently more multifaceted and complex nature of field cultivation relative to animal husbandry, it also stems in part from the *RR*'s identification of *agri cultura* as the paramount subject of *res rusticae,* that is, as the conceptual core under which the two kinds of *pastio* are sometimes (erroneously) included.[89] In other words, *agri cultura* functions as the hegemonic and coordinating concept amongst the three discrete subjects that constitute—jointly and severally—*res rusticae.* In this respect, it is worth considering whether Varro's anthropologizing account of the linguistic and conceptual development of *agri cultura*—specifically, from its primevally undifferentiated state—may, in fact, have some basis in actual historical and sociolinguistic conditions. In this final section, I briefly pursue some of these threads in order to further nuance the nature and implications of Varro's disembedding of *res rusticae* from the broader, more inchoate, category of the *agricola,* or perhaps better, "what a farmer does."

Contrary to what one might expect, evidence for the *iunctura* of *agri cultura* as a set linguistic unit is not securely attested until the mid-first century BC. While Cato the Elder possibly entitled his farming manual *De Agri Cultura,* the manuscript traditions are muddled, alternating between the former and *Res Rusticae*[90]—an equivocation perhaps tellingly underscored by the fact that Cato never once employs the phrase in the body of his work.[91] In fact, the earliest extant attestation for a collocation of *agri* and *cultura* comes from Cicero's speech on behalf of the Manilian Law (*Leg. Man.* 15; delivered in 66 BC) and is found only occasionally thereafter for a total of sixteen Republican attestations[92] outside Varro's fifty uses (forty-eight in the *RR* alone). Linguistic attestation and conceptual existence are not necessar-

---

89. As we saw earlier, previous agronomists are always said to have included *pastio* under *agri cultura* and never vice versa (e.g., 1.2.12–13, 3.1.8).

90. See Reynolds (1983) 40–42 and Von Albrecht (1997) 1.401–2. Cf. n. 91.

91. For the closest approximations, see 2.1 (*fundus cultus siet*), 61.1 (*agrum . . . colere*), and 61.2 (*cultura*). Moreover, in *De Senectute* (ca. 45/44 BC), Cicero has Cato refer to his work as "*de rebus rusticis*" (53). Cf. Aul. Gell. *NA* 10.26.8. In keeping with Varro's tendency to criticize predecessors on his own terms, the reference to Cato's work *de agri cultura* should be understood as descriptive and not necessarily as evidence for the title.

92. Elsewhere, Cicero uses it some five times: *De Or.* 1.249; *Rep.* 5.4; *Fin.* 3.4; *Off.* 1.151 and 2.12. Similarly, Caesar employs the phrase six times: *BGall.* 3.17.4; 4.1.2; 4.1.6; 6.22.1; 6.22.3; and 6.29.1. In Lucretius, the phrase appears only once (5.148).

ily coterminous,[93] but it seems not unreasonable to observe that *agri cultura* as a *fixed* phrase appears much less frequently than what might be expected of a practice that holds the ideological weight that it does in Roman culture. And at the very least, it is suggestive that Latin discourse about farming as an abstract notion in the Roman world was infrequent before Varro.[94]

While *agri cultura* as a fixed expression is sparsely attested among Republican writers, the collocation of *ager* and *col-* root words is not. Ignoring the most obvious and frequently attested compound (*agricola*) for now, *ager* appears in conjunction with the verb *colere*, "to cultivate," as early as Plautus, Terence, and Cato,[95] from which evidence we might plausibly surmise that the typical way of describing the cultivation of a field employed various forms of *ager* and *colere* from the middle Republic onwards. With Cicero, we have sufficient evidence to identify securely this collocation as a standard (though not necessarily fixed) idiom.[96] In sum, the sheer number of pairings of *ager*

---

93. This observation is all the more true given that the extant works of the second and first centuries BC represent but a small fraction of the total literary output. Note also that the majority of subject matter of our data set is not agricultural in nature or purpose.

94. This may also stem from archaic and, to a lesser extent, Republican Latin's preference for avoiding abstract nouns (cf. Von Albrecht [1989] 110). Perhaps *agri cultura* was formed— almost as a calque—on the model of γεωργία, which is securely attested as far back as the fifth century BC (e.g., Thuc. 1.11.1); receives some consideration as one of two ideal modes of wealth acquisition in Aristotle's *Politics* 1 (1258b17–19); and is, perhaps unsurprisingly, a common term in the much-later *Geoponica*. Further exploration of the intertextual relationship between Varro's *RR* and Aristotle's *Politics* (or its tradition; cf. n. 42 in chapter 7) may be illuminating. In particular, Varro's emphasis on the proper distinction between three distinctive types of *res rusticae* might be read as a response to Aristotle's apparent twofold distinction between animal husbandry and γεωργία, the latter of which would seem to include matters that Varro would assign to *pastio villatica*. Democritus's lost *Peri Georgias* is another possible source candidate.

95. For example, a character in Plautus's *Rudens* declares that he sees a *cultum agrum* (214), while Terence's eponymous Phormio describes a "field of his father that must be tended" (*agrum nostro de patre colendum*; *Phorm.* 364–65). On the prose side, Cato rhetorically asks "*quid est agrum bene colere*" in his farming manual and famously declares that he spent his youth in the "cultivation of field[s]" (*agro colendo*) amongst the "Sabine rocks" (*saxis Sabinis*) in his speech *De Suis Virtutibus* (F 51 Malcovati). For this claim, see Astin (1978) 105–7 and Reay (2005) 331–34.

96. The instances are too numerous to list in full, but it will be useful to review the *range* of expressions. For example, Cicero sometimes writes that an *ager* has been either cultivated (*cultus*; *Rosc. Am.* 33.4) or not (*incultus*; *Leg. Agr.* 2.70). A variation of this practice is the supinate or noun use, which actually seems to be as common as *cultura* and *ager* (e.g., *Leg. Agr.* 2.88; *Rep.* 2.4). At other times, he uses forms of the *col-* root verbally (e.g., *ager . . . coleretur*, *Leg. Agr.* 2.88; *Tusc.* 2.13) or in gerundive constructions (e.g., *in agro colendo*, *Rosc. Am.* 39; *Nat. D.* 2.151). Other linguistic possibilities exist for Cicero as well (e.g., *agresti cultu*, *Rep.* 2.4; *cultor agrorum*, *Tusc.* 1.69). Among Cicero's contemporaries, a similarly wide range of collocations of *col-* and *ager* is found: Caesar makes use of both the gerundive (*BGall.* 4.1.7) and the verbal (*BGall.* 5.12.2) constructions, Sallust employs the gerund with an accusative (*Cat.* 4.1), and Cornelius Nepos uses the verb and direct object (*Pausanius* 3.6).

with various forms of *col-* indicates that the pairing of the two terms was a—if not *the*—normative way to talk about field cultivation by Varro's lifetime. Yet, while not completely eschewing these other linguistic possibilities,[97] Varro certainly favors the abstract phrasing of *agri cultura.*

Three tentative conclusions regarding *agri cultura* emerge from this brief overview. First, while the dictates of transmitted literary history clearly preclude placing too much weight on any *argumentum ex silentio,* the lack of secure attestation of *agri cultura* in extant second-century BC literature— particularly in Cato's treatise—provides an admittedly hypothetical, but potentially instructive (and certainly intriguing), *terminus post quem* for the normative use of the phrase in the late second or early first centuries BC. Second, the striking imbalance between the number of instances found in Varro and his contemporaries (at a rate of over three to one) corresponds with the sheer amount of attention paid to the term in the *RR* and is indicative of the work's theoretical nature. Third, the not-uncommon occurrence of *ager* and *col-* words suggests that Varro's contribution involves not the outright invention, but rather, the appropriation of existing terminology and its reinvestment with a delineated technical meaning. In this last respect, what Plato seems to have done for *rhetorike* in the mid-fourth century[98] and what first-century jurists were already doing for jurisprudence,[99] Varro is now doing for agronomy.

Corroborating evidence for these points may be further detected in the term's ongoing infrequency in the first century AD. Thus, of the two writers most likely to use *agri cultura,* Pliny the Elder and Columella, the former employs the phrase a respectable eleven times,[100] but the latter only seven.[101]

---

97. For example, Varro uses the gerundive construction at *RR* 1.3 and the verb at *Ling.* 5.36.

98. The work of Schiappa—especially (1990) 457–70 and (1999) 14–29—has been central to the contention that Plato not only invented the term *rhetorike,* but reframed "the semantic field constituted through the Greek theoretical vocabulary . . . in nontrivial ways with [its] introduction and use" (Timmerman and Schiappa [2010] 10). Note that their further observation that "prior to the coining of *rhetorike,* the verbal arts were understood as less differentiated and more holistic in scope" could easily be applied, *mutatis mutandis,* to my analysis of Varro's account of the previous agronomical tradition (cf. p. 41) and his intervention within the state of that discourse at Rome.

99. The two jurists most commonly associated with this trend are Q. Mucius Scaevola Pontifex (d. 82) and Servius Sulpicius Rufus (106–43). Whether one adopts the view of the jurists as extreme isolationists in their craft (particularly associated with Watson [1995]) or sees various sociocultural circumstances as particularly formative to the development of their knowledge and profession (per Harries [2006], Rawson [1985] 201–14, and, to a much lesser extent, Frier [1985]), this comparison, I believe, is valid, for both positions agree that the late Republic was a particularly formative period for Roman jurisprudence.

100. *HN* 1.8; 1.10; 1.14; 1.15; 1.18a (thrice); 8.180; 18.22; 18.44; 18.201.

101. *Rust.* 1.pref.25; 1.1.2; 1.1.5; 1.8.2; 6.pref.7; 11.1.10; 11.2.79.

Instead of *agri cultura,* Columella's preferred term is *agricolatio,* an insepa-rable word that actually permits inclusion of animal husbandry in its field of reference (e.g., *Rust.* 6.pref.5) and is found only in his treatise a total of twenty times.[102] The broader semantic range of *agricolatio,* its otherwise unat-tested status, and its accorded prominence within Columella's work all sug-gest that the man coined this term, possibly as a programmatic neologism.[103] That an agronomist, whose work historians of Roman agriculture esteem most favorably (and far more so than the *RR*), apparently felt the need to coin a new conceptual term nearly a century after Varro's discursive project would seem to testify to an ongoing state of flux surrounding *res rusticae* and its technical terminology: either the lack of adoption of Varro's newly articu-lated account, or Columella's challenge to it, or some combination thereof.[104]

But in respect to Varro's treatise, what do we make of the claim that *agri cultura* was so ill-defined as to include *pastio* and other nonagricultural prac-tices when the linguistic evidence is suggestive of the term's relative infre-quency pre-Varro? Notwithstanding the possibility that Varro is embellishing (or fabricating) this putative agronomical failing, two, admittedly charitable, answers appear likely. First, it is probable that previous agricultural writers did actually "succumb" to this discursive and semantic failing *according to the terms Varro sets.* Thus, because of their failure to adhere to his theoretical explication of *agri cultura,* Varro can in fact plausibly—albeit retroactively—censure agronomists like Cato and the Sasernae.

The second possibility pertains to the linguistic and semantic relationship between *agri cultura* and *agricola.* In the first place, the former term refers to an activity (i.e., field cultivation) and the latter to an agent (i.e., a farmer). Moreover, *agri cultura* likely does not appear in its fixed form until the late second or early first centuries, yet *agricola* is attested much earlier than it and appears quite frequently in texts contemporary to Varro's *RR.*[105] Furthermore,

---

102. *Rust.* 1.pref.5; 1.pref.10; 1.pref.12; 1.pref.25; 1.1.1; 1.1.9; 1.1.12; 1.1.15; 1.1.17; 1.9.4; 2.2.15; 2.16.1; 2.21.6; 3.3.2; 3.3.7; 3.3.14; 3.10.18; 3.21.4; 4.1.1; and 6.pref.5. Note that *\*colatio* is otherwise unat-tested. To the best of my knowledge, the only other word that uses this "suffix" is *percolatio,* "percolation," in, for example, Vitr. *De Arch.* 8.6.15.

103. What seems likely to me is that *agricolatio* refers to a category of practices broader than *agri cultura* and less imprecise than *res rusticae*; perhaps the state of being (*-tio*) a farmer (*agricola*) is the sense that lies between. In future work, I hope to pursue the implications and purpose of this neologism more closely.

104. One possibility is that the highly circumscribed and overly tidy bounds of Varronian *agri cultura* simply did not fit the practical Roman *agricola*'s messier reality, which Columella's *agricolatio* more closely seeks to capture; that it did not take off either is perhaps a testament to the way that Roman agricultural manuals may be divorced from the actual practitioners of actual agriculture.

105. For example, Plautus (*Rud.* 617), Lucretius (2.1165, 4.592, 5.1360, 6.1260), Catullus (34.21, 62.57, 62.59) all attest to its usage, while Cato (twice in the preface to *De Agri Cultura*),

as an abstract term derived from *colere*, *cultura* primarily denotes the process (i.e., the activity) of field cultivation, whereas *colere*, the root of *-cola*, had a much more general meaning from its outset. In particular, the latter appears to have originally meant something like "to live in" or "to inhabit" and is only subsequently applied thereafter in the sense of "to take care of" or, in a farming context, "to tend" or "to cultivate."[106] Indeed, Varro puns off these two distinct senses of *colere* in the *RR* a number of times. Thus, the *maiores* used to "dwell in" (*colere*) the "countryside" (*rus*) as opposed to maintaining residence in the city (2.pref.1), while Theophrastus's books are more suited for those who "inhabit the schools" (*scholas colere*) of philosophers than those who "tend fields" (*agros colere*, 1.5.1). Accordingly, if we understand the *-cola* suffix of *agricola* to have a preemptively broader sense than Varro's *cultura*, it is easy to see how the term could have plausibly incorporated any number of rustic activities in addition to field cultivation.

On this understanding, an *agricola* was any person who lived on a farm (*ager*[107]) and who derived his livelihood from a field (*ager*) by planting crops, raising livestock, quarrying a mine, or, for that matter, some combination thereof; in all of these instances, the farmer is engaging in the activity (or activities) with a view to procuring a living from the *ager* in whatever way he may. It is only with the linguistic emergence of *agri cultura* as an abstract term describing a specific activity (i.e., sowing or planting)—as opposed to the multifarious set of practices a field dweller engages in—that the broader, more expansive, and now ill-defined semantic range of *agricola* becomes problematized. Thus, by prescribing a specific set of activities for a particular piece of land and contextualizing this discursive intervention within contemporary Roman conditions, Varro seeks to resolve the linguistic and technical "problems" of *agri cultura* as a field with the historical experience of *res rusticae* as subjectively practiced by *agricolae*.

But what do we make of Varro's anthropological *ratio*, which holds that Rome's original *agricolae* were instructed by *pastores* (2.pref.4) and practiced an inchoate and undifferentiated form of *res rusticae* (i.e., *both* agriculture *and* animal husbandry; 3.1.7)? Why, in particular, does neither *pastor* nor *pastio* precipitate such discursive challenges to Varronian *res rusticae*? For one thing, the *RR*'s distinction between *agricola* and *pastor* would appear

---

Cicero (unsurprisingly), and Nepos also employ it extensively in their own writings.

106. For *colo* (*TLL* s.v. *colo*), compare I. *i.q. incolere, habitare* to II. *i.q. curare, tractare, diligere, sim.* For *cultura* (*TLL* s.v. *cultura*), it suffices to compare the relative length of *cultura* in a farming setting (I: roughly three columns) to its minimal other usages (II and III: less than one column). For Cicero's innovative use of *cultura* as a rustic metaphor for rhetorical training, see Connors (1997) 96–97.

107. Cf. Cato's usage of *ager* in appendix 3.

to hinge not only on the activity practiced by each figure (e.g., 1.2.13; 3.1.8), but also—and perhaps more crucially—on their respective juridical statuses; whereas slaves who maintain herds are construable as *pastores* (2.10.1ff.), slaves engaged in field cultivation never admit recognition as *agricolae,* but are instead *servi, mancipia,* or, most famously, "speaking tools" (*instrumenta vocalia*; 1.17.1ff.).[108] In contradistinction to *pastor,* then, *agricola* denotes the free owner (i.e., the *dominus*) of both the means (i.e., the farm and its operations) and the ends of production (i.e., its *fructus*). The appellation of *pastor,* on the other hand, would seem to indicate only that the designated person engaged in the activity of *pastio*—regardless of that person's juridical or ownership status. In this respect, the asymmetrical valuation of *agricola* and *pastor* in the *RR* is consonant with evidence found in Cato the Elder's treatise. Consider, for example, the latter text's description of the prayer that accompanies the estate's *suovetaurilia* (*Agr.* 141.2–3). By singling out "[his] shepherds and [his] flocks" (*pastores pecuaque*) as specific beneficiaries within the preeminent domain of "[the *dominus* or *agricola*], [his] house (*domus*), and household staff (*familia*)," this prayer would seem to imply that the *pastores* mentioned here are part and parcel of the *agricola*'s property and, therefore, are likely slaves.[109] On the basis of this text, then, it would appear that the Catonian *agricola* inherently owned the means to—and perhaps only vicariously "practiced"—field cultivation and, possibly, animal husbandry; *pastores,* on the other hand, engaged specifically and solely in the latter practice, potentially did not own the animals they tended, and were even themselves subject to another's ownership. To put it yet another way, an *agricola* effectively refers only to a person of free status—who might engage in pastoralism and, in this respect, may even be considered a *pastor* himself—but a *pastor* was not necessarily an *agricola* by virtue of praxis and juridical status. And it is because of this disparity in the sociolinguistic valences underlying *agricola* and *pastor* that *agri cultura*—despite the putative priority of *pastio* as an earlier mode of Roman rustic enterprise—functions as, or rather, is rendered, the primary domain for the description of activities surrounding the farm.[110]

---

108. For other instances of *pastor* referring to a herdsman of servile status, see pp. 133–36 and 162 in chapters 4 and 5.

109. It is possible that the *pastores* are free hired hands (cf. *mercennarii* in *RR* 1.17.2 or, perhaps, a dispossessed *pastor* of the sort such as Meliboeus in Vergil's *Eclogue* 1), but the more plausible inference remains that those mentioned here were slaves. Cf. White (1970) 355–56. When slaves, *pastores* would function as extensions of their *dominus*'s personhood; see *RR* 2.10.1–11 for servile *pastores* as part of the *pecudes* owned by *domini* of large ranches (*magnae pecuariae*) and pp. 232–35 in chapter 7 for consideration of how this might play out allegorically in the *RR*.

110. A material reality may also attend the two term's differing valences. Whereas the *pastor* needs only the animals that he intends to husband and access to suitable land for their

## CONCLUSION

In this last section, I have argued that there are good linguistic grounds for understanding the centrality of *agri cultura* in Varro's account of *res rusticae.* I have also suggested that the creation of *res rusticae* as a new field through the technical delineation and disembedding of *agri cultura, res pecuaria,* and *pastio villatica* from the broader category of *agricola* partially depends on the sociological background of Roman farming. Concurrent with these phenomena, moreover, is the historical shift from the elite as hands-on farmers to their status as absentee landowners; whether factual or perceived and, in this sense, ideological, either scenario prompted a revaluation of these traditional activities, and in subsequent chapters, I will return to the implications of these supposed developments more fully. But by surveying and comprehending, appropriating and refining, systematizing and explicating, agronomical precepts and their terminology—"material" (*res*) contingent upon a large amount of *scientia,* scattered throughout various Greek and Carthaginian predecessors, and discussed insufficiently and not unproblematically by Roman ones—Varro not only institutes a new *ars* of *res rusticae* in general, but also elevates it to the level of an object worthy of the methodological approach of philosophy. And in so doing, he renders the technical field of *res rusticae* consonant with the elite praxis of *res rusticae.*

For Varro, then, writing about rustic enterprise is an activity imbued with philosophy. In the following chapter, I present a reading of *RR* 1, which explicates the cultivated and productive tension of the dialogue's conceit and its agronomical precepts. As we shall see, the first book employs this new field of *agri cultura* to comment on contemporary issues of political importance, specifically, the concept of Italia and its potentially uneasy status vis-à-vis Rome.

---

maintenance, the *agricola* requires not only more capital—seed, land, and implements—but also a greater stability in circumstances than the shepherd. Most subsistent peasants would have engaged to varying degrees in both field cultivation and pastoralism (i.e., mixed use), but it remains that the *agricola* was in a better situation to engage in animal husbandry than a *pastor* was to cultivate fields. Particular circumstances could—and did—vary according to individual situations (for which, see White [1970] 272ff.), but if we assume the general applicability of the above observation, it further ensues that the *agricolae* would tend to be of a higher socioeconomic class, which might also explain the applicability of the term *pastor* to persons of servile status. Of course, further work that accounts for the economic realities and the varieties of pastoralism would be required to substantiate this suggestion.

# CHAPTER 3

# *Agri Cultura* and the Italian Farm in *RR* 1

~

[Marcus:] Ego mehercule et illi et omnibus municipibus duas esse censeo patrias, unam naturae, alteram civitatis. . . . Sed necesse est caritate eam praestare e qua rei publicae nomen et universae civitatis est, pro qua mori et cui nos totos dedere et in qua nostra omnia ponere et quasi consecrare debemus; dulcis autem non multo secus est ea quae genuit quam illa quae excepit. Itaque ego hanc meam esse patriam prorsus numquam negabo, dum illa sit maior, haec in ea contineatur.

[Marcus:] By god, I am of the opinion that both that guy and all *municipes* have two *patriae*: one by *natura,* the other by citizenship (*civitas*). . . . But it necessarily follows that the latter *patria* takes precedence in our affections whose name "*res publica*" belongs to the entire citizen body, on behalf of which we should die, to which we should surrender ourselves wholly, and in which we ought to put and, as it were, consecrate all belongings; only a little less sweet is the former *patria* that procreated us than that one which took us in. And so, I will never deny that the former is my *patria,* so long as the latter *patria* is greater and the former one is contained in it.

—Cicero, *De Legibus* 2.5[1]

Iuravit in mea verba tota Italia sponte sua, et me belli quo vici ad Actium ducem poposcit; iuraverunt in eadem verba provinciae Galliae, Hispaniae, Africa, Sicilia, Sardinia.

---

1. I have used the edition of J. G. F. Powell (2006). With the exception of the second sentence, for which I have modified the translation of Zetzel (1999) 131, the translation is mine. For an alternative translation, see Dyck (2004) 259.

All Italy of its own accord swore an oath of allegiance to me, and demanded that
I be the general for the war in which I conquered at Actium. The provinces of
Gaul, Spain, Africa, Sicily, and Sardinia swore that same oath.

—Augustus, *Res Gestae* 25.2

IN THE CONTEXT of 37 BC, the year in which Varro wrote *De Re Rustica,*
it is easy to overlook the degree to which the relationship between Rome and
"Italia" continued to be negotiated, reconceptualized, and even contested. To
be sure, the originally Greek appellation of "Italia" had long readily served
as the Romans' own name for the geographical totality of the peninsula,[2]
while the juridical status of "Italians" vis-à-vis Rome was "settled" by universal enfranchisement following the Social War in 88 BC.[3] Yet, Julius Caesar's extension of citizenship some forty years later to the inhabitants of the
area bounded by the Po River to the south and the Alps to the north[4]—not
to mention Mark Antony's ultimately aborted attempt to extend the same
enfranchisement to the denizens of Sicily[5]—simultaneously reveals and rec-
tifies the potential disjunction between the geographical and the juridical
senses of Italia. Moreover, any attempt to speak of a singular sense of a cultural, conceptual, or ideological "unity" between the city and the peninsula
mystifies the complex and highly variegated historical realities of Italia,[6] for

---

2. Itself originally a Greek term in all likelihood, "Italia" as a geographical appellation
was thought in antiquity to have initially circumscribed various southern portions of the
peninsula and, from there, to have gradually crept up the rest of the peninsula to the end of
the Appenines, to the River Po and, eventually, to the Alps; see, especially, Dion. Hal. *Ant.
Rom.* 1.35; Strabo 5.1.1 and 5.1.11; Radke (1967) 35–51; Gabba (1978) 11–12; Cornell in *OCD*3 s.v.
Italy; and Dench (2005) 157–62, the last of whom notes the possibility of coexisting "non-
Greek conceptualizations of Italia" (cf. *idem* [1995] 213–16).

3. Sherwin-White (1973) remains the classic discussion of Roman citizenship, its gra-
dations, and its gradual extension to all of Italy. Needless to say, the bibliography on
the relationship between Rome and Italy before the Social War is extensive; see, among
others, Brunt (1965a) 90–109 (whose views are slightly revised in his 1988 work); Badian
(1970/71) 373–421; Gabba (1976); and Dyson (1992). For the "Romanization" of Italy more
generally, see Salmon (1982), Keaveney (1987), and David (1996), all of which provide
useful narratives, but tend to overemphasize the resulting unity of Rome and Italy (e.g.,
as a "single civic whole" in David, 173; cf. Keaveney, 189–93) by the mid-first century BC.

4. For the enfranchisement of Gallia Transpadana, see Dio Cass. 41.36.3, Strabo 5.1.1, and
Sherwin-White (1973) 157–59.

5. See Cic. *Att.* 390.1 [= 14.12.1] and Sherwin-White (1973) 230.

6. See especially the important discussion of Gabba (1978) 11–28, whose refusal to identify a unitary sense of Italian national consciousness in antiquity (among other things)
provides a spiritual "blueprint" for more recent approaches that emphasize the complexity of the relationships of the various parties, their motivations, and their attitudes. Note
also that his analysis of "Italia" into three senses—geographical, juridical, and ideologi-

an ever-modulating nexus of Roman, Greek, and local (e.g., Etruscan, Oscan, etc.) elements continued to linger, admitting manifold configurations so as to render the land a sort of patchwork quilt of cultural identities well into the first century BC.[7] Ideologically, the stakes are perhaps most clearly illustrated in Cicero's famous attempt to resolve the competing claims of hometown and metropole to civic devotion, wherein the Arpinate *novus homo* acknowledges two *patriae* for each Italian citizen: the subordinate *municipium* from which one hails and the greater Roman *res publica* with which one's political priorities should ultimately lie. In stark contrast to Cicero's unequivocal subordination of Italia to Roma stands Vergil's prioritization of the peninsula as the larger font of Roman virtues[8] or, for that matter, Octavian/Augustus's careful cultivation of *tota Italia* in 32 BC as the final arbiter of the city's politics.[9]

It is against this larger backdrop of contemporary debates about the relationship of Italia to Rome—as well as in accordance with the approach sketched in Part I of this book—that this chapter considers *RR* 1's representation of Italia. In the first section, I explore how the opening of the dialogue constructs Italia as a geographical and agricultural entity within the space of *res rusticae* and, specifically, of *agri cultura*. Some elements of Varro's presentation are quite overt (e.g., the *laudes Italiae* with which the dialogue begins), while others require substantial explication for the modern reader (e.g., the significance of the Temple of Tellus as a setting). To Varro's contemporary

---

cal—underlies the present discussion. Dench (2005) 93–221 offers a nuanced exploration of the multifarious ways in which the relationship between Italy and Rome continued to be reconceived and negotiated from the fourth century BC to the mid-second century AD. Cf. Giardina (1994) 1–89. Nicolet (1991) 173–76, 189–207 provocatively—and convincingly—argues that it is only with Augustus's division of the peninsula into eleven regions that a distinctly geographical (as opposed to tribal) relationship between Rome and Italy arises. For an intriguing, but ultimately unpersuasive, account of an Italy unified by the physical environment and the modes of livelihood it necessitated (especially, transhumance pastoralism) long before Roman expansion and conquest, which in turn harnessed this unity and transformed it into a unified "Roman state in Italy" by imposing Roman legal categories and through the consensus generated by public lawmaking, see Williamson (2005) 131–238.

　　7. For an excellent discussion of the linguistic and material evidence, see Wallace-Hadrill (2008) 73–143.

　　8. For Vergil's creation of a national identity for Roman Italy in the *Aeneid,* see the pair of articles by Toll (1991) 3–14 and (1997) 34–56. Habinek (1998) 88–102 considers Horace's resolution of the Italian question over the course of his poetic career and through the construction of an elite canon. For the significantly different representations of Italy provided by Cicero, Vergil, and Augustus, see Ando (2001) 123–42.

　　9. Cf. chapter 10.2, in which Augustus relates his election to the position of *pontifex maximus*; the greatest multitude ever "from all of Italy" (*cuncta ex Italia*) came to Rome to appoint him. For the classic treatment of these passages, see Syme (1939) 276–93. Cf. Brunt and Moore (1967) 67–68 and the salutary critique of Ando (2001) 134–35.

reader, however, even these latter aspects would almost certainly have been readily apparent, and my discussion thus seeks to illuminate their relevance to the literary and ideological program of Varro's work. The second and third parts investigate the *exempla* Varro employs for illustrating the produce of *agri cultura*. Beyond generally portraying Italian fecundity as unrivalled, the method and content of Varro's examples also strengthen the impression of Italia as a unified geographical entity by comprehending potentially disparate regions under a totalizing and coherent ideology. Moreover, Varro's strategies for exemplification reinforce the status of the newly expanded juridical entity of Italia as the agricultural epicenter of the *oikoumenē*: one that is both distinct from and superior to the rest of the world. In the fourth section, I argue that Varro consciously maps his conceptualization of agricultural space onto the terminology of geopolitical space. This process is most ostensible in the difficult ninth chapter of *RR* 1, which "scientifically" reconciles his multifarious analysis of soil quality with the lexical—and, ultimately, ideological—position that different regions (*agri*) may in fact come together to form a single country (*terra*). By delineating how the terrestrial diversity of separate, potentially disparate, regions might coalesce into a single organic entity, Varro seeks to naturalize and normalize the otherwise ideologically fraught conceptual unit of Italia. In the fifth and final part, I consider the infamous conclusion to *RR* 1: the mistaken assassination of the temple caretaker (*aedituus*). Examination of this enigmatic ending reveals a richly suggestive range of literary tropes and historical echoes, which simultaneously invite and defy positivistic identifications of Fundilius, the "Estate-Owner," with figures as diverse as C. Helvius Cinna, Cicero, and Caesar. However one chooses to approach the identity of the caretaker, his death nonetheless both concludes the discussion of Italian fecundity and precludes the participants' promised dinner. Thus, by invoking the political turbulence and violence of the late Republic and its civil wars, the idealizing picture of Italia and its agricultural ascendancy is revealed to be a fiction: a satirical fantasy fatally undermined by the ongoing horrors of Roman internecine strife.

## ITALIA AND THE TEMPLE OF TELLUS

Like many of Cicero's dialogues, *RR* 1 begins with an ostensibly straightforward description of the setting: its time, place, and participants. But unlike the majority of Cicero's works,[10] the introductory scene has an uncanny pertinence to the ensuing discussion (1.2.1):

---

10. See chapter 1, pp. 17–19.

Sementivis feriis in aedem Telluris veneram, rogatus ab aeditumo, ut dicere didicimus a patribus nostris, ut corrigimur a recentibus urbanis, ab aedituo. Offendi ibi C. Fundanium, socerum meum, et C. Agrium equitem R. Socraticum et P. Agrasium publicanum spectantes in pariete pictam Italiam.

On the festival of the Sementivae I had come to the temple of Tellus, invited by the *aeditumus* (temple-caretaker), as we learned to say from our fathers, but by the *aedituus,* as we are corrected by modern urbanites. There I ran into Gaius Fundanius, my father-in-law, Gaius Agrius, a Roman Socratic *eques,* and Publius Agrasius, a publican, all gazing at an Italy painted on the wall.

On the day of the Sementivae, a traditional agricultural festival following the planting season, Varro finds himself at the Temple of Tellus, the earth goddess, and in front of a painted representation of Italia.[11] For a discussion of *agri cultura,* the setting of *RR* 1 is entirely appropriate—and even, as it would seem, inspirational, for the *Italia picta* adorning the temple's wall is soon to induce in a *locus amoenus*-like fashion the forthcoming *laudes Italiae.*[12] The dialogue's conceit also involves a certain amount of satirical fantasy, for the encounter is random: "What are you doing here?" asks Varro the interlocutor, as he happens upon (*offendere*) the interlocutors (1.2.1). Invited by the temple's *aeditumus,* Varro is (and remains) unclear as to his relationship with the hosting caretaker, who has been summoned away by the presiding aedile (1.2.2) and whose name, as we later learn (1.2.11), is conveniently L. "Fundilius," or "the Estate-Owner."[13] That the other chance attendees also happen to bear fortuitous monikers—another Estate-man in the case of Gaius Fundanius (*fundi*) and two Mr. Field(er)s in the visages of Gaius Agrius and Publius Agrasius (*agri*)[14]—only further underscores the lurking satirical play, which will reso-

---

11. *Pace* the often-adopted views of Martin (1971) and Heurgon (1978), both of whom see the first book as written ca. 55 BC on the basis of perceived contradictions (e.g., multiple dedications) and questionable assumptions, Flach (1996) 7–15 has, in my opinion, convincingly shown that the dialogue almost certainly takes place sometime between 45 and 37. Cf. Diederich (2007) 182–83 n. 1045. As Flach correctly points out, nothing actually challenges Varro's claim to be writing in his eightieth year (= 37 BC), and the range of 45 to 37 is further corroborated by various other post-45 BC references (e.g., the reference to Caesar's calendar at 1.28.1).

12. In a similar fashion, Cicero's *De Re Publica* takes a visual image as its starting point; see p. 178 in chapter 6 for discussion. Cf. the ekphrastic openings of the *Pinax of Cebes* and Longus's *Daphnis and Chloe.*

13. Cf. Green (1997) 427–28. The *aeditumus*'s identity is an issue to which I shall return.

14. Note that the opening essentially flags the upcoming linguistic play with the seemingly unnecessary pedantry on *aeditumus* versus *aedituus* (1.2.1). There is some evidence to

nate all too neatly with the dialogue's themes. And, as it turns out, Varro and these agronomical conversationalists have all come for a promised dinner party, but the host's absence holds the *cena* in abeyance and instead prompts a discussion of the produce they might otherwise have been eating under a representation of the source of that withheld sustenance.

To be sure, the environs is certainly rich in material for a discussion of field cultivation. But aside from proffering some whimsy, how do these features—puns, setting, and props—shape our reading of the text? Generally anticipating the book's recurring thematic engagement with the agricultural world, these elements specifically bring the *space* of agriculture—its farms and fields, its countries and soils—to the foreground of the dialogue; after all, the auspiciously named interlocutors will be discussing *agri cultura in* a temple to Tellus, the earth goddess, and *in front of* a painted representation of Italia. Perhaps more importantly, the very structure of the temple itself and its ornamentation evoke seminal moments in the political and agrarian history of Rome's extension of *imperium* over Italia, and it is these aspects to which I now turn.

Because the material record is almost entirely nonexistent, we know quite little about the form and function of the Temple of Tellus in the late Republic—an unfortunate loss, since the written sources suggest that the temple was no insignificant structure. Located in the Carinae, the well-to-do district on the western side of the Oppian Hill, the temple appears to have undergone a number of changes in form throughout its history and sources offer two competing aetiologies.[15] One account suggests that the Senate and Roman people built the temple on the site of the razed house of Sp. Cassius, who was consul of 486/5 BC and executed that same year for his apparently tyrannical designs.[16] The other tradition attributes the temple's building to the battlefield dedication of the Roman general P. Sempronius Sophus during an

---

identify C. Fundanius with a tribune of the plebs in 68; see *MRR* 138.

15. Discussions of the Temple of Tellus and the Carinae can be found in the topographical dictionaries: L. Richardson (1992) s.v. "Tellus, aedes"; 378–79; cf. s.v. "Carinae"; 71–72; *Lexicon Topographicum Urbis Romae* (1993) v.5 s.v. "Tellus, aedes"; 24–25. F. Coarelli. Cf. v.1 s.v. "Carinae"; 239–40. E. Rodriguez Almeida. Cf. Spencer (2010) 71–73. For the debate over the temple's location, see Ziolkowski (1992) 132–35; 155–62.

16. See, for example, Livy 2.41.1; Val. Max. 6.3.16; and Dion. Hal. *Ant. Rom.* 8.79.3. Further complicating the matter is confusion between the temple's exact honoree; most sources speak of the temple as the *aedes Telluris,* yet Pliny tells us that the temple's precinct featured a bronze statue—indeed, the first at Rome—of Ceres (*HN* 34.15). In addition to the similar purviews of Ceres and Tellus, this "confusion" may arise from their joint honoring during the Sementivalia (Ov. *Fast.* 1.657.ff.). Cf. Pliny *HN* 34.30, where Cassius places a statue of himself *apud tellum Telluris.* For a good discussion of these issues in their sociocultural context, see Roller (2010) 148–52.

engagement with the Sabine tribe of the Picentes in 268 BC.[17] In an attempt to reconcile these conflicting accounts, some scholars have posited an initial establishment of an archaic cult to Tellus in 486/5 BC with some kind of renovation in 268 BC. Given the paucity of evidence, such a synthetic approach is reasonable enough.

Needless to say, the competing accounts—as well as the complete absence of archaeological evidence—render the search for the historical origin and form of the *aedes Telluris* speculative at best. But what the literary sources *do* offer is a glimpse of the temple's *imagined* origin and form, which provide insight into its ideological significance for our sources and their contemporaries. In this respect, the tradition surrounding Sp. Cassius is particularly relevant. Perhaps reflecting the tumultuous political climate and the rise of inordinately powerful individuals, first-century BC accounts of the foundational years of Republican government are replete with narratives of Romans whose personal designs collided with the fledgling *res publica*. In Livy's history alone, we find, among others, the sons of Brutus (*Ab Urbe Condita* 2.5.1ff.), Appius Claudius Crassus (e.g., 3.44–48), and Spurius Maelius (4.13). As yet another would-be tyrant, Spurius Cassius thus represents an archetype for his late Republican counterparts. Yet, the case of Cassius merits special attention in the context of the *RR,* for it is his proposals that (at least in Livy) aetiologize the root of the agrarian conflicts that pervade narratives of Roman history. Having been defeated by the Romans in the previous year, the Hernici (an ancient Italian tribe) signed a treaty, which gave the victors two-thirds of their territory (2.41.1). As consul, Cassius proposed the division and equal allocation of these lands between the plebs and the Latin allies. In addition, he tacked on a number of "public lands" (*agri publici*) that were being held "by private individuals" (*a privatis*) (2.41.2). The proposal was met with much hostility and resistance from patricians and plebeians alike and marked a watershed in the history of the Roman *res publica* (2.41.3): "Then for the first time, an agrarian law was proposed, from then on never instigated without the greatest disturbances up to this very day" (*Tum primum lex agraria promulgata est, numquam deinde usque ad hanc memoriam sine maximis motibus rerum agitata*). In response to this measure, which the other consul, Verginius, decried as "a road to kingship" (*regno viam*), Cassius was tried, convicted, and executed at the hands of either the Senate and the people or his own father.[18] His house was subsequently razed and a statue of Ceres erected in its place. Yet, the status of the temple itself remains somewhat unclear, for Livy's

---

17. See Flor. 1.14.2 and Frontin. *Str.* 1.12.3.

18. Cf. Val. Max. 6.3.16, who claims that Cassius was crushed with his own house in the course of its demolition.

statement that the house's "location was in front of the Temple of Tellus" (2.41.11) does not shed any definitive light on whether the temple had actually been founded at this particular juncture. Of course, this is not the only difficulty with Livy's account. Most notably, it resonates all too conveniently with the ongoing agrarian struggles over the allocation and use of public land (*ager publicus*) from the Gracchi (133 BC) onwards.[19] Indeed, Cassius's proposed distribution of spoils to the allies and Latins specifically recalls the *lex frumentaria* of C. Gracchus in 123 BC.[20]

Whatever the historicity of this narrative, it remains that the very space occupied by the Temple of Tellus evoked the paradigm of recurring agrarian conflict: in this case, the supposedly seminal one. The cast of characters further reinforces this evocation, for, in addition to the presence of Publius Agrasius, or "Mr. Public Land," both Cn. Tremelius Scrofa and C. Licinius Stolo are introduced by way of their connections to agrarian measures (1.2.9–10): the former as Varro's colleague on Caesar's land commission of 59 BC[21] and the latter in terms of his eponymous ancestor who introduced the Lex Licinia of 367 BC, "which prevent[ed] a Roman citizen from occupying more than 500 *iugera*" of *ager publicus*.[22] Thus, to the very site evocative of the first would-be arbiter of public land comes the descendant of the first *auctor* of a successfully passed agrarian law. The intention behind this collocation is a bit trickier and requires that we recall the late Republic's recurring conflicts over *ager publicus*, which held particular importance for the relationship between Rome and Italy. Referring to lands owned by the Roman state, but available to Roman citizens for use, *ager publicus* occupied a potentially nebulous legal category: situated roughly between the private property of individual Roman citizens and, theoretically, all provincial land that was subject to Roman *imperium*, but not owned by any one citizen and often occupied or possessed by subaltern locals.[23] Public land holdings in Italy itself—remnants of various periods of Italian resistance to Roman rule—continued to exist and, as late

---

19. Ogilvie (1965) 340 also notes a possible reference in *hanc* (2.41.3) to Caesar's (59 BC) and Octavian's (30 BC) land legislation.

20. Ibid. 339.

21. For Scrofa, see p. 16 in chapter 1, p. 32 in chapter 2, and Nelsestuen (2011) 317–28.

22. The traditions surrounding the Lex Licinia are diverse, but the core of the tradition is the restriction of 500 *iugera* of *ager publicus* to each individual; see, for example, Livy, 6.35.4–42.9; App. *B. Civ.* 1.8; and Roselaar (2010) 95–112. As discussed by Gargola (1995) 136–43, the date of the law is questionable, but does appear to be (or, at least, reflect) the earliest one governing the use of *ager publicus*.

23. For the legal status of *ager publicus* in the Republic, see Roselaar (2010) 86–136. Cf. Gargola (1995) 130–31.

as 63 BC, remained a highly contentious issue for Italian landholders.[24] Allusion to *ager publicus* thus had the power to recall the historically tumultuous relationship between Rome and Italia. And by using the Temple of Tellus as a setting for *RR* 1, Varro evokes this problematic legacy of Roman-Italian relations and imparts to the dialogue the sense that the ensuing discussion of Italian *agri cultura* is about more than just the technical aspects of farming.

If only because of its closer temporal proximity, the tradition that emphasizes Sempronius's contribution to the site perhaps merits more historical credence than the stories surrounding Spurius Cassius. Yet, it also provides an even more specific connection between the Temple of Tellus and Rome's history vis-à-vis Italia. Coming off the hard-fought victory over King Pyrrhus of Epirus, the Tarentines, and Magna Graecia in general in the 270s BC, the Romans turned to the punishment of those who sided with the enemy, including the Sabine Picentes. During one such retributory engagement in 268 BC, an earthquake ominously interrupted the battle, thereby portending ill for the Roman forces. Performing the part of the exemplary commander, Sempronius promised in the pitch of battle the temple as a votive appeasement for Tellus.[25] Once again, the history of the Temple of Tellus is intertwined with the history of Rome's hegemonic interactions with the peninsula. But the culmination of the wars that precipitated Rome's operations against the Picentes also represents another watershed in one strand of Roman historiographical tradition. According to Florus (1.18.1), Roman *victoria* in the Pyrrhic and Tarentine Wars both marked the conclusion (*consummaret*) of its conquest of *tota Italia* and "inaugurated" (*auspicaretur*) its future "triumphs overseas" (*triumphos transmarinos*).[26] Where the account becomes simultaneously problematic and suggestive is in the former claim, that is, the

---

24. 63 BC is the year in which Rullus proposed his ten-man commission for the purpose of selling publicly owned land in Italy—particularly in Campania—in order to buy other land for distribution and colonization; see Roselaar (2010) 46–48. For Italia's vulnerability—especially, Capua and *ager Campanus*—to claims made regarding *ager publicus*, see Cic. *Leg. Agr.* 2.73ff. Even if the charge of Hardy (1924) 68–98, which accuses Cicero of gross misrepresentation of Rullus's bill, stands, Cicero's general emphasis on the decemvirs as having the powers of tyrants offers powerful insight into the controversial nature of such laws. For a more positive view of Cicero's critiques, see Williamson (1990) 266–76.

25. In the Roman exemplary tradition, the mark of a good commander included his ability to calm the soldiers at the appearance of natural phenomena. See, for example, Livy's account (44.37.5–9) of Sulpicius Gallus, who explained a lunar eclipse as a routine natural phenomenon, thereby quelling his soldiers' fears and ensuring victory over the Macedonians in the Battle of Pydna in 168 BC. Cf. Cic. *Rep.* 1.23 and the comments of Beard, North, and Price (1998) 2.174.5.

26. But note that Salmon (1982) 57–72 downplays the historical significance of the Pyrrhic War, instead placing more importance on the appearance of Roman-minted coins from 268 BC onwards.

notion that the successful conclusion to this war represented the "completion" (*consummaret*) of Roman control of Italy. From strictly geographical and historical perspectives, this conclusion may appear to be a bit hasty,[27] but it becomes more palatable if we understand Florus's claim from an exemplary perspective, wherein the historicist dimension of the claim (i.e., that Rome had conquered *tota Italia* by the late 270s BC) is less salient than the fact that the amount of *tota Italia* under Roman control had now reached a *degree* hitherto unprecedented.[28] In other words, Florus is claiming not so much that Rome had literally brought the conquest of "all Italia" to a complete and decisive end, but rather, that this *victoria* marked the emergence of Rome as the hegemonic arbiter of the Italian peninsula as a whole.

However we might precisely understand the claims of Florus, it remains that the use of the Temple of Tellus as the setting of Book 1 conjures up the troubled political and military history of Rome vis-à-vis Italy in manifold ways. Moreover, if we recognize the Pyrrhic War as an ideological watershed for Romans of the first century BC, wherein the Roman state was construed in some sense to have "completed" (*consummare*) control of Italy, it is tempting to speculate that the *Italia picta* of the *aedes Telluris* either was part of Sempronius's original vow in that Picenian battle of 268 BC—that is, over two hundred years before the date of *RR* 1 (less likely)—or was added at a later date to commemorate the later interpretation of that putative "unification" (more likely).[29] In either case, however, it remains that the Temple of Tellus and its

---

27. Discussion of the shortcomings of the ancient historiographical tradition has been a leitmotif of recent scholarship; see, for example, Roller (2009) 214–16 and the bibliography cited ad loc. (esp. n. 3). Given the ongoing *oscillazione* between the geographical, juridical, and ideological senses of Italian in the middle and late Republic (cf. Gabba [1978] 12), it is worth considering what Florus meant when he speaks of *Italia* and, especially, *tota Italia*. His preemptive gloss of Campania, Lucania, and Apulia as *tota Italia* does not square well with the Antonine period (in which he writes), when the bounds of Italia were definite, long-established, and venerable, so one possibility is that he is adapting a passage from an earlier source (cf. Strabo 5.1.1), for which Italia could roughly be equated with Magna Graecia and, later, the areas up to the northern Apennine chain. Unfortunately, this explanation may not account for the context's implied inclusion of Picenum, an area northward and, therefore, usually outside this earlier formulation of Italia. Another possibility is that Florus is using "Italia" in contradistinction to Rome, that is, simply as shorthand for those areas outside Roman control at the time. Yet another possibility is that Florus is simply speaking hyperbolically so as to link Rome's first "overseas" success with its (future) incorporation of Italy, thereby presenting a more or less all-encompassing and unbroken narrative of Roman imperialistic achievement.

28. Cf. Roller (2009) 226–28 and, especially, Alföldy (1986) 349–65, the latter of whom heavily informs the observations of the former.

29. The most recent treatment of this "artifact," Roth (2007) 286–87, is rightly skeptical of any claims to an authentic 268 BC origin. For an overly positivistic description of this "painting"—the commission of which is inexplicably attributed to Sempronius's son in 252 BC—see Holliday (2002) 105–6.

ornamentation embed and enshrine—perhaps even extol—Rome's acquisition of hegemonic control over the peninsula.

## *Laus Italiae* in Painted Form

But what is the form and content of this *Italia picta*? Despite the increasing attention paid by modern scholarship to ancient conceptions of literary, geographical, and cartographic space,[30] fundamental questions remain, which are usually framed dichotomously: was it a "map" of some kind or some other representation, such as a mural of the goddess Italia?[31] Although the question's formulation as an "either/or" scenario potentially oversimplifies the matter, I favor the former understanding—that is, that the *Italia picta* was a map—on the basis of Varro's text as well as other evidence.

Any consideration of the *Italia picta* must begin with the artifact's persuasive reconstruction by Roth (2007: 286–300), who cogently explores its relationship with the Temple of Tellus and the thematic presentation of Italian agriculture as found in the ensuing *laudes Italiae*. By understanding this *laudes Italiae* as an *ekphrasis* of the map, he demonstrates that the work was likely a "hodological" representation of Italia, where "hodological" refers to the organization of the artifact's geographical representation according to points connected by lines (e.g., roads, rivers, etc.) and embedded in the perspective of the observing subject.[32] Adducing the Nile Mosaic found at the Praenestine Temple of Fortuna as a comparandum,[33] Roth also convincingly argues that this "map" should be viewed as a *chorographia,* a regional

---

30. At least in the case of the Romans, modern discussions of ancient conceptualizations of space have tended to focus on the degree of cartographic sensibility. For two representative positions within this larger debate, see Brodersen (1997), which generally discounts the notion that Romans had access to cartographic representations of space or, more broadly, conceived of space in terms that resemble modern cartography (e.g., a concern for scalar accuracy); and Dilke (1985), whose work provides a useful, but often uncritical and overly positivistic, survey of mapping in the ancient Greco-Roman world. As will become clear, my position that the *Italia picta* is a "map" does not entail a corresponding claim of cartographic accuracy and thus remains outside this debate.

31. The most famous and roughly contemporaneous visual representation of personified Italia is found on the so-called Gemma Augustana, for discussions of which, see Zanker (1988) 231 and Galinsky (1996) 120–21.

32. As a term, *hodological* was coined by Janni (1984). With its emphasis on roads at the expense of scalar accuracy, the itinerary of the so-called Peutinger Table exemplifies this conception of space. For some useful studies of the Tabula Peutingeriana, see Salway (2005) 119–35 and Talbert (2004) 113–31; (2010). Whereas Salway tends to emphasize the ornamentality of the map and the originality of its designer, Talbert views the map as an important artifact of a broader, Roman cartographic sensibility.

33. Cf. Coarelli (1990) 225–51.

geography, which probably included a series of "natural features, buildings, or specific historical events," and represented "cultural space, mapped out by distinctive natural features and agricultural practices, and connected by the infrastructure of the road system."

Adroitly marrying the material background to its context within the *RR*, Roth provides a compelling explanation for Varro's choice of the Temple of Tellus—with its *Italia picta*—as a setting for Book 1's technical discussion of field cultivation.[34] Before I turn to the written *laudes Italiae*, which complement the *Italia picta*, I would like to push the comparison between the artifact in the Temple of Tellus and the Nile Mosaic at Praeneste, for, as the single best comparandum, it may shed further light on the nature of this nonextant "map," particularly in its temporal dimensions.

Since its discovery in the late sixteenth or early seventeenth century AD, the so-called "Nile Mosaic" has received considerable scholarly attention.[35] As its name suggests, the Nile Mosaic is a mimesis of the Nile's course and delta, both of which were defining features of Egypt in the Greco-Roman imagination.[36] At the top, the mosaic features the deserts of Nubia, while the Delta occupies the bottom portion. In between, the Nile drifts back and forth, ebbing and flowing in its increasingly foreign and fantastic course. The view imposed by its original context on the spectator is from bottom to top, thereby corresponding to the traditional spatial conception of the Nile in antiquity.[37] Moreover, the mosaic's vignettes evince a gradual shift from a human-dominated landscape of civilization in the Delta to the uninhabited, zoological sands of the Nubian desert. The Nile Mosaic thus conceives of the meandering river in spatial, temporal, and cultural terms and, while it may not strictly qualify as a map, it does present an *image of a map*, which incorporates elements of *chorographia* and presents the Nile's course in the fashion of an itinerary.[38]

---

34. But note that Roth rightly raises the possibility that the artifact may be Varro's literary invention (295). I would second this possibility—especially given the *RR*'s nature as a work of satirical, potentially fictive, tendencies. In what follows, however, I (like Roth) accept its existence.

35. For an overview of its discovery and transmission, see Coarelli (1996) 241. Other important studies include Meyboom (1995), Burkhalter (1999) 230–60, and Ferrari (1999) 359–86.

36. For excellent plates, see Meyboom (1995), who views the mosaic as evidence for the second-century BC spread of Egyptian cults in Italy.

37. So Ferrari (1999) 365 rightly observes.

38. So *idem* 376–80 rightly concludes. Cf. the observation (379) that the Nile Mosaic offers "an imaginary itinerary through time: from the empire of the successors of Alexander, through the venerable ruins of the Egyptian civilization, and across the threshold of culture into the timeless landscape of nature." Note also that *chorographia* is an ancient literary genre closely connected with the painting of landscape vignettes (Ptol. *Geog.* 1.1; 4–5).

As for this artifact's location and the occasion of its production, we unfortunately do not possess any ancient narrative that provides the rationale behind the mosaic's placement in the Temple of Fortuna at Praeneste. Indeed, we are even unsure as to the artifact's physical genesis: whether it is an importation of an eastern piece, a copy of an eastern work, or a native Italian creation. The last case is perhaps the weakest, for there is no persuasively discernible reason for why this particular work or subject should appear in the temple that it did. While an Italian artist or patron could simply have desired the piece for ornamental purposes (which undoubtedly played *some* role in the mosaic's production), the precise choice of location still remains unexplained.[39] Moreover, on the premise that details of the mosaic would seem to be connected with the exploratory voyage of the Greek geographer Pythagoras, who reportedly navigated the Nile in the service of Ptolemy Philadelphus (ca. 280 BC), many scholars conclude that the artifact is probably a copy.[40] If we accept the admittedly speculative connection between this voyage and the mosaic, we may tentatively identify the genesis of the mosaic in its original context as a commemorative votive: one that consecrated the memory of the successful charting and, consequently, "conquest" of the Nile River.

To recap, then, the Nile Mosaic exhibits four basic features. First, it is an artistic representation intended to adorn the East Hall of the Temple of Fortuna at Praeneste. Second, it is a spatial mimesis, representing a more or less geographical conception of the Nile and admitting characterization as an "itinerary" as well as a "chorography." Third, a temporal and cultural arrangement accompanies the patently spatial orientation of the Nile Mosaic: from the civilized world of the knowable present to the timeless and hazy limits of the Nubian desert. Finally, the mosaic possibly commemorates a successful, state-sponsored exploration of the Nile.

So what might we make of the Temple of Tellus and its *Italia picta* in light of the comparandum at Praeneste? While recognizing that the complete loss of the former artifact inherently limits understanding its form and function and notwithstanding the minor differences in form and dedicatee,[41] the

---

39. But cf. n. 36. Wallace-Hadrill (2008) 111–13 suggests that the Italian *negotiatores* at Delos, who had deep connections with elite families at Praeneste, "[provide] a context for the economy of the building, and the evident knowledge of and attraction to eastern models," including (presumably) the "explicitly Alexandrian presentation of the Nile and its temples, peoples, flora and fauna" (113).

40. Following Phillips (1962) and Steinmeyer-Schareika (1978) 52–97, Ferrari (1999) 384 connects the pomp at the bottom of the mosaic to a surviving description of Ptolemy's celebration of the founding of games. Cf. Coarelli (1990) 225–51 and the salutary caution of Burkhalter (1999) 230–60.

41. In addition to the fact that each artifact is found in a temple dedicated to a different god, the Praenestine artifact is a mosaic, whereas the *Italia picta* is most probably a painting.

potential similarities between the two artifacts are rather intriguing. First, it would appear that both artifacts served as ornamentation for their respective temples and represented a spatial mimesis in the itinerary and chorographic traditions. Moreover, the foundational accounts of Sempronius's battlefield vow of the Temple of Tellus and Pythagoras's successful navigation of the Nile tentatively suggest that both works commemorated the "control" of space by representing that space. Finally—and here we are on more secure ground—both works seem to have provided a cultural geography, representing a selection of features (natural, agricultural, etc.) and possibly tying them to relevant political events. And in the case of the Temple of Tellus, it is the Roman "conquest" and "unification" of Italia of which the *Italia picta* provides a visual and vivid reminder.

## Scientific and Rhetorical *Laudes Italiae*

After sorting out the circumstances of their fortuitous assemblage, Varro, Fundanius, Agrius, and Agrasius retire to some nearby benches to await the return of their host (1.2.2). The conversation begins with Agrasius's query (1.2.3): "Those of you who have traversed many lands (*terrae*), have you seen any land more cultivated than Italia?" (*vos, qui multas perambulastis terras, ecquam cultiorem Italia vidistis?*).[42] Of course, the question is rhetorical (cf. *ecquam*), as Agrius and Fundanius proceed to confirm in extended responses commonly referred to as "praises of Italy" (*laudes Italiae*).[43] While the opening statement's content (i.e., Italy's fecundity) and form (i.e., a performative question posed in comparative terms) are "conventional" from a later critical perspective and suggest that the *RR* has entered into territory occupied primarily by rhetorical commonplaces,[44] such an estimation ignores that the passage predates all other securely attested *laudes Italiae* and, more importantly, glosses over its integral connection to the overall theme of the first

In itself, however, this latter difference is not so significant given that we know that mosaics were frequently representations of paintings; see Ling (1991) 7.

42. For this passage in the context of Roman elite *ambulatio* as a cultural and philosophical practice, see O'Sullivan (2011) 96–100. Note that there may be a tinge of irony here, for Agrasius's sojourns as a *publicanus* would have been anything but philosophical.

43. On the basis of Serv. *ad Georg.* 2.136, modern scholarship tends to characterize any praise of Italia as a set rhetoric piece, wherein the speaker bestows unqualified praise upon Italia: "[Vergil] now begins a *laus Italiae*, which he pursues according to rhetorical precepts, for he says that Italia both possesses everything good and lacks everything bad."

44. Thomas (1982) 39, however, rightly implies that Servius's identification of *laus Italiae* as a rhetorical trope does not mean that it was such in the first century BC. Cf. Dench (2005) 189–91.

book: Italian *agri cultura*. Continuing to highlight the importance of Italy within *RR* 1, the dual praises will, as we shall see, present a model for reading *RR* 1 as both a "technical" and a "literary" work, the conjunction of which encourages a "political" reading of the text: in this case, a new and reconciliatory ideology for the relationship between Rome and Italia.

In response to Agrasius's opening query, Agrius, the "Socratic equestrian" (1.2.1), dutifully provides the expected affirmation by supplying (predictably) a philosophical—in particular, an Eratosthenean—rationale for Italian fertility.[45] Italia is "so wholly cultivated" (*tam tota . . . culta*; 1.2.3), he responds, because of its natural geographical advantages. First dividing the world into northern (i.e., European) and southern (i.e., Asian) halves and then subdividing the former into more northern and more temperate portions, Agrius endeavors to show that Italia is situated precisely in the most temperate, healthful (*salubrior*), and profitable (*fructuosior*) part of the *orbis terrae*. Regardless of the fidelity with which Varro has summarized it,[46] Eratosthenes's "philosophical" (or what we would more readily consider to be "scientific" or "technical") account attributes Italy's fecundity to its temperateness: its medial location between the frigidity of northern Europe and the heat of Asia to the south.

Not too hot and not too cold, Italy thus benefits from its tempered exposure and access to the elements and, thereby, has a "scientific" justification for its unsurpassed fecundity. Perhaps finding Agrius's account a bit too Hellenic for his more traditional tastes, Fundanius interjects a line from Pacuvius's *Antiope*: "if there is day or night all the time, all the fruits of the earth (*terra*) perish because of the fiery vapor or extreme cold."[47] On the one hand, the quotation buttresses Agrius's Graecizing claim with a Latin source, thereby initiating the *RR*'s programmatic preference for Roman authorities.[48] On the other hand, it also effects a transition to a new mode of discourse: from the philosophical (i.e., scientific/technical) one of the Hellenizing Agrius to the

---

45. On the basis of his character description as an *eques Socraticus* (1.2.1) and his climatological analysis (which, per the nature of ancient geography, often entails ethnographical and ethical analyses; cf. Clark [1999] *passim*), it may be possible to apprehend a Posidonian element in Agrius's characterization as well; cf. Nicolet (1991) 65–66.

46. As Flach (1996) 231 notes, the basic assignment of Europe to the north and Asia to the south appears also in Varro, *Ling.* 5.31. For a concise discussion of Eratosthenes's contributions to geography, see Aujac (1998) 247–62.

47. F 26–28 Warmington = F 28 Ribbeck.

48. For the *RR*'s programmatic preference for Roman authorities, see pp. 42–46 in chapter 2. Spencer (2010) 73–75, on the other hand, understands Agrius's use of Greek science and Fundanius's quotations of literature as indicative of Varro's use of "pan-Mediterranean Greek semiotics" (75), which is part of Varro's interrogation of Roman identity as it practically works and in opposition to Catonian-style traditionalism.

literary one of the thoroughly traditional Fundanius. The importance of the
*RR*'s tendency to shift between and, even elide, registers cannot be underestimated, for it recurs, as we shall see, elsewhere in the text and, in fact, provides
a model for reading the stylized literary backdrops of each dialogue with the
ostensibly more straightforward technical discussions.

Moving from Pacuvius's to his own authority, Fundanius then effuses
(1.2.6–7):

> Contra quid in Italia utensile non modo non nascitur, sed etiam non egre-
> gium fit? Quod far conferam Campano? Quod triticum Apulo? Quod vinum
> Falerno? Quod oleum Venafro? Non arboribus consita Italia, ut tota poma-
> rium videatur? An Phrygea magis vitibus cooperta, quam Homerus appellat
> ampeloessan, quam haec? Aut tritico Argos, quod idem poeta polupuron?
> In qua terra iugerum unum denos et quinos denos culleos fert vini, quod
> quaedam in Italia regiones? An non M. Cato scribit in libro Originum sic:
> "ager Gallicus Romanus vocatur, qui viritim cis Ariminum datus est ultra
> agrum Picentium. In eo agro aliquotfariam in singula iugera dena cullea
> vini fiunt?" Nonne item in agro Faventino? A quo ibi tricenariae appellantur
> vites, quod iugerum tricenas amphoras reddat?

> On the other hand, what useful product not only does not take root, but also
> not thrive in Italia? What spelt am I to compare to the Campanian? What
> wheat to the Apulian? What wine to the Falernian? What oil to the Venaf-
> ran? Is not Italia so planted with trees as to seem to be wholly an orchard
> (*pomarium*)? Or is Phrygia, which Homer calls "*ampeloessan,*" more cov-
> ered with vines than Italia? Or what about Argos and its wheat, which the
> poet calls "*polupuron*"? In what land (*terra*) does one *iugerum* return ten
> and fifteen *cullei* of wine, which certain regions (*regiones*) of Italia produce?
> Or does not Cato write in his *Origines* thus: "the Ager Gallicus, which lies
> on this side of Ariminium and beyond the Ager of the Picentes and was
> given out in viritane assignments, is called Roman. In this region (*ager*)
> in many places, ten *cullei* of wine are produced in every single *iugerum*"?
> Isn't this also the case in the Ager Faventinus? Where the vines are called
> "*tricenariae*" by the fact that one *iugerum* returns three hundred *amphorae*?

Teeming with rhetorical questions and exemplifying Italy's fecundity in terms
of specific agricultural produce, Fundanius's compensatory *laus Italiae* exhibits many features common to the later rhetorical tradition.[49] Thus, no grain

---

49. For a concise list of examples of the *laudes Italiae,* see Thomas (1982) 39. Those of

is finer than the Campanian, no wheat better than the Apulian, and so on. In the case of fruit-bearing trees, their overall superiority transcends individual regions to encompass the whole (*tota*) of Italia—so much so that the peninsula would itself seem to constitute an orchard (*pomarium*). In these respects, this *laus Italiae* not only sets the terms for the later and more famous praises of Italy, but even outdoes them in offering a superlatively concise praise meted equally between individual regions (*agri*) and the land's (*terra*) overall bounds.

Yet, this second *laus* merits closer attention for several reasons. For one thing, while comparison of Italy to other countries (*terrae*) is found in other writers (most notably Vergil), the references to specific earlier *auctores* are not.[50] So, while it may be the case that Phrygia and Argos are covered respectively with vines and wheat, their fertility pales in comparison to that of Italia—over and above Homer's epithets. Fundanius's speech continues in this comparative vein, with Homer then pitted against Cato the Elder. Unlike the poet, whose agronomical boasts are found wanting in an Italian context, Cato's examples hold their weight and reinforce Italia's agricultural superiority: so Italian Cato trumps Homer the Greek. This notion of Italian agricultural superiority over Greece and Phrygia adroitly illustrates two recurring features of Book 1's presentation of Italian agriculture. It is not just that the fecundity of Italia stems from its various regions and their exemplary products, but also that Italian agriculture is superior to that of other, non-Italian lands.

The method of exemplification also merits attention. The speech first emphasizes Italian fecundity in terms of staple products: grains, grapes, and olives. These products are in turn linked to specific regions: Campania, Apulia, Faventia, Venafrum, the Ager Gallicus, and Ariminium. Finally, and most crucially, the praise of *specific* regions and products is extended *generally* to Italia as a whole. Thus, Apulian wheat contributes to the overall state of Italian fertility. Or in the case of vines, a common Italian quality implicitly lies at the root of "all" (*tota*) Italy's status as an orchard (*pomarium*) as well as of the superiority of the regional Falernian and Faventian varieties of grapes over

---

the *Quellenforschung* persuasion have tended to view this passage as the link between the putative (but not extant) Polybian/Posidonian tradition and the praise of Italy found in Vitr. *De Arch.* 6.1.10–11; cf. *idem* 61 n. 15–17, who rightly discounts this suspect approach.

50. For comparison of Italia to other *terrae*, see Verg. *G.* 2. 136–39; Dion. Hal. *Ant. Rom.* 1.26.3; Strabo 6.4.1; and Pliny *HN* 37.202–3. Any authority or authorities invoked by the other *laudes Italiae* are generalizing impersonals ("it is said"), generalizing third-person plurals ("they say"), or, at most, the "ancients." See, for example, Dion. Hal. *Ant. Rom.* 1.31.8.

the Phrygian ones.[51] In sum, both kinds of exempla collaborate to create an overall impression of Italian fecundity.[52]

But what of the "rhetorical" nature of the *laus Italiae*? The connection between particular geographical regions and signature agricultural products is not uncommon in ancient texts; indeed, Varro elsewhere refers to certain types of figs as the "Chian" or "African" variety (1.41.6). Yet, this strategy is generally not a feature of the topos of Italian agricultural superiority. When both Vergil (*G.* 2.150; 181–83) and Pliny (*HN* 3.41), for example, extol Italian olives and grapes, their praise is always formulated in terms of the broader category of "Italia"—and *not* the specific regions in which they are actually grown. By eschewing the regional focus found in Varro's *laus*, Vergil and Pliny instead present Italian fecundity as a uniform whole. In part, this tendency is subject-oriented—after all, *laudes Italiae* are fundamentally about "Italia"—and it is not inconceivable that later writers simply assume the reader's cognizance of individual regions' particular excellences within the terms of their more general praise. Even so, Varro's emphatic connection of specific products with particular regions constitutes a deliberate attempt to construe "Italia" through its variegated and multifarious nature.

In support of this proposition, it may be relevant to compare the only other "praise of Italy" that names specific regions, which is found in the roughly contemporaneous account of Dionysius of Halicarnassus. Like Fundanius and by way of rhetorical question no less, Dionysius substantiates general Italian fecundity through exemplary regions and their specific produce (1.37.2): grains three times per year in Campania; olives in Messapia, Daunia, and Sabine country; and grapes in Etruria, Alba Longa, and Falernia. There is some overlap in regions between Dionysius's and Varro's lists (e.g., Campania, Falernia),[53] but the more significant point of similarity would seem to

---

51. Reference to *tota Italia* as a *pomarium* occurs within the context of, on the one side, Venafran olives and Falernian grapes, and, on the other, Phrygian grapes. While Latin has specific words for an oliveyard (*oliveta*) and vineyard (*vinea*), *pomarium* can serve as a generic term for any kind of orchard or garden planted with trees and for the intention of bearing fruit. Cf. *arbustum*. See *TLL* s.v. *pomarium* 1.a.A. As discussed later, Varro seems also to be punning off the morphological and phonological analogue, *pomerium*.

52. Cf. Spencer (2010) 73: "inconveniently diverse Italian local identities disappear once their landscapes are rezoned as Rome, from a Roman perspective, and regions are redefined in terms of quintessential crops rather than as unique ethnoscapes: Falernum becomes a sea of vines, Campania waves of spelt. Eventually, such examples are trumped by some dramatic totalizing perspectives regenerating *Italia* implicitly as an ethnically unified whole, a 'Rome' greater than the sum of its parts." While I agree that this *laus* diminishes the vast ethnic diversity of Italy, I do think that it—as well as *RR* 1—attempts to preserve some degree of regional diversity and does not wholly subsume individual regions under a category of "Italia" that ultimately collapses into "Rome."

53. Campanian fertility—especially in terms of grains—is well attested in the literary sources (e.g., Pliny *HN* 18.3), while Falernian wine was famous for being of the highest quality

be their consensus on Italian superiority in the trifecta of ancient agricultural produce: cereals, olives, and grapes.

The two accounts diverge significantly, however, in their geographical focus and manner of organization. Unlike Varro's text, which markedly shifts from a collocation of central and southern Italian areas (Campania, Apulia, Falernia, Venafrum) to a more northerly orientation (the Ager Gallicus, Picenum, and Ager Faventinus), Dionysius's exempla are almost exclusively focused on central Italy:[54] Campania (central-west), Messapia (southeastern), Daunii (central-eastern), Sabine country (central), Etruria (northwestern), Alba Longa (central-west), and Falernia (central-west, but a bit farther south). In fact, the more readily discernible principle of organization for Dionysius's account is the number three: three harvests in Campania, three regions for wine, and three more for olives. Fundanius, on the other hand, is unhampered by any numerical trope and incorporates a decidedly wider range of areas: central, southern, and northern.

In the ideologically fraught context of conceptualizing and representing Italy, the *RR*'s more inclusive approach merits closer attention. As mentioned above, the first half of the *laus* focuses on south-central Italy: Campania, Apulia, and the more specific regions around Falernum and Venafrum (i.e., northwestern Campania). The second half, after the (denied) comparison with Phrygian viticulture and Greek grain, then shifts northward to the regions of the Ager Gallicus, which is situated on the northeastern coast of Italy, and the Ager Faventinus, which is located inland approximately 100 miles northwest. By virtue of the fact that the first set of communities is situated on the Via Appia and Via Latina, and the second on the Via Flaminia and Via Aemilia, both halves of Fundanius's speech evince a Romanocentric hodological perspective.[55] But given the backdrop of the *laus* (i.e., the Temple of Tellus) and the polemical nature of the passage (e.g., Italia is more fertile than Greece), we might wish to consider the cultural and temporal ramifications concomitant with the geographical shift. Thus, the first half focuses on the southern-central regions of Campania and, to a lesser extent, Apulia—areas that, from a Roman point of view, had longer-standing cultural recognition as "Italian." The second half concentrates on the more northern regions of the Ager Gallicus and Cisalpine Gaul—regions that came to be considered "Italian" more recently than the central and southern regions. In this way, Fundanius's

---

(e.g., Hor. *Carm.* 2.3.8). As Heurgon (1978) 105 observes, Venafrum was known for its olives (Strabo 5.3.10; Pliny *HN* 15.8).

54. As Phillip Horky has observed to me, the manner of organization resembles the counterclockwise periegesis evinced in (among others) Eratosthenes and Apollonius of Rhodes.

55. So Roth (2007) 291–92. For classic treatments of Roman roads, see Chevallier (1976) and Laurence (1999).

speech exemplifies Italian fecundity in terms of not only south and north, but also old and new.

The temporal implications of this balanced and more complete spatial distribution may be pushed further. From a purely Roman perspective, the first four exemplary regions of central and southern Italy—Campania and Apulia, Falernus and Venafrum—gradually came under its control in the course of the mid-fourth to early third century BC: a process that culminated in victory over Pyrrhus. The Ager Gallicus, on the other hand, came under Roman control in 283 BC after the Romans defeated the Gallic tribe of Senones, that is, roughly contemporaneous with the consolidation of the southern portion of the peninsula; however, it was not until 232 BC that the apportionment of the land to Roman colonists occurred, to which the quotation of Cato refers.[56] Only then would the Ager Gallicus have been called *Romanus*.[57] Likewise, the area of Faventia did not come under the control of the Romans until at least 222 BC, and the town itself may only have been founded in the 120s BC.[58] Varro's inclusion of these areas in his *laus Italiae* is, then, a calculated move that reinforces the relatively more recent incorporations of areas traditionally considered "Gallic" into Roman "Italia"[59] and subtly underscores the role and historical thrust of Rome's position as *arbiter Italiae*.[60]

---

56. For the defeat of the Senones, see Polyb. 2.19.7. Cato *Orig.* F 46 Cornell [= F 2.10 Jordan = F 43 Peter]. Cf. Polyb. 2.21.7–8 and Cic. *Sen.* 11. See Cornell (2014) 3.93 for discussion.

57. *Pace* the translations of Ash and Hooper (1934), Chassignet (1986), and Roth (2007), all of whom render the name of the region as "Gallo-Roman" (*ager Gallicus Romanus*), the traditional way to refer to the region was simply as the Ager Gallicus (Cic. *Clu.* 22, 24; *Sen.* 11; Varro *RR* 2.3.9; Livy 21.25.2; Plin. *HN* 3.112). Cato's point is that *ager Gallicus* became *Romanus* upon the viritane distribution of its land. Cf. Cornell (2014) 3.93. For subsequent shifts in the region's name, see Columella, *Rust.* 3.3.2 (Picenum) and Serv. *ad Aen.* 10.198 (Bononia). For the joint pronouncement of an *ager* for a newly established *urbs,* see Gargola (1995) 81–82.

58. See Salmon (1969) 112 and Roth (2007) 292, esp. n. 23.

59. Interestingly enough, Pliny the Elder, who writes about a century after Varro's *RR* and who (idiosyncratically) uses the Augustan division of Italia into regions as his primary method of organization for his geography, still refers to these areas as the start of "Gallia Togata" (*HN* 3.112). Cf. Dio Cass. 48.12.5.

60. To be sure, Varro does not explicitly draw attention to the preeminence of Rome, and in the context of *RR*'s prioritization of Italia, the presence of the city is minimized. Moreover, the few instances of Rome as an example of Italian agriculture (e.g., 1.50.2) figure it as any other region of the peninsula. Interestingly enough, Latium as a discrete spatial entity only figures explicitly into the *RR* once (1.10.1), as opposed to its relatively more frequent attestation in *De Lingua Latina* (e.g., 5.32; 5.100). In any case, Rome's presence may be subtle, but its political preeminence—however embedded it may be—nevertheless remains.

## PATTERNS OF EXEMPLIFICATION FOR ITALIAN
## *AGRI CULTURA*

Spanning diffuse spatial (south and north, west and east) and temporal (early third to late second centuries BC) frames, Fundanius's *laus Italiae* offers two ways of construing "Italia": as an entity that incorporates smaller regions (*agri*) and as a corporate identity that marks itself off in contradistinction to other *terrae*. As we shall see, this twofold approach also informs the dialogue's technical discussion and, more specifically, Varro's strategies for illustrating the precepts of *agri cultura*. In terms of sheer numbers, "Italia" appears more often than any other single geographical entity, yet it also serves as the central conceptual unit underlying *RR* 1's construal of agricultural space. In this last respect, this qualitatively preeminent notion of *Italia* functions as the fundamental frame of reference for his discussion as well as the "nodal" point of agricultural interaction between the numerous intra-Italian exempla and their less frequent non-Italian counterparts: incorporating the former and framing them collectively in opposition to the latter.

So as to begin to substantiate these claims, all of the first dialogue's geographical references have been collected and arranged in appendix 4 according to the tripartite system of classification found in the opening *laus Italiae*'s formation of the world: intra-Italian regions (*agri*), the *terra* of Italia itself, and other *terrae* (e.g., Phrygia and Argos).[61] On this analysis, *RR* 1 contains a total of sixty-two references to various Italian regions, fifteen references to Italia in general, and thirty-nine to non-Italian areas.[62] Of these instances, when we subtract the citations of other authors, we retain roughly the same

---

61. Note that I have placed each geographical reference in the order in which it is found in the dialogue and, when applicable, I have denoted collocations of *exempla* with a box. I have also included a loose description of the subject under discussion and whether or not Varro is quoting from another authority. Quotations from Theophrastus and Cato the Elder often contain geographical references and, in the case of Theophrastus, feature mostly non-Italian *exempla*. This is not to say that Varro is blindly quoting here, for (cf. Skydsgaard [1968] 64–68) Varro can adapt and modify the passages for his own purposes (e.g., 1.7.6–7, which is a reworking and supplementation of Theophrastus's *Hist. Pl.* 1.4.3 and 1.9.5). In any case, while I do not want to ignore these quotations, thereby implicitly denigrating them as simply "derivative," I will privilege Varro's own contributions. For example, in this last instance, it is suggestive that Varro's additional examples of Consentia and Reate are both Italian and, in this sense, complement, supplement, or even contend with Theophrastus's comparatively eastern focus. Thus, instead of simply looking at the sheer numbers, my discussion focuses mostly on collocations of spatial exempla, which offer greater insight into the spatial conceptualization with which Varro was working.

62. It is certainly not insignificant that Varro's agricultural purview is, as has often been observed (e.g., White [1973] 447), far broader than Cato's focus on Latium and Campania.

proportion: forty-two, fourteen, and twenty-six. In either case, references to Italian regions and Italia itself significantly (and unsurprisingly) outnumber the non-Italian category (roughly two to one) and thus collaborate with the emphasis found in Fundanius's literary *laus Italiae*. The majority of these examples are found in groups, but isolated spatial exempla can and do occur. For example, Italia is mentioned alone in 1.9.1 (see below), while the use of oxen in Campania (1.20.4) and the threshing floor employed by the Bagienni (i.e., in Liguria; 1.51.2) are discussed without reference to other regions. More of these isolated examples, however, are non-Italian, that is, transmarine or "foreign," cases: Athens (1.2.20; 1.37.1; 1.37.5), Corcyra (1.4.5), Gaul (1.32.2), and Hispania Citerior (1.52.2).[63] Notwithstanding these exceptions, however, Varro's usual practice is to include a number of examples, which, from a pragmatic standpoint, is conducive to his theoretical overview of *agri cultura*; it is simply easier to conceptualize general practices inductively from specific exempla rather than vice versa.

Within Italy, Fundanius's praise, as we saw before, explicitly ties specific products to particular regions in support of the larger claim of an overall Italian fecundity. Moreover, these exempla are generally oriented around two points of geo-temporal focus: southern (i.e., "older"), and northern (i.e., "newer") Italia. The notion of "balance" or "complementarity" implied herein can be found elsewhere in the *RR*,[64] but the most explicit example actually comes from the second dialogue, where Varro (*qua* interlocutor) discusses the transhumance of his sheep (2.2.9): "For my flocks, which would summer in the mountains of Reate, used to winter in Apulia, since the public trails between these two places encompass the separated grazing places, just as a yoke (*iugum*) connects its buckets." Humorously punning on the meaning of *iugum* as both a "yoke" and a "mountain range," Varro's badinage neatly illustrates the fact that the Apennines run through both the central Italian city of Reate and the southeastern region of Apulia and, in this respect, "connect" the two otherwise remote areas.[65] By presenting Apulia as the ideal winter

---

63. Note that a few occur in a nonagricultural context: 1.2.20, for example, treats the Athenian prohibition of allowing goats onto the Acropolis, while 1.4.5 mentions Corcyra as the location of the fleet that Varro apparently saved from pestilence in 67 or 48 BC; see appendix 6 for further discussion of the latter.

64. See Dench (2005)189–191, who also notes the "composite" presentation of Italia, wherein the "different parts of Italia complement each other" (with reference to *RR* 1.2.6, 1.6.3, 1.7.10, 2.1.16, and 3.17.9).

65. For the role that transhumance played in connecting various Italian peoples geographically—often on a large scale—and culturally, see Williamson (2005) 134–46. While she is correct to observe that both short-distance transhumance (i.e., the movement of herd animals between highlands in the summer and lowlands in the summer *within* a more localized region) and long-distance transhumance (i.e., that same pattern of movement but *between* regions and on a much larger scale, which is what Varro is describing here) were practiced

quarters for flocks that summer in the mountains of Reate, this passage is also indicative of how Varro can use individual regions to present a *range* of Italian environmental conditions. In *RR* 1, a similar polarity underlies the representation of the Apulian plains as a "heavier" and "hotter" climate, counterbalanced by the "lighter" and "more healthful" climate of the mountainous regions around Vesuvius (1.6.3). Elsewhere, the typology of soils is eventually framed in terms of a threefold scheme of negative (x), positive (y), and an intermediate therein (z): "poor [x], rich [y], or medium [z]" (*macra an pinguis an mediocris*) as found in Pupinia (x), Etruria (y), and Tibur (z) (1.9.5–6). Regions can also illustrate the wide range of Italian agricultural practices. Thus, the variety of trees used for demarcating boundaries is exemplified in the use of pines in Sabine country, cypresses around Vesuvius, and elms near Crustumeria (1.15), while Umbria, Picenum, and Rome likewise proffer different methods for harvesting grains (1.50.1–2).

So far, the passages discussed evince an intra-Italian perspective, exemplifying agricultural products, conditions, and practices within Italia. But in addition to its use as a spatial unit that encompasses numerous regions, cities, and natural features, Italia can also identify a space separate from and against other geographical spaces. In other words, Italia admits signification equally as a "space that demarcates" as well as a "space that incorporates." Within the ideologically charged environment of the late Republican and Triumviral periods, where the standing of Italia vis-à-vis Rome and its provinces had already become a point of contention, the attribution of an Italian superiority over other *terrae* is just as important to the concept of Italia as is the incorporative mode, for it suggests, above all, that Italia was not just geographically distinct from, but even qualitatively better than, the rest of the Mediterranean.[66]

---

from an earlier period than historians commonly acknowledge, she overemphasizes the Italian "unity" resulting from these common, though not ubiquitous, practices. In part, she is also arguing against the more conventional scholarly view, which holds that it was only with the coming of Rome that the necessary influx of capital, existence of regional marketplaces, and legal protections and security that long-distance transhumance came into its own; see especially Toynbee (1965) 2.286–95, Gabba (1979) 15–73 and (1988) 134–42, Pasquinucci (1979) 79–182, and Spurr (1986a) 125–26. For attempts to balance environmental explanations with social, economic, and political ones, see Garnsey (1988) 196–209, J. Thompson (1988) 213–15, and Dench (1995) 116–25, all of whom also stress that a variety of pastoralist forms were practiced throughout Italy: short- and long-distance transhumance as well as husbandry within a mixed farming context.

66. For further discussion of how the *RR* responds to the precarious ideological valuation of Italia and the provinces in the late Republic and Triumviral periods, see pp. 215 and 231–36 in chapter 7. It may be useful here to consider Dench (2005) 154, who notes Rome's "peculiarly proprietorial attitude [towards Italy] that is rather different from the conceptualization of overseas peoples and places under the *imperium* of Rome."

One recurring tactic for carving out a place for Italia as a *terra* superior
to other *terrae* is the consistent comparison of non-Italian areas with Italia
writ large—and *not* with its individual regions. The discussion of the types
of vineyards (1.8.1–2) perhaps best exemplifies this tendency. This juncture in
the dialogue finds Scrofa responding to Stolo's quotation of Cato's nine types
of fields ranked according to their quality (the precise criterion is presumably
their potential for long-term profitability; *Agr.* 1.7). For an unspecified reason,
Scrofa rejects Cato's top choice of a vineyard. Instead, he considers meadows
to be the best kind of *ager* to possess.[67] But rather than explaining why meadows are the best kind of field, Scrofa digresses into a description of the various
kinds of vineyards and their profitability (1.8.1–2):[68]

> Refert, inquam, quod genus vineae sit, quod sunt multae species eius. Aliae
> enim humiles ac sine ridicis, ut in Hispania, aliae sublimes, ut quae appel-
> lantur iugatae, ut pleraeque in Italia. Cuius nomina duo, pedamenta et iuga.
> Quibus stat rectis vinea, dicuntur pedamenta; quae transversa iunguntur,
> iuga: ab eo quoque vineae iugatae. Iugorum genera fere quattuor: pertica,
> harundo, restes, vites—pertica, ut in Falerno, harundo, ut in Arpano, restes,
> ut in Brundisino, vites, ut in Mediolanensi; iugationis species duae: una
> derecta, ut in agro Canusino, altera conpluviata in longitudinem et latitudi-
> nem iugata, ut in Italia pleraeque.

> It matters, I say, what kind of vineyard it is, because there are many kinds.
> For some are low-lying and without props, as those used in Spain; other
> kinds of vineyards are raised aloft, which are called "yoked" (*iugatae*) as
> most in Italia are. There are two names for this [latter] kind: "stakes" (*peda-
> menta*) and "yokes" (*iuga*). Those in which the vineyard stands straight
> up are "stakes"; those which are yoked transversely are "yokes." The four
> general kinds of yokes are as follows: poles, reeds, ropes, and vines—for
> example, the pole type [is employed] in *ager Falernus* (Falernum), the reed
> in the *ager Arpanus* (Arpi), the rope in the *ager Brundisium* (Brundisium),
> and the vine in the *ager Mediolanensis* (Mediolanum). Of the two modes of
> yoking, the one is in a straight line (*derecta*), just as in the *ager Canusinum*

---

67. There is possibly a satirical undertone here. Columella (*Rust.* 6.pref.4) relates the story
that Cato, when asked about the three best ways to become wealthy through farming, replied
that the first was good pasturing (*pastio*), the second mediocre pasturing, and the third poor
pasturing. Scrofa's response that not all agree with Cato's preference for a vineyard—expressed
in *Agr.* 1.7—and some instead prefer meadows (for pasturing) is possibly playing off the potential inconsistency in Cato's own agronomical thought.

68. Skydsgaard (1968) 14 considers this passage to be a somewhat confusing digression
from the order of topics announced in 1.5.3; cf. n. 56 in chapter 2.

(Canusium), and the other horizontally and vertically in the manner of a *compluvium,* as in most of Italia.

Scrofa begins by distinguishing between the fundamental differences of Italian and Spanish viticulture (1.8.1): the former involving trellises, the latter without any kind of prop.[69] The propless practice employed in Hispania does not receive any more attention until the end of the passage (1.8.5), where the Asian and Pandaterian[70] (but not Spanish) customs are adduced to illustrate the susceptibility of this practice to pests. For my purposes, the comparison between, first, Italian and Spanish and, second, Italian and Asian/Pandaterian viticulture is indicative of the *RR*'s tendency to compare non-Italian spaces with Italia as a whole and *not* specific regions therein. Thus, after the Asian and Pandaterian examples are introduced, Varro introduces a third possibility, "where only those vines that show themselves to be fruit-bearing are raised from the earth" (*ubi ea modo removetur a terra vitis, quae ostendit se adferre uvam*; 1.8.6). "This practice," he explains, "is used in Italia by the Reatini" (*hac consuetudine in Italia utuntur Reatini*).[71] The prequalification of *Reatini* as *in Italia* is key here, for it corroborates the *RR*'s practice of contrasting non-Italian lands generally only with Italia as a whole and not with specific, intra-Italian regions.

After making the initial distinction between the horizontal "stakes" of Spain and the vertical "yokes" of Italia, Varro then offers four different types of yokes: poles in Falernum, reeds in Arpi, ropes in Brundisium, and vines in Mediolanum.[72] On the one hand, this passage (as convoluted as it may be) illustrates the wide variety of practices employed in Italian viticulture. But rhetorically, the passage also exhibits a balanced pattern of exemplification; four kinds of trellising represent the majority of Italian practices, which are chiastically framed by their reference to Italia (*ut pleraeque in Italia . . . ut*

69. For a still useful overview of Roman methods of training vines (complete with diagrams), see the exposition of White (1970) 231–36.

70. Note that Pandateria (mod. Ventotene) is an island off the western coast of Italia and part of the Pontine archipelago. Most famous as an island of exile (e.g., Julia, Augustus's daughter, spent some time there; Tac. *Ann.* 1.53), Pandateria was probably not considered "Italian," just as Corsica, Sardinia, and Sicilia generally were not.

71. Flach (1996) prints the text as *Uriatini,* for which he has manuscript support. I have chosen to print *Reatini,* which Keil (1889) and Heurgon (1978) use, simply because Reate, as Varro's hometown, is often cited securely elsewhere (1.7.7; 1.14.3; 2.pref.6; 2.1.14; 2.2.9; 2.6.1; 2.6.2; 2.8.3; 2.8.5; 2.8.6; 3, *passim*). In either case, it remains that the text invokes an intra-Italian region.

72. The practice employed at Canusium is an exception to the *compluvium* practice as well as a further subvariety of this fourth kind (i.e., figs, not vines), as made clear shortly thereafter.

*in Italia pleraeque*). In this respect, this passage approximates the practice that is established in the *laus Italiae*: a fourfold exemplification framed by overarching mentions of Italia. Moreover, the four regions cover the contemporary scope of Italia: Falernum in Campania (central), Arpi in Apulia (east-central), Brundisium in Apulia (southeastern), and, perhaps most significantly, Milan in Transpadane Gaul (northern).[73] While the specific regional *exempla* adduced are not exactly the same as that of the *laus Italiae*, the basic outline encompasses both southern and central—that is, "older"— Italia and the more recent northern additions. In this respect, Scrofa's discussion of Italia's vineyards replicates the geographical inclusivity of Fundanius's opening *laus Italiae*.

Elsewhere, however, the invocation of Italia functions solely as a unit of comparison with other *terrae*. In discussing the cultivation of figs (1.41.1–6), for example, Scrofa advocates a preference for working from young, graftable offshoots of the plant rather than the plant's seeds. Where grafting is not possible, he maintains that the figs should be dried and planted thereafter in a nursery. To exemplify this practice, Varro writes (1.41.6), "Of this variety were the following kinds of figs: the Chian, Chalcidian, Lydian, African, and the rest of the overseas kinds brought into Italia" (*sic genera ficorum, Chiae ac Chalcidicae et Lydiae et Africanae, item cetera transmarina in Italiam perlata*). In addition to surveying the produce of other *terrae*, this brief passage implicitly buttresses the idea of a general Italian fecundity, which is able to provide a sufficiently fertile locus of planting for desirable agricultural products that are, in this case, not even native to its bounds. It also implies a willingness on the part of Italian agriculturalists to introduce such products, a tendency that accords with *agri cultura*'s overall goal of producing profit.[74] Finally, the use of *transmarina* bolsters the idea of Italia as a distinct geographical entity, bounded by water and separate from the eastern regions of Chios and Chalcidike and the more southerly regions of Lydia and Africa.[75] Able to incorporate the fruits of other *terrae*, Italia stands at the pinnacle of agricultural potential in the *RR*.

---

73. Phillip Horky has astutely pointed out to me the possibility of a cosmological reading of this passage, wherein the various horizontal, vertical, and transverse configurations of trained vines in the *vinea* might be taken to correspond to (possibly to map out?) the various cartographical coordinates of the exemplified Italian locations. In keeping with the generic nature of the *RR*, a strictly rigorous and precise analogical reading of this passage is both out of place and bound to fail, but the implication that the *compluvium* method prevails in most of (*pleraeque*) Italia is perhaps suggestive nonetheless.

74. For references to the concern for *fructus* of *Italici homines*, see 1.2.8 and 1.3. Cf. pp. 47–48 in chapter 2 and pp. 189–96 in chapter 6.

75. For Lydia as a region in "southern" Asia, see p. 87 in this chapter.

## EXCEPTIONAL "EXCEPTIONS" TO *RR* 1'S
## AGRICULTURAL EXEMPLIFICATION

*RR* 1's dual modes of conceptualizing Italia—as a "space that incorporates" heterogeneous regions as well as a "space that demarcates" itself from the rest of the Mediterranean—complement each other, for they jointly sketch an overarching Italian fecundity unfound elsewhere in the known world. Given this overwhelming focus on Italia, the first dialogue spends little time exploring the agricultural potential or efficacy of other *terrae,* but if we recall Agrius's scientific *laus Italiae,* which attributed Italian agricultural superiority to its superlatively medial and temperate location within the *oikoumene,*[76] it is perhaps not unreasonable to consider where the other *terrae* of southern Europe fit into this scheme. Conditioning from our Hellenically infused Roman sources might suggest the Greek East as a possible candidate, yet Fundanius's "correction" of Homer (as well as the notoriously rocky lands of Greece and Macedonia) eliminate its consideration as a competitor to Italian fecundity. And Gaul—that is, the Transalpine *terra*—might also be thought to challenge Italia were it not for Scrofa's personal claims to have seen a number *(aliquot)* of places "where neither vine nor olive nor fruit would grow" *(ubi nec vitis nec olea nec poma nascerentur;* 1.7.8).[77]

The western land of Hispania, however, would seem to be a slightly different story and occasionally occupies an exceptional position within Varro's cognitive geography. At times, a rigorous distinction between Hispania and *(tota)* Italia is maintained, as in the aforementioned treatment of vineyards (1.8.1) or in Scrofa's brief comment on the types of containers used for storing wine: Italia uses *doleae,* whereas Hispania employs *orcae* (1.13.6). Elsewhere, however, Hispania—like Italia and unlike non-Italian areas—admits divisibility and invites direct comparison to intra-Italian regions. For example, with regard to systems of measurement, Scrofa observes that "in Hispania Ulterior, they measure in *iuga,* in Campania with *versus,* and among us in the *ager Romanus* and *ager Latinus* with *iugera*" (1.10.1). The extent of each unit of measurement receives specification in the ensuing discussion, but what matters here is the manner in which Hispania Ulterior is mentioned in conjunction not with Italia, but rather, with the intra-Italian regions of

---

76. Note also that Agrius's scientific *laus Italiae* defined Italia in a delimitative manner: as part of Europe, both "north" of and separate from Asia, and within Europe, south of and "more temperate" than the excessive cold and ice found in the "interior" (i.e., north).

77. That Scrofa figures his observations in terms suspiciously similar to those of Fundanius's *laus* (*Quod* vinum *Falerno? Quod* oleum *Venafro? Non arboribus consita Italia, ut tota pomarium videatur?;* 1.2.5)—for which he was not even present—is suggestive of a programmatic element to his statement.

Campania, Latium, and Rome. There are at least three possible reasons for this "aberration." First, although his brief list is by no means comprehensive from either an Italian perspective (e.g., the use of the stade in Magna Graecia is omitted) or a universal Spanish perspective (note the qualifying *ulterior*[78]), Scrofa is emphasizing the *regional* diversity of systems of measurement, and it is simply not in his immediate rhetorical interests to compare larger spatial entities (i.e., Hispania and Italia writ large). Second, Varro served as one of Pompey's legates in Spain during the Sertorian and civil wars, commanding several legions, cultivating close relationships with the inhabitants, and presumably becoming somewhat acquainted with the land and its practices during his tenure.[79] Perhaps Scrofa's inclusion of Hispania among Crustumeria, Reate, Tusculum, Ager Gallicus, Ager Sabinus, and Ager Tarentus as the only non-Italian example of enclosures for estates (1.14.3–4) and Stolo's later pairing of Hispania Citerior and Apulia as examples of regions wherein granaries are built aboveground for storing the harvest (1.57.3) also simply reflect Varro's personal experience with Hispania. Third, it cannot be a coincidence that all three of these "exceptional" exempla—as well as the other two mentions of Hispania—illustrate agricultural practice or technology and do not, at least in the way that they are framed, bear on the relative fecundity of Hispania vis-à-vis Italia. In this respect, the desire to substantiate the agricultural preeminence of Italia as a whole may simply not be paramount and, consequently, the instinct to avoid comparisons of non-Italian *terrae* with Italian regions would be absent as well. But whatever the precise reason for Hispania's special status in Varro's work, it remains that Spanish agriculture comes under discussion to nowhere near the extent to which the Italian situation does. If anything, *RR* 1's stinting presentation of Hispania—a land personally familiar to Varro and subject (*a la* Eratosthenes) to a similar climatic situation—throws into relief the overwhelming focus on Italian *agri cultura*.

The only other instances where Italian regions are directly compared to non-Italian lands occur in citations: one from Saserna and two from Theophrastus. The former citation comes up in Scrofa's extended consideration of the requisite number of slaves for a farm (1.18.1ff.). After rejecting Cato's prescriptive approach as overly rigid (1.18.1–5), Scrofa turns to Saserna's method, which calculates the requisite number of slaves according to a ratio of the amount of work a slave can be expected to complete successfully within a

---

78. From an early period, the Romans had divided Hispania into two distinct administrative regions, *ulterior* and *citerior*; see Pliny *HN* 3.6; 3.18; and 3.29. In a sense, then, Roman Hispania was never a unity to begin with. For an account of Roman control and administration of Hispania, see Richardson (1986).

79. Cf. p. 5 in the introduction and Van Ooteghem (1954) 125.

given timespan to the quantity of land under cultivation. Thus, one slave should be able to cover one *iugerum*'s worth of work in four days (1.18.6). The problem with this approach, so Scrofa maintains, is that "if this [number] was enough for Saserna's farm in Gaul, the same does not necessarily apply to a region in mountainous Liguria" (*si hoc in Sasernae fundo in Gallia satis fuit, non continuo idem in agro Ligusco montano*).[80] This objection—which amounts to the idea that varying conditions demand different responses and various accommodations—thus caps Scrofa's general antipathy towards his predecessor's set formulae and clears the way for his own rationale, which entails a thoughtful combination of comparative autopsy, personal experience, active imitation, and proactive experimentation (1.18.7–8).

But what about the nature of the geographical comparison? To what does Saserna's *in Gallia* refer? Is it Gallia Cisalpina, Narbonensis, or Transalpina? Moreover, did Saserna himself claim that his formula also applies to Liguria, or is that Scrofa's own argumentative insertion? For that matter, to what does Liguria refer?[81] Our fundamental lack of knowledge regarding Saserna (or, for that matter, the Sasernae[82]) intractably impairs any attempt to answer

---

80. The logic is abbreviated and can be construed in two ways. On the one hand, a farm in the mountains is limited in size by the terrain and would, therefore, require *fewer* slaves than Saserna's Gallic farm. On the other hand, Scrofa may be implying that the difficulty of the terrain necessitates the employment of *more* slaves. Of course, we would be in a better position to ascertain the nature of this passage if we knew what kind of farm Saserna envisioned in his treatise; see Martin (1971) 81–84 for the intractable problems with ascertaining the nature of this work. But whatever the underlying rationale for Saserna's injunctions, Scrofa's point is clear: differences in terrain require a more flexible approach than Saserna's overly prescriptive one.

81. In general, there is confusion in the ancient sources over the bounds of Liguria. As we know from Polybius and Livy, the area admitting designation as "Ligurian" in the third century BC ranged from the Rhone River to the west, the Arno River in the east, the Apennines to the north, and the coast of the Adriatic to the south. In other words, "Liguria" traversed the western Alps and could hypothetically be construed as part of both Gaul and Italia. In his reorganization of Italia (Pliny *HN* 3.46ff.), Augustus designated Liguria as the ninth of eleven regions (3.49), thereby providing the territory with an administrative definition and a fixed geographical location within Italia. For a discussion of this geographical reorganization and the evidentiary problems with determining the form (and date) of Augustus's "geographical 'work,'" see Nicolet (1991) 171–78. Still, it is suggestive of the region's ongoing indeterminacy that the roughly contemporaneous Strabo discusses Liguria in his treatment of both Transalpine Gaul (4.6.3) and Italia (5.1.4). In short, the existence of a number of related peoples who inhabited both the Italian and Gallic sides of the northeastern Alps presented a challenge to ancient geographical conceptions of Liguria.

82. Note Varro's (and Columella's) seemingly inexplicable tendency to attribute this work sometimes to a (singular) "Saserna," at other times to the (plural) "Sasernae," which raises the further question of whether the father-son duo jointly composed one treatise or individually authored two separate ones; see White [1973] 459–60, esp. n. 34, for further discussion. Cf. n. 31 in chapter 1. Throughout this book, I have followed Varro's particular ascription in the passage that happens to be under consideration.

these questions, which in turn crucially affects our evaluation of this passage, but it is worth pointing out that the comparison—Liguria as opposed to Gaul—turns out in all scenarios to depend upon the relative proximity of the two areas. Thus, Scrofa's point is that terrain—and *not* geographical proximity alone—is what matters for *agri cultura,* which accords with the terms of his theoretical account (cf. pp. 63–65). This last point may appear to complicate the notion of an overall Italian fecundity. But, as we shall see in the next section, the *RR*'s presentation of *agri cultura* in fact attempts to account for the challenges presented by an entity as geographically and topographically diverse as Italia was. With that said, it is simply impossible to explicate with certainty the dynamics of this geographical comparison within the parameters we have set.[83]

We are on more secure ground when it comes to the Theophrastan quotations (1.44.1–3), one of which appears to recount the examples provided by the original source: Etruria, the *Ager Subaritanus* in Italia, Gadara in Syria, Byzacium in Africa, and Olynthia in Macedonia.[84] Unlike Varro, Theophrastus has no Italian agenda and, therefore, has no vested interest in avoiding comparison of Italian regions with non-Italian lands. The other quotation occurs in Scrofa's claim that the soil's quality is the primary determining factor for what can be grown on that land (1.7.6–7). In support of this position,

---

83. If we assume that *Gallia* refers to Transalpine Gaul and that the terms of the comparison are set by Varro (and not Saserna), one possible solution for the reasoning behind the comparison can be found in Liguria's status as a shadowy pivot region in the cognitive geography of the ancients. With the enfranchisement of all regions "inward" of the Alps and the full extension of the appellation "Italia" to the regions therein, it is not unreasonable to suppose that Liguria, a region that had mostly occupied the Cisalpine side, became firmly "Italianized." Cf. Cicero's description of the region's harshness in terms of the inhabitants' agricultural prowess and durability (*Leg. Agr.* 2.95) and Vergil's inclusion and description of Ligurians in the *laus Italiae* of the *Georgics* as "trained in hardship" (*adsuetum malo; G.* 2.168). Thus, by contrasting a Gallic farm with a Ligurian farm and, by extension, the agricultural situation in Gaul and Liguria, the historically liminal status of Liguria allows it to serve as a metanymic entity for Italia and the division therefrom. To be sure, Liguria and its mountainous terrain are not exemplars of Italian fertility *per se,* but that would not necessarily exclude them from contributing to *RR* 1's depiction of a wide variety of Italian agricultural practices. The result is that even those Italian regions deficient (though not necessarily lacking fundamentally) in the otherwise exemplary Italian fertility can serve as *exempla* for *agri cultura.* Of course, if *in Gallia* refers to Cisalpine Gaul, then the contrast is simply between two Italian regions.

84. As Skydsgaard (1968) 74 discusses, this passage partly stems from Theophr. *Caus. Pl.* 1.20.4. As indicated by the *dicunt* (1.44.1; cf. 1.44.3), everything after "*in Italia*" is most likely also a quotation from Theophrastus, but it is not attested in his extant oeuvre. The possibility remains that Varro is working from some indeterminate intermediary. Cf. Flach (1996) 314–15, who notes a possible reference to Theophr. *Hist. Pl.* 8.6.2 and rightly observes that this use of *Italia* is probably the earlier sense restricted to the south.

he cites examples given by Theophrastus:[85] evergreen plane trees "in Crete around Cortynia" and in Cyprus; an evergreen oak "at Sybaris, now called Thurii"; evergreen fig trees and vineyards "near Elephantine" (in southern Egypt); biannually producing vineyards "around the coast of Smyrna"; and Epirote alder trees that thrive in rivers. These examples, which come from *Historia Plantarum* 1.4.3, evince a distinctly Greek and eastern perspective: Epirus, Crete, Cyprus, and Egypt. Even in the one Italian example, Thurii, Theophrastus cites a historically Greek portion of Italia and uses the archaic Greek name, Sybaris, for the site razed in 510 BC, leaving it to Varro to provide the gloss.[86] Nonetheless, Varro supplements these exempla with two Italian ones of his own: a semiannual apple crop in the *Ager Consentinus* and the prosperity of reeds grown in lakes in the *Ager Reatinus*. In this case, even the quotation of Greek source material can be made to bear on *RR* 1's depiction of Italian agricultural excellence.

## THE AGRIPOLITICAL GEOGRAPHY OF ITALIA

So far, we have seen how the dialogue's setting and opening establish Italia as (a) a variegated landscape of individual regions, which are (b) complementarily coherent with one another and (c) collectively distinct from and superior to the rest of the *orbis terrae*. This notion of an overarching and preeminent Italian fecundity is then borne out in the dialogue's technical portions, where Italia conceptually governs the patterns of geographical exemplification and where the majority of these examples evince a decidedly Italian perspective and generally replicate the earlier *laudes Italiae*. In short, the concept of Italia is the central organizing principle of *RR* 1's presentation of *agri cultura,* and the geographical exempla only reinforce its centrality.

At this point, we may want to consider whether the technical discussion accounts for Italia's fruitfulness just as Agrius's scientific *laus* rationalizes (and not merely asserts) its advantages in terms of climatic factors. We need look no further than Varro's construal of agricultural space as explicated in chapter 2 (pp. 57–65). There, we saw that *ager* refers to a portion of land (i.e., a "field") in the countryside, which serves as a location for planting and which

---

85. A direct (albeit rearranged) citation of Theophr. *Hist. Pl.* 1.9.5, this passage has factored extensively into Varronian *Quellenforschung,* for which, see Skydsgaard (1968) 64–70. Cf. 70–72, where Varro's reorganization, abbreviation, and supplementation of the Theophrastan passage suggests that he is not engaged merely in "indifferent copying" and that "Varro knows his Theophrastus, and knows him well" (72).

86. On this basis, Skydsgaard (1968) 71 and n. 20 suggests that Theophrastus's source predates the foundation of Thurii in 443 BC.

contains *terra*. *Terra,* on the other hand, is land viewed in its generative and material aspects and is therefore qualitatively different from *ager.* On this basis, *agri cultura* is a "science" (*scientia*) that teaches "what must be planted and done in each field (*ager*) so that the earth (*terra*) always returns the greatest profits" (1.3). We also saw that the discussion of the types of *terra* (1.9.1–7) is crucial to understanding the dynamics of *RR* 1's agricultural landscape. Initially providing ninety-nine different kinds of *terra,* Scrofa subsequently reduces them to three general types: poor, rich, or medium exemplified in, respectively, Pupinia, Etruria, and Tibur (1.9.5–6). But the passage prior to this simplification is worth quoting in full, for its discussion of the three ways in which *terra* may be used contains the roots of Italia's agricultural supremacy (1.9.1–3):

> Ea tribus modis dicitur, communi et proprio et mixto: [1] communi, ut cum dicimus orbem terrae et terram Italiam aut quam aliam; in ea enim et lapis et harena et cetera eius generis sunt in nominando comprensa. [2] Altero modo dicitur terra proprio nomine, quae nullo alio vocabulo neque cognomine adiecto appellatur. [3] Tertio modo dicitur terra, quae est mixta, in quo seri potest quid et nasci, ut argillosa aut lapidosa, sic aliae, cum in hac species non minus sint multae quam in illa communi propter admixtiones. In illa enim cum sint dissimili vi ac potestate partes permultae, in quis lapis, marmor, rudus, harena, sabulo, argilla, rubrica, pulvis, creta, cinis, carbunculus, id est, quae sole perferve ita fit, ut radices satorum comburat, ab iis quae proprio nomine dicitur terra, cum est admixta ex iis generibus aliqua re, tum dicitur ut cretosa, sic ab aliis generum discriminibus mixta.

> *Terra* (*ea*) is used in three ways: *communis, propria,* and *mixta*: [1] *communis,* such as when we say the *orbis terrae* [i.e., the world], Italian *terra,* or any other. For in this *terra,* stone, sand, and other things of this kind are incorporated into the term. [2] In the second way, *terra* is employed in its specific sense, that is, it is spoken with no other word or adjective added. [3] *Terra* is used in the third sense, that is, mixed, for that *terra* where something is able to be sown and to grow, such as clay *terra* or rocky *terra,* and so on, since there are no less as many forms among this *terra* as there are among the *communis* one on account of the mixtures. For since there are in this *terra* [i.e., *communis*] a great number of parts with differing strength and power, which include stone, marble, rubble, sand, loam, clay, red ochre, dust, chalk, ash, carbuncle (that is, what the *terra* becomes from such an intense sun that it scorches the roots of plants), when that which is called *terra* in the *propria* sense becomes mixed from these kinds of parts (sc. *partes*) in some

way, then it is called, for example, "chalky" [*terra*], and so "mixed" (*mixta*) from the other distinctions of types.

In this grammatically tortured (and perhaps slightly parodic[87]) passage, Scrofa claims that the word *terra* can be used in three senses: *communis, propria, and mixta*. The latter two, as we saw in chapter 2, are integral to understanding how *ager* and *terra* relate to one another and how *cultura* affects both entities. Thus, *terra propria* is the aspect of the land that neither the farmer nor *agri cultura* can modify (1.4.4), and it is this sense of *terra* that operates in *RR* 1's definition of *agri cultura* (1.3). The farmer can, however, account for the physical substance of *terra mixta*, that is, the one of ninety-nine possible combinations of elemental *terra* (i.e., *propria*), aggregate (e.g., clay, stone, sand, etc.), and moisture. And knowledge of these distinctions thus enables the farmer to adjust his operations to account for *terra mixta*: the other elements that are contained within the *ager* and combine with the given *terra* (i.e., *propria*).

Yet, Scrofa also includes *terra communis,* that is, the sense of *terra* used when talking about "the Earth, Italia, or any other [*terra*]" (*orbem terrae et terram Italiae aut quam aliam*). Scrofa does not fully explicate the constitutive components of *terra communis,* but the implication is that it is defined in opposition to nonland (e.g., water, the heavens) and in terms of scale, that is, a quantitatively large enough area of land that encompasses (cf. *comprensa*) a number of other objects, such as rock (*lapis*) or sand (*harena*), as well as smaller collective entities (e.g., regions, cities). Thus, the *orbis terrae* denotes the world's terrestrial landmass, which includes other *terrae* (e.g., Italia, Hispania, etc.) and other landforms (mountains, plains, coasts, etc.). Likewise, *terra Italia* incorporates a number of regions, which are denoted (throughout *RR* 1 and per Latin spatial terminology in general) as *agri*.

From a modern lexicographical perspective, Varro (through Scrofa) is discussing categorically different kinds of *terra*—literal (i.e., *propria* and *mixta*) and metaphorical (i.e., *communis*)—and each should accordingly occupy different headings.[88] Yet, the way that Scrofa defines the *communis* and *mixta*

---

87. For the *RR*'s potential parody of the pedant's expert knowledge, see Kronenberg (2009) 76–93. Elsewhere, I have argued that Stolo's eminently brief citation of Diophanes (1.9.7), the redactor of a redactor of Mago, implicitly criticizes the length and complexity of Scrofa's extravagant scheme; see Nelsestuen (2011) 345–46. For Columella's possible critique of this passage, see *Rust.* 2.2.1–2.

88. See OLD s.v. *terra,* where entries 1–4 and 6 refer to more or less the physical substance of soil (albeit in different aspects), while 7 corresponds to a specific land or country and 9.b. to the *orbis terrarum,* both of which fall under Varro's *communis* heading. Cf. L&S s.v. *terra*: "I. *In gen.* land, ground, soil; II. *In partic.* a land, country, region, territory."

senses in parallel ways and plays with the overlap between "different" discourses—in this case, between agronomical and, for the lack of a better
word, geopolitical terminology—is crucial to understanding the *RR*'s critical approach to seemingly simplistic, tedious, or pedantic verbal and semantic matters and, more importantly, their potential bearing on contemporary
political issues. More immediately, however, it rationalizes the seemingly
unnecessary inclusion of *terra communis* in his agronomical discussion and
explicates the repeated (and otherwise inexplicable) declaration that "there
are no less as many forms among *terra mixta* as among *terra communis* on
account of the mixtures."

Let me begin by presenting the three senses of *terra* in the form of a chart:

| SENSE | EXAMPLE | CHARACTERISTICS |
|---|---|---|
| 1. *Communis* | Italian *terra* | Geopolitical [+ substance] |
| 2. *Propria* | *Terra* | Generative force |
| 3. *Mixta* | Rocky *terra* | Generative + substance |

The underlying logic of the passage seems to be that the *communis* sense of
*terra* resembles *terra mixta* in terms of the varieties of non-*terra* elements
potentially found in each. To be sure, the two terms fundamentally differ in
terms of scope: *communis* refers to some larger area (usually of "geopolitical" significance), whereas *mixta* has no such essential quantitative criterion.
Despite these differences, however, Varro twice emphasizes the similarities
between the two. Thus, the various other materials (i.e., sand, stone, etc.)
found in (but inessential to the definition of) a *terra communis,* when combined with *terra propria,* would seem to result in *terra mixta.* And this last
*terra* is what the farmer needs to account for in his cultivation of the land.
Nevertheless, from a logical standpoint, there is no need for Varro to specify
the presence of these other objects in *terra communis,* as *terra mixta* remains
intrinsically defined by the combination of *terra propria* with non-*terra*
components.

The reason, then, for the emphatic similarity between *terra communis*
and *terra mixta* remains unstated within the passage itself, but *RR* 1's general
thematic emphasis on Italia—its agricultural diversity and its overall fecundity—provides a context for understanding this convoluted passage. As we
saw earlier, the programmatic praise and general exemplification of Italia
emphasize the superiority of its *terra* over other *terrae.* In this respect, Italia is *qualitatively* superior to other lands. At the same time, specific regions
(*agri*) and their exemplary crops are subsumed under the quantitative notion

of Italia. The diversity of these *agri* is presumably the result of the nature of local soil conditions, that is, *terra mixta*. Thus, *RR* 1 provides for the distinctiveness of the various Italian regions (i.e., *agri*)—a distinctiveness that stems from the nature and quality of each particular region's *terra mixta*—yet it also emphasizes a shared and *communis* Italian *terra*. Given that all of Italia does not have the same *terra mixta*—otherwise, all the regions would grow the same products equally well (e.g., Ligurian wine would be on par with Falernian)—the reasonable inference is that Italia simply has some peculiar or exceptional quality to it *on the whole*. Whether Italian fecundity stems from its beneficent climate (cf. the scientific *laus*), an unspecified substrate underlying the specific regions and their particular *terrae mixtae,* or (what seems most likely) a combination of the two remains unarticulated. But this interpretation accounts for the repeated emphasis on the similarity between *terra communis* and *terra mixta*. Thus, this passage should be understood as Varro's attempt—however inadequate, problematic, or convoluted it may be— to rationalize how Italia incorporates a wide variety of regions (i.e., *agri*), yet still maintains a coherent and corporate agricultural identity.

On this view, Varro is essentially eliding the agricultural and geopolitical senses of *terra* as part of his effort to construct a larger Italian *terra*. But in so doing, he concurrently projects the literal senses of *terra* as generative force and physical substance onto the metaphorical notion of *terra* as geopolitical unit. Simply put, then, Italia emerges as both a *terra communis* and a *terra mixta*.

In the broader context of his most explicit objective—the discussion of *agri cultura*—this manipulation of semantics entails a further corollary. By mapping the geopolitical and agricultural spheres onto one another, the notion of Italia as a singular geopolitical unit (*terra*) that incorporates numerous regions (*agri*) suggests that *RR* 1 is also conceptualizing Italia as a *fundus*. For, as the term that best encapsulates the area for the activities of *agri cultura* (i.e., a "farm"), a *fundus* can likewise incorporate a number of different fields (*agri*). The traditional Roman association of politics and farming suggests that such a metaphorical leap is not so difficult for a Roman like Varro—fully committed as he was to both political and intellectual life—to make. Moreover, the metaphorical representation of Italia as the *fundus* of rustic enterprise is not an otherwise foreign concept within the *RR,* for the text offers at least two other such figurative paradigms for Italia.

The first occurs in the midst of the discussion of Cato's land preferences and Scrofa's subsequent digression into vineyards. After mentioning his own partiality for meadows, Scrofa invokes the authority of the orator, C. Caesar Vopiscus, who claimed that the meadows (*prata*) of Rosea were so fertile as to be the "udder" (*sumen*) of Italy (1.7.10). The exact circumstances of Vopiscus's speech are unclear, although his pleading as aedile (90 BC) of a case before Roman censors in a matter dealing with Rosea suggests that the issue pertained to a recurring dispute over the unintended draining of these meadows.[89] Whatever the context, his metaphor plays off the folk etymology that Italia came from *vitulus*, or "calf,"[90] of which Varro himself is well aware and on which he puns in *RR* 2.[91] The significance of this representation in *RR* 1, however, should not be underestimated, for the notion of Italia as a rustic organism quite explicitly reinforces its conception as a corporate entity with multifarious but coherent parts, that is, an organic unity.

The other paradigm occurs in Fundanius's *laus Italiae*, which claims that the whole (*tota*) of Italia is an orchard (*pomarium*; 1.2.7). Given the emphasis on wine, olives, and grains, this metaphor is an odd one. Why is Italia said to be a *pomarium* and *not* a vineyard (*vinea*) or an *arbustum*,[92] an olive-yard (*olivetum*), or a grain-producing field (e.g., a *campus frumentarius*)? The answer lies in the opportunity for punning on *pōmārium* with the phonetically similar *pōmērium*.[93] Aside from proffering the sorts of puns that a Menippean satirist might enjoy, *pōmērium*, the Latin word for "boundary," usually denotes the politico-spatial and divinely sanctioned limits of a city-state.[94] Thus, the pun quite clearly—and succinctly—reiterates the presentation of Italia as a singular and unified entity. Yet, by moving beyond the traditionally urban notion of the term, the *RR* is also pushing its literal bounds and imput-

---

89. In addition to building Rome's second aqueduct, the Aqua Anio Vetus, in 272 BC, Manius Curius Dentatus, also drained Lake Velinus, which apparently had the (unforeseen?) effect of draining the Rosean plains as well. See Flach (1996) 253 and Cic. *Att.* 90.5 [= 4.15.5]. For the draining of land—often appropriated from recently subdued Italians by the Roman state—to improve agricultural production, see Williamson (2005) 152 and bibliography *ad loc*. Scrofa's appeal to an oration from this dispute thus adds yet another layer to *RR* 1's evocation of the delicate history of Roman-Italian interactions. It is perhaps not insignificant that a similar dispute appears to have prompted the visit of Appius Claudius Pulcher to Q. Axius in Book 3 (3.2.3); see p. 181 in chapter 6.

90. Cf. Dench (2005) 191, where she cites this passage as an example of Varro's conception of Italia as an "interconnected" and "organic whole."

91. Cf. pp. 168–69 in chapter 5.

92. For the *arbustum*, an "orchard" planted for the explicit purpose of training vines on the trees, see White (1970) 236.

93. In addition to sharing the same gender and number of syllables (as well as being orthographically similar), both words have similar vowel lengths and consonantal structure.

94. See L. Richardson (1992) s.v. *pomerium*. Cf. Varro *Ling.* 5.143–44. Note also that Stolo's response to Scrofa's request for determining what constitutes *agri cultura* specifically singled out the need to follow those agronomists "who defined [it] with a smaller boundary" (*qui minore pomerio finierunt*, 1.2.13); cf. p. 58 in chapter 2). In a sense, then, the redefinition of the *pomerium* of *agri cultura* aids the refiguration of Italia as a *pomarium*.

ing an additional, explicitly political, and possibly religious connotation to the concept of Italia within Roman *res publica*. No longer a simple city-state, Rome and its *territorium* had come to comprise Italia and the Mediterranean at large. By figuring *tota Italia* as a *pomarium,* however, Varro is ascribing a privileged place for Italia as the new *pomerium* of Roman empire.

## THE DEATH OF FUNDILIUS AND THE END OF *RR* 1

The various elements of *RR* 1—the literary "ornamentation" of the dialogue form as well as the technical discussion of field cultivation—collaborate to present Italia as the pinnacle of agricultural efficacy and fecundity. By portraying an Italia defined by its corporate agricultural preeminence and unified in spite of its regional diversity, Varro responds to contemporary debates concerning the relationship between the *urbs* of Rome and its peninsular cohorts; just as *agri cultura* is central to the tripartite *praedium* envisioned by the *RR,* so Italian *terra* now serves as the base—indeed, the *fundus* and veritable *pomarium/pomerium*—of Roman *imperium.*

Yet, it is this recurrent emphasis on Italia's putatively unsurpassed fertility that perhaps renders the infamous end to *RR* 1—the freedman's announcement of the temple caretaker's murder—all the more jarring and unsettling. The apparent dissonance between the dialogue's abrupt and demoralizing denouement and its otherwise positively buoyant staging has not gone unnoticed; most commentators rightly view the incident as exemplary of the tendency for the political violence endemic to the late Republic to erupt without warning,[95] while Kronenberg has even gone so far as to argue that the concluding incident consummates *RR* 1's general subversion of the "rational optimism" of expert knowledge to overcome the natural world and its operative principles based on chance (*casus/tuche*).[96] In keeping with my approach to the *RR* as a text that walks the line between the technical and the philosophico-satirical—as well as the historical and the fantastical—the assassination of the sacristan, a certain L. Fundilius (1.2.11), merits further investigation.

The context is as follows. As Stolo is completing his discussion of storage, the freedman (*libertus*) of the sacristan (*aeditumus*) bursts onto the

---

95. See especially Green (1997) 432, who rightly views this scene as part of the *RR*'s programmatic engagement with politics. Cf. Martin (1971) 219 and White (1973) 486. The emphasis of Flach (1996) 338 on the problems with identifying Fundilius speaks to his tendency to approach the *RR* as a technical treatise with occasional references to the contemporary political scene. Cf. Diederich (2007) 183.

96. See Kronenberg (2009) 90–91; cf. 101–2.

stage,[97] weeping, begging forgiveness for the interlocutors' extended wait, and requesting the group's presence at tomorrow's funeral (1.69.1). Generally agitated, the group solicits further information. In turn, the freedman explains that his *patronus* had been stabbed in a crowd by an unseen person, whose unidentifiable voice exclaimed that a mistake had been made; that his ensuing attempts to save his former master, despite their diligence and piety, failed; and that, for this reason, he requests the pardon of the would-be dinner guests (1.69.2–3). In turn, "bearing no ill-will we step down from the temple and, lamenting human misfortune more than wondering that it happened at Rome, depart one and all" (*non moleste ferentes descendimus de aede et de casu humano magis querentes quam admirantes id Romae factum, discedimus omnes*; 1.69.3).

And so, the otherwise upbeat and, at times, positively lighthearted dialogue abruptly ends on this *almost* bewildering note of melancholy— "almost" except that the interlocutors hardly appear to be surprised or even upset at the incident. Instead of consoling the bereaved or, for that matter, one another, the would-be dinner guests bemoan "human misfortune" (*casus humanus*) in the most general of terms. Indeed, the interlocutors' reaction to the assassination itself—especially a "mistaken" one—is certainly understated (perhaps even blasé) and would instead seem to reflect their general disenchantment with those human affairs tied to the political sphere.[98] Fundilius's death thus provides a fitting end for a dialogue written in 37 BC and set in the turbulent, post-45 period of ongoing civil disturbances and strife.

But who *is* this L. Fundilius? By way of a not-so-subtle pun, his name, "Estate-Owner," invokes the *fundus,* that is, the space that encompasses all the activities of *agri cultura* just discussed. In terms of the satirical staging, moreover, Fundilius's death precludes the promised dinner party—that is, the consumption of the agricultural produce discussed by the hungry interlocutors for quite some time—which was the entire premise behind the chance meeting of Varro and his agronomically minded compatriots. With the demise of "Fundilius" *qua* the "Estate-Owner," then, comes the end of *RR* 1's idealizing treatment of the *fundus,* its praise of Italian agriculture, and its figuration of Italia as the *fundus* of Roman enterprise.

In addition to a purely literary reading of Fundilius, however, it may be possible to detect a historical personage. In this respect, Linderski has

---

97. That the *libertus* runs onto the scene may be a play off the *servus currens* of New Comedy, especially when we consider *RR* 1's other references to play parts (e.g., 1.26; 1.56, as noted by Brendan Reay in personal correspondence). Cf. Kronenberg (2009) 102 n. 22, who cites Hunter (1985) 141: "No subject for general reflection is more common in New Comedy than the role of Luck or Chance (Tuche, Fortuna) in human affairs."

98. Cf. Green (1997) 432.

plausibly connected this Fundilius with a Reatinian *gens* of the same tribe as Varro's own family.[99] That there is no other record of the Lucius Fundilius in question is unsurprising if we presume that his main claim to fame was the oversight of the Temple of Tellus. Nor is it likely that his position as *aeditumus* reflects a servile or lowly origin and, therefore, fundamentally impairs his visibility within the historical record.[100] In fact, the present case testifies to the sacristan's condition as, at the very least, not so humble: he has his own personal freedman (*libertus*), and his social standing is such that he is successfully able to host two ex-praetors, a former tribune of the *plebs,* and a member of an old consular *gens.*[101] Thus, we are left with an intriguingly absent *aeditumus,* who apparently possessed substantial social connections (or, at the very least, enough status to chase them with some success); whose name provides a sufficiently appropriate trope for the subject of *RR* 1; and whose inopportune death offers a most convenient end to the dialogue.

Insofar as the evidence permits, the tentative identification of Fundilius as a member of the Reatinian *gens* is certainly prudent and plausible enough. Yet, it may also be worth considering a few other scenarios in light of the historical and satirical backdrop. One possibility involves denying outright the historical existence of Fundilius. While understanding him merely as an onomastically appropriate construct heightens the dialogue's fantasy, such an interpretation may do so at the expense of the poignancy of the man's death. A far more fruitful approach would be to split the difference between satirical fantasy and historical veracity, that is, to approach the man as a quasi-historical composite of various historical figures: an omni*absent* Fundilius who simultaneously invites historical comparison to other victims of late Republican political violence, but frustrates, even defies, positivistic identification. Although he does not frame his proposal in these terms, such an approach would seem to underlie Osgood's suggestion of the mistaken killing of C. Helvius Cinna as a possible antecedent.[102] Seeking to avenge the recent death of their beloved benefactor, a riotous mob of Caesar's devotees went on the prowl for the assassins and their supporters, among whom was numbered a praetor of the previous year, L. Cornelius Cinna. Upon encoun-

---

99. (1989) 126 n. 96. Cf. *CIL* 14.4273, which offers the first-century AD epitaph of a freedman, C. Fundilius Doctus, found in the sanctuary of Diana at Nemi.

100. As Cavazza (1995) 58–61 has shown in his survey of appearances of *aeditumus,* its cognate, *aedituus,* and similar terms (e.g., *custodes [aedis]*), the only consistent feature to these temple caretakers is that the term *aeditumus* never applies to the freedmen and slaves who attend to the temple's well-being.

101. Varro and Scrofa were praetors, while Fundanius was tribune of the *plebs* and Stolo came from a noble *gens*; see Linderski (1989) 117.

102. (2006) 211.

tering another Cinna—commonly identified with the Neoteric familiar of Catullus[103]—and despite his pleas otherwise, the crowd sated their anger with the blood of the inopportunely misidentified victim.

Indeed a case of mistaken assassination, the murder of Helvius Cinna would nonetheless appear to have little relevance to the Temple of Tellus. We do, however, know of one late Republican individual with direct connections to that *aedes* who also met an untimely demise as a result of political violence: M. Tullius Cicero.[104] In *De Haruspiciis Responsis,* a speech that reacts to Clodius's maneuvers to retake the site of Cicero's house, the *novus homo* from Arpinum denounces the sacrilege of his enemy's brother, Appius Claudius Pulcher, who had apparently removed a religious artifact from the Temple of Tellus.[105] Claiming that "many" (*non nulli*) think that the temple's desecration was a matter of particular concern to him, Cicero maintains that his impetus for action not only derives from the fact "that the Temple of Tellus is under my superintendence (*curatio mea*)," but also that famine and agricultural sterility (*in hac caritate annonae, sterilitate agrorum, inopia frugum*) further fuel his *religio telluris* (31). Composed in 56, at a time when his return from exile was recent and the security of his recovered property still tenuous, Cicero's claims to the oversight of the Temple of Tellus might be written off as mere rhetorical hyperbole—except that this "curatorship" (*curatio*) seems to have still been in effect two years later. In a letter to Quintus dated to September of 54 BC, Cicero relates the progress of work on the temple as well as his placement of a statue of Quintus in its precinct (*Q. Fr.* 21.14 [= 3.1.14]). While he never refers to himself as the *aedituus* of the Temple of Tellus, both passages imply that Cicero sought to cultivate the image of himself as acting in a similar capacity.

There is yet another important connection between Cicero and the Temple of Tellus, one that integrates both man and edifice into the final days of the Republic. Serving as the site for the first meeting of the Senate two days after the assassination of Caesar, the temple witnessed a pair of speeches delivered by Antony and Cicero. The conciliatory tone of each speech is well

---

103. For the problems with the identity of the murdered Cinna, see *MRR* 2.320–21, 2.324, and 3.100; Osgood (2006) 13; and, most generally, Wiseman (1974) 44–58.

104. Proscribed in 43, Cicero subsequently met his end after a conflicted attempt to flee Italy; see App. *B. Civ.* 4.5–20; Dio Cass. 47.8; and Plut. *Cic.* 47–49; and Rawson (1983) 292–96 and Osgood (2006) 25–43, 61 for discussion.

105. The exact nature of this artifact, which is called a *magmentarium,* is unclear. See Varro *Ling.* 5.112. For the suggestion that it was a *lararium,* see L. Richardson (1992) 379. It may be worth observing that this Appius Claudius Pulcher is the very one who figures so prominently as an interlocutor in *RR* 3. Cf. chapter 6.

established.[106] The chosen place of convocation has tended to be associated with the proximity of the location to Pompey's former house, which was now occupied by Antony.[107] While it is true that Antony convened the meeting, it should be clear from the above discussion that there was, at least, an equally plausible connection between the Temple of Tellus and Cicero. Perhaps playing off this connection in his first (and most restrained) philippic against Antony (*Phil.* 1.1.1), Cicero claims to have "laid the foundations of peace" in that temple and to have proposed the general amnesty of the conspirators. For various reasons, the seeds of peace scattered that day failed to take root. In the eyes of Cicero—and perhaps also a Pompeian and fellow proscribed of the sort such as Varro—the site quickly came to symbolize Antony's tyrannical designs (*Phil.* 2.89–90) and the general failure of negotiations with Caesarians (*Att.* 402.1 [= 16.14.1]). And with the vision of reconciliation *in Tellure* having given way, Antony had Cicero proscribed and killed less than two years later.

A fair amount of evidence connects Cicero with the Temple of Tellus, and it is certainly enticing to read the erstwhile *pater patriae* into the figure of the "Estate-Owner." Yet, his assassination was by no means "mistaken" (*perperam*; *RR* 1.69.2). Before we admit that the question of Fundilius's identity may ultimately be an inscrutable one—and, perhaps, intentionally so—it is worth considering what, from the vantage of an elder statesman writing in 37, would likely have been the most relevant political assassination: that of C. Julius Caesar. Might it be possible that the character of Fundilius the "Estate-Owner" was meant to invoke the figure of the assassinated *dictator in perpetuum*? Reference to his various dictatorial measures pertaining to the administration and maintenance of Rome and Italy[108]—as well as his infamous regulation of his own household (Suet. *Iul.* 74.2; cf. 6.2)—could all reasonably be brought to bear on this question. Still, the "mistaken" nature of the assassination remains difficult to square with Varro's earlier political activities and affiliations.[109]

It is here that we might consider more closely the use of the adverb employed to describe the manner of the killing: *perperam*. So far, I have translated the word as "mistaken" or "mistakenly," basically in the primary

---

106. For the testimonia regarding Cicero's and Antony's speeches, see Crawford (1984) 244–47.

107. See L. Richardson (1992) 379 and Ramsey (2003) 85.

108. For (among other things) Julius Caesar's reduction of the grain dole, see Suet. *Iul.* 41.3, Dio Cass. 43.21; his enfranchisement of Transpadane Gaul, Dio Cass. 41.36.3; and his imposition of tariffs on foreign goods, e.g., Suet. *Iul.* 43.1.

109. Cf. introduction.

sense of the Latin *error.*[110] But it is generally—if not mostly—used with a moral connotation to it: often in a legal context and not infrequently understood as the direct antonym of *recte.*[111] Thus, characterizing the assassination as "mistaken" may not quite capture the sense of *perperam,* for the word does not *necessarily* imply that the killing was the result of misapprehension; instead, *perperam* allows for the possibility—perhaps even encourages the interpretation—that the murder was (solely? also?) the result of a *moral* misjudgment. Indeed, depending on how one construes the syntax of *perperam fecisse*—is it coordinated with (i.e., through asyndeton) *exaudisse vocem* or subordinate to it (i.e., by means of embedded indirect discourse)?—as well as whose indirect speech is being represented (is it the freedman's commentary, the assassin's admission, or even the narrator's estimation?), the sentence offers a multitude of interpretative cruces. Is *RR* 1.69.3 stating that the "Estate-Owner" was *wrongly* killed, or could it be implying that the *wrong* "Estate-Owner" was killed? Might Varro be deploring the assassination of Caesar, condemning the ascension of Mark Antony (and possibly Octavian) upon the demise of the former, or merely relating the unfortunate death of L. Fundilius of Reate?

Be it Cinna or Cicero, Caesar or Fundilius, identification of the "estate-owning" caretaker remains inherently problematic. But such is the nature of a work that purports to represent the real world in its technical discussion and dabbles in the philosophical and satirical to the extent that the *RR* does. However tenuous the connection between Fundilius and any or all of these figures may be, it remains that the death of the caretaker—an act that ends the discussion of Italian fecundity and precludes the promised dinner—unquestionably invokes the internecine struggles of the civil wars that destroyed the lives of individual Romans and, from the vantage of *RR* 1, the putative livelihood of Italia. Thus, the fantasy of the dialogue, which has presented an idealizing picture of Italian agriculture, is shattered by the ongoing horrors of civil strife.

That the dialogue concludes with the political strife of Rome shattering the utopian vision of Italian agriculture is itself not insignificant, for it implies that Rome as the principal city of Italia—that is, its metaphorical *caput* or metropole—remains the ultimate arbiter of peninsular destiny. Thus, the *RR*'s construction of Italia as a unified *terra* still acknowledges the supremacy of Rome and the Romanocentric view of Italia as ultimately proprietary endures. More generally, *RR* 1 functions as an implicitly political text that provides

---

110. Cf. *TLL* s.v. *perperam* I.B: *quorum consilia errore frustrantur.*

111. For its appearance in legal contexts and/or documents, see *TLL* s.v. *perperam* II. A.1–2. For the pairing of *perperam* with *recte* as its antonym, see, for example, Cic. *Caecin.* 69 and *Dig.* 46.8.22.4.

an agricultural, or rather, agronomical, commentary on the effects of Roman political strife on Italia. In this way, it provides a conception of Italia as a *fundus* managed by the Roman state and offers a paradigm for the relationship between Rome and the peninsula that had come to hold an important, even privileged—if somewhat precarious and unresolved—position within Roman *imperium* over the Mediterranean.

# CHAPTER 4

# The Song of Faustulus

## Pastures and Provinces in *RR* 2

καίτοι γ᾽ ἐν τῇ ἡμετέρᾳ πόλει τοὺς ἐπικούρους ὥσπερ κύνας ἐθέμεθα ὑπηκόους τῶν ἀρχόντων ὥσπερ ποιμένων πόλεως.

And, you know, in our city we placed the guardians under the rulers, just like dogs under shepherds.

  —Plato, *Republic* 440d4–6

Hos super advenit Volsca de gente Camilla
agmen agens equitum et florentis aere catervas,
bellatrix. . . .
illam omnis tectis agrisque effusa iuventus
turbaque miratur matrum et prospectat euntem,
attonitis inhians animis ut regius ostro
velet honos levis umeros, ut fibula crinem
auro internectat, Lyciam ut gerat ipsa pharetram
et pastoralem praefixa cuspide myrtum.

Beyond these ones came Camilla of the Volsci,
leading a column of horsemen, bands blooming with bronze,
a *bellatrix*. . . .
Upon her the youth poured forth from all the buildings and fields
and a throng of mothers gazed and watched as she went,
amazed in their thunderstruck minds how queenly honor
covered her slender shoulders with purple, how the brooch

interweaved her hair with gold, how she herself bore a Lycian quiver
and a shepherd's crook fixed with a spear.

   —Vergil, *Aeneid* 7.803–5; 812–17


IN THE *REPUBLIC,* Plato famously analogizes his ideal *politeia* along pastoral lines: the rulers stand as the shepherds of the city's pastures, while the
guardians' doglike qualities aid them in their watch over the sheep, which (by
implication) correspond to the *demos.* By exploiting the iconic image of shepherd, faithful dog, and flock to capture the social and political structure of the
city in which justice perfectly obtains, Plato's analogy insinuates itself into a
long literary and intellectual tradition surrounding the caretaker of animals,
which, despite its longevity, ubiquity, and rustic lack of pretension, is anything
but uniform, artless, or simple. Indeed, it is perhaps precisely *because* of the
lowly herdsman's seeming unaffectedness that the profession admits multiple, sometimes even countervailing, forms of figuration:[1] as the wretched and
solitary poet, like Hesiod in his *Theogony* (23, 26); as rulers of states, perhaps
best captured in the Homeric epithet of *poimen laon* (e.g., *Il.* 7.230); as primeval and monstrous figures of *phusis,* like Geryon or the Odyssean Cyclops;
as primitive pioneers of post-lapsarian civilization;[2] as rustic figures of idle
repose and song, like the herdsmen of Hellenistic *bucolica*; and as aggressive,
sometimes bellicose, thieves, like Autolycus or the Trojan prince, Paris. For
the Romans, the most renowned *pastor* was undoubtedly Romulus, whose
humble beginnings as the foster son of a lowly shepherd, Faustulus, underpin
his later heroics—as much destructive as they are constructive. As caretakers
and defenders of docile animals, herdsmen can also be aggressors to would-
be predators, and they would thus seem to embody a paradox, which Vergil's
Camilla—a royal shepherd, like Romulus, cheated of a throne—wholeheart-
edly embraces. Already an enigma in her status as a woman fighting in a
man's war, Camilla wields a staff that doubles as crook and blade, thereby
neatly encapsulating her utterly dualistic role in the *Aeneid* as caretaker of
flocks and master of men.

   In the following two chapters, I present a reading of the second dialogue
of *De Re Rustica,* which argues that Varro exploits the field of values that

---

   1. For an excellent treatment of the herdsman in Archaic Greek literature through Plato,
see Gutzwiller (1991) 23–79, for whom herdsmen generally appear "only for the purpose of
communicating something about another figure of more value to the society—king, warrior,
poet, seer, even deity" due to the fact that their mundane ubiquity "more sharply define[s]
the activities of other figures considered worthy of artistic focus" (24).

   2. Dicaearchus, F 56 Mirhady [= 49 Wehrli]; cf. F 54 Mirhady [= 51 Wehrli = *RR* 2.1.3–9]
and F 55 Mirhady [= 48 Wehrli = *RR* 1.2.15–16]. Cf. Plato, *Laws* 677b1ff.

shepherds and other herdsmen variously inhabit so as to present new paradigms of *pastores* for the expanded world of Roman *imperium* in the late Republic. I begin by unpacking the significance of the dramatic setting: in Epirus, in 67 BC, and against the backdrop of Pompey's military operations against the pirates, in which Varro participated as legate and for which he received the rare and prestigious naval crown. I then turn to the cast of interlocutors, which is divided between the "Greek" Romans of Epirus and the "Italian" Romans on campaign. While the dialogue actively cultivates a distinction between the two groups, both end up being figured as *pastores*: of animals, in the case of the former, and of humans, in the case of the latter. A contemporary work, Vergil's *Eclogues,* factors substantially into my discussions, and the third section of chapter 4 and the second section of chapter 5 engage in a comparative analysis and interpretation of these two texts, which may have much more in common than critics have previously recognized. At the very least, such a comparison casts light on the nature of Varro's project of renovating the theory and the praxis of animal husbandry (*pastio*) and the figures of its practitioners (*pastores*) for the contemporary Roman world. By inflecting his technical discussion with various epic, bucolic, and other literary features, Varro presents us with a Camilla-like allegory of animal husbandry, in which the Roman elite preside as economic, military, and political *pastores* over the pastures of the Mediterranean.

## STAGING THE DIALOGUE

In the previous chapter, we saw that *RR* 1's staging—its temporal and physical setting, cast of characters, and off-stage happenings—shaped and colored its account of *agri cultura* to an extent that allowed us to read the dialogue *also* as a metaphorical exposition of Italia as the *fundus* of the Roman imperial estate. Unlike the first dialogue, which presented a clear exposition of its dramatic backdrop, *RR* 2 provides no such straightforward prologue to the time, place, and cast of its *sermo* and, as it would seem, begins *in medias res*.[3] Perhaps fitting for a dialogue that, as we shall see, contains a number of Homeric allusions, this stylistic choice certainly complicates any effort to discern the possible relationship between setting and subject. Consequently, we are left to tease out the conversation's historical conditions from the various comments and events that occur in the course of the dialogue.

---

3. Most editors since Keil have posited a lacuna, but see Flach's convincing arguments against this proposition (1997) 185. For the first appearance of "*in medias res*," see Hor. *Ars P.* 147–49, who famously associates this compositional technique with Homer.

For this reason, I begin with the dialogue's setting: its date, place, and occasion. Merely identifying the general context is no difficult task, for Varro himself states that the conversation occurred with "large ranch-owners in Epirus" and was located "at that time in the Pirate War when I myself was in charge of the fleets of Greece between Delos and Sicily" (*tum cum piratico bello inter Delum et Siciliam Graeciae classibus praeessem*; 2.Pref.6). Though perhaps prudently omitting the name of his commanding officer given the prevailing political situation of 37 BC, Varro clearly places the conversation in the context of his service as legate under Pompey's unprecedented military command some thirty years prior to the *RR*'s date of composition.[4] The precise date and occasion of the *sermo* requires a bit more searching, but several hints in the course of the dialogue point to the Parilia, a festival held on the twenty-first of April in honor of Pales, who was the patron deity (or deities) of the shepherd.[5] Little is known about Pales[6]—including the deity's gender and number or, for that matter, the day's ceremonies—but it would appear that Menates, whose departure initiates the dialogue (2.1.1), may be the *aeditumus* responsible for the deity's maintenance in Epirus.[7] Moreover, this festival's date is consonant with the duration of Pompey's campaign, which we know to have begun at the tail end of winter and to have lasted for three months.[8] Thus, we can be reasonably certain that *RR* 2 is set in Epirus on April twenty-first, 67 BC.

But identification is far from explanation and only raises the following questions: why the date of the Parilia, why Epirus, and why 67 BC? In respect

---

4. Varro was one of 18 legates; for a discussion of these men and their relative jurisdictions, Van Ooteghem (1954) 172–76 remains fundamental. Cf. *MRR* 2.168.

5. The evidence includes the following: the reference to the Parilia (2.1.9) in Varro's account of the *dignitas* of *pastio*; Lucienus' playful request that Murrius act as his *advocatus* and witness as he pays his homage to Pales (2.5.1); the ongoing thematic representation of the interlocutors as shepherds (cf. below); and, most importantly, the later announcement by Menates's freedman that the sacrificial cakes and other preparations had been made ready (2.8.1). For the dating of *RR* 2 to the Parilia, see J. H. Jones (1935) 214–15, Heisterhagen (1952) 23, and Flach (1997) 40–41.

6. For a prudent discussion of this difficult god (or goddess), see Beard, North, and Price (1998) 1.174–76. Ovid preserves a description of the ritual activities associated with the festival at *Fasti* 4.721–806, which included the offering of ritual cakes and the leaping of a fire by both "herdsman" and flock. For the problems with Ovid as source as well as with the location (rural? urban?) of the ritual performance, see North (1996) 140–41. Cf. Tib. 1.1.35–36, 2.5.87–90; and Prop. 4.1a.19–20 and 4.4.73–78. On the last of these passages, Hutchinson's comments (2006: 132) may be right, but still cannot be substantiated: "The Parilia in the first century BC should be thought of . . . as a single festival, but with different activities in city (ritual purification associated with Vesta) and country (leaping over hay fires, cf. Pers. 1.71–72)." See also Beard (1987) 1–15, who argues that the changing nature of the rituals reflects the vitality of the Parilia in constructing and performing "Romanness."

7. For this suggestion, see Linderski (1989) 118. Cf. *RR* 2.8.1 and see Flach (1997) 185.

8. For the dating of the war, see Cic. *Leg. Man.* 35 and Seager (1979) 37.

to the first query, appeal to the fittingness that a conversation on animal husbandry (*pastio*) take place on a festival held in honor of the patron deity of shepherds (i.e., Pales) might be thought to suffice. Thus, the celebration of the appropriate deity on its specific day and the attendant discussion of pertinent subject matter are features common to both *RR* 1 and 2.[9] There is, however, at least one fundamental difference between the settings of the first two dialogues; whereas the first conversation takes place at the appropriate temple in Rome, the location of the second is decidedly *not* Rome—nor even Italia—but rather, Epirus. Thus, unlike the first book, wherein the occasion of a pertinent festival (i.e., the Sementivalia) in an appropriate place (i.e., the Temple of Tellus) contributes to the presentation of an inimitable Italian fecundity, Book 2 relocates the Parilia from its proper place in Roman Italy[10] to *transmarinus* Epirus.

This transference becomes all the more marked when we recognize the ideological significance of this ill-attested festival. By Varro's day, the Parilia had come to be celebrated as the foundation day—a "birthday" of sorts— for the city of Rome, an association that stemmed from its pastoral progenitors.[11] As Varro himself will observe in his treatment of the *dignitas* of *pastio*, Faustulus, the foster father of Romulus and Remus, was a shepherd, and so were the twins themselves, whose statuses as *pastores* are attested by the fact that "they founded the city particularly on the Parilia" (*quod Parilibus potissimum condidere urbem*; 2.1.9; cf. 2.Pref.4). Thus, the second dialogue takes this shepherds' festival—intimately connected with the very foundation of the city itself—and displaces it abroad.

What are we to make of this quintessentially Roman festival's transference to Epirus within the context of 67 BC? A strictly historicizing mode of explanation might appeal to the fact that the celebration of this Roman festival abroad anticipates a burgeoning trend of dispersion in Roman religious practices from the city itself to other localities—Italian and otherwise—under Augustus.[12] Yet, the displacement of this religious festival from Rome and its

---

9. Note also that both Fundilius and Menates never make an appearance in the dialogue, instead being represented only by their freedmen.

10. For the problems with identifying the location of the Parilia, see n. 6. Interestingly enough, most modern accounts omit mention of the possible role or function of the Temple of Pales, which was vowed and built by M. Atilius Regulus as part of his defeat of the Salentini in 267 BC. For the difficulties in locating this temple on the Palatine and the paucity of references to its function, see L. Richardson (1992) s.v. "Pales, Templum" 282–83 and Coarelli (2007) 132.

11. Among other texts, see *Fasti Antiates Maiores* (II XIII 2.9; 84–55 BC), Cic. *Div.* 2.98, and Prop. 4.4.73–74.

12. See, for example, Orlin (2007) 73–91.

relocation to Epirus in particular accomplishes several literary ends as well. Most obviously, the choice of Epirus over other areas under Varro's jurisdiction allows him to plausibly introduce into his cast of characters a number of Romans who, as it would appear, owned properties and herds of animals in the area. The choice of Epirus thus rationalizes Varro's presence among Roman expatriates, adds plausibility to his claim to be relating an actual conversation, and, most importantly, provides a contextual backdrop for the conversation's recurring play on the status of these men as Romans abroad.

In addition to adding a veneer of biographical plausibility and a tinge of unfamiliarity to these otherwise thoroughly Roman interlocutors, the backdrop of Epirus resonates with the region's historical legacy as a significant locus of transmarine conflict with Rome. In the first place, it was the breeding ground for Pyrrhus, the Hellenistic warlord and king (319–272 BC). His Hellenophilic appeal to common ancestry with the Tarentines (via his claim of ancestral descent from Neoptolemus and, consequently, Achilles) and concomitant military aid to the same in support of their struggle against the Romans in southern Italy temporarily stemmed the Romans' march southward (279–75 BC) and would loom large in Roman historical consciousness. Nonetheless, with his return home in 275 BC and the fall of Tarentum some three years later, Pyrrhus failed to replicate the success of that first Trojan War. While the text does not explicitly invoke that episode of Hellenic intrusion into the shores of Italia, the first Roman incursion into the land of Epirus during the Second Macedonian War (200–197 BC) does itself receive mention in the form of a quotation from Ennius; after Varro and Scrofa have each finished their respective parts, the latter requests their Epirotic counterparts (cf. *O Epirotae*) to "return to us again" (*rursus vos reddite nobis*) so that he and Varro "may see what the *pastores* from Pergamis or Maledos[13] are able" (*videamus, quid pastores a Pergamide Maledove potis sint*; 2.2.1) to say about animal husbandry. As Skutsch has argued, these hexameters—especially with their use of the archaic form of *potis*—strongly suggest that they are lines adapted from book 10 of Ennius's *Annales,* in which the Roman general Flamininus would appear to have enjoined some local shepherds to return after completing their appointed task—most likely their guiding of one contingent of the Roman army through an unguarded mountain pass to attack the rear of Philip V's army.[14] This allusion thus casts the Roman expa-

---

13. *Pace* the despair of Ash and Hooper (1934) 330, Pergamis and Maledos are, according to Flach (1997) 209 and the bibliography *ad loc.,* to be identified with the region of Chaonia and the town of Maleshovë in, respectively, northwestern and southern Epirus. Cf. Skutsch (1985) 513.

14. F 10.340–42. For the shepherds' aid in that conflict, see Livy 32.11 and Plut. *Flam.* 4.4.

triates in the role of Epirotic shepherds and invokes a historical conflict in which the lowly practitioners of animal husbandry actually came to the service of Roman military might and imperial aspiration. I will return in chapter 5 to this nexus of *res rustica* and *res militaris,* which, as we shall see, plays an integral thematic part within *RR* 2. Similar to how *RR* 1's Temple of Tellus and its *Italia picta* invoke various watersheds in Roman-Italian agrarian and political history, the Epirotic backdrop of *RR* 2 marks both the beginning of Rome's emergence as a Mediterranean power and a crucial step in its eventual ascendancy over that world.

Yet, the significance of Epirus lies not simply in its historical legacy as another obstacle in the path of Rome's retrospectively unstoppable march toward Mediterranean dominion, for the place was also a staging ground for Varro's military maneuvers in 67 BC. But what does Varro gain by setting the dialogue in the context of Pompey's war with apparently marauding raiders? For a partial answer, we must turn to one of the rationales for the Lex Gabinia, which granted unprecedented powers to Pompey over all the shores of the Mediterranean: the pirates' disruption of the trade routes on which Rome and Italy had increasingly come to rely for their grain supply.[15] While the threat posed by the so-called pirates may in fact have been exaggerated—the menace was, after all, eliminated within three months of the law's passage and Pompey's assumption of command[16]—Pompey's success nevertheless came to be understood as having achieved the safeguarding of the grain routes as well as the solidification of Roman control over the Mediterranean.[17] Ironically enough, some thirty years later and at roughly the same time as the *RR*'s composition, the security of the grain supply was a justification for the war against another "pirate": Sextus Pompeius.[18] I shall return to this more recent case of piratical activity later; for now, it will suffice to observe that by setting the

---

For further discussion, see Skutsch (1985) 510–14, who notes that the enjoined task could also be some sort of precautionary appeal to Charops, a pro-Roman Epirote, for his endorsement of the shepherds' credibility prior to their help. For Varro's use of quotations from Ennius in general, see Magno (2006) 75–82.

15. Dio Cass. 23.1; App. *Mith.* 93; Livy, *Per.* 99. Cf. Plut. *Pomp.* 25.1; 26.1. See also De Souza (1999) 166, who views the concern for the grain supply as "the one thing which no one could ignore at Rome."

16. But see *idem* 167–72, who maintains that the threat was a substantial one and attributes the brevity of the campaign to Pompey's efficient and sound practice of *clementia* for those who abandoned their piratical ways.

17. According to Cic. *Leg. Man.* 34, one of Pompey's first moves was to secure three state granaries at Sardinia.

18. App. *B. Civ.* 5.80; cf. 92. For the role that the blockade of grain shipments played in Sextus Pompeius's campaign against Octavian, see A. Powell (2002) 114–17, who depicts Sextus as a shrewd commander whose policies were to emphasize his moral superiority over his opponents, while creating unfavorable conditions for them in Italy.

dialogue in Epirus during this specific crisis, Varro underscores not only the sort of public service that prevented him from enjoying the *otium* necessary for a "more agreeable" (*commodius*) write-up of *res rusticae* (1.1.1), but also his efforts on behalf of the city's grain supply. In these respects, setting the dialogue in 67 BC allows Varro to introduce unambiguously political dimensions to the setting, which will dovetail nicely with the technical discussion of rustic matters.

While the Pirate War of 67 BC evokes the inestimable importance of Rome's grain supply, the subject of Book 2 is not *agri cultura,* but *pastio* (or *res pecuaria*). Given that the prescriptive injunction of appropriate activity for the requisite sphere of a *praedium* lies at the heart of Varro's theory of *res rusticae,*[19] how then are we to understand the apparent disjunction between the backdrop of Book 2 and its subject, insofar as I have framed it up to this point? On the one hand, we might see it as further evidence for the destabilization of the unfounded optimism in the *ratio* and *scientia* of *agri cultura* purveyed by the first dialogue's Menippean know-it-alls. Analogous to the way that the second preface supposedly debunks *RR* 1's lie of Italian agricultural self-sufficiency (2.pref.1–3), such discrepancies espouse mutually divergent worldviews, fatally undermine the *RR*'s overall intellectual project, and ultimately offer up a devastating satire of Roman agricultural ideology and political life.[20] On the other hand, we may frame this "contradiction" more positively and observe that Varro's service as nautical bulwark for Rome's overseas grain supplies now partly fulfills a task once realized solely by the *agricola* of yesteryear.[21] On this view, the image of Varro *qua* naval commander both highlights his own part in the safeguarding of the grain supply and the Roman state, and proffers a renovated and complementary paradigm of a contemporary "farmer."

In the end, neither solution is, in my opinion, wholly satisfactory. Instead of dismissing the potentially countervailing representations of farming presented in each book as irreconcilably ironic or seeking to square them perfectly with one another in an ultimately uneasy union, these disparate images adroitly illustrate what I have referred to as the "constructive tension" that pervades the *RR* in terms of its form (i.e., as philosophico-satirico-technical dialogues) and content (i.e., a theoretical account of farming), and that prompts the reader to search for additional layers of meaning to the text's otherwise generally straightforward agronomical precepts.[22] For now, it will

---

19. See pp. 47–52 in chapter 2.

20. So Kronenberg (2009) 99–102. Cf. pp. 22–23 in chapter 1.

21. Cf. pp. 152–54 in chapter 5.

22. I will return to this idea of a "constructive tension" and the protreptic role it plays for

suffice to observe that this tension is not limited to the apparent conflict over the viability of Italian grain production, but may be understood to pervade a number of the dialogue's other aspects as well. For example, it threatens to spill over into the definitional program, as *pastio* is a sphere of activities clearly demarcated from, yet still closely affiliated with, *agri cultura*; as Varro puts it in the highly suggestive terminology of political alliance, "a great *societas* exists between them" (*quarum societas inter se magna*; 2.Pref.5). And as we have already seen, *RR* 2 cultivates this tension between its occasion (i.e., the Parilia), displaced setting (i.e., Epirus and *not* Rome), and its subject matter of *res pecuaria*, the legacy of which is itself intimately tied through the figure of Romulus to the foundation and identity of Rome itself. By building on and exploiting these (and other) tensions, *RR* 2 will proffer a new set of paradigms for the Roman elite as the political, military, and economic *pastores* of Rome's pasture provinces.

## A CAST OF SHEPHERDS

In keeping with its setting on the Parilia, the dialogue repeatedly figures the interlocutors as herdsmen, and this casting of elite *pecuarii* in humble shepherds' guise sporadically seeps into the technical discussion and inflects it with possibilities for metaphorical interpretation.[23] To elucidate the dynamics of this masquerade first requires that we have a clear understanding of the pastorally inclined cast of characters. Excluding the ever-absent Menates, the brief appearance of his freedman (2.8.1), and the late entrance of the freedman of an otherwise unmentioned Vitulus,[24] there are seven participants, each of whom takes up at least one part of the account of *pastio*:

readers in chapter 7's consideration of the overall model for *imperium* presented by the three dialogues of *De Re Rustica*. See also p. 11 in chapter 1.

23. Green (2012) 32–39 collects most of these references and provides a good overview of them and their political associations, but interprets the various references in terms of a single and uniform model.

24. For Menates, whose name appears to be Etruscan and whose freedman (*libertus*) makes a brief appearance in 2.8.1, see Flach (1997) 185 and bibliography *ad loc*. Vitulus, on the other hand, remains unmentioned until the appearance of his own *libertus* leads to the departure of Varro and Scrofa for the man's estate (2.11.12); while he would seem to be an entirely different person, could Vitulus simply be some kind of endearing, quasi-diminutival, pun on Vaccius (i.e., the "Calf" for the "Cow")? See pp. 168–69 of chapter 5 for another symbolic interpretation. Note also that, if (a) Orsini's difficult emendation of P<a>et{a}<u>m at 2.1.1 is to be accepted (for discussion of which, see *idem* 186) and (b) this Paetus to be identified with L. Papirius Paetus, a *familiaris* of Atticus and mostly known from Cicero's correspondence (*Fam.* 114, 188–91, 193–98, and 362 [= 9.15–26]), this individual could be understood to be another Roman landowner at Epirus.

| NUMBER | SUBJECT | SPEAKER |
|---|---|---|
| | *Origo* and *dignitas* of *pastio* (2.1.1ff.) | Varro |
| | *Scientia* of *pastio* (2.1.11ff.) | Scrofa |
| 1 | Sheep (2.2.2) | Atticus |
| 2 | Goats (2.3.1) | Cossinius |
| 3 | Pigs (2.4.1) | Scrofa ("Sow") |
| 4 | Cattle (2.5.1) | Vaccius ("Cow-man") |
| 5 | Asses (2.6.1) | Murrius |
| 6 | Horses (2.7.1) | Q. Lucienus |
| 7 | Mules (2.8.1) | Murrius |
| 8 | Dogs (2.9.1) | Atticus |
| 9 | Herdsman (2.10.1) | Cossinius |
| | *De lacte et caseo* (2.11.1) | Cossinius [or Vaccius] |
| | *Tonsura* (2.11.6) | Cossinius [or also Atticus[25]] |

With the exceptions of Varro, Scrofa, and Atticus, the others are ill attested in the historical record. The presence of Varro and Scrofa under the aegis of Pompey's command needs no further comment at this point, while Atticus—most famous as the close friend of Cicero—is well known to have had an estate in the area (at Buthrotum) and to have been on intimate terms with Varro as well.[26] Of the other interlocutors, Cossinius is one of the Epirotic cattle owners and most likely synonymous with the Roman *eques* and friend of Atticus.[27] Regarding Vaccius, however, all we know is what the dialogue

25. In the final two supplementary points of discussion (i.e., milk/cheese-making and shearing), there is some confusion as to the identity of the speaker. A more conservative editor may wish to assign all of the discussion to Cossinius, as there is no *explicit* indication of a change in speaker. Flach, on the other hand, chooses in his 2006 edition to assign various parts to Vaccius, Atticus, and Cossinius, presumably on the basis of whom he deems to be the appropriate speaker for each part (e.g., Atticus discusses sheepshearing on the basis of his earlier ovine assignment). Note that these assignments are not found in his 1997 edition and commentary.

26. We have no other evidence for Scrofa's role in the Pirate War, but his status as proconsul over Gaul in the mid- to late 70s BC suggests that his participation is not far-fetched; see Nelsestuen (2011) 318–19. Atticus's estate at Buthrotum is well documented. For example, Cicero contemplated taking up Atticus's offer to spend his time in exile there (*Att.* 52 [= 3.7]). For the close relationship between Atticus and Cicero in general, see Shackleton-Bailey (1965) 3–57. We also possess epigraphical evidence that attests to Atticus's close relationship with another Greek city, namely, Ephesus. See, in particular, the discussion of C. P. Jones (1999) 89–94. On the basis of 2.1.2–3, Shatzman (1975) 400 mistakenly infers that Varro had a cattle-raising estate in Epirus.

27. Possibly the son of the praetor L. Cossinius killed by Spartacus in 73 BC (Plut. *Crass.* 9; cf. Cic. *Balb.* 53), this Cossinius is usually identified with the friend of Cicero and Atticus

itself tells us, namely, that he too was a wealthy cattle owner in Epirus (2.5.12; 18).[28] Likewise, Murrius is now an Epirote, but originally hails from Reate, as he repeatedly observes (2.6.1; 2.8.6) to his fellow townsman Varro.[29] Finally, there is Q. Lucienus, a "friend to us all" (*familiaris omnium nostrum*) and seemingly the only senator among these Epirus-dwelling Romans (2.5.1).[30] In the inclusion of these characters—largely obscure and mostly undistinguished as they are—Linderski saw Varro as providing a "paean to the Italy of agricultural entrepreneurs" (1989: 116), but one in which the principle of the fitting (*to prepon*) dictates the lowly cast of characters for the humble subject of *res rusticae* (118). Such an evaluation captures, I would contend, only part of the *raison d'être* of these particular interlocutors, for it is also the dissonance between their Roman-Italian origins—embedded in their names and sometimes invoked in their speeches—and their present status as (mostly) equestrian transplants that, as we shall see, adds another ludic layer to *RR 2's* representation of *pastio* in dialogue form. Like the Parilia itself, these thoroughly Italian interlocutors are displaced from their homeland to Epirus, and this state of expatriate existence—especially in contradistinction to the politically engaged paradigm offered up by the likes of Varro and Scrofa—may attest to or inform their possibly humble backgrounds, lack of political ambition, political marginalization, perhaps even fictional status, or some combination thereof.[31]

At no place does the dialogue explicitly articulate the precise relationships among the interlocutors or even the seemingly haphazard manner in

---

(Cic. *Att.* 19 [= 1.19], 20 [= 1.20], 21 [= 2.1]; 338 [= 13.46]; *Fam.* 289 [= 13.23]). For discussion, see Nicolet (1974) 856–57. Cf. Shackleton-Bailey (1965) 1.341. No mention of his Epirotic landholdings is made outside the *RR*, though he does serve as the go-between for Cicero and Atticus in the case of at least one letter (*Att.* 19.11 [= 1.19.11]), which perhaps corroborates his owning of an estate in Epirus. See Linderski (1989) 117.

28. I cannot find any other Vaccius otherwise attested, but see Cic. *Dom.* 101 and Livy 8.19.4 for brief accounts of a certain Vaccus whose house was razed.

29. See Linderski (1989) 118 and esp. n. 89, which provides possible epigraphic evidence for the man. Cf. Flach (1997) 237.

30. See Wiseman (1971) 238 s.v. 234. Q. Lucienus. Cf. Shatzman (1975) 461.

31. It may be that Varro's apparently tertiary cast in *RR* 2 inverts the Ciceronian dialogue's practice of employing the uppermost political stratum of Romans in dubious intellectual roles. See pp. 16–17 in chapter 1. Interestingly enough, Epirus was historically associated with Roman exiles, for it became a sizable colony of sorts for many of Catiline's fellow conspirators (loosely centered around P. Autronius Paetus) after their conviction in 62 BC. It is explicitly for this reason that Cicero was wary of traveling to and residing in Atticus's villa during the former's own exile in 58 BC. For discussion and citations, see Kelly (2006) 108–25, 189–92. By setting his dialogue in a locale historically associated with political exiles, could the Varro of 37 BC be alluding to his own or his contemporaries' more recent experiences with political disenfranchisement, loss of property and status, and exile?

which they have all congregated together, but it does fashion the seven participants into two distinct groups: the "large-scale cattle-ranchers" (*magni pecuarii*) who own estates in Epirus (Atticus, Cossinius, Vaccius, Lucienus, and Murrius) and those who, in lieu of specific residential and economic considerations in Epirus, are present only because of their involvement in Pompey's campaign (Varro and Scrofa).[32] While the criteria for this distinction actually turn on the economic commitments, political engagements, and/or concomitant military duties of each individual, the way that each group is differentiated manifests itself instead along cultural and ethnic lines: the sojourning Romans are Italian, whereas the Epirus-dwelling Romans become "Hellenic." To be sure, the seven interlocutors recognize that they all are actually Roman citizens and Italians; consequently, a wry undercurrent of humor attends this representational conceit of the dialogue. Nonetheless, this bifurcation allows the dialogue actively to play upon the identities of the interlocutors by cultivating and even occasionally subverting the figuration of the politically involved interlocutors (Varro and Scrofa) as "Romans" and their Epirotic compatriots (Atticus, Cossinius, and company) as "Greeks."

This recurring play on the interlocutors' putatively different ethnicities and cultural heritages is present as early as Varro's acquiescence to the opening request of Cossinius and Murrius to resume their interrupted conversation of yesterday,[33] and his prompt delegation of the discussion of *pastio's* status as a *scientia* to Scrofa on the grounds that the latter is, "to quote Greek to half-Greek shepherds, 'a man by far better than me'" (*ut semigraecis pastoribus dicam graece, hos per mou pollon ameinon*; 2.1.2).[34] Scrofa subsequently follows up this jocular casting of the Italian Cossinius, Murrius, Vaccius, and Atticus as *semigraeci pastores* by addressing them as "the animal-husbandry athletes of Epirus" (*Epirotici pecuariae athletae*). After the discussion of the origin, dignity, and science of *pastio* (in the course of which a number of Homeric epithets are invoked[35]), Scrofa invites the *Epirotae* to speak what they can about each one of the nine subjects. So the eighty-one-part exposition

---

32. For the identification and solidarity of the "Greek" participants, see 2.2.20—Atticus (speaker): "we"; 2.3.10—Cossinius: Cossinius, Murrius; 2.5.18—Vaccius: Vaccius, Atticus, Lucienus; 2.7.1—Lucienus: Lucienus, Atticus; and 2.10.11—Cossinius: Cossinius, Atticus.

33. Note that the reference in 2.1.1 to an interrupted conversation (*quae coeperas nuper dicere, cum sumus interpellati*) and separate conversation "yesterday" (*here*) was formerly taken as indicative of a lacuna (although it is most unlikely that *RR* 2 spanned two days). Cf. n. 3.

34. The Greek quote is Homeric: *Il.* 7.114, 16.709, and 21.107. Cf. Flach (1997) 188. For *RR* 2's recurring Homeric motifs, see below.

35. These epithets include (2.1.6) *polyarnas* ("of many flocks"), *polymelos* ("of many sheep"), and *polybatas* ("of many herds").

of *pastio* is engendered in the midst of these ethnic jocularities, where some Romans are "Romans," but the other Romans are "Greeks."

This fashioning of the Epirus-dwelling Romans as Greek *pastores* continues explicitly throughout the first third of the dialogue, but does allow for some play on the trope. Cossinius, for example, subverts it upon his assumption of the discussion from Atticus (2.3.1):

> Cui Cossinius, "Quoniam satis balasti," inquit, "o Faustule noster, accipe a me, cum Homerico Melanthio cordo, de capellis et, quem ad modum breviter oporteat dicere, disce."

> To [Atticus] Cossinius says, "Since you have bleated on for quite long enough (*satis*), my dear Faustulus, hear from me as a Homeric Melanthius, a late-born lamb (*cordus*), about goats, and learn how one ought to speak concisely."

A number of elements underlie Cossinius's playful casting of Atticus as "Faustulus," the guardian and foster father of Romulus and Remus. On the one hand, Atticus, in having just completed his discussion of the number of *pastores* per sheep, had appealed to the practice "that nearly all of us do in Epirus" (*illut fere omnes in Epiro facimus*; 2.2.20), which, in conjunction with the all-too-obvious opportunity for punning offered by his assumed cognomen (cf. Cic. *Fin.* 5.4), trenchantly ironizes Cossinius's fashioning of "the Athenian" as a (proto-)Roman shepherd. After all, Atticus is in many respects the consummate example of an elite Roman whose philhellenic mode of life is *not* entirely commensurate with his thoroughly Roman pedigree and birthplace in the city.[36] Still, the appellation of "Faustulus" is not entirely inappropriate either, for despite his cognomen, residence at Epirus, and cultural proclivities, Atticus's avoidance of a traditional political career certainly would have left him with the pastoral *otium* necessary for calculating the proper sheep-to-shepherd ratio, and, in any case, "the Athenian" still remained Roman.[37] On the other hand, Cossinius's manipulation of the shepherd motif is not as simple as wholesale ethnic inversion, for he traces the etymology of his own name to the Greek word *chorion* in a torturous pun and explicitly casts

---

36. For the life of Atticus, see Shackleton-Bailey (1965) 3–59.

37. Note also that the dialogue itself acknowledges his two different names: originally Titus Pomponius, adoption by an uncle rendered him Quintus Caecilius (2.2.1). Interestingly, no mention is made of Atticus's Epicureanism, which seems to have motivated his apolitical stance.

himself as Melanthius, the treacherous goatherd of Odysseus.[38] Whether or not there is some pointed barb to his representation as an Italian Melanthius, Cossinius nonetheless casts himself as a Hellenizing goatherd of Roman Epirus. In sum, these countervailing appellations and puns equally reinforce and subvert the identity of the displaced Romans as "Greeks" who remain Romans, albeit expatriate ones.

At the heart of this dramatized destabilization of identity lies the historical existence of a significant landowning class of Roman elites in Epirus. Through its playful representation of such transplanted Romans as Greek shepherds, *RR 2* stages a drama in which Roman identity—originally tied to membership in the *populus* of the city itself, but gradually staked on a juridical status increasingly dislocated from the *urbs* and extended geographically to *tota Italia* most recently—is simultaneously problematized and, as we shall see, reaffirmed. By no means, however, were these particular individuals unique within the bounds of Roman *imperium* over the Mediterranean in the mid-first century BC, for literary, historical, and epigraphic evidence amply attests to the large numbers of Romans and Italians living abroad and participating in the economic, social, and religious life of various Mediterranean communities in multifarious modes and capacities.[39] In this respect, Varro's depiction of Romans living abroad transcends the scope of his own personal experience to evoke two larger issues as well: first, the widespread emergence of significant expatriate communities in the provinces in general, and second, the intellectual recognition of such communities as aspects of a broader

---

38. For the erudite and strained nature of the joke, see Flach (2006) 14. Among other things, the joke puns off the supposed etymological relationship between *cordus* and *cossinius*. For the explanation of a *cordus* as a lamb born post-term, see 2.1.19. As Odysseus's goatherd who colluded with the suitors on Ithaka and insulted his disguised master upon the latter's return, Melanthius is, so to speak, the black sheep of the other shepherds found in *RR 2*: Faustulus, Romulus, and Eumaeus (see below). Given that little is known about the historical Cossinius, any further point to this potentially questionable characterization would appear to be lost to the modern reader.

39. Perhaps the most well-known example is the Italian community at Delos in the late second century through the mid-first century BC. While these Italians appear to have largely made their living there as *negotiatores* and to have transferred their operations and residence after the island's sack in 69 BC, the epigraphic evidence attests to the size of the group, its strength as a recognizable and robust community, and its presence as a quasi-autonomous community vis-à-vis the island's other inhabitants; for discussions, see Hasenohr and Müller (2002) 13–16, Deniaux (2002) 29–40, Baslez (2002) 55–66, and Hasenohr (2002) 67–76. As the individual contributions of Hasenohr and Müller's 2002 volume, *Les Italiens dans le Monde Grec,* variously demonstrate, such Italian communities not infrequently came to exist in various parts of the Mediterranean, including the Narbonne (Christol, 41–54), Athens (Follet, 79–88), Boeotia (Müller, 89–100), Macedonia (Rizakis, 109–32), Asia Minor (Ferrary, 133–46), and Rhodes and Caunos (Bresson, 147–62). For a list of elite Roman landowners of provincial estates, see Shatzman (1975) 460–61.

historical phenomenon within the contemporary sociocultural landscape of Roman imperial experience. The play on the ambiguities of their identities as expatriate Romans should thus also be understood as a synecdoche for the larger "problem" that they (as one specific instantiation of a historical phenomenon) embody.[40] Through the ludic representation of their identities as Romans abroad, whose provincial holdings were made possible by and are, in fact, dependent on the *res publica*'s dominion over extra-Italian lands and subjugation of non-Italian peoples, *RR* 2 dramatizes the tension between the Romans' traditional identification with shepherd-farmers of a humble city-state and the "challenge" that Mediterranean empire and its attendant possibilities for possession of land and livelihood outside Italia presents to this ideology.[41] As I shall argue below, in highlighting this phenomenon, *RR* 2 not only problematizes it, but also rationalizes it within a technical discussion of *pastio* and, in so doing, implicitly proposes a "solution" to it.

## A VERGILIAN COUNTEREXAMPLE: GREEK SHEPHERDS IN A BUCOLIC ITALY

But let us turn briefly to another text in which there is, to borrow the oft-cited phrase of one scholar in another context,[42] a "pastoral masquerade" at

---

40. Cf. Steel (2001) 21–74, who explores the many ways in which Cicero exploits to his forensic advantage the challenge that residing—temporarily (e.g., Verres in his governorship over Sicily) or permanently (e.g., C. Appuleius Decianus in Asia Minor)—in a province poses to a Roman's identity.

41. It is worth recalling that, according to Varro (2.pref.4–5; 2.1.3–5; 3.1.7–8; cf. pp. 48–51 in chapter 2), the pastoral origin immediately gives way to a mixed agricultural mode of livelihood concomitant with the founding of Rome. The founding of the city thus "settled" the Roman *pastores* in the *urbs* and would have rendered them "settled" in their mode of life as *agricolae*. For the historical tensions between predominantly transhumant Italian societies like the Ligurians and (possibly) the Samnites (cf. Dench [1995] 116–25) with their more fluid conceptions of political boundaries, and Roman categories and conceptions of ownership and usage, which rigidly fixed boundaries and often privileged mixed agriculture at the expense of pastoralism, see Williamson (2005) 156–74. By virtue of their transmarine wandering across political bounds, the Epirotic Romans would almost seem to resemble migratory *pastores*; but if we understand Italia as the *fundus* of a mixed agricultural estate and the provinces as its pastureland, the Romans in Epirus actually contribute to the same mode of life originally established by Romulus and company—just now on a vastly larger scale. See pp. 159–60 in chapter 5 and pp. 231–36 in chapter 7.

42. So Reitzenstein (1893) 228–39 in describing the cultic outgrowth of the poetic coterie of Theocritus and his Coan compatriots from a group of herdsmen devoted to Artemis per Prolegomena B—an improbable account of the origins of bucolic poetry that is not to be factored into the present discussion.

play: Vergil's *Eclogues*. Critics have seldom read these texts in tandem,[43] a lapse in scholarly attention that is both surprising and not. On the one hand, the two texts do exhibit some overlap in content, as each concerns animal husbandry—albeit in quite different ways and to dramatically different ends. Moreover, the date of composition for each work is roughly contemporaneous, with most scholars dating the *Eclogues* (or, at least, the majority of them) slightly earlier (42–39 BC) than Varro's professed date of composition of 37/6 BC.[44] On the other hand, this oversight is unsurprising when we acknowledge the efficacy of the conventional scholarly binary of "literary" vs. "technical" in deterring substantive comparison of these two texts;[45] whereas the *Eclogues* tend to be understood as art for art's sake, which is "marred" only by the occasional (and still artistic) irruption of the "real" world into its fictive, (mostly) autonomous, and idyllic landscapes of otherwise pure poetry,[46] Varro's *RR*

43. Most approaches to the relationship between Varro and Vergil focus on the former's function as a source for the latter's *Georgics* and, to a lesser extent, *Aeneid*; see Salvatore (1978) and Kronenberg (2009) 32–33, esp. n. 111. A noteworthy exception is Leach's 1974 monograph, one aim of which is to demonstrate the thoroughly "Roman viewpoint" (23) that Vergil brings to the writing of his *Eclogues,* which she pursues through sporadic attention to the agricultural writings of Cato and Varro.

44. The traditional dates given for Vergil's life and literary career are derived from the scholiast tradition of Suetonius-Donatus and Servius. Beginning with Bowersock (1971) 73–80, there have been many (and often tenuous) attempts to date specific poems beyond the traditional *terminus ante quem* of 39 BC to the mid-30s. Cf. Clausen (1972) 201–5. For further discussion and bibliography, see Thibodeau (2006) 618–23 and Volk (2008) 9. Given these uncertainties, I have kept the traditional dates and framed my discussion in terms of an intertextual relationship, which does not assume one author's knowledge of the other.

45. More precisely, the prevailing twentieth-century mode of reading the *Eclogues* in highly formalist terms (often under the influence of the New Criticism) and vis-à-vis the so-called pastoral tradition has discouraged comparison with nonpoetic and, to a lesser extent, poetic works of "other" genres; see the invaluable discussions of Connolly (2001) 89–116 and Martindale (1997) 107–24. Cf. Hubbard (1998) 1–4. Such approaches tend to place particular hermeneutic weight on the poem's formal aspects and its engagement with the bucolic tradition: the setting within an artificial Sicily or Arcadia, the amoebaean structure of the shepherd's songs, the fundamental and pervasive analogical structure of the poetry, the created communities of shepherds convening in an ideal landscape, and so on. For a sampling of such approaches, see Snell (1953) 281–309; Rosenmeyer (1973); Schmidt (1987) 239–64; Gutzwiller (1991) 14–19; Alpers (1997) 79–93; Hubbard (1998) 19–44; and Rumpf (2008) 64–78. The result is that these poems are read as largely self-contained and self-referential poetic experiments within the "pastoral," or perhaps more accurately, "bucolic," genre (or "mode"). For two poles of the debate over the validity of "pastoral" as a historically accurate or generally useful generic notion, see Halperin (1983) 1–23 and Alpers (1997) 44–78. While I will speak of a "bucolic genre" in the ensuing discussion, I do so for the sake of simplicity and am fully aware that it may be more accurately described as a "subgenre" of ancient *epos*.

46. One recurring theme of Putnam's 1970 monograph is the nearly constant crisis in which Vergilian pastoral finds itself; see, for example (26): "To suggest in a 'bucolic' poem that there are opposing ways of life is to court disaster for the myth; to suggest that the pastoral scene is accountable to something else is to destroy it." Compare Leach (1974)

is relentlessly technical and practical—one might even say "georgic"[47]—and, therefore, the two texts are *prima facie* incompatible. That Vergil is, by most accounts, the greatest of the Roman poets, whereas the positive adjectives applied to Varro are more circumscribed and usually slightly backhanded, certainly does not help the matter.[48]

The differences that undoubtedly exist between the two works, their genres, and their authors may not, however, seem so vast once we acknowledge the similarities: like Vergil in his Roman-Italian reimagining of Theocritean bucolica, Varro actively engages with a prior tradition (i.e., agronomy), revises it for the Latin-speaking readership of his contemporaries, and fundamentally transforms it into a new form (i.e., the newly disembedded and theoretical field of *res rusticae*). Moreover, in a manner similar to the poet's occasional incorporation of the "political" into a traditionally apolitical form of poetry that is partly defined in opposition to epic, the agronomist intermittently implants the formal and generic elements of philosophy and satire, which encourages additional, specifically political, ways of reading the technical content. A comparative reading of the *RR* with the *Eclogues* will further show not only how the former appropriates and subverts bucolic conventions (perhaps a reflex of the parasitic nature of satire; cf. pp. 19–27), but also that both works respond—albeit in quite different ways—to a similar set of anxieties and concerns: in particular, each author uses the variously literal and metaphorical displacement of his *pastores* to symbolize his project, problematize its possibility within the late Republic, and, ultimately, reassert its viability within the tempestuous political conditions of the 40s and 30s BC.

As we have seen, *RR* 2 stages a *sermo* among wealthy Roman-Italian cattle ranchers, whose holdings and operations lie abroad in Epirus and who play

---

25–50: "Thus we cannot seriously complain of the interruption of pastoral tranquility, for disturbance is the ultimate justification of its existence" (36). For an intertextual approach to Vergil's use of Theocritean bucolic, see Hubbard (1998) 46: "even within Vergil's own work, this idealized Arcadian life of pastoral innocence seems evident more in its violation or transcendence than in its presence. Arcadia is simultaneously Vergil's own construction and an object of deconstructive counterpoint." Payne (2007) 166 observes that, in contrast to the purely fictional world created by Theocritus, which is thematized by the herdsmen's own fictionalizing songs, the *Eclogues* "fashion . . . a bucolic world that partially merges with the historical world, and whose legibility as an image of contemporary reality rests upon the visible presence of its author and his contemporaries within it."

47. For the antinomy between "georgic" and "pastoral," see Ross (1990) 59–75 (as well as the salutary counterpoint by Halperin [1990] 77–93). Cf. Rosenmeyer (1973) 21–26, whose designation of "Hesiodic" is roughly analogous to what others mean by "georgic." Cf. Halperin's definition (1983: 249–57) of the "bucolic" as a subgenre of *epos*, which takes its thematic, formal, and linguistic cues "oppositionally" from more traditional forms of *epos*, including Hesiod's mythological and didactic works.

48. Cf. n. 21 in the introduction.

at being Greek *pastores.* In these respects, the various sorts of displacement—spatial, temporal, and political—experienced by these elites afford them the *otium* to discuss animal husbandry and to enjoy the economic rewards of Roman *imperium.* The *Eclogues,* however, present us with a quite different image of *pastores.*[49] Taking his cue from Theocritus, Vergil frames the *pastores* primarily as shepherds and goatherds, that is, as the guardians of the smaller and, in a sense, more menial animals.[50] Thus, notwithstanding a few herders of cattle or an occasional other animal,[51] the primary identities of the personae in the *Eclogues* are, like those of Atticus and Cossinius, shepherds and goatherds. Unlike Atticus and Cossinius, however, whose *otium* consists of playing herdsmen on festal days and whose vicarious statuses as Faustuli and Melanthioi hinge rather on their ownership of sheep and goats and their use of others for the work of animal husbandry, Vergil's *pastores* themselves engage in the actual work of tending the very animals on which their daily livelihood would appear to depend and spend their *otium* in the singing of songs for songs' sake.

Yet, it is not just in the sphere of the work performed that Vergil's shepherds diverge from their counterparts in *RR 2,* for there is a clear disparity in social, economic, and even juridical status as well. Let us take the Corydon

---

49. In keeping with the conventions of the pastoral, Vergil never provides a formal introduction or convenient précis for any of the herdsmen who populate his poetic countryside, but instead offers us sporadic and accretive hints about each figure in the course of the poems, and only insofar as those tantalizing details have some bearing on the personae and the poem. The gradual and accretive unfolding of the bucolic world and its inhabitants shares some affinity with the Homeric practice of beginning *in medias res.* If Halperin's view of bucolic poetry as an oppositionally formed subgenre of *epos* is correct, perhaps this similarity is intentional.

50. In *Ecl.* 1 for example, Tityrus tends sheep (1.8) and Meliboeus tends goats (1.12–15), while Thyrsis and Corydon, the two *Arcades* alongside the banks of the Mincio in *Ecl.* 7, care respectively for sheep and goats (7.3–4). For additional examples, see *Ecl.* 3, where Damoetas watches the flock of Aegon's sheep (3.2–3), and Menalcas his parents' goats (3.8; 32–34); and *Ecl.* 5 and 9, where Mopsus (5.12) and Moeris (9.6; 62) each have goats (the animals of their respective counterparts, Menalcas and Lycidas, remain unspecified).

51. For cattle herders, see particularly Damon and Alphesiboeus in *Ecl.* 8 (8.2), but also the Meliboeus of *Ecl.* 7 (7.11). But see Coleman (1977) 211 for other, though less plausible, interpretations. To be sure, the identification of each persona is not strictly delimited to a specific type of animal, as it emerges in the course of each poem that several of these *pastores* also husband other animals or, at least, have access to them. Thus, we may infer that the shepherd Damoetas, in addition to possessing a goat stolen from Damon (3.17–18), owns some cattle from his willingness to wager a calf (*vitula*) in the ensuing competition (3.29–31). The cattleman Meliboeus of the seventh *Eclogue* clearly owns goats (7.9) and probably sheep as well (15). And it is likely that the lowly Moeris (9.30–31) and even lowlier Tityrus (1.9; 53–54; cf. 45) possess cattle as well as bees. As Leach (1974) 96 observes, "the majority of the persons in the *Eclogues* are not merely herdsmen, but cultivators as well," an estimation that is particularly valid for the dispossessed Meliboeus (1.70–73) and Moeris (9.3)

of *Eclogue* 2 as an example. In this poem,[52] which relates the shepherd's unre-
quited love for the boy Alexis, "the apple of the master's eye" (*delicias domini*;
2.2), Corydon addresses the absent object of his desire, cataloguing his various possessions and, in so doing, providing us with a fair number of details
regarding his daily existence. Contrasting the state of the countryside in its
repose from the swelter of midsummer's day to his own burning desire in
what amounts to a play on the "sympathy figure,"[53] Corydon laments that
Alexis never inquires as to "how rich in flocks I am, how overflowing in
snowy milk" (*quam dives pecoris, nivei quam lactis abundans*; 20), adding the
further boasts that "a thousand lambs of mine wander in the Sicilian mountains; I lack fresh milk neither in the summer nor in the winter" (*mille meae
Siculis errant in montibus agnae; non aestate novom, non frigore defit*; 21–22).
Changing his tack slightly, Corydon proceeds to imagine Alexis "inhabiting the lowly countryside and meager huts . . . and driving the drove of kids
with a green switch" (*sordida rura / atque humilis habitare casas . . . / haedo-
rumque gregem viridi compellere hibisco*; 28–30) with him.[54] He then returns
to his absentee wooing and ups the ante by promising the boy two roebucks
(*capreoli*) he has recently found (40–42) as well as the various flowers, nuts,
and fruits he could readily gather (45–55). But all of these vaunts, wishes,
promises, and flights of fancy are for naught, as Corydon abruptly realizes in
what may as well be the rejection of the would-be beloved, were the suitor
actually to articulate his desire to the boy: "You are a *rusticus*, Corydon" (*rusticus es, Corydon*; 56). Yet, as sun begins to set and the day draws to a close,
not all is lost, for despite his burning love and *dementia*, Corydon turns back
to his work and consoles himself with the acknowledgement that, should the
boy continue to spurn him, he will nonetheless find another Alexis.

In terms of its artistry, *Eclogue* 2 is an excellent example of Vergil's program of appropriating Theocritean and Hellenistic bucolic and transforming it into thoroughly original Latin poetry for a Roman context. To the
extent that Corydon is a thoroughly fictional composite of previous literary
traditions,[55] any reconstruction of his putative (read: non-) existence runs the

---

52. That the opening narrative turns out to be "spoken" by Menalcas of *Ecl.* 5—and not
"Vergil"—need not concern us here, though it is worth observing that this passage is symptomatic of the *Eclogues*' shifting identification of the poet with his herdsmen; see Putnam
(1970) 192, Hardie (2002) 21, and Payne (2007) 162.

53. For the "sympathy figure" in ancient bucolic, see Coleman (1977) 9.

54. Line 30 admits two distinct interpretations, for which see Clausen (1994) 75.

55. Vergil draws upon Theocritus's goatherd of *Idyll* 3 and famously love-sick Polyphemus of *Idyll* 11 as well as elements of the Alexis poem found in Meleager (*Anth. Pal.* 12.127 =
79 Gow-Page) to inflect the poem and its herdsman with a self-consciousness that transcends
its sources; see DuQuesnay (1979) 35–69 and Hubbard (1998) 54–68. In so doing, the poet

risk of stripping away his poetic vitality and of historicizing in a quite vulgar fashion Vergilian bucolic's world of imagination and art. But the comparison of a fictional shepherd with men who play at being shepherds in *RR 2* will prove illustrative for a number of reasons. First, if we take his claims at face value, Corydon's focus on the myriad of sheep and plenitude of unending milk he owns would seem to make him a wealthy man; in particular, a flock of one thousand sheep would put him far beyond the scale of any other *pastor* in the *Eclogues* and, indeed, even beyond the likes of Atticus and Cossinius, who, as the latter informs us (2.10.11), have flocks of, respectively, eight hundred and seven hundred sheep.[56] But it is not just a thousand sheep that Corydon claims to possess, but rather, a thousand *female lambs* (*agnae*),[57] which would make his flock larger than any found even among the represented *magnae pecuariae* of Epirus. Unless we are to believe that the shepherd is actually a Sicilian sheep baron, Corydon is clearly engaging in a bit of hyperbole, which can perhaps be chalked up to his Polyphemus-tinged "suitor's license"[58]—an interpretation congruent with the "lowly countryside" (*sordida . . . rura*) and "humble cottages" (*humiles casae*) that permeate his existence. To put it simply, Corydon is lowly, humble, and poor; by his own admission he is, after all, a *rusticus*.

Corydon's abject state may extend even to his juridical status, for it seems that he is a slave of the same *dominus* who resides with Alexis in the city.[59] On

---

renders Corydon a more sympathetic and humorous, and, at the same time, less pathetic, shepherd, whose poetic vitality lies in an exquisite balance between a charming boorishness inherent in his *carmen incompositum* and an elegiac suffering of hopelessness, which nonetheless does not render him absolutely helpless.

56. Cossinius is talking primarily about the ratio of shepherds to animals, which he fixes for himself at 1:80. Cf. Atticus's prescription of 1:100 at 2.2.20. The upshot of all of this for Corydon is that if he himself owns a flock of some thousand sheep, he would certainly need to employ (or own) some ten to twelve shepherds. For two landowners whose holdings would have dwarfed even Corydon's audacious claims, see Brunt (1975) 619–35.

57. As Hubbard (1998) 60 astutely observes, Vergil's reworking of Polyphemus's one thousand animals (Theoc. *Id.* 11.34) implies Corydon's shrewd appeal to "Alexis" sense of refinement and delicacy."

58. So Coleman (1977) 96 puts it.

59. Alexis is described as "the apple of the master's eye" (*delicias domini*; 2) and the genitive *domini* would seem clearly to refer to Alexis's master and to denote the boy's servile status. For *deliciae* as a term of erotic endearment often used by a master for a favorite slave, see *OLD* s.v. 3 and *TLL* s.v. II. A. Yet, as most critics interpret it, the lack of any qualifier for *domini* suggests that the *dominus* (likely named Iollas; cf. 62) was the master of Corydon as well; see, for example, Putnam (1970) 83, Clausen (1994) 62, and Van Sickle (2010) 80. For rejection of this inferred servility, see DuQuesnay (1979) 64–65, especially n. 221. Either way, as Coleman (1977) 91 observes, the "shepherd's plight is equally hopeless." The residence of Alexis and *dominus* in the city is reasonably inferred from lines 61–62; see Putnam (1970) 109.

this view, the *dominus* is an absentee animal owner and it is consequently *he* who turns out to be a vicarious *pastor* of a similar ilk to Atticus, Cossinius, and company. This interpretation also casts new light on the nature of Corydon's material vaunts, for it may not be the *quantity* of sheep that Corydon so much exaggerates, as the ownership—his word is *meae*, not *mihi*, as one commentator astutely observes[60]—to which he mendaciously lays claim. In other words, Corydon may in fact tend a flock (or, rather, part of one) that collectively comprises a thousand female lambs, but he does so only on the basis of his status as servile *pastor* under the dominion of his absentee and masterly "shepherd"/owner.

In the case of *RR* 2, it is worth observing that, aside from the aforementioned bantering of the interlocutors and brief remembrances of Faustulus and his foster sons, the term *pastor* nearly always refers to a *servile* guardian of a flock or herd.[61] Rather than reflecting any inherent semantic nuance of the word itself, however, the usage found in *RR* 2 most likely reflects the elite perspective and language of its cast of large-scale, absentee cattle ranchers, wherein *pastores* are tantamount to the very animals they tend and, like dogs and mules, comprise one-ninth of *res pecuaria* only insofar as they have some bearing on the produce/profit (*fructus*) seized from the other animals: either for the sake of that profit (*propter eam*) or derived from it (*ex ea*) (2.1.12). For Atticus and Cossinius, the upshot of this analysis is that the jocular figuration of each other as *pastores* is ironic as well, for it plays on the dissonance between their actual social and juridical status and that implied by the appellation of *pastor* as they would normally use it.

In the shepherds that collectively populate his *Eclogues*, Vergil thus presents nearly the inverse image of Varro's pastoral elite: rustic and humble, generally poor or, at best, of exceedingly modest means, and, as it turns out, not infrequently servile.[62] This, so to speak, "contradistinctive" relationship

---

60. Cf. Coleman (1977) 95–96, who rightly notes the implausibility of the care of a thousand sheep "even for use *precario* in gathering his *peculium*."

61. For the exchanges between interlocutors, see *RR* 2.1.2, 2.1.6, and 2.2.2. For the characterization of Romulus and Remus as *pastores*, see 2.pref.4 and 2.1.9. While the juridical status of the *pastor* is occasionally not pertinent (e.g., 2.pref.5, 2.3.5), it is generally safe to assume that the term itself implies the servility of its bearer. Cf. p. 71 in chapter 2 and p. 162 in chapter 5.

62. Insofar as his servile status is concerned, Corydon is not alone in the *Eclogues*, for Tityrus of *Ecl.* 1 was formerly a slave and is now a freedman, while it is not improbable that at least some of the other shepherds are (or were) are slaves as well. For example, Menalcas and Damoetas in *Ecl.* 3 are likely slaves as well; see Currie (1976) 411–20. As Clausen (1994) 44 notes, "for the most part, [Vergil] leaves the question of status, slave or free, vague so as not to disrupt the harmony of his pastoral landscape." One might, however, observe that the occasional inclusion of such details speaks to Vergil's inclusion of such mundane and "real" details as one of his signature contributions to the tradition. In the case of Corydon,

between the *Eclogues* and *RR* 2 is, however, not limited to the social and juridical statuses of each work's respectively fictitious and (largely) histori-cal personae, but extends to other elements as well. For example, in keeping with Vergil's poetic program of appropriating the thoroughly Hellenic bucolic world of Arcadia and Sicily for and within a Roman context, the convening shepherds and goatherds often either inhabit the countryside of Italy or evince an Italian character or disposition in some way.[63] But even in those poems in which the geographical location is either not so precisely imputed or stated, or in fact is said explicitly to be elsewhere than Italy,[64] other details—gods, trees, and dialect—contribute to the distinctively Italian character of Ver-gilian pastoral.[65] Yet, for as much as they may haunt an Italian countryside, evince Italian mannerisms, and sing in Latin, these *pastores* are not infre-quently beholden to Greek values and concerns—particularly in the erotic sphere, as we saw in the case of Corydon's desire for Alexis—and always bear Greek monikers.[66] Even alongside the banks of the Mincio, that most specific Italian locale Vergil proffers us, Meliboeus describes Corydon and Thyrsis as

his servility underscores his lowly, sordid lifestyle and perhaps adds further comedic and elegiac tinges to his *incompositum* pastoral song (cf. DuQuesnay [1979] 40–42 and Kenney [1983] 79–82).

63. A countryside ravaged by land dispossession would seem to point to northern Italy as the location of *Eclogues* 1 and 9: a supposition not the least prompted by the allegorical readings promulgated since Servius and, in the case of 9, seemingly substantiated by the explicit reference to Mantua and Cremona (9.27–28). In the case of *Ecl.* 7, Meliboeus relates the alternating compositions of Corydon and Thyrsis as he happens on them on the banks of the Mincio (13), a river that begins in the Alps and runs through Lake Garda to the Po alongside Vergil's native Mantua.

64. Such poems might include *Ecl.* 2, which is the only one set explicitly against the Theo-critean backdrop of Sicily; 4, which has no dramatic setting by virtue of its prophetic form; 6, which, in the words of Coleman (1977) 203, does not provide a "single evocative landscape"; and 10, which imagines love-sick Gallus on a sojourn in Arcadia.

65. The appearance of Greek gods found in the previous bucolic tradition (e.g., Pan, 2.31–33; 4.58–59; 5.59; 8.24; 10.26) is balanced by the sporadic appearance of thoroughly Ital-ian deities like Pales (5.35), Ceres (5.79), the Fauni (6.27), and Silvanus (10.25). See Coleman (1975) 61–62, whose estimation of these details as "intimations . . . of the life of the actual Italian countryman" perhaps goes too far in its claim. Perhaps the most visually striking of these Italian details is the proliferation of *fagi*, "beech-trees," in Vergil's bucolic landscape. As a native to Italy (and especially northern regions like Mantua), the *fagus* is neither in-digenous to Arcadia nor Sicily nor has a secure poetic lineage older than Catullus, another northern Italian like Vergil, prompting Ross (1975) 72 to characterize it as "the tree of the *Eclogues*." But see now the counter-suggestion of Lipka (2002) 133–38. Cf. Hubbard (1998) 48–49, who understands the *fagus* as a "conscious correction" of Theocritus's pine (*Id.* 1.1); the latter offers a "far from satisfactory . . . locus for pastoral music." For the colloquial tone to the herdsmen's language, one that is "redolent of contemporary rural dialects in Latin," notoriously subject to ancient parody, and perhaps evoked in Horace's famous estimation of the work as *molle atque facetum* (Hor. *Sat.* 1.10.44–45), see Coleman (1975) 59.

66. See F. Jones (2011) 89–91 for discussion.

"Arcadians both" (*Arcades ambo*, 7.4; cf. 26). Thus, one essential strand of the *Eclogues*' poetic conceit entails the transference of Greek shepherds into the rustic countryside of Italy. And it is also in this respect that the *pastores* of the *Eclogues* further constitute a near-mirror image of *RR* 2's Romans who play at being Greek shepherds in Epirus.

Comparative analysis of the essentially inverse relationship between the populated worlds of *RR* 2 and the *Eclogues* could easily extend to each work's formal properties and generic affiliations. Along these lines, one final point of comparison between the two works remains to be made: the way that each interrogates the conditions and the viability of its existence within the contemporary Roman world of the 40s and the 30s BC. In the case of the *Eclogues,* it has become a leitmotiv of modern scholarship to stress the complex ways in which these poems variously and self-consciously explore—indeed, even interrogate—the bucolic tradition in which they are situated: be it through the intrusion of distinctly non-Theocritean elements (like the world of Roman politics), the mapping of generic contours vis-à-vis other genres, or even the unbridled expression of a bucolic ideal so optimistic that it may ultimately be untenable.[67] It is not without reason, then, that more than one critic has discerned varying degrees of crisis in Vergilian pastoral;[68] by allowing all sorts of alien influences to encroach on his pastoral landscape, Vergil calls into question the genre's autonomy, which is a hallmark for any type of field, but particularly so for bucolic, which might be described ultimately as "song for the sake of song." On this view, then, it is the very essence of the *Eclogues*' generic manifestation that problematizes the notion of bucolic as a vital and viable genre for Rome of the first century BC.

The *RR* also responds to a crisis in terms of not only its generic and formal properties, but also its very content and project. Like the *Eclogues*' efforts to transfer Arcadian shepherds to and to habituate bucolic poetry within Italia, *RR* 2 also labors to renovate an old and traditional subject for a present-day audience of transformed horizons: in this case, an account of animal husbandry for contemporary Roman ranchers whose pastures are no longer coterminous with those of the *maiores*. For *RR* 2, this struggle manifests itself not only in the ludic figuration of displaced Romans at Epirus as both "Greeks" and "shepherds," but also in, as we shall see, the incorporation of

---

67. For Vergil's sporadic inclusion of the political world, see pp. 131–32 and nn. 45–46. For *Ecl.* 10's exploration of the bucolic tradition by means of its relationship to elegy, see Conte (1986) 100–129. Cf. *Ecl.* 6's engagement with the didactic tradition, another offshoot of ancient *epos*; see Clausen (1994) 174–209. For *Ecl.* 4's overly exuberant expression of a pastoral ideal, see Putnam (1970) 136–65.

68. Cf. n. 46.

still other generic elements—specifically, the multifarious threads of ancient *epos*—within the already hybridized text of *De Re Rustica.*

## *EPOS* AND THE TECHNICAL IN *RR* 2

We are now at a point where we may return to the exchange between Atticus and Cossinius in the company of the other Hellenizing Italians assembled at Epirus and grasp the way in which *RR* 2 interweaves the technical material with its generic dabbling in *epos*. Atticus's discussion of sheep, the "first-born beast" (*primigenia pecuaria*) that humans took possession of and tamed (2.2.2; cf. 2.1.4) and the first animal of the dialogue, initially sketches the desirable qualities or the felicitous conditions of the first four parts of *pastio*—age, *forma,* breed, and the legal aspects of purchase—in a quite straightforward fashion. Thus, one should purchase sheep that are neither elderly nor mere lambs (2.2.2); of the proper quantity and quality of wool (2.2.3); and of a good stock, which can be ascertained from the physical appearance of the ram and lamb (2.2.4). In keeping with Atticus's viewpoint as an owner—but not actual *pastor*—of sheep, the discussion of the legal aspects of the sale matches the length of the previous three *partes,* wherein he also provides some examples of the various factors to be taken into consideration (e.g., how lambs and elderly sheep are to be counted in the sale) as well as examples of the formulae to be used in the sale. In sum, the discussion provides an adequate, if cursory and somewhat pedestrian, overview of the main points to be considered in the pursuit of *fructus,* that is, the produce/profit that constitutes the *raison d'être* of Varronian *pastio.*

His ensuing four-part discussion of pasturage, breeding and rearing, feeding, and health, however, begins to take subtle, yet still perceptible, turns, encompassing a number of other discourses in the course of its otherwise technical overview. For example, after surveying the care of the sheep kept under cover in pens near the homestead (2.2.7–8), Atticus considers those that wander in "various places far and wide" (*longe . . . et late in diversis locis*) or, in modern technical parlance, that are subject to the practices of transhumance husbandry.[69] Presumably so as to combat the elemental and sea-

---

69. See White (1970) 306, whose account of animal husbandry remains strongly beholden to the Roman agronomists, especially Varro in this particular case. For the social and historical importance of transhumance pastoralism in Italy, see Gabba (1988) 134–42, though his views surely need to be tempered (cf. Thompson [1988] 213–15) and Frayn [1984] 45–65). Horden and Purcell (2000) 82–87, 549–52 is a valuable corrective to accounts of pastoralism and, among other things, differentiates between "horizontal" transhumance, which can involve the movement of vast quantities of animals over long distances (and which is presumably

sonal changes and conditions, these latter flocks, so Atticus maintains, are to carry with them "wicker-work and nets, by which they are to make camps (*cohortes*) in the wilderness" (*portant secum crates aut retia, quibus cohortes in solitudine faciant*; 2.2.9). Originally denoting the area to which a flock or herd was relegated on the farm (e.g., Cato, *Agr.* 39.1), *cohors* is the appropriate word for the sort of makeshift enclosures that shepherds might be thought to use while sojourning in the backcountry. Yet, it is precisely the ability of a *cohors* to organize a flock within a demarcated space that, as Varro observes elsewhere, informs its transference from the farm and, by 37 BC, more common application to the military world, which this use of *cohortes* undoubtedly evokes.[70] Indeed, the image of the flocks ranging back and forth over long distances from their winter quarters to their summer abode with pack in tow conjures up that of a Roman army on campaign: a personified group of wooly legionaries marching with a view to bivouacking at the day's end.

By virtue of the martial imagery, Atticus's discussion of pasturage so far smacks more of epic connotations than of bucolic ones. But flourishes of the pastoral world also emerge in the course of Atticus's account. Returning to those sheep that remain attached to the local homestead, Atticus focuses his discussion on the proper times of day to send out the sheep to graze (2.2.10–11). Unsurprisingly, the proper time is not fixed absolutely, but turns out to depend on the season and, more specifically, that time when the moisture and, consequently, the *iucunditas* of the grass is at its peak. On its own, this passage constitutes a commonsense approach to the pasturage of sheep and agrees with other technical discussions of animal husbandry as well.[71] Moreover, commentators on the ancient bucolic tradition have not overlooked this passage as a comparandum for similar sentiments in Theocritus and Vergil, citing it as evidence of bucolic's inclusion of the occasional realistic detail that contributes to the poetry's charm.[72] Yet, there may be something more to the otherwise practical instruction being purveyed here by Atticus. In addition to the succulence of the grass, so Atticus continues, attention must also be paid to minimizing the flock's exposure to the sun; consequently, shepherds

---

described here) and the more common form of "vertical" transhumance, which involves more local movements (usually from lower to higher pastureland in the summer) of smaller herds. Cf. n. 65 in chapter 3 and n. 41 in the present chapter.

70. See *Ling* 5.88. Cf. *OLD* s.v. *cohors*; *L&S* s.v. *cohors*; and *TLL* s.v. *cohors*. Note the similar multivalence of *cratis*, which can mean both "wickerwork" (i.e., a "hurdle" for building temporary structures) and a "fascine" used for constructing battlements (e.g., Caes. *BGall.* 5.40).

71. Cf. Columella, *Rust.* 7.3.23–25 (who intermittently quotes Vergil's *Georgics* 3.324–37 with approving commentary interspersed); Pliny *HN* 8.199; Palladius 12.13.5; and Flach (1997) 216–17.

72. See, for example, Clausen (1994) 37, 244, 275. Cf. Coleman (1977) 72–73.

are to drive their flocks in the summer's midday heat "under shade-bearing rocks and spreading trees" (*sub umbriferas rupes et arbores patulas*). Chiastic in its structure, this prepositional phrase resonates with highly poetic language redolent of the bucolic and epic traditions. On the one hand, the mention of the shade offered by rocks and spreading trees recalls the pastoral convention of herdsmen meeting thereunder.[73] On the other hand, the use of *umbrifer-* also marks the language as poetic, but its earliest extant appearances are in two of Cicero's poetic creations: his translation of *Iliad* 1 and the much-derided *De Consulatu Suo*.[74] Thus, this phrase invokes both ends of the *epos* spectrum: the trunk of its heroic tradition and the offshoot of its bucolic branch.

The inflection of the practical with the poetic continues in the ensuing instruction on the care of newly birthed lambs but takes an even more distinctly bucolic turn. As Atticus observes, a balance must be struck between ensuring that the lambs get their fair share of the mother's milk and protecting them from accidental harm inflicted by their ewes. The vocabulary and imagery throughout underscore the officious care (cf. *diligentia*; 2.2.17) that must be taken for these lambs, and verges at times on the precious: the lambs are to be delicately filled up (*satulli*) with milk (2.2.15); to be protected from harming themselves by their constant frolicking (*toto die cursantes inter se*; 2.2.16); to be weaned in such a way "that they do not grow feeble by longing" (*ne desiderio senescant*; 2.2.17) for their mother's milk; and to be driven out with the rest of the flock only when that desire abates out of their forgetfulness of it (*cum oblivione iam lactis non desiderat matrem*; 2.2.18). The use of the diminutive and the image of animals at play all have clear bucolic analogues, as do the senses of desire and loss, both of which are particularly suggestive given Vergil's inflection of bucolic with the elegiac in *Eclogue* 10.[75] Thereafter, the charming and bucolic tone of Atticus's discussion ceases and he returns to the more practical point of dividing up the new additions to the flock amongst the various categories of function (2.2.18–19): the rams and wethers, wool producers, ewes, milk producers, and so on. Health is treated only summarily and amounts to a restatement of Scrofa's previous theoretical instruction, namely, that the head shepherd (*magister gregis*) is to consult the pertinent written instructions (*scripta*; 2.2.20; cf. 2.1.23) that he apparently carries with him. With the final point, the aforementioned matter of the propor-

---

73. So Alpers (1997) 79–93. Note also the use of the word *patulas* to describe the tree; were we able to fix the priority of the *Eclogues* (as well as Varro's knowledge of them), we would almost certainly recognize here a nearly direct allusion to that work.

74. For Cicero's translation of a portion of *Iliad* 1, see *Div.* 2.63–64 [= F 23 Büchner]. This portion of *De Consulatu Suo* is preserved in *Div.* 1.17–22 [= F 6.73 Büchner].

75. Cf. n. 67.

tion of herdsmen to flock size (cf. p. 128), Atticus concludes his account with the guidelines that "basically all of us in Epirus" observe.

In this first part of the ninefold account of *pastio,* several observations stand to be made. First, by applying Scrofa's theoretical framework to the matter of sheep, Atticus has provided a synoptic, if cursory and somewhat superficial, account of the praxis of "shepherding" or, more precisely, sheep *owning.* In so doing, he puts the theory of *pastio* into practice and demonstrates its value as both an organizing principle and a framework for the contemporary owner of animals, whose needs for information and content are essentially managerial and, in this respect, relatively minimal in comparison to those of the actual *pastor* of the actual work. Second, in the course of providing this elite-focalized account of shepherding, Atticus switches between a number of discourses—military, epic, and bucolic—so as to inflect his technical overview with the now more pertinently elite spheres of war and poetic/literary production. Finally, insofar as Atticus's account simultaneously reflects the reorientation of elite perspectives and interests from the hands-on production of yesteryear to the ownership and vicarious management of the present day and renovates shepherding for the modern Roman elite, it is also emblematic of *RR* 2's account of animal husbandry (*pastio*) and, indeed, all of *De Re Rustica*'s treatment of *res rusticae.*

Despite his suggestions to the contrary, Cossinius's treatment of goats continues many of the same trends of Atticus's discourse. As we saw earlier, his initial words fashion both himself and Atticus as famous shepherds and, moreover, position his ensuing account of goats explicitly against his counterpart's treatment of sheep (2.3.1). Whereas Atticus's ovine bleating (*balasti*) would appear to have gone on for far too long (*satis*), Cossinius promises not only to speak briefly (*breviter*) on goats, but to do so in a way that is instructive of the brevity proper for his would-be Faustulian counterpart. His account thus purports to be didactic (cf. *disce*) in both content (i.e., goats) and method (i.e., "how briefly one ought to speak"). Against the backdrop of Atticus's pastoralizing account of sheep and the more general context of Roman elites playing at being Greek shepherds and goatherds, Cossinius's framing of his part in a competitive, almost agonistic, fashion evokes the bucolic convention of amoebaean refrain: the competing songs sung in responsion to one another. But in place of the aesthetic criteria to which Theocritean and Vergilian herdsmen (sometimes inexplicably) appeal,[76] Cossinius grounds his claims in the pragmatism of brevity and, in

---

76. See Henderson (1998a) 213–28, who finds that the value of the herdsmen's contest in *Eclogue* 3 ultimately inheres in the way in which it forces the reader to confront her own values, criticality, taste, and social judgment.

this respect, aligns himself with the poetics of conciseness, which Varro himself proclaims is the *modus operandi* of the *RR* at many points (e.g., 2.pref.6:
*qua de re pecuaria breviter ac summatim percurram*). Moreover, Cossinius
further underscores the antithesis between Atticus's garrulous shepherd and
his own succinct goatherd through his playful allusiveness to pertinent and
renowned mythic *pastores*—the adoptive father of Romulus and Remus in
the case of Atticus's Faustulus, the treacherous servant of Odysseus in his
own case—both of whom stand as ancillary, proto-bucolic figures within the
grander narratives of epic.[77] In this respect, Cossinius not only continues
Atticus's prior practice of inflecting his account with *epos*-related elements
of both the grand tradition of Homer and the oppositional bucolic strand of
Theocritus and his successors, but also functions as a programmatic spokes-
man for the *RR*'s technical poetics.

Simply on the criterion of length, Cossinius makes good on his promise
to be briefer than Atticus—his speech is roughly half as long as Atticus's—but
duration is not the only point of contrast, for goats, as it gradually emerges,
turn out to be nearly the polar opposites of sheep in many respects. Initially,
Cossinius's treatment of the first four points follows Atticus's comments quite
closely, and this brevity depends on his ability to refer back sporadically to
the ovine prescriptions of his precursor. Thus, one should obtain animals of
a proper, *fructus*-bearing age: neither too young nor too old (though the former, Cossinius states, just as Atticus had observed, are certainly better than
the latter). Like Atticus as well, Cossinius focuses on the physical characteristics, albeit adjusted so as to account for the difference in *genera* (2.3.2). It
is with breed, however, that the differences between goats and sheep truly
begin to emerge, for the seed of sheep turns out to be slower (*tardius*; 2.3.3)
than that of goats, which results in their respective states of quietude (*pla-
cidiores*) and of activity (*mobilius*). Cossinius proceeds to gloss *mobilius* with
*velocitas* in the following line's quotation of Cato's *Origines* [= F 47 Cornell],
which would seem to confirm that he is thinking primarily of their physical movements, but the ensuing discussion repeatedly makes clear that this
mobility also characterizes their mental states. Thus, in the case of sale, Cossinius chiastically observes that "no man, sound of mind, promises sound
goats" (*capras sanas sanus nemo promittit*), for goats are never without fever
(2.3.4). Perhaps this lack of *sanitas* stems in part from the possibility that

---

77. For Melanthius (and Eumaeus) as Homeric precursors to the herdsmen of Theocritean bucolic, see Halperin (1983) 224–27: "But by far the most important Homeric precedent for the encounter between Simichidas and Lycidas [of Theoc. *Id.* 7] is the meeting of
Eumaeus and the goatherd Melanthius in [Hom. *Od.* 17], which results in the first pastoral
competition in Greek literature—the exchange of insults between the two herdsmen" (225).

goats, unlike all other living beings, breathe through their ears—or, at least, so Archelaus and many "rather inquisitive shepherds" maintain (2.3.5). In terms of their physical and mental natures, then, goats are basically the antipodal images of sheep.

Other ovicaprine points of contrast continue to emerge in the remaining five *partes*. In the first place, while the process of feeding goats is similar to that of sheep, the place of pasturage is not, for goats favor forest glades over the sheep's preferred meadows (2.3.6). More fundamentally, however, whereas sheep are useful (*utile*) for improving the quality of farmland on account of their manure and are therefore to be led out onto it (2.2.12), goats, if given the chance, feed on the field's produce, their teeth are "hostile to planting" (*inimici sationis*), and, consequently, they ought to be entirely excluded from the field (2.3.7). The goat's fundamental lack of *sanitas* is reiterated in the eighth point's treatment thereof, and the master of the flock must consult his customary written instructions particularly for the inevitable wounds that arise from their customary infighting with their horns and pasturing in thorny places (2.3.8). Beyond the potential material damage and loss as a result of the antisocial tendencies and unsound feeding habits of goats, this lack of *sanitas* would also seem to infect even their owners, as the case of Gaberius may attest, whose purchase of a thousand goats for the sake of a large profit ended in disaster when disease wiped out the herd (2.3.10). In these respects, the spirit and, so it would seem, tenuous sanity of goats stand in antithesis to the characteristic docility and, as Atticus would have it, pastoral quietude of sheep.

Just as in Atticus's treatment of sheep, Cossinius's account of goats adheres to the ninefold schema proffered by Scrofa and exemplifies its utility as a framework for the prospective owner of goats. In terms of content, Cossinius does not ostensibly inflect his discussion with "other" discourses in the manner that Atticus did with manifold elements of *epos*. But his recurring musings on the unsound mental health and antisocial behavior of goats do pick up on the brief thread of personification found in his counterpart's treatment of sheep and, like Atticus's account, range outside the strictly technical world of *pastio* with a view to considering the interests, needs, and anxieties of the contemporary large-scale owner of animals. Thus, while goats are certainly different beasts than sheep and do present their own unique challenges in husbandry, the essential similarity in both method and perspective speaks to an essential similarity between Atticus and Cossinius *qua* elite cattle ranchers as well, and betrays a certain churlishness in Cossinius's attempt to distinguish his account from that of his counterpart. In this last respect, Cossinius may be understood to reengage in the bucolic masquerade of Atticus, playing the part of the truculent goatherd, whose claims to qualitative difference from the shepherd ring hollow to a literate, learned, and urbane audience. Thus, the figure of Cossinius ends up providing a marginally differentiated version of the renovated paradigm offered in the image of Atticus: the elite Roman owner of land and animals as a contemporary *pastor* in the provinces abroad.

# CHAPTER 5

# Provincial Pastures

## The Amoebean Refrain of Romulus in *RR* 2

Viri magni, nostri maiores, non sine causa praeponebant rusticos Romanos urbanis. Ut ruri enim qui in villa vivunt ignaviores quam qui in agro versantur in aliquo opere faciendo, sic qui in oppido sederent quam qui rura colerent desidiosiores putabant. Itaque annum ita diviserunt, ut nonis modo diebus urbanas res usurparent, reliquis septem ut rura colerent. Quod dum servaverunt institutum, utrumque sunt consecuti, ut et cultura agros fecundissimos haberent et ipsi valetudine firmiores essent ac ne Graecorum urbana desiderarent gymnasia. Quae nunc vix satis singula sunt, nec putant se habere villam, si non multis vocabulis retineant Graecis, quom vocent particulatim loca procoetona, palaestram, apodyterion, peristylon, ornithona, peripteron, oporothecen. Igitur quod nunc intra murum fere patres familiae correpserunt relictis falce et aratro et manus movere maluerunt in theatro ac circo quam in segetibus ac vinetis, frumentum locamus qui nobis advehat, qui saturi fiamus, ex Africa et Sardinia, et navibus vindemiam condimus ex insula Coa et Chia.

Great men—our ancestors (*maiores*)—not without reason did they rank the country-dwelling (*rusticos*) Romans higher than the city-dwelling (*urbanis*) ones. For, it is the case that, just as in the countryside (*ruri*), those who live in a villa are more slothful than those who are engaged on a field (*ager*) in some task, so too did they deem those entrenched in a city more slothful than those who inhabited (*colerent*) the countryside (*rura*). And so, they divided the year in such a way that they took possession of urban affairs on only the ninth days, and inhabited the countryside on the remaining seven days. So long as they observed this practice, they met both goals, namely, the maintenance of their most fertile fields by *cultura* and their own health, and they did not at all long for the city's

Graecian gymnasia. As it stands, one such complex is scarcely enough, nor do people think that they have a villa unless they keep it with many Greek names, since they call the places with distinct names: the ante-room (*procoetion*), gymnasium (*palaestra*), locker-room (*apodyterion*), colonnade (*peristylon*), aviary (*ornithon*), pergola (*peripteron*), fruit-gallery (*oporotheca*). Therefore, as it stands (*nunc*), the heads of households have basically slunk into the city—abandoning the scythe and plow—and have preferred to move their hands in the theater and circus rather than the cornfields and vineyards; and the grain-supply, by which we become full (*saturi*), we hire someone to bring it to us from Africa and Sardinia; and we store the vintage in ships from the islands of Cos and Chios.

—Varro, *De Re Rustica* 2.Pref.1–3

CITING THE *maiores'* greater estimation of rustic Romans, the preface to *RR 2* evokes the preface to *De Agri Cultura* of Cato[1]—that champion and, depending on one's own *existimatio,* innovator or outright inventor of the *mos maiorum*'s affinities for the *agricola*[2]—only to wryly upend it by tracing the supposed decline of Italian *agri cultura* through the infiltration of Greek architectural and linguistic units. With fields and vineyards giving way to the circus and theater, this Hellenic cooption has issued forth in the present condition (*nunc*) of Italian *patresfamiliae* wholly "saturated"—and rendered "objects of satire" (*saturi*)—by African and Sardinian grain and the vintages of Cos and Chios. Once a producer but now a consumer, Italia *qua* agricultural powerhouse—a felicitous vision seemingly shattered by the death of Fundilius at the close of *RR* 1 (cf. pp. 109–15)—would thus appear to have been put to definitive rest.

The sincerity of Varro's lament over the *luxuria,* moral decline, and loss of agrarian identity attendant to Roman *imperium* was never in question for Columella and, in fact, serves as fodder for his own rehashing of the trope of agricultural decline (1.pref.15–20). But one modern reader is almost certainly correct in pointing to the hyperbolic and possibly ironic rhetoric Varro heaps on this passage, which perhaps renders it as improbable as the *laudes*

---

1. Compare the weight that both Cato (*Agr.* Pref.1–4) and Varro (*RR* 2.pref.1–3) place on the "ancestors" and their greater estimation of rurally engaged Romans in terms of moral worth, physical/military fitness, and social value. Note, however, that for Cato it is specifically the *agricola* who merits the ancestors' *existimatio*, whereas Varro frames the claim in terms of the broader category of "country-dwelling Romans" (*rustici Romani*) and against "city-dwelling" (*urbani*) ones. In future work, I hope to explore the intriguing intertextual relationship between *RR* 2.pref.1–3 and *Agr.* Pref.1–4 more fully.

2. See, for example, Blösel (2000) 53–59 and Reay (2005) 331–61. For *existimatio* in *De Agri Cultura*'s preface and Roman culture more generally, see Habinek (1998) 45–59.

*Italiae* of the previous dialogue and potentially destabilizes all moral and intellectual signification in *De Re Rustica*.[3] Yet, for however much this passage may exaggerate the demise of Italian *agri cultura* and call into question such "partial and superficial understandings of the world,"[4] Varro's lament also provides us with a transition from the fields of Italia to the transmarine lands of Africa, Sardinia, Cos, Chios, and, in the case of the dialogue itself, Epirus. Moreover, although he deplores wholesale dependence on provincial produce in terms of its ill effects on the moral and physical status of imperial Romans, Varro's lament ultimately betrays that the Mediterranean provinces could (and did) spring up as greener pastures of lucrative agricultural and, as *RR* 2 explores, pastoral opportunities for exploitation. In conjunction with the previous chapter's examination of the Epirotic Romans as contemporary, Faustulean herdsmen of provincial pastures, this chapter explores the figuration of Varro and Scrofa as their Romulean counterparts, whose "husbandry" consists metaphorically of the control of subject humans in these same meadows. By analyzing the interdependent relationship between these two paradigms of *pastores*—both intratextually within *RR* 2 and intertextually with, again, Vergil's *Eclogues*—I argue that Varro's dialogue presents a model for Roman imperialism, which entails the exploitation of the provinces as not only literal, but also metaphorical, pasturelands within the Roman (e)state (*praedium*).

## SCROFA AND VARRO AS MILITARY HERDERS OF MEN

If shepherds and goatherds can serve as symbols for the contemporary, elite owner of animals in provincial pastures, swineherds signify a qualitatively different, though still related, paradigm of *pastio* in the provinces. Initially reinvoking the implicit distinction between the two groups of interlocutors—those "who depart[ed] . . . from an Italian port" (*quis e portu . . . Italico prodit*) and their Epirotic counterparts (2.4.1)—Cossinius turns the discussion over to Scrofa by helpfully anticipating the eponymous duty of the "Sow" to discuss *pecus suillum*. Rather than readily accepting his part (as Vaccius the "Cow-Man" will later do in the case of cattle; 2.5.2), Scrofa first feels compelled to dispel the company's ignorance of his name's origin (2.4.1–

---

3. See Kronenberg (2009) 101–2; cf. 106–7. For Wiseman (2009) 96–98, however, this passage "presupposes an earlier Varronian treatment of the subject, no doubt in the *Antiquities*," was "a reflection of his own family tradition," and attests to Varro's fervent belief that Romulus "had established the principle of equality at the very origin of Rome."

4. Kronenberg (2009) 102.

2). Contrary to what they might think, Scrofa's *gens* does not have a "piggish cognomen" (*suillum cognomen*), nor was he "born from a Eumaeus" (*ab Eumaeo ortum*). By denying affiliation with the loyal swineherd of Odysseus, Scrofa deftly invokes the most famous mythological *exemplum* of pig farming as well as the logical antithesis to Cossinius's treacherous Melanthius,[5] thereby resuming the ludic representation of the interlocutors as famous shepherds. Yet, in keeping with the dynamics of the dialogue's pastoral masquerade, Scrofa rejects that Homeric and Greek paradigm and, instead, offers his own, distinctly Roman origin for the name. As he recounts, his grandfather, while serving as quaestor to the absent praetor, Licinius Nerva, in Macedonia during the revolt of 143, marshaled the army in response to the enemy's uprising and, in his speech of exhortation, promised total victory "just as a sow (*scrofa*) scatters her pigs (*porcos*)."[6] The subsequent rout of the enemy earned Nerva the title of *imperator* and the grandfather the cognomen which our Scrofa carries as "no less than the seventh man of praetorian rank in [his] family." Whereas the Scipiones took the names of conquered lands, the Tremelii apparently settled for a barnyard honorific. Thus, Scrofa's recounting of his familial cognomen's origins constitutes a rejection of not only the Homeric prototype to which he might otherwise lay claim, but also, by virtue of its enshrining of his grandfather's military achievements, the bucolic strand of *epos* as well; after all, martial prowess has no place within the pastoral landscape and the swineherd has but a marginal existence amongst his bucolic brethren.[7]

While the Varronian Scrofa vehemently denies any swinish or Eumaean—that is, Homeric, "Greek," servile, and possibly ignoble[8]—associations with his inherited cognomen, Macrobius preserves a countervailing and decidedly less laudable aetiology. According to the early fifth-century AD grammarian, some slaves of Scrofa's grandfather killed a neighbor's wayward sow and, in an effort to conceal their furtive destruction of another's property, the grand-

---

5. Hom. *Od.* 15.403ff. Note also that the recurring Homeric figurations may draw inspiration as well from the relative geographical proximity between Epirus and the *Odyssey*'s setting on the island of Ithaca.

6. See Livy, *Per.* 53 and Eutr. 4.15. Cf. Perl (1980) 98–99.

7. The complete omission of swineherds in Theocritean bucolic and the sole mention of *subulci* in *Ecl.* 10.19 has prompted the alternative, but not-to-be-adopted, reading of *bubulci* by some scholars; see Clausen (1994) 299, who suggests a native Cisalpine inspiration ("where the oak forests produced a plentiful supply of acorns and swine abounded") for lines 19–20. Coleman (1977) 280 characterizes this passage as "deliberately prosaic" and "distinctly unpastoral."

8. Recall, however, that before Eumaeus was a slave, he was the son of a king on the island of Syria; see Hom. *Od.* 15.351–484.

father placed it under some blankets on the bed on which his wife was lying (Macrob. *Sat.* 1.6.30). When his neighbor demanded the sow's return and was conducting a search of Tremelius's estate, the latter pointed to his wife's bed and swore an oath that there was "no sow in his villa except . . . that one lying in those blankets." By means of this "most clever oath" (*facetissima iuratio*) Tremelius became the "Sow." Thus, Scrofa's compunction to peremptorily explain his cognomen and his prefatory denial of its swinish (and Eumaean) origin may testify to this tradition's existence in the first century BC and add another parodic layer to the *RR*'s multivalent representation of Scrofa.[9]

But whatever the actual origin of the cognomen may be, the aetiology Scrofa does produce nonetheless testifies to the potential of barnyard terminology to honor and to commemorate political and martial activity and, in so doing, to metaphorize it.[10] As "the Sow" who scattered Macedonian piglets, Scrofa's grandfather made good on his promise to exert control over those revolting subordinates of the Roman pen, thereby rendering himself the master of the litter. Thus, within *RR* 2's discussion of animal husbandry, the inherited legacy of the grandfather—as well as the political circumstances that have brought the scion to Epirus—aligns Scrofa with the figure of the herdsman, who oversees and controls the livestock under his purview, yet with one crucial twist: Scrofa is a *pastor* of men.

Although acknowledging his primary interest in *agri cultura* (cf. *agri . . . cultura ab initio fui studiosus*; 2.4.3), Scrofa (like his grandfather) refuses to flee (*defugere*) from the task at hand and agrees to speak *de pecore suillo* (2.4.2). After all, he rhetorically asks, "Which of us tends a farm, who does not have swine and who has not heard our fathers say that lazy and extravagant was he who hung in his meat-locker a slab of bacon from a butcher rather than from his own farm (*domestico fundo*)?"[11] Initially, his treatment

---

9. See Kronenberg (2009) 114 n. 15 and Nelsestuen (2011) 315–51, esp. 333–37. Perhaps the mention of Eumaeus, a character with a complex backstory as present slave, but former royal (cf. n. 8), slyly hints that there might be more to the origin of the *gens*'s honorific than Scrofa is willing to admit?

10. Cf. Kronenberg (2009) 114–16, who makes a similar point (albeit to different ends).

11. The full quote is as follows: "Quis enim fundum colit nostrum, quin sues habeat, et qui non audierit patres nostros dicere ignavum et sumptuosum esse, qui succidiam in carnario suspenderit potius ab laniario quam e domestico fundo?" This simultaneously ideological (e.g., the invocation of the *maiores* and their *existimatio*), intertextual (cf. Cato, *Agr.* Pref.2), and practical claim appeals to the reality that a self-sufficient *agricola* would likely cultivate pigs as a secondary source of livelihood (i.e., in a mixed-farming setting) and speaks to the continuing ideological importance ascribed to animal husbandry. The metaphorical context of Scrofa's swineherding statesman, however, perhaps encourages a political interpretation of the comment as well. If we understand *nostrum* not as a partitive genitive dependent upon *quis* (cf. Flach [1997] 240, who notes the extensive gap between the

of swine threatens to trump the conciseness of Cossinius, as Scrofa summarily dispatches the first four points in a way that still compares favorably with his predecessors. Thus, potential owners are simply to choose pigs of a good age (*bona aetas*), good physical appearance (*bona forma*), and good breed (*bonum semen*), with the latter two parts receiving minimal, though still functional, elaboration; a "fullness of limbs" (*amplitudo membrorum*) is the primary criterion for *forma* (2.4.3), while the quality of a breed is easily determined by appearance (*facies*), offspring (*progenies*), and region (*regio caeli*; 2.4.4). Under the rubric of purchase, Scrofa offers a sample legal formula and briefly notes the possible further stipulation of the herd's freedom from fever and diarrhea (2.4.5). Roughly one-quarter of the length of Cossinius's already compressed first four *partes,* the account of Scrofa would appear to be on pace for the *palma* of concise *res pecuaria.*

Despite this promising start, however, Scrofa's account over the next five *partes* (2.4.5–22) is increasingly marked by discursive meanderings, which tend to veer in two directions: the first practical, the second decidedly less so. On the one hand, he provides significantly more detail on certain points than is found in Cossinius's and even Atticus's corresponding treatments. This tendency is especially true of his discussion of feeding (*nutricatus*), in which he prescribes quite specific instructions for the care of newly birthed piglets (or *porculatio,* as he prefers to call it; 2.4.13) over precisely fixed periods of time. On the other hand, he repeatedly delves into matters that are, strictly speaking, extraneous to the conversation's technical program; while Greek and Latin etymological ruminations on the terminology of swine (2.4.9–10; 17), the historical role of pigs in various sacrificial contexts (2.4.9–10), and the portentous size of the animal and of its litter (2.4.11–12; 18) may be of cultural import or simply intrinsically interesting and thus offer a certain amount of pleasure to his listeners (and readers), these *miscellanea* would appear to have little to no ostensible bearing on the *pecuarii*'s practical pursuit of *fructus* through pig farming. In these respects, it is not without some irony that Scrofa—perhaps more so than any other interlocutor of *RR* 2—violates the bounds of his (own) otherwise rigorously defined, practically calibrated, and production-oriented ninefold schema.

The tension between the practical and the pleasurable that characterizes Scrofa's treatment of swine renders the man and his account emblematic

two words), but as an adjective modifying *fundum,* we might be able to interpret *domesticum* geopolitically, that is, as referring to the "homeland" of Italy. Could Scrofa's comment be thus read as an appeal to the maintenance of swineherding (perhaps military order?) in Italy? If so, interpretation of this oblique plea in the context of a dialogue so otherwise focused on the Mediterranean beyond Italy would require further explication than I can give here.

of the *RR* in terms of its generic nature—philosophical, satirical, and technical—and its approach to the subject matter of *res rusticae*. But lest we fall victim to vaguely characterizing Scrofa as "programmatic" of the work in which he figures so prominently, it is worth asking whether we can say anything more specific about him and his account at this particular juncture in *RR* 2. Given Scrofa's resistance to the bucolic figuration of the prior two interlocutors, his inherited legacy of military conquest, and the current political and military circumstances that have brought him to Epirus, it is worth asking whether his status as *pastor* of men informs, or somehow bleeds into, his account of swineherding. In the case of *nutricatus,* it would seem so. Stressing the importance of the swineherd's (*subulcus*) control of his animals, Scrofa goes so far as to claim that he "ought to train them to do everything to the sound of a horn" (*debet consuefacere, omnia ut faciant ad bucinam*; 2.4.20; cf. 3.13.1). The professed reasons for this practice include the benefits of orderly, more efficient feeding and the avoidance of losing pigs in the woods. But, on a metaphorical level, the use of the war horn (*bucina*) as well as the emphasis on order invests the discussion with a distinctly martial aspect. While the marshaling of pigs with a war horn may seem odd, the general practice is attested elsewhere, most notably in Columella's discussion of the management of cattle with a *bucina* (*Rust.* 6.23.3), which not merely implies, but openly asserts, an affinity with military protocol.[12] By virtue of evoking *res militaris,* then, Scrofa's discussion is thus also reminiscent of Atticus's previous representation of transhumant sheep as soldiers on campaign, with the *pastor* as commanding officer (2.2.9).[13] Yet, there is one crucial difference between Atticus's shepherd and Scrofa's swineherd: whereas the former model figured the Roman commander as the *pastor* of internal discipline, the latter provides a farmyard paradigm for Roman control over external, hostile peoples through military conquest. Unlike Atticus's beneficent shepherd, Scrofa's swineherd is decidedly more antagonistic towards his charges; notwithstanding this difference in orientation, however, both examples of herdsmen ultimately contribute to the representation of Roman commanders as the *magistri virorum,* or masters of men.

---

12. For Columella, the sounding of the horn prompts the cattle to return to their stables, whereupon the herd can be reviewed "within the stablekeeper's camp" (*intra stabularii castra manserint*) and "just as if according to military discipline" (*si velut ex militari disciplina*). Cf. Flach (1997) 263–64.

13. See p. 140. *RR* 3 offers another implicit representation of the Roman people as sheep. As Green (1997) 431–35 has astutely observed, the reference to maintaining sheep and birds at a villa (3.2.11) plays off the dialogue's setting, the Villa Publica; the context of the aedilician elections, the site of which was the Ovilia ("the Sheep pen" and a structure adjacent to the Villa Publica); and Appius's aviary of Roman birdmen.

One final image of a Roman commander as a herdsman remains to be discussed. Immediately after Scrofa finishes speaking and shortly before Vaccius takes his turn with cattle, Q. Lucienus briefly appears prior to departing with Murrius for a spell (2.5.1): "'Bonjour (χαίρετε), my fellow Epirotes (*Synepirotae*),' he says, 'For, Scrofa and my dear Varro, the shepherd of the people (ποιμένα λαῶν), I greeted this morning.'" Addressing the "Epirotes" in Greek, Lucienus then refers to Varro as "the shepherd of the people" (ποιμένα λαῶν) and thus employs "the usual Homeric address to kings and generals."[14] In this respect, the appellation reevokes the heroic epic tradition and aptly plays off the motivating context of the otherwise happenstance *sermo de re pecuaria*: Varro's service as Pompey's legate and commander of Roman naval forces. For one thing, the Roman naval forces of the late Republic consisted of foreign *auxilia* and were generally composed of conscripted locals.[15] While we do not have any specific evidence for the source of Varro's sailors, an inscription from Cos during the Mithradatic War (84–82 BC) some twenty years earlier provides a useful comparandum. Preserving the hierarchy of command for a Greek fleet in the service of Rome, the inscription (*IGRom.* 1.833) records that an Aulus Terentius Varro served as legate (πρεσβευτής) over a fleet captained by various Greeks and thus composed of local forces. Aside from this Terentius Varro, no other Romans are mentioned. Thus, while manned by Greek sailors and Greek captains, this Greek fleet ultimately remained under the command of a Roman admiral. Recalling Varro's formulation of the setting as "at that time when I was in charge of the fleets of Greece between Delos and Sicily in the Pirate War" (*tum cum piratico bello inter Delum et Siciliam Graeciae classibus praeessem*; 2.Pref.6), it is probable that Varro's stay on mainland Epirus partially entailed the mustering and outfitting of local ships and sailors, that is, "the fleets of Greece." In this respect, the Homeric appellation in the original Greek is especially fitting, for it not only continues the thematic connection between herdsmen and commanders, but even invokes the specific historical context that brought Varro *qua* "herdsman" to Epirus as, literally, the commander of Greeks.[16] Even more so than Scrofa,

---

14. So Ash and Hooper (1934: 364) have succinctly put it. For examples, see Hom. *Il.* 7.230 and *Od.* 4.24. Cf. the complete list in Flach (1997) 267.

15. For the reliance on locally commissioned fleets in the late Republic, see Saddington (2007) 201–2. As noted by De Souza (1999) 67, Pompey relied upon the Rhodians in this capacity; see Flor. 3.6.8 and *SIG* 749.

16. Interestingly enough, L. Domitius Ahenobarbus, the fellow Pompeian who famously raised a fleet at Massilia and opposed Caesar vigorously in that siege in 49 BC only to die subsequently on the fields of Pharsalus in 48 BC, apparently staffed his makeshift fleet with *coloni* and *pastores* from his estates (probably in Etruria); see Caes. *BCiv.* 1.56 and Brunt (1975) 621 for discussion. Note also that with the figuration of Varro as *poimen laon*, we may

then, Varro's status as herdsman stems from his mastery over foreign others: in this case, Epirotes and other eastern *auxilia*.

But it is not simply that Scrofa and Varro reduplicate the image of the Roman commander as *pastor*, for a further parallel exists between them or, more precisely, between Varro and Scrofa's grandfather, which is left for the reader to discern. Just as the cognomen enshrined the victory of Scrofa's grandfather under Nerva, so Pompey distinguished Varro's service in the Pirate War with the granting of a *corona rostrata* (Pliny *HN* 16.3–4).[17] The only other recorded instance of this award is Octavian's bestowal of the crown on Agrippa for his defeat of Sextus Pompeius the "pirate" in 37–36 BC.[18] Moreover, the future Augustus's notorious representation of this particular civil conflict (ongoing in various forms from 42 BC onwards) as a war with pirates and slaves—as well as the fact that at stake in both 67 BC and 37 BC was the security or control of the city's grain supply—further connects the two campaigns.[19] It very well may be that the composition and setting of *RR* 2 in the twin shadows of father and son's piratical activities constitutes some kind of political act by Varro, but any conjecture over what that act may mean is intractably hampered by our ignorance of which came first: Varro's composition of *De Re Rustica* (undertaken in 37 BC, perhaps completed in 36 BC?) or Agrippa's defeat of Pompey's son off the cape of Naulochus on September 3 in 36 BC. In any case, the likelihood that *RR* 2 silently alludes to the contemporaneous war with the "pirate" Sextus Pompeius by setting the dialogue during his own father's Pirate War adds yet another political dimension to the text's account of *pastio*.

We are now at a point where we may recap. As we have seen, by invoking various features of the heroic and bucolic strands of ancient *epos*, *RR* 2 presents an array of herdsmen figures with which the various interlocutors

---

wish to reconsider Scrofa's denial of the Homeric prototype, for it may not be so much the Homeric aspect nor even the Hellenic associations that prompt Scrofa's emphatic denial of Eumaean origins, but the decidedly unmartial implication that that swineherd brought to the table; were Scrofa more aptly cast as a Menelaus to Varro's Agamemnon, or a Eurylochus to the latter's Odysseus, perhaps he would not have protested so much.

17. Cf. Pliny *HN* 3.101 and 7.115. The precise rationale for this award is obscure, though the terrestrial civic and siege crowns suggest that the maritime honor commemorated either saving a citizen's life at sea or being the first to board an enemy ship; see Maxfield (1981) 74–76.

18. For the account of this incident, which was part of a series of measures undertaken by Octavian to raise troop morale and encourage loyalty, see Dio Cass. 49.14.3; cf. Verg. *Aen.* 8.684 and Serv. *ad loc.* Maxfield (*ibid.*) also observes that, while Dio and Seneca (*Ben.* 3.32.4) claim that Agrippa was the only person to have received the *corona rostrata,* there is no reason to doubt Pliny's testimony for Varro's recognition.

19. *Mare pacavi a praedonibus. Eo bello servorum.* . . . (Augustus, *RG* 25.1). See the notes of Brunt and Moore (1967) 66–67.

are affiliated in manifold ways. Though the representations of these shepherds, goatherds, and swineherds are neither constant nor uniform, all of these herdsmen figures—be they literal or metaphorical—collectively proffer two countervailing, though still related, paradigms for masters of animal husbandry: as large-scale owners of animals in provincial lands outside Italia, and as military commanders honored, enriched, and ennobled by their martial and political activities in those same lands. In both cases, elite Romans abroad play the roles of *pastores* in Mediterranean pastures. Thus, in addition to overlaying its technical discussion with a modicum of literary charm and play, *RR*'s bucolic masquerade provides a twofold renovation of *pastio*, in which the provinces serve as literal and metaphorical pasturage to be exploited in various ways by the contemporary Roman elite on behalf of the Roman estate.

## PAIRS OF PARADIGMATIC HERDSMEN: *ECLOGUE* 1 AND *RR* 2

In the previous section, I argued that *RR* 2 presented two *distinct* paradigms for elite Romans as "herdsmen" of Mediterranean pastures: as owners of large flocks in provincial lands and as commanders of armies abroad. Yet, this relationship of difference does not entail mutual exclusion; although their reliance on one another is not explicitly articulated in the course of *RR* 2, both the *pastor* of animals and the *pastor* of men require the other for the successful pursuit of their respective practices. Here again, Vergil—more specifically, *Eclogue* 1—proves instructive for explicating this relationship of interdependence as well as for gaining greater insight into the poet's transference of Greek shepherds into Italia and his project's possible bearing on *RR* 2.

Generally regarded as the most programmatic of Vergil's signature treatment of bucolic poetry, the first *Eclogue* presents the reader with an image of two "displaced" shepherds, Meliboeus and Tityrus, both of whom have recently experienced sudden and substantial, but diametrically opposed, reversals in their respective political and juridical statuses, material circumstances, and spiritual existences. In the case of Meliboeus, this free landowning citizen has just been dispossessed of his plot and must now leave the countryside to wander as an exile;[20] whether as a result of proscription or,

---

20. In keeping with Vergil's standard practice in the *Eclogues* (cf. n. 49 in chapter 4), Meliboeus's experiences must be inferred from the sporadic and accretive hints given over the course of the poem: particularly lines 1.1–5, 11–12, and 64–72.

more likely, due to mere confiscation,[21] Meliboeus's forced displacement from the bounds of his *patria* (cf. 1.3–4) and, as it turns out, concomitant loss of his status as *boukolos* thus also metapoetically symbolize Vergil's expansion of the bounds of Theocritean bucolica so as to incorporate—even to the point of being threatened by—the "external" world of politics and history. For Tityrus, on the other hand, the profound changes in juridical, social, and economic status are unquestionably more felicitous than those experienced by Meliboeus. Yet the *senex fortunatus* (cf. 46) likewise offers another paradigm of the "displaced" pastor: as he reveals, it was only through a trip into the big city and an audience before the *iuvenis* that Tityrus was able to secure his long-sought *libertas,* the usufruct (or outright ownership) of land he had once worked as a slave, and, perhaps most importantly, the bucolic *otium* that he now enjoys as a *pastor.*[22] Regardless of whether or not it is the Triumvirs' seizure of lands for reallocation to veterans (including, apparently, Vergil's familial estate at Mantua) that specifically underlies the widespread upheaval in the countryside (cf. *undique totis/ usque adeo turbatur agris;* 11–12),[23] Tityrus first had to experience physical displacement from the countryside into the city before he could enjoy his renewed commitment to the spirit, ideals, and *otium* of his bucolic brethren. As was the case for Meliboeus and his exile, then, the political world ends up being decisive—perhaps overly so—for Tityrus's pastoral existence.

Within *Eclogue* 1's depiction of "Greek" shepherds and appropriation of Hellenistic bucolic, the figures of Meliboeus and Tityrus present two quite different and, in many ways, opposite paradigms of *pastores* at the end of the Republic: the one free, but now dispossessed, abject, and a political refugee

---

21. For discussion of the two possible reasons for Meliboeus's dispossession—as well as the de facto "identical" result of each scenario—see Osgood (2006) 119–20. As Kelly (2006) 3 rightly observes, however, proscription fundamentally differs from exile (voluntary, statutory, or the closely related *relegatio*) in that the proscribed was a *hostis* ("public enemy") and remained so even after his physical departure from Roman territory.

22. For Tityrus's experiences, see *Ecl.* 1.6–10, 27–35, and 40–52. Many of the details of his trip, his manumission, and the injunction to continue his work require reconstruction and are inherently open to interpretation; for representative and useful approaches, see Leo (1903) 1–18; Williams (1968) 307–12; Putnam (1970) 43–45; Leach (1974) 120–30; Coleman (1977) 81–82; DuQuesnay (1981) 115–24; and Osgood (2006) 114–16.

23. From Servius onwards, such allegorical (and biographical) interpretations of *Ecl.* 1 (and 9, with its similarly dispossessed Moeris; cf. Hor. *Sat.* 2.2) have held various degrees of purchase among readers. The problems these readings pose remain well known and will not receive much attention here, though it is worthwhile to observe that they tend to identify Vergil with either the "mask" of Tityrus or of Meliboeus: an estimation that largely hinges on the critic's overall estimation of Vergil's political leanings or "mood." For useful explorations of these issues, see Hardie (1998) 18–20; Osgood (2006) 108–44, esp. 112–18 and 131–34; and Payne (2007) 159–69.

of some sort; and the other formerly a slave, but now manumitted, flush with material resources, and, at least to a greater extent than before the tumult, politically enfranchised. Yet, to insist on a stark distinction between the two *pastores* is to ignore the extent to which the poem relies on each figure for voicing and engendering the other's experiences.[24] Fleshing out each figure by means of the other, Vergil uses the dialogic exchange of the herdsmen to create a sum unity—greater than either one of its parts—of a bucolic countryside metaphorically and literally riven between its Theocritean roots and Roman-Italian graft. The interdependence of each paradigm extends beyond the poetic and metapoetic realms to encompass the material, historical, and political as well, for each figure's rural livelihood and pastoral existence (or lack thereof) ultimately depends on the city of Rome itself.[25] As we are implicitly told in the poem and as we explicitly know from other contemporary sources, the dispossession of some did in fact benefit others.[26] In this last respect, the exchange between Meliboeus and Tityrus also poses the question of whether the latter's good fortune comes at the expense of the former. Thus, the herdsmen essentially become ways to think heuristically about a series of binaries that held great purchase at Rome: the relationship between the city and the country, between the enrichment of some and the deprivation of others, and between the political and the poetic. Yet, in typically Vergilian fashion, *Eclogue* 1 offers no easy answers to these simultaneously historical and transcendental questions. The fact that there is ultimately no discernible trace of an invidious tone in the words of either the dispossessed or, notwithstanding his self-centered elation,[27] the newly enfranchised possessor, might be understood as Vergil's nod to idyllic relations between *pastores* caught up in a distinctly nonbucolic situation.

---

24. Note that it is Meliboeus who describes, even creates, the pastoral existence of, or better, *for* Tityrus (1.46–58), while it is Tityrus's virtuosic *adynata* (59–63) that presage Meliboeus's pitiable lament of his and his fellow exiles' extravagant wanderings (64–78), which constitutes the poem's climax.

25. See Putnam (1970) 20–81, who views the disparate situations of the two herdsmen as symbolizing the duality of Rome, which both provides succor to the poet and his pastoral life of the mind and destroys it (61): "Both the pain [of Meliboeus] and the happiness [of Tityrus] are caused by Rome."

26. This point tends to be fundamentally obscured by modern scholarship's heavy reliance on the memorable (and lamentable) literary depictions of dispossession. See the nuanced discussion of Osgood (2006) 126–31, 137–40, who adduces epigraphic evidence that attests to the gratitude of the triumvirs' veterans for the improvement of their material lot and subsequent prosperity.

27. For the argument that Tityrus is ultimately "drawn out of his complacency and self-absorption by the beautiful song" of Meliboeus, which prompts the former's closing offer of one last night's hospitality (79–83)—an act of "newfound pastoral generosity"—see Perkell (1990) 171–81.

In terms of presenting dual paradigms of *pastores, Eclogue* 1 offers up an instructive model for understanding the two paired paradigms found in *RR* 2—albeit in different terms and to quite different ends. In place of humble Greek shepherds inhabiting an Italian countryside, *RR* 2 presents the Epirotic Roman ranchers as the living exempla of the sorts of commercial and economic opportunities inherent in provincial animal husbandry, while the sojourning commanders of Scrofa and Varro embody the militaristic side of those figurative opportunities. Moreover, like the poetic and material codependence of Tityrus and Meliboeus, the very existences of the ranchers and commanders turn out to be mutually implicated as well; whereas the ranchers are dependent on Roman political and military supremacy for the security of their estates and operations, the commanders "rely" on the provinces for the honor and glory that provide fodder for their ambitions and, in the case of Scrofa, his eponymous patrimony. Roman reliance on provincial exploitation extends also to its material livelihood, for the city of Rome itself had come to count on its Mediterranean possessions. Not only had the provinces' imported wine and grain come to supplement or, as the preface to *RR* 2 hyperbolically claims, to supplant Italian foodstuffs, but Romans also relied on their wealth, manpower (primarily in the form of cavalry and naval *auxilia*), and even, as we shall see in the next section, superior breeds of animals.

Like Vergil's first *Eclogue*, Varro's *RR* 2 presents an internal pair of paradigms, each of which is distinct from, yet still in some sense complicit with, its antithetical counterpart. I would like to conclude this section with two broader comparative observations concerning these two roughly contemporaneous texts. First, just as Vergil's bucolic world incorporates the political, so Varro's technical dialogue dabbles in the poetic and the bucolic. In this respect, each text is indicative of the sort of literary creativity and generic experimentation already burgeoning in the late Republic and coming to fruition in the Augustan period. Second, while both texts are thematically interested in a poetics of displacement, there remains a profound difference in orientation between the two; whereas Vergil transfers his harried Greek shepherds into a vaguely contemporary, yet still sublimely imprecise setting, Varro quite explicitly relocates his elite discussants to a previous and precise time when Romans—*qua* ranchers and campaigners—were shepherding the provincial lands of the Mediterranean and *not* the Italian homestead. In these respects, the dialogic conceit of *RR* 2 avails itself of the bucolic world, inflects it with the various epic resonances I traced above, and resituates that world in the geographically and temporally specific locale of Roman Epirus in 67 BC. Varro thus endows his dialogue with a simultaneously historicizing

and idealizing veneer, which, unlike the idyllic worlds of Theocritean and
to a lesser extent Vergilian bucolic, both evokes a particular historical past
and specifically echoes contemporary experience. In this way, he stages a
normative and prescriptive drama *of* and *for* literal and metaphorical animal
husbandry, in which provincial pastures and Italian farmland were not yet
being confused to the extent that Varro would claim them to be (2.pref.4)
against the chaotic backdrop of the 40s and 30s BC.

## ANIMAL HUSBANDRY IN PROVINCIAL PASTURES

From a historical perspective, the conceit of the dialogue's representation of
the interlocutors as "herdsmen" abroad relies on Roman domination of other,
non-Roman-Italian peoples in the Mediterranean. From an ideological perspective, however, the intelligibility and normativity of this association of animal husbandry with military prowess and political supremacy hinge also on
the exemplum of Romulus as the shepherd-cum–warrior king who founded
Rome and expanded its boundaries through aggressive military action. By
displacing this traditional paradigm across the sea—to areas outside Italy and
yet still under Roman *imperium*—Varro renovates the venerable profession of
Romulus for the greatly expanded world of first-century BC Rome, whose citi-
zenry now hails from a whole peninsula and whose power has come to span
the entire Mediterranean. The characters of Scrofa and Varro thus emerge as
contemporary *pastores* of a Mediterranean *empire*, whose tending of herds
of non-Italian peoples concurrently renders this provincial periphery as the
"pastureland" of Rome's imperial estate (*praedium*). At the same time, relocating this potentially bellicose form of animal husbandry from the confines
of the Italian agricultural *fundus* to the fields of the provinces also removes
the Romulean *pastor* from the recently unified geographical and juridical
totality circumscribed by the straits of Messina, the foothills of the Alps, and
the Tyrrhenian and Adriatic Seas;[28] after all, although the "alliance" (*societas*)
between *pastio* and *agri cultura* may be great (*magna*) and "he who owns an
estate (*praedium*) ought to have knowledge of each *disciplina*" (2.pref.5), it
is the descendants of the city's founders—and *not* those original shepherd-

---

28. Note that this prescriptive and mixed-agricultural vision of *res rusticae* (cf. n. 41 in
chapter 4) may also mystify centuries of Roman-Italian conflict over the control of pastures
and arable lands throughout the peninsula and seek, in a sense, to "reconcile" the historically tenuous relationship between farmers and herders by largely removing the latter from
the bounds of Italia. For the recurring conflicts over the control of pasturelands and arable
fields (esp. the Samnite Wars) in the middle and late Republic, see Skydsgaard (1978) 7–36.
For the relatively recent "unification" of Italia, see pp. 73–75 in chapter 3.

farmers—who converted fields (*segetes*) into pastures (*prata*) on account of *avaritia*, in contravention of law, and out of ignorance of the difference between the two forms of *res rusticae* (2.pref.4).

Yet, as we have also seen, *RR* 2 is a technical discussion of actual *pastio* on actual pastures, and this final section thus considers how the text exemplifies nonmetaphorical *pastio*—the literal art of husbanding animals with a view to gleaning profit—in these changed geopolitical conditions of the late Republic. Unsurprisingly, the various local cattle enterprises of the Epirotic Romans provide the most visible evidence for such *pastio*. As we saw earlier, both Atticus and Cossinius are wont to adduce their own flocks and herds as models for various aspects of *pastio,* and this penchant for exemplification through personal experience is common to Vaccius, Lucienus, and Murrius as well.[29] As counterparts to the neo-Romulean Scrofa and Varro, whose status as shepherds stems from military control of non-Romans, the *Synepirotici* instead hold sway over the region via their extensive cattle holdings. Unlike Faustulus, however, their status as *pastores* rests somewhat vicariously on their ownership of animals and, far from being directed towards the procurement of daily sustenance, the concerns of these herdsmen instead turn on the profitability of their herds. And perhaps even more crucially, by employing subjugated labor in the form of slaves on pasturelands outside Italy, these contemporary *pastores* of Roman *imperium* exploit the material rewards of empire for their alienated and distinctly non-subsistent interests. Somewhat ironically, then, the Epirotic Romans, like their martial counterparts, end up treating humans like animals, and it is this willingness to construe humans as one part of *pastio* (2.10.1ff.; cf. 2.1.12) that enables Atticus, Cossinius, and company to play their neo-Faustulean parts as herdsmen of provincial pastures.

The dialogue's dramatization of the new opportunities for *pastio* abroad transcends its displacement from Italy and its physical setting in Epirus to embrace as well the entire Mediterranean within the *sermo*'s geographical scope. Unlike the *RR*'s first and third books, which have a decidedly Italian focus in terms of geographical exempla, Book 2 evinces a distinctly pan-Mediterranean one with respect to both quantitative and qualitative metrics. In appendix 5, I have compiled a list of all spatial references in *RR* 2.[30] Of the 164

---

29. The complete list of interlocutors' appeals to personal practice is as follows: Varro's flocks of sheep, 2.2.9; Atticus's flocks of sheep, 2.2.20; Cossinius's, Menas's, and Murrius's herds of goats, 2.3.10; Scrofa's pigs, 2.4.3; Vaccius's and Atticus's herds of cows, 2.5.12; Vaccius's, Atticus's, and Lucienus's herds of cows, 2.5.18; Murrius's drove(s) of donkeys, 2.6.1; Lucienus's and Atticus's herds of horses, 2.7.1; Murrius's mules, 2.8.3; Varro's mules, 2.8.6; and Cossinius's and Atticus's flocks of sheep, 2.10.10–11.

30. For its principles of organization, see n. 61 in chapter 3.

references to places in the dialogue, only 53 refer to Italian regions or cities and 19 to Italia itself. Of the other 92 references, roughly two-thirds (62) are to the Greek east and the remaining one-third (30) to non-Italian, non-Greek areas, such as Spain and Syria. To put these numbers in percentages, roughly 44 percent of the examples come from Italia, while the other 56 percent come from the rest of the Mediterranean. When compared to Book 1's composition—66 percent Italian, 34 percent non-Italian—the quantitative difference in the distribution of *RR 2*'s geographical exempla clearly underscores the dialogue's greater focus on *pastio transmarina*. Thus, just as the spatial examples employed in *RR 1* connect the dialogue's setting with its thematic emphasis on Italian agriculture, so the second dialogue—located abroad and during Rome's bid to solidify its mastery of the Mediterranean and its coasts—associates *pastio* with its transmarine spatial bearing.

If we turn from quantitative to qualitative analysis, the situation becomes a bit more complex—not least because the ideological relevance of *pastio* to Rome itself preempts a wholesale connection of animal husbandry with regions outside of Italy but under Roman *imperium*. In what follows, I will explore two partially overlapping spatial patterns evident in the dialogue. The first involves those passages that evince a preference for some aspect of non-Italian *pastio*, a trend that runs counter to the apparent Italian superiority in all things agricultural. The second pattern entails the comparative evaluation of non-Italian and Italian practices. When taken in conjunction with the dialogue's general emphasis on the transmarine territories, these two patterns point to the renovation of *pastio* for the late Republican Roman "shepherd," whose accessible pastures included, if not in point of fact, then certainly symbolically, the entire Mediterranean world.

In contrast to Book 1's insistence on the agricultural preeminence of Italia, *RR 2* will readily acknowledge the superiority of non-Italian regions for *pastio*. In part, this trend may be a consequence of empirical observation and actual experience. For example, despite his earlier appeal to the *maiores* for the moral import and economic thrift of producing homegrown pork (*succidiam . . . e domestico fundo*; 2.4.3), Scrofa acknowledges that "the Gauls generally produce the best and largest slabs. . . . [which is reflected] in the fact that even now forequarters from Comaci and haunches from Cavari are imported each year from Gaul to Rome" (2.4.10).[31] Elsewhere, the interlocutors will acknowledge a particular region's superior breed of animal. Thus, after observing that "it matters in what regions cattle are born," Vaccius proceeds to claim that, "within Italy" (*in Italia*), the Gallic breed is superior in

---

31. The Comaci and Cavari are both tribes located in Gallia Narbonensis (Pliny *HN* 3.5).

terms of work capacity to their Ligurian counterparts,[32] but that "the foreign
(*transmarini*) cattle of Epirus are not only the best of all Greece, but even
better than the ones of Italy" (2.5.9–10). Vaccius thus implicitly establishes
a threefold tier of cattle breeds: the Greek-Epirotic kind at the top and the
Italian-Ligurian at the bottom. What goes unmentioned, however, is that
Roman *imperium* has unfettered the contemporary *pastor*'s knowledge of,
and access to, all three breeds. Indeed, unlike *agri cultura* (the quality of
which intrinsically stems from the region's *caelum* and *terra*; 1.4.1–4), *pastio*
is not so inextricably tied to land; after all, animals can—indeed, *must*—be
moved from one location to another, and with few apparent consequences.[33]
While these examples suggest that we are far from the world of *RR* 1, where
Italy's excellence in *agri cultura* innately flourishes with unmatched fecundity, they also attest to the pastoral possibilities offered by Roman control of
the Mediterranean. Gone are the days when one had to rely solely upon the
household pigs for middling bacon or inferior domestic cattle for fieldwork.
Indeed, even the need to husband one's own animals has been rendered
obsolete by the advent of slave herdsmen (2.10.1–11), who turn out to be tantamount to the very animals they themselves tend. Perhaps unsurprisingly,
the *RR* does not entertain the possibility of "herds" of Italian slaves; instead,
as Cossinius asserts, the slaves most "suited for engaging in *res pecuariae* are
neither Bastulan nor Turdulan," but Gallic, while Illyrican women "in many
regions do not yield to the men in terms of work" (2.10.7). In short, Mediterranean pastures under Roman control are expansive, varied, and teeming
with potential utility (*utilitas*) and produce (*fructus*) for the contemporary
*pastor*.

One further instance of this pattern will suffice, for it neatly illustrates
both the new scope of these possibilities within Roman *imperium* and the
dialogue's penchant for blurring the lines between literal and metaphorical
interpretation. According to Scrofa (2.4.11–12), a certain Atilius, "a Spaniard
hardly deceitful and learned in many things," used to tell a story about a

---

32. Whether they are imported from Transalpine Gaul, bred from Gallic stock, or native to some part of Cisalpine Gaul remains unclear (although the implicit contrast between
"*in Italia*" and "*transmarini*" testifies to the probability of the last interpretation). Cf. n. 82
in chapter 3. For the diminutive size of Ligurian cattle, see Columella, *Rust.* 3.8.3 and Flach
(1997) 281.

33. The dialogue does not explore the impact of variations within regional microclimates
on the raising of animals in any systematic or comprehensive way, though the interlocutors will occasionally acknowledge the impact that an area may have on the animals, as, for
example, in the case of Atticus's injunction to use the same water source for a herd on the
grounds that change (*commutatio*) can render the wool spotted (*varia*) and harm the uterus
(2.2.14). For transhumance, which can be practiced on both long and short ranges, see p. 94
and n. 65 in chapter 3 and nn. 41 and 69 in chapter 4.

massive piece of bacon (roughly twenty-three pounds) sent to the senator L. Volumnius from a sow slaughtered in Lusitania (i.e., in Hispania Ulterior). There is little historical evidence for Volumnius and, apart from this reference, none for Atilius and the Lusitanian sow,[34] but Volumnius's senatorial status implies that he either served as some magistrate of the region or, at the very least, had some form of patron-client relationship with it.[35] Whatever the case may be, the story of the Lusitanian sow does not merely provide pleasure, for it exemplifies the potentially wondrous size of produce to be found in provincial pastureland and also insinuates the way in which imperial control or even informal political influence over a region could constitute a new, in this case, metaphorical, form of *pastio*. Like Scrofa's eponymous grandfather, the case of Volumnius illustrates the beneficial impact of transmarine Roman *imperium* on swineherding for the state; unlike the public dividends procured by the former, however, a twenty-three-pound slab of pork would only have filled the senator's private larder.

The second pattern within the dialogue's geographical exemplification involves the recurring comparison of non-Italian examples with Italian ones. Some of these comparisons are quite brief and unremarkable, like the one concerning the length of sheep's tails, which are apparently long in Italy but short in Syria (2.2.3). For this reason, I focus on three prominent examples, the first two of which occur once again in the discussion of bacon. After stating the superiority of Gallic slabs, Scrofa provides two other examples, taking care to cite his sources for each one. The first comes in the form of a quotation from Cato's *Origines,* which, as Scrofa formulates it, is meant to buttress his earlier claim of the massive size of Gallic slabs, but frames the credit in terms of the "Insubrians in Italy" (2.4.11). Ethnically Gallic, the Insubrians were a subalpine tribe in northern Italy,[36] which makes it slightly unclear as

---

34. For the problems with identifying these figures and this episode, see Flach (1997) 251–52. In the case of L. Volumnius, the only other piece of evidence comes from an oblique reference in Cic. *Fam.* 132 [= 7.32]. Cf. *MRR* 2.498. The suggestion of Fear (1996) 48 that this Atilius Hispaniensis was a wealthy Roman émigré—"a gentleman farmer with interests in amateur scholarship; just the kind of man that Varro would have associated with when he was governor of Ulterior"—cannot be corroborated any further, but remains intriguing and, if true, adroitly complements the expatriate(d) theme of *RR 2*. On the other hand, the description of Atilius as "hardly deceitful" (*minime mendax*) may not inspire confidence in the man's existence and story for those who privilege irony in reading the *RR*.

35. On the basis of the dialogue's date, Flach (1997) 252 speculates that he could have served under Pompey in the latter's campaign against the rebel Sertorius in the 70s BC. For the potential revenue through gifts and bribes a Roman elite might gain from a magisterial relationship with a provincial area, see Shatzman (1975) 53–55; cf. 59.

36. See F 48 Cornell [= F 2.11 Jordan = F 39 Peter]. Note that the Insubrians only received Roman citizenship in 49 BC, which means that they were neither citizens in Cato's day nor

to whether or not this particular quotation simply reinforces Scrofa's previous claim, or provides some Italian counterbalance to the Gallic superiority in pork production, or perhaps even accomplishes both ends simultaneously. The subsequent example—Atilius's aforementioned case of Volumnius's pork barrel in Spanish Lusitania—is then followed by a more unequivocal illustration of this principle in the form of Varro's interjection. After relating his observation of an Arcadian sow so fat that a mouse burrowed into her side, built a nest, and reared its offspring, Varro concludes that it was "a thing I heard happened in Venetia also" (*hoc etiam in Venetia factum accepi*; 2.4.12). Gallia Narbonensis, the Italian Alps, Lusitania, Arcadia, and finally Venetia (in Transpadane Italia)—the world of porcine *mirabilia* is much larger and more varied than one might suspect. Yet, the relative balance between non-Italian (three) and Italian (two) regions testifies to *RR* 2's ongoing concern with supplementing its broader Mediterranean focus with a few *exempla* closer to the Roman-Italian homestead.

The most memorable example, however, is to be found in the thrice-repeated comparison of Arcadia and Reate. In Scrofa's opening exposition of the eighty-one-fold nature of *pastio,* his insistence on the importance of breed chiastically appeals to the *nobilitas* that Arcadian asses have in Greece, in Italy those of Reate (*Arcadici in Graecia nobilitati, in Italia Reatini*; 2.1.14).[37] Later, Murrius—a self-proclaimed Reatinian by birth (2.6.1), but an Epirote in terms of estate ownership and residence (cf. 2.4.1)—reiterates this claim in his treatment of *pars asinaria*; Peloponnesians prefer to buy from Arcadia, whereas Italians look to Reate (2.6.2). But his claim to have actually sold Reate-bred asses to Arcadians asserts the absolute superiority of the Italian breed (2.6.1)—the only such instance in *RR* 2. In case his audience missed it the first time, Murrius further underscores this bold contention in his subsequent discussion of the importance of the donkey's breed when siring a mule (2.8.3):

> Qui non habent eum asinum, quem supposuerunt equae, et asinum admissarium habere volunt, de asinis quem amplissimum formosissimumque possunt eligunt quique seminio natus sit bono, Arcadico, ut antiqui dicebant, ut nos experti sumus, Reatino. . . .

---

probably even considered "Italian" at that time; whether or not the character of Scrofa recognizes this historical difference in perspective remains an open question. For discussion of the textual and interpretative problems, see Cornell (2014) 3.94–95.

37. Cf. Kronenberg (2009) 114–15, who interprets this passage (among others) as indicative of *RR* 2's implicit "equation between ruling people and herding animals."

Those who do not have a donkey, which they have suckled at a mare, and wish to have a stud-ass, should select from the sturdiest and most comely asses they can, one which is born of a good seed: the Arcadian, as the ancients used to say, but as we have found, the Reatinian. . . .

Invoking the importance of breed and physical appearance as markers of quality studs,[38] Murrius extends the superiority of Reatinian donkeys to the sphere of mules (i.e., the offspring of a jack donkey and a mare). Interestingly enough, Murrius's claim that he and his contemporaries have found (*nos experti sumus*) that the Reatinian asses are better than Arcadian ones preferred by the ancients (*antiqui*) recalls one of Scrofa's programmatic methodological claims in the previous dialogue; whereas the "most ancient farmers" (*antiquissimi agricolae*) used their own trial and error (*experientia*) and their descendants followed suit in *imitatio,* contemporary farmers ought to employ a combination of the two methods according to "some system" (*ratio aliqua*) and not by chance (*alea*) (1.18.7–8; cf. 1.7.6). In the case of asses and mules, then, *experientia* trumps *imitatio,* and implicit within this claim is a further, almost optimistic, one: that contemporary Italian practitioners of *pastio* may surpass their ancient counterparts.

Yet, further reflection may lead one to reconsider the tenor of these passages. On the one hand, Arcadia seems to have been almost proverbial for its fine donkeys, while there is no obvious reason to doubt the quality of the Reatinian ass and, at least after Varro, the region seems also to have enjoyed a fine reputation for the animal.[39] On the other hand, in addition to *RR 2*'s decidedly pan-Mediterranean focus in general and otherwise complete reticence about the absolutely superior virtues of Italian livestock, both Reate and Arcadia are replete with personal and literary resonance which possibly freights the surface claims with additional meaning. In the first place, Reate was the hometown of not just Murrius, but also Varro himself; as we know, it was the ancestral seat of the agronomist's family as well as the location of his stable of horses, donkeys, and mules (2.pref.6; 2.8.6; 3.2.4).[40] Elsewhere, Varro extolled the region's apparently bountiful fecundity in writings no longer extant, going so far as to invest it with a Delphi-like, mythical aura as the

---

38. As we shall see in chapter 6 (pp. 193–95), the concern with aesthetics is an important thread of Book 3 as well as of the *RR* in general.

39. For the quality of Arcadian asses, see Plaut. *Asin.* 333–34, Columella, *Rust.* 7.1.1, and Pliny *HN* 8.167. Pliny also cites Reate in conjunction with Arcadia, though it is clear from the context that he is working directly from Varro's text. Interestingly enough, while Columella opens his book on the lesser animals (*de minore pecore*) with qualified praise of the qualities of the Arcadian ass, he entirely omits any mention of Reate's asses.

40. Cf. F 502 Bücheler of Varro's *Menippeans.*

"navel of Italia" (*umbilicus Italiae*; Pliny *HN* 3.108). In the case of Arcadia, an even more longstanding and richer historical, mythological, and literary tradition surrounds the region. Perhaps the most pertinent one for our purposes, however, is the thread that associates Arcadia with the bucolic landscapes of some of Theocritus's rustic *Idylls*.[41] The question thus arises: could the mention of Arcadia as the land of the vulgar, but sturdy and useful ass be intended to invoke the mythopoetic landscape of lush verdure found in Theocritean and perhaps even Vergilian bucolic as well? *RR* 2's other dabblings in *bucolica* may provide indirect support for this last contention, but if it does, a further question arises: how, then, are we to square the comparison of Italian Reate with a Hellenic Arcadia of such literary repute?

If Arcadia can stand as generic shorthand for bucolic poetry, one possible solution is to rethink our understanding of Reate and its consummate livestock along similar lines. While Reate does not, so far as I know, have any (meta-)literary connotation (beyond what Varro created for it), mules and asses do, but an explication of this meaning requires turning to another contemporary text—namely, Horace's first book of *Sermones*—and entails some conjecture. As various scholars have perceptively observed, mules constitute a programmatic animal in Horatian satire.[42] In 1.5's journey to the heart of satire, mules serve as pack animals for Horace's mundane, trivial, and ultimately frustrating account of the monumental rapprochement of Octavian and Antony at Brundisium in 40 BC (or is it at Tarentum in 38? or ultimately Athens in 37?), thereby serving as the "proper vehicle for Horatian Satire."[43] In the following *Sermo*, Horace's admissions that "[he] was not born to a distinguished father, and [he] did not ride around the countryside on a Tarentine nag" (*Satureianus caballus*; 1.6.58–59) anticipate his later assertion that he instead rides a "castrated mule" (*mulus curtus*; 1.6.104–5). In rejecting a Tarentine nag, Horace simultaneously puns on the much-vaunted equestrian status of C. Lucilius and criticizes his predecessor's old and tired form of satire, which is symbolized by the broken-down condition of a mount otherwise befitting a man of his status. Moreover, the rejection of a horse coincides with the seemingly apolitical stance struck by Horace (again in contradistinction to Lucilius and his unbridled, often *ad hominem, libertas*) and is consonant with his use of chariot imagery to symbolize and denounce the avaricious pursuit of wealth (1.1.113–16) and of political honor and *gloria*

---

41. See n. 45 in chapter 4.

42. See Freudenburg (1993) 205–7 and Gowers (1993a) 57.

43. So Gowers *ibid.* formulates it in a rhetorical question. Note also that she makes the subsequent connections with 1.6 as well, and, in general, I am greatly indebted to her reading of 1.5 for my understanding of the poem.

(1.6.23–24).[44] By adopting a mule—and a gelded one at that—as his steed of choice, Horace thus differentiates his satire from the broken-down old horse of Lucilian satire and, by virtue of its lowlier status, embraces an animal perhaps more becoming to the humbler status of a freedman's son. As for donkeys in Horace's *Sermones,* there is but one in the form of a mock-epic simile in 1.9. Upon realizing that the inopportune pest is simply not going to leave him alone, Horace's "little ears drooped, just as a lil' donkey (*asellus*) of uneven temper, when a weighty load is placed on its back" (1.9.20–21).[45] In this case, Horace's failure to shake the boor (another Lucilian inspiration) renders his satirical persona a temperamental, yet ultimately impotent and servile, little ass.

It would seem, then, that asses and mules may serve as programmatic animals for satirists—particularly marginalized or "apolitical" ones—whereas horses are the appropriate equines for those of a more exalted lineage or standing.[46] Does such a distinction somehow find its way into *RR* 2? The association of horses with the socially or politically enfranchised would seem to motivate the senatorial Lucienus's seamless assumption of the *pars equina* at 2.7.1 (though this connection is as much cultural as it may be satirical).[47] While there is nothing particularly satirical about the content of the Reatinian Murrius's treatment of asses and mules, the consistent ascription of these two animals to the Reatinian estates of Varro—an author renowned as much for his *Menippeans* as for his voluminous "antiquarian" output—may itself be suggestive of this association.[48] While this connection remains tenuous, in a

---

44. So DuQuesnay (1984) 48 rightly interprets 1.6.23–24.

45. For the "mock-epic" quality of this simile, see Anderson (1982) 92, who also cites the famous comparison of Ajax to an ass at Hom. *Il.* 9.556ff., but inexplicably denies the possibility of Horace's allusion to it.

46. For another example of an animal as a programmatic marker of genre, see Horace's swan in *Od.* 2.20.

47. It may not be insignificant that this period, partly due to the political and social upheaval of the civil wars, also marks the beginning of increasing attention to the *equites*. The future Augustus will take various, mostly unprecedented, steps to strengthen the equestrian class as a whole and to integrate them—formally and informally—within the administration of the empire; see, for example, Suet. *Aug.* 46 and Nicolet (1984) 89–128.

48. Two other points might be brought to bear on this argument, one slightly stronger than the other. First, the description of another of Varro's estates (at Casinum) and, in particular, its aviary in *RR* 3, not only is the most memorable portion of *De Re Rustica* in general, but functions as the most overt instance of "satire" in the work as well. See pp. 199–200 in chapter 6. Second, it is tempting to understand Murrius as a cypher for Varro by virtue of its resemblance to the transliterated Greek translation of the author's name: *myrios* ≈ *murrius* ≈ *varius* ≈ *varro.* If we accept this (admittedly tenuous) interpretation, we may be able to detect another satirical element to the *RR*: the reduplication of the author as character. For this theme in the *Menippeans,* see Leach (1999) 139–79.

text that enigmatically resonates with so many "other" generic features, it is hard not to read meta-literarily into the fact that Italian Reate consistently trumps Greek Arcadia in the quality of its asses and mules. If we accept this suggestion, however, perhaps Varro (*qua* author) intends the reader to understand that the Reatinian brand of satire he interweaves into *RR* 2 partially resembles, but ultimately trumps, Arcadian bucolic.

Or it may simply be the case that Reatinian asses are actually just superior to the already excellent Arcadian ones. But such is the sort of recurring ambiguity that a lack of contextualizing knowledge may prompt for the critical reader of Varro's *De Re Rustica*.

## CONCLUSION

In these two chapters, I have sought to interpret the staging of the dialogue in conjunction with its technical content. As we have seen, Varro's literary creation is, to say the least, multifarious, drawing upon bucolic and epic literary conventions so as to exploit existing cultural associations between *pastio* and the world of political governance and to create new ones as well. By intermittently figuring the motley assemblage of interlocutors as literal and metaphorical *pastores* abroad of both animals and men, Varro renovates animal husbandry—in its praxis and as an art and science—for an imperial context and, in so doing, fashions the provincial lands of the Mediterranean as the pastureland of the Roman imperial estate.

As the conversation winds down, Cossinius wraps up the eighty-one-part account of *pastio* with the promised supplements concerning milk and cheese production (*de lacte et caseo*; 2.11.1–5) and shearing (*tonsura*; 2.11.5–12), each of which now reliably veers into matters anthropological—the digestive qualities of various cheeses and the sacrificial use of milk, the advent of barbers into Rome in the case of shearing—and is perhaps fitting for a conversation that has not infrequently blurred the lines between animal and man. Just as the interlocutors are concluding the day's conversation—a discussion that has explored the changed realities of both literal and metaphorical animal husbandry in the context of a Mediterranean empire—the freedman (*libertus*) of a hitherto-unmentioned Vitulus bursts onto the scene. Instead of panicking at the death of his former master, however, this one calmly and politely requests the presence of Scrofa and Varro at his patron's estate "lest [they] make the festal day shorter" (2.11.12). In comparison to the ending of the first book—an unexpected, but not unprecedented, assassination marring an otherwise idyllic discussion—the thoroughly peaceful conclusion to a dialogue set during a foreign war with piratical bandits is rather ironic. Perhaps this contrast is meant to underscore the difference that thirty years can make? Or maybe it juxtaposes the Romans' success in external affairs with their failure when it comes to domestic ones? Whatever the purpose may be, it is not insignificant that the two interlocutors figured as military herdsmen of Rome depart separately from the other *pastores* and conveniently to the estate of a man whose name, "Vitulus," Varro (*qua* interlocutor) previously etymologized as the source for "Italia" in at least two different ways.[49] In this way, the literal departure also transacts a metaphorical one from the pastures of Epirus back to the homestead of Italia and to Rome, the *villa urbana* of Book 3.

---

49. At 2.1.9, Varro states that L. Calpurnius Piso, the annalist, claimed that Italia came from *vitulus*, "calf." Later on, he interrupts Vaccius's discussion of cattle to note that Timaeus, the writer of universal history, claimed that the name came from the Greek *italus* (2.5.3; cf. F 42 Jacoby). Immediately thereafter, Varro gives another account, which maintained that Italia was so named from Hercules' pursuit of a bull named *italus* from Sicily to Italia (cf. Dion. Hal. *Ant. Rom.* 1.35.2). See Dench (2006) 157–60 for an instructive discussion of the various traditions.

# CHAPTER 6

# Tending the Villa of Rome in *RR* 3

Firmano saltu non falso Mentula dives
fertur, qui tot res in se habet egregias,
aucupium omne genus, pisces, prata, arva ferasque.
Nequiquam: fructus sumptibus exsuperat.
Quare concedo sit dives, dum omnia desint.
Saltum laudemus, dum modio ipse egeat.

Prickula is said to be wealthy with his Firmian estate—not falsely, for he has so many wonderful things within it: all kinds of bird, fish, meadows, fields, and game. It's all in vain: the profit (*fructus*) is swallowed up with the expenses (*sumptibus*). Therefore, I grant that he's wealthy, though all things are lacking. Let us praise his estate, though he himself lacks all measure.

   —Catullus, *Carmen* 114

Nam omnem nostram de re publica curam, cogitationem de dicenda in senatu sententia, commentationem causarum abiecimus, in Epicuri nos, adversari nostri, castra coiecimus, nec tamen ad hanc insolentiam sed ad illam tuam lautitiam. . . .
Proinde te para. Cum homine et edaci tibi res est et qui iam aliquid intellegat. . . .

All of my concern for *res publica,* all my thought about pleading in the Senate, all my preparation for cases, I have cast aside; and I have taken myself into the camp of my adversary, Epicurus—still, not for purposes of extravagance, but for that refinement of yours. . . . Therefore prepare yourself. You are dealing with a hungry man who now knows a thing or two [about luxurious dinners]. . . .

   —Cicero, *Fam.* 193.1–2 [= 9.20.1–2]

IN *CARMEN* 114, Catullus returns to the attack on Mentula—this time, using his *fundus* at Firmum as point of entry.[1] It is, however, not the quality of the land and its resources that are susceptible to reproach, for the estate's *res* are in fact excellent (*egregiae*) and diverse, consisting of fields (*arva*) for *agri cultura*, meadows (*prata*) for *pastio*, and the habitats necessary for birds, game, and fish. Rather, Mentula's estate, which has earned the man the estimation of *dives* and should make him wealthy in point of fact, is swamped in expenses (*sumptus*) that drown the profit (*fructus*). As Cato said (*Agr.* 1.6), "know that an *ager* is like a man: although it may produce income (*quaestuosus*), if it's full of expenses (*sumptuosus*), not much is left." In the case of Mentula, then, his overly sumptuous and, therefore, economically unviable estate imputes a "foul character"[2] to the owner and upends the man's pretensions to the luxury and status of such contemporaries as Q. Hortensius, L. Lucullus, and even M. Terentius Varro himself. And though Catullus does not articulate it as such, the tricolon of animal resources—birds, game, and fish—corresponds precisely to the third part of the tripartite estate (*praedium*) of Varronian *res rusticae*: so-called *pastio villatica,* which is a new form of animal husbandry practiced in or around the villa (3.3.1) and which "as a whole has not been distinguished separately by anyone, so far as I know" (*neque explicata tota separatim, quod sciam, ab ullo;* 3.1.8).[3] As we shall see, Varro's innovative account of *pastio villatica* appreciates the practice's potential for astounding returns that come at the cost of incredible risk—both economic and moral—to the entrepreneur, which perhaps renders Mentula's spectacular failure in *production* all the more understandable and more derisible.

The *fructus* of *pastio villatica* also functions as a symbol of status for Cicero, yet not in the same way that Catullus's Mentula conspicuously failed to achieve. Instead, it is the *consumption* of that *fructus* in refined dinner parties that, for Cicero, emblematizes his effective retirement from public life by 46. Displaying a marked change in tone from his famous contempt for the "affishionados" (*piscinarii,* e.g., *Att.* 19.6 [= 1.19.6]) some fifteen years earlier, Cicero's letters with this particular correspondent, L. Papirius Paetus,[4] are stuffed with culinary references to the erstwhile statesman's burgeoning experiences with the elite world of prestige eating, central to which is the produce

---

1. Note that the attack continues in a similar vein in 115 as well. My reading of Catullus 114 is indebted to Harvey (1979) 329–45.

2. So *idem* 344 phrases it.

3. For an overview of *pastio villatica,* see Rinkewitz (1981).

4. See *Fam.* 114; 188–91; 193–98; 362 [= 9.15–26]. Cf. n. 24 in chapter 4.

of *pastio villatica*. To Cicero's (somewhat jocular[5]) chagrin, peacocks and dinner parties have supplanted senatorial hearings and *res publica*. But where the produce of *pastio villatica* symbolizes political withdrawal for Cicero, Varro will make use of it in a much more complex and supple manner in *RR* 3. As this chapter explores, *pastio villatica* is an area of *res rusticae* that, when practiced with a view to profit (*fructus*) and pleasure (*delectatio*), turns out to be good farming practice in the *luxuria*-laden conditions of contemporary Rome. Yet, these same exploitative and pleasure-seeking values of the villa freight its allegorical application to the political and cultural life of the city with considerable baggage, which in turn makes it an especially fitting area of rustic enterprise for the Rome of the tumultuous late Republican and Triumviral periods.

Unlike the first two dialogues, *RR* 3 has attracted much more scholarly attention—mostly because of its memorable setting, its colorful cast of characters, and, above all, its fantastic description of Varro's ornate aviary.[6] The dialogue has also benefited from a handful of attempts at synthetic interpretation, among which Green's article (1997: 427–48) stands first and foremost. On the basis of *RR* 3's association of *pastio villatica* with the city of Rome through the dialogue's staging in the Villa Publica, she argues that Varro's treatment of aviaries and use of bird motifs enables him to figure humans as animals and to allegorize contemporary Rome as a birdcage owned by Octavian and his partisans.[7] Her suggestion that Varro's purpose was to provide "farming as a Xenophontic, or Cincinnatan, metaphor for wise government" (431) represents a sea change in critical approaches to the *RR*, yet implicitly subscribes to the view that "farming" (as both praxis and ideology) was uniform, static, and normative in the late Republic. In addition to the fact that the villa took many physical forms,[8] was subject to a complex process of cul-

---

5. Shackleton-Bailey (1977) 331 may go too far in his estimation that "the Paetus correspondence is rarely more than half-serious," but humor and irony are hallmarks of this sequence of letters.

6. For examples, see van Buren and Kennedy (1919) 59–66 and Fuchs (1962) 96–105 on the description of Varro's ornate aviary; Linderski (1989) 105–28 and Tatum (1992) 190–200 on the cast of characters; and Nicolet (1970) 113–37, Richardson (1983) 456–63, and Linderski (1985) 248–54 on the date.

7. Note that her argument partly relies on the shared legal status of humans and birds as naturally free beings that can nonetheless become the property of another (cf. *Digest* 41); see pp. 436–39.

8. The range in forms of and complexity in construing the "villa" partly reflects linguistic variation amongst ancient sources and partly derives from the regional and socioeconomic diversity of the material evidence. Linguistically, Columella famously provides a tripartite division of the villa (*Rust.* 1.6.1–24) into (1) the *villa urbana* (i.e., the domicile of the owner), (2) the *villa rustica* (i.e., the working and living quarters for the household slaves

tural negotiation,[9] and could consequently have a range of connotations,[10] her approach underestimates *RR* 3's efforts to present a new vision of the role that it specifically plays within an agricultural estate (*praedium*) as well as the implications of Varro's rigorous distinction between the three spheres of *res rusticae*. As well, her approach does not consider the practical side of Roman farming as, above all, a production-oriented enterprise—an aspect that Purcell's roughly contemporaneous article (1995: 151–79) does treat. By using *RR* 3's opening debate on what constitutes a villa to examine a wide variety of textual and material evidence, he successfully argues that production and profit were of paramount concern to virtually all Romans (be they lowly holders of small plots or elite owners of large-scale estates[11]), demon-

---

as well as those structures housing both the herd and pack animals), and (3) the *villa fructuaria* (i.e., the places of storage and production). While neither Cato nor Varro formally acknowledges the third category as a discrete one, both authors do distinguish between the *villa urbana* and the *villa rustica* (e.g., *Agr.* 4; *RR* 1.13.6) and include the structures, equipment, and operations of the *villa fructuaria* within the latter. The precise location of *pastio villatica*—is it at the *villa urbana* or at the *villa rustica?*—is problematic, for the sheer diversity amongst the practices included under this category means that some (e.g., the raising of dormice in *gliraria*) could have taken place in the *villa urbana* proper, whereas others were probably located at or, at least, close to the *villa rustica*. In discussing this form of animal husbandry, both Columella and Varro tend to speak of its presence in or around the *villa* unqualified (e.g., Columella, *Rust.* 8.1.3), though Columella's observation that the location of *vivaria* (cf. Varro's *leporaria*) is often placed within view of the "master's living-quarters" (*dominicas habitationes*; 9.pref.1) may suggest that *pastio villatica* implies the *villa urbana*. For the reason that the ancients did not find it necessary to qualify the *villa* under consideration, I will speak simply of the *villa* henceforth, fully aware of the possible ambiguity surrounding this term. While the types of villas discussed in *RR* 3 are sometimes assigned to the category of a *villa suburbana*, that is, a villa "distinguishable from a town house only by being on the outskirts of town" (Percival [1976] 54–55), I avoid this term primarily because Varro himself never uses it in either *RR* 3 or anywhere else (but see 2.3.10's reference to a *suburbanum* [*praedium*]). The difficulties of applying the terminology of the "villa" to archaeological sites have become a scholarly *topos* since at least *idem* (cf. 13–5) and especially in more recent and archaeologically grounded studies. See, for example, Purcell (1995) 167–68; J. T. Smith (1997) 3–12; and Marzano (2007) 2–3; 82–99 *passim*. Cf. Terrenato (2001) 5–6: "the term 'villa' has been given to a variety of sites that differ in size, architecture, function and chronology, to the point where the boundaries of the type and terminological consistency appear today blurred and in need of comprehensive redefinition."

9. See Spencer (2010) 62–134 for a thought-provoking survey of the way that villa landscapes could provide meditations on the relationship between agriculture, Roman citizenship, and identity. Cf. Bodel (2012) 45–60, whose brief survey of the roles that Cato, Cicero, and Varro played in formulating "villaculture" provides an intriguing précis for future work.

10. For example, Lucullus's villa could signify excessive luxury, *RR* 1.2.10; cf. Cic. *Off.* 1.140. Elsewhere, the villa could be associated with withdrawal from political life; Cic. *Att.* 163 [= 8.13].

11. See especially Purcell (1995) 154–61, who rightly observes that even the estates of the obscenely wealthy (e.g., Lucullus) and their overt gestures towards nonproduction speak to the normative centrality of production at Roman estates.

strates the inextricability of the putatively opposed goals of actual production and showy pleasure, and concludes that Roman villas in general are geared towards the production of profit and that "productivity and consumption permeate the whole society" (173). By virtue of its emphasis on produce and profit, *RR* 3 emerges on his view as a treatise that prescribes thoroughly traditional terms of production for the newly emergent "prestige delicatessen market, the *macellum*" (172–73).

For the interlocutors of this allegorical dialogue that doubles as handbook for *pastio villatica,* the pursuit of profit and, where congruent, pleasure lies at the forefront of their minds: from the profit-focused "Mr. Worth" (Axius) to even Varro himself, whose aunt successfully participates in this newfangled, potentially lucrative form of husbandry (3.2.14–15). Yet, this concern for profit, which at times borders on the obsessive and is associated explicitly with an increase in *luxuria* and implicitly with a decline in traditional morality, has the power to disconcert as well. For Kronenberg (2009: 73–129), Varro's treatise actually "debunks the myth of the virtuous farmer by revealing that the farming life became associated in Roman culture with morality . . . because of the material benefits it provides the Romans"; in her view, the treatise's contentions that "farming is about nothing if not profit, and what is profitable is simply assimilated to what is moral" (97) thus denounce by way of irony and allegory Roman political culture in general. Kronenberg's argument holds some weight, for profit does hold a central place in the work's articulation of *res rusticae* (cf. pp. 47–52 in chapter 2), especially in its most lucrative form of *pastio villatica.* And she is certainly correct to observe that, within *De Re Rustica,* "Varro does not imply that there is a source of value beyond *utilitas* and *voluptas*" (107). But the strength of her argument, which lies in her reading of the text *against* normative Roman political culture, is also its weakness, for her focus on what the work does *not* do (e.g., provide a meaningful or philosophical account of morality) causes her to minimize, undervalue, or even ignore what it *does* do: the articulation of a new account of *res rusticae* and the delineation of genuinely useful technical precepts.

By building off these important, but countervailing, contributions, I provide a new close reading of the text, which correlates the date of composition (37 BC) with the setting (50 BC) and the technical content (*pastio villatica*). While the treatise does raise serious financial and ethical questions about the practice of villa husbandry, it nonetheless provides an account that makes it a viable practice in contemporary Rome. In particular, *RR* 3 adheres to an ideology of production that actively explores the ways in which *pastio villatica* can provide a form of rustic enterprise, which is compatible, though imperfectly so, with both the contemporary *luxuria* resultant of Rome's imperial wealth and the venerable farming practices of the *maiores*. And in their meta-phorical application, the precepts of *pastio villatica* and those particularly memorable moments of allegory, irony, and trenchant critique—especially the accounts of the aviaries of Merula, Varro, and Lucullus as well as the treatment of bees—offer up sporadic critiques of Roman political culture and imperfect solutions to its problems. The result is a dialogue that remains pro-foundly ambivalent over the current practice of *pastio villatica*—and poli-tics—in the city of Rome, but that nonetheless constructively renovates it as another sphere of the *praedium* for the contemporary Roman *res publica*.

## THE VILLA-STILL-PUBLICA AND THE SHADOWS OF CAESARIAN DICTATORSHIP

Set in the Villa Publica of the Campus Martius during the aedilician elec-tions (3.2.1), *RR* 3 stages its *sermo* in a place and on an occasion of transparent political relevance. The precise dramatic date of the dialogue has prompted scholarly debate, but textual and historical evidence securely establish 50 BC as the year of its setting.[12] The question is: why the election of aediles in 50 BC? While it may be relevant that aediles were *not* elected in the following year nor in the year of the *RR*'s composition,[13] it is doubtlessly the election's occasion on the eve of civil war between Caesar and Pompey that motivates this date. From the vantage of 37/6 BC, the year 50 BC marked the decisive point of transition from an ailing, but still functional, Republican govern-ment to the openly pitched cycle of internecine strife of the 40s and 30s BC, the unprecedented *dictator in perpetuum* of Julius Caesar, and the eventual

12. The debate has traditionally turned on whether the year is 54 or 50 BC. For those scholars who endorse 50 BC, see especially Badian (1970) 4–6, Linderski (1985) 248–54, and Flach (2002) 29–30. As Linderski cogently argues, the two strongest pieces of evidence mar-shaled by those in the 54 BC camp (most recently, Shatzman [1968] 350–51 and Richardson [1983] 456–63)—the mention of the recent (*nuper*) triumph of Metellus Scipio in 54 BC (or, as Linderski suggests, probably in 53) and the evocation of Appius Claudius Pulcher as an augur—do not in fact rule out the later date, while the temporal references in 3.2.15–16 ac-tually preclude 54 BC; given that Appius was proconsul of Cilicia from 53–51 BC (cf. Taylor [1960] 63 n. 63), 50 BC thus emerges as the sole viable candidate. Cf. Nicolet (1970) 113–16.

13. Dio Cassius (41.36.2) records that there were no aediles elected in 49 BC, but see Grueber's postulation only weakly endorsed by Broughton (*MRR* 2.258). For the lack of ae-diles in 36 BC as well, see 49.16.2. Note also that this setting perhaps alludes back to *RR* 1, where the absence (and eventual mistaken assassination) of Fundilius, the *aeditumus* of the Temple of Tellus, is due to his summons by the presiding aedile (1.2.2). Cf. Green (1997) 431. Note also that Varro's satire entitled "Serranus (περὶ ἀρχαιρεσιῶν [= on elections])" would seem to have connected agricultural imagery and the famous farmer-statesman (cf. p. 226) with popular elections.

domination of the Second Triumvirate. And on the cusp of this impending political tempest stand Varro and his interlocutors about to discuss the profitable and pleasurable production of luxury animal products. Yet, despite the date's obvious significance, the dialogue opens rather uneventfully and, aside from potential tampering with ballots (3.5.18), remains free from political disturbance. Indeed, *RR* 3 never *explicitly* refers either to the piqued political tensions plaguing the city of Rome in 50 BC or, for that matter, to the contemporary political landscape of 37/6 BC. This silence should not, however, be mistaken for absence, for the dialogue engages these issues in an oblique manner and often cast in cultural and moral terms.

Indeed, the choice of the Villa Publica for the precise backdrop may be indicative of such elusive allusion. As the curtain opens onto Varro and Q. Axius,[14] both of whom have just voted and are waiting to accompany their candidate homeward once the results have been announced, the sun's heat (*sole caldo*) prompts the latter to suggest that the pair of Reatinians avail themselves of the shade provided by the Villa Publica rather than the "halved planks of their *candidatus privatus*" (*privati candidati tabella dimidiate*; 3.2.1). Aside from the vexed meaning of this last phrase,[15] the dialogue's exposition is *prima facie* straightforward; after all, comitial voting took place in that area known as the Saepta or, more affectionately, the Ovilia ("Sheep-Pen"), which was a massively rectangular, pen-like area that constituted either part of the Villa Publica or, more likely, a separate space lying immediately adjacent to it.[16] Varro and Axius thus naturally head from there to

---

14. Q. Axius was probably a "Sullan senator" (Nicolet [1966] 586; Shatzman [1975] 474–77) and apparently a friend of both Varro and Cicero (*Att.* 60 [= 3.15]; 90 [= 4.15]; Suet. *Iul.* 9; Aul. Gell. *NA* 7.3). Q. Axius should also be identified with the moneylender mentioned in *Att.* 12.1 [= 1.12.1] and is almost certainly the man who owes Cicero some money in 49 BC (*Att.* 202 [= 10.11]; 205 [= 10.13]; 207 [= 10.15]). See *MRR* 2.475; Taylor (1960) 197; Wiseman (1971) 216; and Shatzman (1975) 308. On the basis of his introduction as a senator (3.2.1) and given his lack of attestation elsewhere, Linderski (1989) 117 infers that Axius most likely attained no position higher than the quaestorship. Note that his eager desire for profit plays off the Greek pun, "Mr. Worth," inherent in his name.

15. Providing an excellent analysis of the problems in interpretation of this enigmatic phrase and overview of scholarly solutions, Nicolet (1970) 113–37 subsequently offers up his own conjecture—*praeteriti candidati tabella diribita*—which is attractive in its intelligibility, but manifestly deficient in its lack of manuscript support. As usual, I have adopted Flach's 2006 text. See pp. 178–79 below for further discussion.

16. For reconstruction of voting practice in this space, see Taylor (1966) 47–58 and 78–113. Cf. Nicolet (1970) 113–37, Coarelli (2001) 37–51, and Albers (2009) 7–22. For standard scholarly discussions of the Ovilia, see L. Richardson (1992) s.v. *Ovile* and *Saepta Iulia*; Coarelli (2007) 263–65, 289–90; and Claridge (2009) 202, 232. Note that scholars tend to refer to the (presumably original) Republican structure as the Ovilia and the rebuilt structure as the Saepta or Saepta Iulia, though Ovilia and Saepta are used interchangeably and consistently throughout both periods. Despite their centrality to the Roman political process, remarkably little is known about both the Ovilia and the Villa Publica.

the Villa Publica as the closest structure so as to avoid the baking sun (*sole caldo*).

Yet, from the vantage of 37 BC, this seemingly offhand comment about the unimpeded sun is loaded with significance, for the Ovilia was no longer the same structure as the one of 50 BC. As early as 54 BC, Julius Caesar had begun to plan a major renovation of the Saepta, a "most glorious undertaking" that, with the moral support and financial backing of Cicero, would have rendered it marbled, covered, and girded "with a lofty portico of upwards of a mile long" (*Att.* 89.8 [= 4.16.8]). By planning to renovate an area so intimately connected with the heart of the Republican political process, Caesar may have been attempting to cast himself as a traditional upholder of *res publica*—perhaps in contradistinction to Pompey, whose Hellenically tinged theater built in 55 BC constituted the first such permanent structure.[17] But whatever his intentions, Caesar's planned work was of such scale and scope that it sought to leave its patron's lasting mark by definitely transforming the Saepta and surrounding area; indeed, so much would seem to underlie Cicero's exceedingly wry quip that this work will be joined to the "Villa-Still-Publica" (*villa etiam publica*; 89.8 [= 4.16.8]).

While the precise state of the undertaking in 50 BC remains obscure in the historical record, work over the next decade appears not to have progressed very far, if at all. In the first place, the promised porticos were added only by Lepidus—presumably as triumvir, in accordance with the deceased Caesar's wishes, and therefore sometime between 44–41 and 37 BC—while it was Agrippa who finally completed and dedicated the project thereafter in 26 BC (Dio Cass. 53.23.2). When combined with Cicero's subsequent silence about the state of the project and his involvement in it—as well as the multifarious distractions that the various political disturbances of the day offered—it seems most probable that the Saepta remained the same in 50 BC as it was some four years earlier: largely unadorned, without porticos, and, as *RR 3* would seem to attest, exposed to the "hot sun" (*sole caldo*). The prominent placement of this seemingly minor detail by an author writing in 37 BC thus subtly, but tellingly, invokes a previous time and prior place in the urban landscape of Rome.[18]

---

17. For discussion, see Taylor (1966) 47–49. See also Agache (1987) 211–34, who makes intriguing, but tenuous, connections between Varro's emphasis on the census-taking, voting, and mustering aspects of the Villa Publica, the coinage issued by T. Didius in 56 BC (which represents the Villa Publica on one side, the defeat of Gaul on the other), and Caesar's designs for the Saepta. Cf. Hamilton (1955) 224–28.

18. So Agache (1987) 211–34 rightly argues. That she adheres to the 54 BC dating does not affect her otherwise excellent discussion of the Saepta and Villa Publica. While there may be something to her explanation of Varro's capturing of this detail as a reflex of his "antiquarian anxiety" (*antiquaire soucieux*) for preserving the past, this estimation ultimately undervalues

But there may be a specifically literary dimension to this loaded detail as well. *De Re Publica*—a work that Cicero was actively composing around the same time as he was apparently supporting Caesar's initiative[19]—opens with the solar phenomenon of a perihelion (i.e., the appearance of two suns, *Rep.* 1.15; cf. 1.17; 1.19), the occasion of which prompts the interlocutors' conversation and comes to symbolize the two senates and two peoples—that is, the factionalized *res publica*—brought about by the recent proposals and death of Tiberius Gracchus (1.31). In contrast to the two suns of *De Re Publica,* there is but one in *RR* 3—though it is a hot, perhaps even fiery (*caldus*), one. If we are willing to construe the *sol caldus* as an allusive inversion of Cicero's perihelion in *De Re Publica* and to contextualize it against the backdrop of an uncovered, portico-less, and pre-Caesarian Saepta on the eve of civil war, what are we to make of this conjunction? One possible line of interpretation would be to understand the sole "fiery sun" as somehow symbolizing Julius Caesar's impending dictatorship. The withdrawal of Varro and Axius to the shade (*umbra*) of the Villa Publica thus takes on new political salience.

Whether the two interlocutors are seeking refuge from the looming dictatorship of Caesar or simply from the sun, another echo of Caesarian politics may be detected in Axius's rejected alternative to the shade of the Villa Publica. As mentioned above, his proposal is framed as a counter to constructing (*aedificare*) shelter from the "halved planks of their *candidatus privatus*" (*privati candidati tabella dimidiata*). The precise meaning of this phrase has prompted various explanations and emendations,[20] but the simplest and most orthodox one explains it as follows: *aedificare* plays off the duties entrusted to the post of aedile sought by the *candidatus,* who remains *privatus* until elected and whose campaign promises remain only "halved" or "half-built" (*dimidiata*) until he is actually elected by ballot (*tabella*) to the aedileship. On this reading, Varro's Axius puns cleverly, if somewhat inelegantly, on the occasion that has brought the pair together and in proximity to the Villa Publica. Yet, there may be a complementary way of construing this

the man and his work and emblematizes reductive approaches to Varro; see p. 3 in the introduction.

19. That Cicero was conversing with Atticus about the state of the work—and entertaining the latter's request that Varro be included in it, no less!—in the same letter (*Att.* 89 [= 4.16]) in which he informs his faithful friend of Caesar's initiative and his own support for it may simply be coincidence, but it is a powerful one nonetheless. Furthermore, in a following letter (90 [= 4.15]), Cicero also mentions his participation in a dispute between the Reatinians and Interamnatians over the draining of Lake Velinus, when he stayed with Axius, the interlocutor of *RR* 3; cf. n. 90 in chapter 3 and n. 29 in the present chapter. The possible allusion to Cicero's *De Re Publica* was first suggested to me by Stephen White (though he may not necessarily agree with the present interpretation).

20. Cf. n. 15. For the orthodox position, see Flach (2002) 192.

sentence as well, for *tabella dimidiata* recalls a measure undertaken by Caesar in his dictatorship (probably in 45 or 44 BC), by which Caesar split comitial power with the *populus*: the people electing one half (*pro parte dimidia*) of the magistrates (excluding the consuls), and Caesar the other half (Suet. *Iul.* 41).[21] On this view, Axius's use of *tabella dimidiata* alludes to this controversial seizure of power by Caesar. To be sure, such an allusion would violate the historical accuracy otherwise sought—and generally maintained—by Varro in his dialogues.[22] Yet, if we are willing to read this treatise in the way proposed in chapter 1—as a technical treatise that sporadically engages in philosophical inquiry and satirical critique—I would suggest that this passage allows for both readings at once and that this dry and intricate double entendre is precisely the sort of sly humor for which Varro was known. On this reading, then, the hot sun and "halved plank/vote" allude to the looming presence of Julius Caesar and, from the outset, the interlocutors are seeking to escape the sun of Caesar's impending dictatorship under the shade of the pre-Caesarian Villa Publica.

## BIRDCAGES, VILLAS, AND THE CRAPSHOOT OF *PASTIO VILLATICA*

Agreeing to Axius's suggestion with a labored reworking of a well-known proverb,[23] Varro heads off with companion in tow to the Villa Publica only to happen upon (*invenire*) an uncanny sight (3.2.2–3):

> Ibi Appium Claudium augurem sedentem invenimus in subselliis, ut consuli, siquid usus poposcisset, esset praesto. Sedebat ad sinistram ei Cornelius Merula consulari familia ortus et Fircellius Pavo Reatinus, ad dextram Minucius Pica et M. Petronius Passer. Ad quem cum accessissemus, Axius Appio subridens, "Recipis nos," inquit, "in tuum ornithona, ubi sedes inter aves?" Ille, "Ego vero," inquit, "te praesertim, quoius aves hospitales etiam nunc ructor, quas mihi apposuisti paucis ante diebus in Villa Reatina ad lacum Velini eunti de controversiis Interamnatium et Reatinorum."

---

21. For this explanation, see Stobbe (1868) 88–112. Presumably, Varro would have disapproved of Suetonius's (mis)use of *dimidia* for *dimidiata* (cf. Aul. Gell. *NA* 3.14).

22. So Nicolet (1970) 124 argues.

23. See Green (1997) 445–46 for an explanation of the proverb, which plays off the episode involving the misconceived moving of the Horatius Cocles statue in the Comitium (Aul. Gell. *NA* 4.5).

There, we happen upon (*invenimus*) Appius Claudius [Pulcher], the augur, sitting on a bench, so that he might be present (*praesto*) for consultation, if any need had demanded it. Sitting on his left were Cornelius Blackbird (*Merula*), born from a consular family, and Fircellius Peacock (*Pavo*) of Reate, while sitting on his right were Minucius Magpie (*Pica*) and Marcus Petronius Sparrow (*Passer*). When we had come to him, Axius with a smirk says to Appius, "Will you receive us in your aviary, where you are sitting amongst the birds?" That one says, "I do indeed—especially you, whose hospitable birds (*aves hospitales*) even now I am belching up, the ones that you set before me a few days earlier in your villa at Reate while I was going to Lake Velinus in regard to the controversies between the Interamnatians and the Reatinians."

By way of the fantastically satirical conceit of the augur, Appius Claudius Pulcher, sitting amongst the birds of Roman Italy, Varro presents his colorful cast of characters. Though introduced in terms of his augurship,[24] Appius achieved far more in his life than simple enrollment into that priestly college. Indeed, as the eldest scion of a most noble and patrician clan, Appius lived up to the precedent set by so many of his ancestors, holding the consulship in 54 as well as the censorship in the present year.[25] By virtue of these offices, he is the most eminent figure of *RR* 3 and, indeed, of the entire *De Re Rustica*. Of the avian characters, far less is known. In the first place, it is only Cornelius Merula who sings at any length and, perhaps in keeping with his status as the other primary interlocutor, who also receives any substantive identification: a one-off reference to his family's consular lineage. While the family is reasonably well known, this particular Merula remains obscure, though it is not unreasonable to assume that he was—or was on track to become—a senator.[26] Thereafter, the standings and contributions of

---

24. Appius's post becomes relevant again when he is summoned by the consul to take auspices to avoid the potential disruption of the election (3.7.1). For the role of augurs in public ceremonies, see Cic. *Leg.* 2.20–21; cf. *Nat. D.* 1.122. It may be not insignificant that, within the invocation of Appius's status as augur, it is only the "sinister" (*sinistra*) side that has any real role in the dialogue, while the *dextri* are largely silent. Perhaps this arrangement portends the election's disruption or, for that matter, the impending civil strife of the following year?

25. For his consulship and censorship, the latter of which would be disrupted by his departure from Italy to join the forces of Pompey in Greece, see *MRR* 2.221 and 247–48. Constans (1921) remains the sole monograph devoted to the man. See also Astin (1988) 30ff.; Tatum (1990) 36–40; and Tatum (1999) 33–36, 191, and 231–34.

26. The most famous Cornelius Merula attested is the *flamen dialis,* who replaced the exiled Cinna as suffect consul in 87 BC and who committed suicide after the latter's return and after piously laying down his priesthood (Vell. Pat. 2.20.3; Val. Max. 9.12.5). As Linderski (1989) 125 n. 86 observes, however, the present Cornelius Merula is not found in the list of supplementary senators in *MRR* 2.486ff.

the remaining fowls quickly fall off: the otherwise unknown Pica from Reate (3.7.11) and Pavo (3.17.1) chirp but once each in the dialogue, while Passer is likewise entirely absent from the historical record and is, moreover, wholly without song. Rounding out this birds' gallery is the obscure Pantuleius "Parra," whose brief appearance as an ill-omened "Barn-owl" bears ominous screeching of electoral fraud (3.5.18). Chosen to fill out the fantastical image of the Villa Publica *qua* aviary, these men were nonetheless likely historical figures—specifically, local elite from Italian municipalities[27]—and thus important guest-friends (*hospites*) and clients of Roman politicians: in this case, perhaps we are to infer, of Appius and possibly of Cornelius Merula as well.[28] Thus, however ridiculous the resulting image of an eminent augur surrounded by a prominent blackbird and lesser birds may be, it also emblematizes the symbiotic political dynamic between Roman politicians of the city and those municipal *nobiles domi,* for whom the former serve as patron, but also rely on for their own sociopolitical clout.

Embracing Axius's explication of the Villa Publica *qua* aviary, Appius then invites the pair of Reatinians in and frames this gesture of hospitality specifically as recompense for Axius's prior act, when the man served him a fine bird platter on his way to preside over an ongoing dispute between the Reatinians and the Interamnatians[29] and to which his digestive troubles presently attest. Insofar as this exchange of hospitality is framed, it continues to foreground the dialogue's recurring juxtaposition of the public and private spheres as well as the dynamics of Roman-Italian political culture, yet further ups the satirical ante. On the one hand, whereas Varro and Axius were said to be "on hand" (*praesto*; 3.2.1) for their *candidatus privatus*, Appius *qua* augur is presently "on hand" (*praesto*; 3.2.2) for consultation during the public election. Moreover, each interlocutor explicitly invokes the sort of villa-centered dining culture that accompanies interactions between amicable members of the Roman

---

27. Based on epigraphic and linguistic evidence, this inference of Linderski (1989) 116–17 is almost certainly correct.

28. The bibliography of patron-client relationships in the Roman world is extensive; see, for example, Gelzer (1969) 62–70. As Wiseman (1971) 33–38 rightly discusses, the categories of relationships between those from the city of Rome proper and Italians are inherently blurry: "the dominance of Rome and the correspondingly large political power wielded by a member of the Roman Senate resulted in the merging of the idea of *hospitium* into that of *clientele.* The Roman could do more for his foreign or Italian host or guest than the latter could do for him, and so became in a sense his patron and protector, expecting in return for his *beneficia* as much political support as his *hospes* could muster in his home town or district" (34–35).

29. For discussions of this debate over the draining of the Lacus Velinus and its impact on the Rosean plains, which seems to have been a longstanding environmental and political problem from 272 BC until at least 15 AD (cf. Tac. *Ann.* 1.79), see Shackleton-Bailey (1965) 2.209 and Flach (2002) 195–97. Cf. Cic. *Att.* 90.5 [= 4.15.5].

political elite, while the occasion for that instance of hospitality continues to underscore the role that an eminent Roman politician might sporadically play in municipal matters pertaining to his clients and thus, strictly speaking, of more local political import. On the other hand, the emphasis on dinner (i.e., fowl) and its resultant effects (i.e., chronic burping) smacks of the satirical obsession with gustatory detail and bodily functions, yet also adds a chilling and macabre note; as the sated augur in an aviary, Appius still belches from the consumption of fowl and, although no one dares to mention it, the cannibalistic undertones to Appius's interminable eructation next to his food's nominal brethren lurk. In this respect, the third dialogue offers a decidedly more unsettling opening image than is found in either of its predecessors, which, in conjunction with the already portentous backdrop of 50 BC, only intensifies the ominous calm of the backdrop.

With the scene set and hospitality seemingly now reciprocated, Axius and Appius continue their bantering exchange, and the discussion gradually enfolds Varro and Merula in its swath as well. Of course, the eventual subject will be *pastio villatica,* a novel, distinct, and potentially lucrative form of *res rustica,* but the conversation only reaches this subject by way of a preliminary debate over what constitutes a villa (3.2.3–18). Throwing down the gauntlet, Appius accosts Axius with the charge that the latter's private villa is "thoroughly polished" (*perpolita*) with the costliest materials, frequented by mares and donkeys, and possessed by one man alone. In contrast, the Villa Publica belongs to the people, hosts citizens and humans,[30] and serves a "useful" purpose for *res publica* (*ad rem publicam administrandam . . . utilis;* 3.2.4) as the site of citizen levies and the census. Thus, Appius frames Axius's private villa as a locus of *voluptas,* without *utilitas,* and the Villa Publica as one of *utilitas,* without *voluptas.*[31] Axius's rejoinder is, to say the least, spirited, with him reversing his counterpart's evaluations point for point.[32]

---

30. The inclusion of the *cives* and *reliqui homines* is likely intended to reflect the dual purpose of the Villa Publica as the location where both the census was taken and foreign embassies were received. Cf. nn. 16–17.

31. So much should one infer from the incomplete second half of Appius's final sentence, which Axius's rejoinder interrupts (3.2.5).

32. As Flach (2002) 198 astutely observes, Axius's use of the ironic particle *scilicet* (3.2.5) in response to Appius's claim may very well testify to the facetiousness of the latter's description of the Villa Publica as a simple, austere structure. Unfortunately, Flach neither provides any hard evidence for this possibility nor does he engage any secondary scholarship on this temple (cf. nn. 16–17). The observations of Green (1997) 433 are thus to be preferred, but note that the context dictates that it is Axius's—not Varro's—Reatinian estate under discussion. Cf. Purcell (1995) 152, who correctly apprehends that Axius's estate is the subject, but takes the following statements of Appius's too literally and consequently fails to understand that it is not the latter's personal villa, but the Villa Publica under his purview in the capacity of augur and censor. See also Linderski (1980) 272–73 and Tatum (1992) 197–98, esp. n. 43.

Chock-full of paintings and busts, the Villa that Appius champions has neither field nor draft animal and hosts neither harvest nor vintage; instead,
his own villa, so Axius claims, is heavily marked by traces of the sower and
the shepherd and is actually "polished" (*polita*) by a large *fundus* and herds
(3.2.5–6). Thus, on Axius's estimation, the putative pleasure villa actually produces practicable profits, whereas the supposedly useful one turns out to
reap no such returns.

In bifurcating their analyses in terms of profit *or* pleasure, the discussion
and, for that matter, the treatise as a whole would thus seem to have come
to an impasse. Each interlocutor fundamentally rejects the other's characterization of the structures in question and they both even seem to regard the
dual ends of Varronian *res rusticae*—the pursuits of *utilitas* for *fructus* and of
*voluptas* for *delectatio*—not as jointly complementary (as they were shown to
be in *agri cultura* and *pastio agrestis*; cf. pp. 47–52 in chapter 2), but rather, as
mutually exclusive. Another cause for perplexity initially stymies the *sermo*,
yet eventually provides a way forward for the discussants. As it turns out,
Axius and Appius are unclear as to the requisite criteria for what constitutes
a villa; so much does the former implicitly acknowledge in his denial that
an extra-urban (*extra urbem*) location is the necessary and sufficient criterion for a villa (3.2.6) and the latter in his openly wry (*subridens*) admission
of ignorance as to what a villa is (3.2.7). Eventually, Merula will resolve the
standstill by inferring (*colligere*) that any structure where animals are stabled
will rightly be called a villa (3.2.10), but the discussion's impasse first enables
the introduction of a third model: the Ostian villa of a certain Marcus Seius.[33] What emerges from the ensuing discussion is that the previous emphasis
on adornment and productive infrastructure—*urbana ornamenta* and *rustica membra,* as Axius subsequently phrases it (3.2.9)—was too narrow and
fails to capture this third model's capacity to produce both profit (*fructus*)
and pleasure (*delectatio*). As Merula has apparently witnessed firsthand, Seius's villa has neither the ornamental trappings of a *villa urbana* nor the sort
of equipment necessary for a *villa rustica* (3.2.8), yet is more delightful (cf.
*magis delectatus*; 3.2.8) than the former and even more profitable (*maioris*

---

33. Seius shows up in a handful of references in Cicero's letters (*Att.* 106.2 [= 5.13.2];
247 [= 12.10]) and seems to have been a supporter of Caesar in 46 BC (*Fam.* 9.7.1). See also
Shackleton-Bailey (1965) 3.214 and Shatzman (1975) 164 n. 96, both of whom note the possibility that this Seius was the son of a curule aedile of 74 BC. Note also the appearance of a
Seius in Varro's *Menippeans* (F 60 Bücheler). Famous for his success in *pastio villatica*, Seius
was also possibly the inventor of foie gras (Pliny *HN* 10.52). Intriguingly, the *gens Seia* show
up in a variety of agricultural and commercial enterprises in Italy, North Africa, and Delos;
see Kolendo (1994) 63, Bertrandy (1995) 61–85, and Deniaux (2002) 29–39, for all of which
references I am indebted to Marzano (2007) 90 n. 35.

*fructus*; 3.2.13) than the latter. Thereafter, the conversation devolves to Merula and then Varro adducing the vast sums extracted from exemplary villas— Seius's villa and its return of 50K sesterces per year, 60K from the Sabine estate of Varro's aunt, the profit of 40K from Cato's tutelary sale of the fish of L. Lucullus's son—to the ongoing astonishment of "Mr. Worth" (i.e., Axius), a man who increasingly embodies the value embedded in his name and now seeks instruction in this most lucrative form of *res rusticae*. Yet, for all the playful banter and jokes at the expense of Axius's greed, the conversation nonetheless provides the basis for the eventual definition of *pastio villatica* (3.3.1): as a science (*scientia*) of how animals can be reared (*pascere*) in or around the villa (*in villa circumve eam*) so as to secure profit (*fructus*) and delight (*delectatio*).[34] Thus, whether knowingly or not, the interlocutors have ended up using Seius's villa as a heuristic model for *pastio villatica*, which allows them to articulate the final sphere of the tripartite estate of Varronian *res rusticae*: a topic that Varro claimed "as a whole has not been distinguished separately by anyone, so far as I know" (3.1.8).

Insofar as the interlocutors eventually winnow playful chaff from a serious core, the opening exchange of *RR* 3 resembles that of the first dialogue (1.2.11–28). Yet, unlike *RR* 1, this *sermo* remains plagued by a number of unsettling uncertainties. In the first place, endemic to the conversation's first half is a fundamental confusion regarding the precise villa under consideration. As previous commentators have frequently observed, when Axius speaks of *tua villa*[35] to refer to that structure for which Appius advocates, it becomes slightly unclear whether he is referring to the Villa Publica or to another villa Appius actually owned in the area, though the *tua* undoubtedly refers to the former by playing off Appius's censorship of that year: hence the man's delineation of the Villa Publica's functions.[36] Even so, one is left to wonder whether Appius's

---

34. The full quote is as follows: "Primum . . . dominum scientem esse oportet earum rerum, qu{e}<i> in villa circumve eam animalia ali ac pasci possint, ita ut domino sint fructui ac delectationi." Note that Flach in his 2006 edition restores the *qui* as the archaic ablative singular form (as he prefers to do elsewhere and against *quae*) and retains the *animalia*, which most editors drop. Either way, the meaning is largely the same.

35. Note Axius's threefold repetition of *tua* (3.2.5–6).

36. So Tatum (1992) 198 n. 43 rightly has it. For an example of the misguided reading, see Purcell (1995) 151–52, which does not detract from his overall point. Cf. n. 32. Green (1997) 432 takes a different tack by understanding Axius as "respond[ing] to the other, symbolic meaning, to the Villa Publica as Rome itself." Her note 15 ad loc. for the possibility of literally understanding the phrase *haec in campo Martio extremo* is intriguing, but difficult to accept without qualification. Moreover, the reference to the grandfathers and great-grandfathers surely plays off Appius's exalted lineage, his "*Appietas,*" as Cicero contemptuously put it (*Fam.* 71.5 [= 3.7.5]). Cicero's remark plays off the venerable lineage of the Appii Claudii, many of whom were among the most prominent men of their day, the most famous undoubtedly

"villa" refers only to the Villa Publica; or sometimes to a villa he owns as well; or, symbolically, to the city of Rome; or even to all three possible referents at once.[37] Likewise, it emerges only post facto that Axius actually owns *two* estates in Reate, which casts a new light on his disagreement with Appius, as each speaker may in fact be referring to different estates.[38] There is a confounding humor, then, to the deliberate ambiguity built into the interlocutors' conversation *de villis,* which contributes to *RR* 3's blurring of the subject (i.e., the villa) and its various literal and metaphorical referents: the Villa Publica, private villas, and, as we shall see, the city of Rome.

The ambiguity surrounding Appius's and Axius's villas extends to the Ostian one owned by Marcus Seius as well and takes a disconcerting turn. After playfully admitting that he does not know the definition of a villa, Appius mentions his desire to purchase Seius's villa, a plan that, owing to his ignorance, may lead him to the imprudent (*imprudentia*) purchase of a "Seian house" (*Seianas aedes*) instead of a villa (3.2.7). It has become a commonplace for commentators to observe the similarity of a story recorded by Aulus Gellius about a roughly contemporary Gnaeus Seius, whose exquisite horse was believed to have brought an untimely demise to its owner (proscribed by Mark Antony) as well as to all the steed's possessors thereafter: hence, the proverbial "Seian horse" (*equus Seianus*; Aul. Gell. *NA* 3.9.1–6).[39] The list of the deceased post-Seius is impressive: the hapless Caesarian, Publius Cornelius Dolabella, in 43 BC; the ill-fated assassin of Caesar, C. Cassius, in 42 BC; and, in an act of proverbial retribution, the right-hand man of Caesar, Mark Antony himself, in 31 BC. Of course, Varro would only have been aware of the first three "Seian" victims in 37 BC. Regardless of the possible relationship between the two Seii, the otherwise obscure joke about the "Seian house" becomes

---

being *the* Appius Claudius Caecus (censor 312 BC, cos. 307, 296). Cf. *Cael.* 33, where Cicero famously conjures up the *imago* of Caecus (through *prosopopoeia*) to shame Clodia.

37. So Kronenberg (2009) 102 n. 24 interprets it. Note also that at 3.17.1, Appius departs *in hortos,* which adds to the confusion, but which Linderski (1980) 272–3—*contra* Shatzman (1975) 323; 346—rightly saw were public gardens attached to the precinct of the Villa Publica.

38. Until 3.2.9, there is no explicit acknowledgment that Axius owns one estate near Lake Velinus—which "has never seen a painter nor *tector*" and thus corresponds closely to Axius's description of his villa at 3.2.5–6—and another one in the plain of Rosea, which is "elegantly polished with stucco" and thus corresponds more closely to Appius's (implied) description of Axius's villa at 3.2.3–4. Merula's subsequent comments strongly suggest that the villa at Lake Velinus had the large *fundus* attached to it and focused solely or primarily on *agri cultura,* was unadorned, and perhaps merited description solely as a *villa rustica,* whereas the one at Rosea focused primarily on *pastio agrestis,* was adorned, and merited description as both a *villa rustica* and a *villa urbana.* For Axius's multiple estates in Reate, see Shatzman (1975) 308.

39. For further discussion, see Flach (2002) 199–200.

intelligible once we construe Appius's comment as a pun off the well-known proverb, thereby not only allowing the authorial Varro to obliquely allude to events of civil war in the late 40s BC, but also inflecting *pastio villatica* with a troubling resonance and undermining its exemplary instantiation.

Perhaps even more problematic are the elements of uncertainty and risk attendant to *pastio villatica* and thematically reinforced throughout. For example, one of the exemplary proprietors is the virtually obscure Lucius Abuccius, "a particularly learned man, whose booklets are in a Lucilian style" (*adprime doctus, cuius Luciliano character sunt libelli*; 3.2.17).[40] According to Varro, his actual returns from his villa were relatively modest—over 20K as opposed to his fields' annual return of 10K—but his claims for the potential profit to be culled verge on the ludicrous: upwards of a 100K should he have had his pick of land near the sea. Given that Abuccius survives in little more than scant testimonia, it is impossible to determine the context in which he made such claims—or even to verify that he did—though it is certainly curious that Varro chooses to cite a man whose defining characteristic is his status as learned satirist and whose figures are nearly twice the amount of the next-highest one procured by proprietors of *pastio villatica*. Indeed, one learned satirist citing another so as to further fan the flames of Mr. Worth's greed is an image not exactly designed to embolden the reader's faith in the veracity of the figures or, for that matter, the viability of *pastio villatica* as a profitable endeavor of *res rusticae*.

The fundamental problem apparently lies in the enterprise's market aspects, that is, what Stolo called *promendo* in the case of *agri cultura* (1.37.4). And any enthusiasm for the profit potential of *pastio villatica* must be tempered by the recognition that its yield depends on the whims of the city's festal circumstances and, in this respect, is a "crapshoot" (*bolus*; 3.2.16):

> [VARRO:] Sed ad hunc bolum ut pervenias, opus erit tibi aut epulum aut triumphus alicuius, ut tunc fuit Scipionis Metelli, aut collegiorum cenae, quae nunc innumerabiles excandefaciunt annonam macelli. Reliquis annis omnibus etiam si hanc expectabis summam, spero, non tibi decoquet non ornithon; neque hoc accidet his moribus nisi raro, ut decipiaris. Quotus quisque enim est annus, quo non videas epulum aut triumphum aut collegia non epulari?

---

40. Lucius Abuccius is usually dated to the first half of the first century BC. For an intriguing assessment of what Varro meant by *Lucilianus character*—namely, a style that was *gracilis*, but one that was not necessarily characterized by invective—see Svarlien (1994) 253–67.

[VARRO:] "But to haul in this score (*bolum*), you will need to have either a banquet or someone's triumph, such as Scipio Metellus' was then [i.e., in 54 or 53 BC], or the collegial dinners, which innumerably light up the *annona macelli* at present. Even if you await this amount in all the other years, your aviary will not, I hope, go bankrupt; nor will it happen that you are cheated—except rarely—in these present *mores*. For how few are the years in which you do not see a banquet or a triumph or *collegia* feasting?"

Framing the issue via a tricolon of public banquets, triumphal celebrations, and collegial dinners, Varro emphasizes the necessity of a public occasion for the profitable sale of the villa's produce. On the upside, however, the state of the "present *mores*" means that such celebratory feasts saturate the city's calendar. The moralizing connotations and negative undertones to this particular claim are patent, which Axius succinctly (and shrewdly) reframes in his subsequent rejoinder: "But it is on account of luxury (*luxuria*) . . . that there is, in a certain way, a daily banquet within the gates (*ianuas*) of Rome" (*Sed propter luxuriam, inquit, quodam modo epulum cotidianum est intra ianuas Romae*; 3.2.16).[41] In this respect, *pastio villatica* would seem to have emerged as an economically viable sphere of *res rusticae* in response to *luxuria* and the Roman people's greater appetite for public feasts, thereby all but ensuring the profitability of villa husbandry and providing the sorts of windfalls that Seius, Varro's aunt, Abuccius, and Cato—Ostian villa owner, woman, satirist, and Stoic alike—have apparently enjoyed and which Axius so greedily desires. The model of private villa husbandry thus envisioned by Book 3 depends upon the participation of those who inhabit the Villa Publica and the figure for which it stands: the city of Rome. And like any villa which one necessarily enters through doors (*ianua*), those who came to dine in the city would have entered through its "gates" (*portae*).[42] By choosing *ianua* over the appropriate word for the city, however, Axius's statement in fact puns on and reifies the dialogue's metaphorization of Rome as a villa: "But it is on account of *luxuria* . . . that there is, in a certain way (*quodam modo*),[43] a daily feast within the *doors* (*ianuas*) of Rome."

---

41. For the connection between *luxuria* and gluttony, see Gowers (1993b) 12–24.

42. Strictly speaking, the difference between the two terms lies in *porta*'s reference to the enclosure (*TLL* s.v. *porta* I. A.), while *ianua* refers to the door(s) that provide(s) access to the enclosure (*TLL* s.v. *ianua* I. A.), although it should be noted that *porta* can sometimes be used in the sense usually assigned to *ianua* (*TLL* s.v. *porta* I.B). Note that *ianua* as a proper *porta* is a post-classical Latin usage (*TLL* s.v. *ianua de usu*).

43. Note that this formula of qualification is found repeatedly in Cicero's *De Re Publica*—perhaps most relevantly, in his use of the agricultural slave-bailiff, *vilicus,* as an analogy for the *rector rei publicae* (5.4 Powell [= 5.5 Ziegler]). See Nelsestuen (2014) 130–73. Cf. pp. 227–28 in chapter 7.

Because its viability is inextricably tied to the market demand occasioned by the intermittent public or collegial feast, *pastio villatica* (unlike *agri cultura*[44]) is a crapshoot (*bolum*). Yet, the declined state of Roman mores has somewhat ironically rendered the practice a relatively safe bet. To frame the matter in terms of the earlier contrasts we saw, public feasts drive the demand for private production of the animal goods, which provide, on the one hand, pleasure for the feasting citizens and, on the other, both pleasure and profit for the producing villa owners. The result is that *pastio villatica* is characterized by a series of tensions: beholden to the volatility of market demand, but reasonably safe in its eventual realization; a private enterprise that feeds on public consumption; and financially lucrative, but morally questionable. Indeed, by its very nature, the practice is somewhat paradoxical, for it is the production of prestige items *at* the (private) villa—items that might be said to fall under the category of "luxury foodstuffs"[45]—that constitutes, supplies, and finances the pleasure offered *in* villas: both private and public. Indeed, by turning *luxuria* and declined *mores* to the advantages of profit and pleasure, it is as if *pastio villatica* is a self-perpetuating practice that feeds—and feeds *on*—the city, which renders it an economically viable, but morally fraught, sphere of *res rusticae*.

A final discomfiting image concludes the preliminary discussion. Just before Merula gives the dialogue's working definition of *pastio villatica*, Axius pleads to be taken on as Merula's student, promising as a fee (*minerval,*[46] 3.2.18) a dinner consisting of the villa produce he so eagerly desires to learn how to rear. Inferring the meal to be of fowl once again, Appius now recants his taste for Axian poultry and jests that the birds would sooner die than be successfully reared as produce, to which Axius responds by pointing out that the birds they eat are always already dead (*mortuos*), so it matters not whether the fowl die from natural causes (*morticinos*) or from slaughter. Recalling the opening connotations of cannibalism, this final image threatens

---

44. In this respect, *pastio villatica* would appear to differ qualitatively from *agri cultura*, which is a game of chance (*alea*) only when *salubritas* is fundamentally lacking (1.4.3) or when the farmer seeks to innovate without a balanced use of *imitatio* and *experientia* (1.18.8). See pp. 62–63 in chapter 2 and p. 165 in chapter 5.

45. See Purcell (1995) 152–53, who views Seius's estate as "one of the most advanced examples of the new fashion for investment in the rearing of luxury foodstuffs for the prestige delicatessen market, the *macellum,* and for prestige eating on the part of the elite and its fared dependents."

46. Ash and Hooper (1934) 438 adduce Juv. 10.116 for the closest parallel of this otherwise unattested form of this "satirical word."

to transgress another culinary taboo—that of eating carrion[47]—thereby casting one last pall over the practice of *pastio villatica* in Rome.

## NOT YOUR FATHER'S *LEPORARIA*: PROFIT *AND* PLEASURE

By relying on declined Roman *mores* and the concomitant increase in demand for gustatory forms of pleasure, and then trading in them as economic commodities, *pastio villatica* is a new and economically viable practice of contemporary *res rusticae* directed towards the twin ends of profit (*fructus*) and pleasure (*voluptas*). As we shall see, the technical portions of *RR* 3 are replete with examples of such simultaneously profitable and pleasurable practices. Yet, the dialogue also raises serious questions about its ethics and morality. While this more critical perspective continues in the technical discussion proper, it is framed primarily in allegorical terms and advanced in the accounts of aviaries and apiaries, which two sections below will examine closely. In the present section, I focus on Merula's analytical and historical account of *pastio villatica* (3.3.1–10) and the interlocutors' technical discussion of specific animals (3.6.1–15.2), the former of which defines and contextualizes, the latter of which exemplifies, how the production of prestige animal products may reap profitable and pleasurable returns.

Once Merula has defined *pastio villatica* (3.3.1) as a *scientia* of "how animals can be nourished and reared in or around the villa in such a way that it brings the owner profit (*fructus*) and delight (*delectatio*)" (3.3.1), he then gets to the text's usual business of division and schematization. Identifying three categories (*genera*) of practice within *pastio villatica* (3.3.1–2)—aviaries (*ornithones*), animal hutches (*leporaria*), and fishponds (*piscinae*)—Merula then specifies the animals (by means of two *species*) to be included under each category (3.3.2–4) and provides a historical pedigree for each *genus* as well. After the initial (*prima*) rearing of chickens for auspicial use in the city and private consumption in the countryside came (*secunda*) the enclosing of

---

47. A relatively rare word, *morticinus* generally is applied to animals and denotes that the adjective's bearer had died on its own (cf. *TLL* s.v. morticinus *i.q. mortuus [fere sua morte; imprimis de animalibus . . .]*), that is, from what English speakers would refer to as "natural causes." The word often carries a pejorative connotation, as evidenced by the examples adduced in *TLL*. Interestingly enough, in the context of a discussion of the luxurious feasting—including the eating of birds fattened and, like *RR*, kept in the dark—Seneca describes those men who dedicate themselves to such practices as "living carrion" (*in vivis caro morticina est*; *Ep.* 122.4).

animals within walls and, specifically, the keeping of bees in the villa's eaves, which preceded the final (*tertia*) addition of freshwater fishponds stocked with local fish (3.3.5). The historical evolution of this contemporary practice thus has three distinct and progressive phases, which correspond to the three categories of, respectively, *ornithones, leporaria,* and *piscinae.*[48] Within each category, two stages (*bini gradus*) further nuance this chronological scheme in distinctly moralistic terms: the "*superiores,* which ancient frugality [added], and the *inferiores,* which later luxury added" (*superiores, quos frugalitas antiqua, inferiores, quos luxuria posterior adiecit*; 3.3.6). In support of this contention, Merula adduces specific examples for each *genus* of *pastio villatica.* In the case of aviaries, the "ancient stage of our ancestors" (*gradus anticus maiorum nostrum*) consisted only of the barnyard where chickens were raised and the makeshift dovecotes maintained (3.3.6). At that time, *fructus* was limited to eggs and offspring. As for the contemporary situation, Merula states (3.3.7):

> Contra nunc aviaria sunt nomine mutato, quod vocantur ornithones, quae palatum suave domini paravit, ut tecta maiora habeant, quam tum habebant totas villas, in quibus stabulentur turdi ac pavones.

> Now (*nunc*), on the other hand, *aviaria* have a changed name—seeing that they are called *ornithona*—which the delicate palate of the owner has obtained, with the result that people have larger buildings (in which thrushes and peacocks are stabled) than they used to have entire villas back then (*tum*).

Reiterating the topos of Greek loanwords as a symptom of increased luxury,[49] Merula's observation of the linguistic shift from the Latin *aviarium* of the past (*tum*) to the Greek *ornithon* in current usage (*nunc*) accompanies the aviary's expansion beyond chickens and doves to include thrushes and peacocks. It also anticipates similar developments in the other two categories of

---

48. In these respects, Merula's account is analogous to the relevant passages of *RR* 1 (1.2.11–28) and 2 (origin: 2.1.3–5; dignity: 2.1.6–11).

49. For examples in architectural terminology, see Varro's remarks at 2.pref.2. For examples in *RR* 3, see *peristeretrophion* (3.7.1); *peristeron* (3.7.2–3); *ornithoboscion* (3.9.2); *ornithotrophion* (ibid.); *chenoboscion* (3.10.1; cf. Columella, *Rust.* 8.14.1); *nessotrophion* (3.11.1; cf. Columella, *Rust.* 8.15.1; 7); and *therotrophium* (3.13.2). Note Axius's explicit ridicule of the use of Greek words by "you Grecophiles" (*vos philograeci*) at 3.10.1 and Hortensius's rejection of the term *leporarium* for *therotrophium* at 3.13.2. The use of such Greek words undoubtedly plays off the location of the kinds of estates envisioned in *RR* 3 in such modish areas as the Bay of Naples, which famously remained culturally and linguistically Greek; see D'Arms (1970) 39–43, 55–61.

villa husbandry. Thus, whereas the *leporarium* owned by Axius's father "never saw anything beyond a little hare (*lepusculum*) from hunting," those of today (*nunc*; 3.3.8) are exponentially larger and incorporate boars and roes as well. Likewise, the few *piscinae* owned by the forefathers had only *squali* and *mugiles,* which the contemporary "dandy fop" (*minthon*[50]) counts as no better than frogs. "Just as our age (*nostra aetas*) with this *luxuria* increased the bounds of *leporaria,* so did we extend the *piscinae* to the sea and call back the deep-sea schools of fish into them," concludes Merula (3.3.10).

By contrasting the limited and rudimentary practices of villa husbandry in the past with the larger and more extravagant operations of the present, Merula's account achieves several ends at once. First, it gives a historical pedigree to *pastio villatica,* which effectively normalizes what may otherwise appear to be a wholly novel rustic practice. Second, the historical excursus also highlights the historically determined and distinctive nature of contemporary *pastio villatica.* Finally, by employing tropes typical of Roman moralizing discourse, it reinforces the figuration of the generalized past as one of austerity (*frugalitas*) and the present as one of extravagance (*luxuria*). In this last respect, *RR* 3 would appear to have much in common with those Roman texts[51] that extol the farmer of yesteryear—often implicitly at the expense of the putatively vitiated one of the present.

Yet, for all of its emphasis on the recent genesis of *pastio villatica* in its present form and for all of its use of moralistic rhetoric, this passage—as well as *RR* 3 in general—does not condemn the production of *fructus* through the "new" villa husbandry. To be sure, traces of nostalgia for the humbler practices of the past clearly peek through in the course of the *sermo.* And, of course, the interlocutors have no qualms with good-naturedly ribbing those Romans whose obsessive pursuit of *fructus* (like Axius's) borders on the avaricious as well as with ridiculing those whose tastes tend towards the ludicrously extravagant. As an example of the latter, Q. Hortensius Hortalus, the renowned orator and statesman, comes under derision for his absurdly excessive affection for the mullets inhabiting his fishpond. So great was his concern, Axius claims, that he maintained fishermen to supply minnows to the mullets and even kept a store of salted fish for them when inclement weather precluded the procurement of live ones (3.17.6–7; cf. 3.3.10).

---

50. Apparently another Greek loanword, *minthon* has presented textual and interpretative difficulties for editors; see Flach (2002) 213, who follows the explanation of Philodemus (*Peri Kakion,* 21.19–20 Jensen) adopted here. Cf. *TLL* s.v. *minthon.*

51. See, for example, Cic. *Rosc. Am.* 52 or Columella, *Rust.* 1.pref.13–19. Cf. Columella *Rust.* 8.16.1–6, who riffs on this passage and its theme of *luxuria* but, like Varro, endorses *pastio villatica* as a profitable venture.

But sporadic nostalgia and derision of a few *pecuarii villatici* do not equate to wholesale denunciation of a contemporary sphere of rustic enterprise. Instead, the impetus behind the interlocutors' disapproval is the imputation of *mis*production: be it in the form of a substantial *failure*, complete *lack*, or even gross *superfluity*. As observed earlier (cf. pp. 173–74), the drive for production infused all levels and spheres of Roman society—including those of the elite—and thus was an acceptable and expected part of Roman behavior in villa and agricultural settings. The flipside to this ideology is that the "pursuit of sterility and the expensive investment are gestures which only work against this background" of production and which attest to the "freakishness" of pure aestheticism and *delectatio*-oriented display.[52] Hence, in the opening debate over the relative merits of their respective villas, both Appius and Axius seek the rhetorical jugular by averring the lack of utility and production at the estate of the other. Or, in Hortensius's case, it is his raising of fish solely for the pleasures of sentimentality and display, but *not* profit, that is worthy of unabashed derision and made even more ridiculous by his expensive and quasi-cannibalistic outlays of additional fish—live and dead— to feed the piscine objects of his affection. Conversely, Lucullus's Xerxean efforts to expand his saltwater *piscinae* to the bounds of the Mediterranean run excessively in both the directions of profit and pleasure (3.17.9; cf. pp. 209–10 below). Thus, it is not so much *pastio villatica* itself, but the failure to practice it *soundly*, that presents a problem for the interlocutors of *RR 3*.

The implication thus emerges that there would seem to be an *ethics* of production somehow operative in *De Re Rustica*. While *RR 3* does not explicitly articulate this system—if only because the sheer variety of animals renders each account largely *sui generis* and, consequently, the utility of generalizations is inherently limited—its rudimentary principles take their foundations from the twofold pursuit of profit and pleasure and are further fleshed out in the technical precepts of Varronian *res rusticae*. I begin with the first animal, namely, peafowl (*pavones*), which Axius entreats Merula to provide in the absence of the departed Fircellius Pavo.

Like most of the other animals now kept at the villa, peafowl are said to have become a staple of profitable *pastio villatica* only "in our time" (*nostra memoria*; 3.6.1). Merula then proceeds by way of a fivefold division appropriate to fowls, which he articulates later on in his account of ducks (3.10.1): breed/kind (*de genere*), mating (*de fetura*), eggs (*de ovis*), chicks (*de pullis*), and fattening (*de sagina*). Thus, regarding the *genus*, peafowl of a "good age"

---

52. So Purcell (1995) 156 and 152, respectively, puts it, observing as well that "the compulsion to make money from the productive environment was all-pervasive in the Roman elite" (156).

and "good form" are to be procured (3.6.2). For mating, peahens of an age above two years and yet not too old ought to be used, and the amount of feed to be given should adhere to Seius's specifications (3.6.3). As for the production of eggs and chicks, not only are the existing eggs to be removed from the care of the peahens by the caretaker before the peacocks tread and to be sold for immense profit, but still other eggs ought to be purchased and placed under (chicken-)hens (*gallinae*) as well (3.6.3–4; cf. 3.9.10). In place of cramming (*sagina*), Merula substitutes prescriptions for the peafowls' housing, the need for clean quarters, and the mixed usage of their droppings (both as fertilizer for *agri cultura* and as bedding for chicks, 3.6.4–5; cf. 3.9.14), and concludes the brief treatment *de pavonibus* with a repetition of his opening remarks on the profit potential of peafowl.

As was the case for *RR* 2, the technical precepts are keyed to the perspective of an owner (*dominus*) and not the actual fowler or servile caretaker (cf. 3.3.4). Moreover, although the instruction is a bit more cursory and less structured than that found in the previous book, it still remains largely practical and sensible. The most conspicuous point of difference, however, is the marked emphasis on the *amount* of profit. Whereas the example of M. Aufidius Lucro's 60K sesterces kicks off the account (3.6.1), rough estimates of the sums to be made from the sale of eggs (five denarii), birds (50 denarii), and entire musters (40K to 60K sesterces) close it (3.6.6). In fact, in terms of its potential profitability, this bird apparently surpasses all others (3.6.3). Yet, Merula's treatment of peafowl is not so blinded by returns to completely eschew pleasure, the other end of Varronian *res rusticae*; as he notes, if one's interests lean more towards *delectatio,* the owner ought to have more males, which are more beautiful (*formosiores*; 3.6.1). And even if the owner is more inclined to profit, it nonetheless remains that an aesthetically pleasing form (*bona forma*) generally corresponds to a good breed (3.6.2), which translates into a better price, and so on. Indeed, the original impetus for this now profit-focused practice was the pleasure afforded by its consumption at Hortensius's inaugural banquet for his augurship, from the precedent of which the peafowl industry subsequently emerged as a viable market for the farmer of the villa (3.6.6). Thus, pleasure originally prompted—and now continues to procure—profit.

In its emphasis on the viability of profit and pleasure as congruent and mutually reinforcing ends, Merula's account of peafowl neatly illustrates the idealized vision of Varronian *res rusticae.* Other examples abound in the case of birds due to the fact that aesthetically pleasing animals were found to be more desirable and, therefore, commanded more money. For example, pairs of beautiful doves (*columbae*) fetch some two hundred sesterces and

particularly fine ones upwards of a thousand sesterces (3.7.10), while size
dictates the price of ortolans (*miliariae*) and quails (*coturnices*; 3.5.2). In the
case of geese (*anseres*), both external appearance and size matter (3.10.2).
And, of course, cramming seeks to swell the bird's size (doves, 3.7.9; turtledoves [*turtures*], 3.8.3; chickens, 3.9.19–21; and geese, 3.10.7), apparently
sometimes enriches the quality of its appearance as well (doves, 3.7.10), and,
of course, increases the diner's delight. At other times, an animal's exoticism
or rarity, which is sometimes brought about by the pastoral opportunities
of Roman *imperium,* renders it a source of pleasure and profit. For example,
Merula divides chickens into three basic kinds: domesticated (*villaticae*),
wild (*rusticae*), and *Africanae*. Whereas the domesticated and wild kinds
are viewed as primarily contributing to, respectively, the production-oriented enterprise of the private villa (3.9.4) and the spectacular trappings of
public ceremonies (*in ornatibus publicis*; 3.9.17), the so-called African *gal-
lina* constitutes the most recent entrée to the dinner spreads of gourmands
(3.9.18). Thus, in a manner reminiscent of Hortensius's introduction of the
peacock to the dinner table (3.6.6), it proffers both considerable profit and
pleasure: financial compensation to the farmer and gustatory delight to the
diner (3.9.19).

The confluence of profit and pleasure is also found in Appius's account
of *leporaria,* though less readily in the case of hares (*lepores*; 3.12.1–7), snails
(*cochlires*; 3.14.1–5), and dormice (*glires*; 3.15.1–2); Appius, for example, never
prescribes pleasing or ideal qualities for the physical appearance of any of
these creatures, though he does allude to the pleasure-inducing and profit-
producing culinary utility of snails (3.14.3) and, moreover, offers up precepts
for the fattening of all three (hares, 3.12.5; snails, 3.13.5; and dormice, 3.14.2).
In the case of boars, his discussion almost completely eschews any technical content,[53] focusing instead on the pleasure that these profitable animals
(3.2.11; cf. 3.3.8) contribute to the delectation of spectacle (3.13.1–3). On the
Tusculan estate of Varro (formerly, of M. Pupius Piso), the boars (and roes)
of the *leporarium* would customarily gather at the sound of a horn for feeding and, thus, offer up a delightful spectacle to the viewer (3.13.1; cf. 3.3.8).
But the Hellenistic *therotrophium* (pointedly, *not* a *leporarium*) of Hortensius's Laurentian villa is of another order quantitatively and qualitatively; not
only were the grounds vastly larger and filled with more kinds of animals,
but the summoning, as Appius wryly puts it, was conducted "Thracian-style"
(θρᾳκικῶς), replete with an Orpheus with his *bucina*-cum-*cithara* and a

---

53. From the standpoint of *De Re Rustica* as a whole, this omission may reflect the fact
that the care of boars would largely resemble that of pigs, which was covered in depth in
2.4.3–22.

raised dining table (*tricilinium*) at which banqueting spectators sat to watch the stage (3.13.2–3).[54] In this instance of Hortensian *pastio villatica,* we are not told whether he cherished these Orphic animals to the degree that he did his fish and, consequently, refrained from their slaughter, though such production of *delectatio* without any *fructus* would presumably have elicited some derisive comment.

The third (and final) category of *piscinae* bears on this discussion as well, but, like the dialogue's treatments of aviaries and bees, presents a unique set of interpretative challenges and will thus be considered later. As we have seen, successful *pastio villatica* is tantamount to the successful production of profit and, where possible, pleasure through the rearing of animals in and around the villa. In this respect, it adheres to the twin goals of *agri cultura* specified and arranged by Scrofa in *RR* 1: *fructus* and *delectatio,* with the former taking priority over, but often being aided by, the latter (1.4.1–2). But it is not simply a matter of obtaining the greatest possible profit and pleasure, for there is a sense of proportion that moderates—mostly implicitly, sometimes explicitly—the proprietor's operations and actions. Throughout the treatments of each animal, the interlocutors intersperse their accounts with considerable and detailed description of the necessary structures and accommodations specific to each animal. In so doing, the dialogue prescribes proper and appropriate infrastructure—what would be referred to as the villa's *membra* (cf. 3.2.9)—which imposes a limit on the number of animals and, thus, prudent bounds for the operations.[55] For example, in specifying the dimensions of the housing for turtledoves, Merula cites his previous strictures for the doves' cotes, but replaces the inset nests (*columbaria*) with unique stakes (*pali*) or brackets (*mutuli*) of strict spacing in terms of length, width, number of rows, and distance from floor and from ceiling (3.8.1–2); but the overriding principle, as he observes, is to procure "a place in proportion to how many [turtledoves] you wish to raise" (*locum . . . proinde magnum ac quam multitudinem alere velis*; 3.8.1).[56] Thus, even in the production of luxury prestige items like turtledoves, there is a sense of moderation and balance that ought to prevail.

---

54. For Hortensius's arrangement as "Golden Age fantasy and imagined visions of Latium's early landscapes and Trojan landfall," see Spencer (2010) 83.

55. One might wish to compare the discussion of herd sizes as the ninth point of *pastio agrestis* in *RR* 2 or the consideration of the proper size of a villa (1.11.1) or the debate over the requisite amount of equipment for the *fundus* (1.22.1–6) in *RR* 1. See also Spencer (2010) 80–81, who traces this connection between "moral worth" and "the definition and use of space."

56. See Flach (2002) 238–39 for his textual emendation and the interpretation.

As a further example of this principle, let us consider a passage from Book 1, which has sometimes been read in tandem with *RR* 3's treatment of the *luxuria*-focused *pastio villatica*.[57] In the midst of Scrofa's discussion of the proper layout of a farm (*fundus*), Fundanius interrupts with an observation that would seem to unambiguously privilege ancient over contemporary practice. According to Fundanius, the owner's profits are greater when he constructs the buildings of the *fundus* "according to the *diligentia* of the ancients rather than the *luxuria* of the men today" (1.13.6). Fundanius explains that, unlike the ancestors' concern for building a *villa rustica* in proportion to the operations, the contemporary focus is on having the "largest and most adorned *villa urbana* possible" (*villam urbanam quam maximam ac politissimam*). He further elaborates that the concern for desirable placement of summer and winter dining rooms currently outweighs the past, production-oriented need for properly ventilated and seasonally appropriate storage areas for wine and oil (1.13.7). In other words, the pleasure offered by ornate living quarters now trumps the pursuit of profit, and present *luxuria* has subverted past utility. As examples of this deleterious trend, Fundanius cites Lucullus and Metellus, whose "villas constructed to public detriment" (*villis pessimo publico aedificatis*) induce others to "contend" (*certant*) with their extravagantly ornate and adorned villas. Precise explanation as to how this competition adversely impacts *res publica* in turn is not explicitly provided, but the immediate context (not to mention *RR* 1's overall emphasis on productive *agri cultura*) suggests that Fundanius is decrying the corresponding lack of production as well as perhaps any other consequences attendant to this shift (e.g., debt incurred as a result of nonsustainability).[58] Thus, in keeping with what we have seen so far in *RR* 3, it is not so much the lavish construction and *elegantia* that are specifically at issue, but rather, it is the unbounded *luxuria*—the "unrestrained passions" (*libidines indomitas*)—at the expense of rational production (cf. *ad fructum rationem*) that is the crux of the matter.

---

57. See Kronenberg (2009) 106, who views this passage as indicative of the morally bankrupt nature of "old-fashioned farming values" in *De Re Rustica*.

58. In *De Legibus* 3.30–31, Cicero advances the claim that Lucullus's greatest point of guilt in pursuing the *magnificentia villae Tusculanae* was not the *libido* and *cupiditas* inherent in that particular project or that single man, but the fact that such *principes* and such projects inspired so many imitators (*permulti imitatores*) of such ills. While the publication of *De Legibus* remains a vexed issue, the sentiment is certainly found elsewhere in Cicero (e.g., *Rep.* 5.1–2) and suggests that Fundanius—knowingly or not—is rehearsing a Cicero-inspired argument regarding the morality of the elite as evidenced through their building practices.

## AVIARIES AND THE FAILURE OF ELITE
## POLITICAL BEHAVIOR

In presenting *pastio villatica* as a discrete area of profitable rustic enterprise, *RR* 3 completes the treatise's promised vision of the tripartite *praedium* (1.1.11): *agri cultura* on the *fundus*, *pastio* on the pastures, and *pastio* at the *villa*. But the status of *pastio villatica* as the newest area of rustic enterprise, which only emerged as a differentiated concept with a requisite level of wealth at Rome (cf. 3.1.7–8), also renders it a particularly good subject for discussing a number of other recent trends in the city. As we have seen, villa husbandry epitomizes contemporary *luxuria* and the proliferation of public feasts. Or, as in the case of chickens, it evokes the conditions that facilitated this *luxuria*, namely, Rome's acquisition of *imperium* over the Mediterranean world. The present section now turns to the specifically allegorical ways in which *pastio villatica* can function as veiled commentary on the political culture of the city.

As Green first saw, the figuration of humans as animals and of animals as humans is central to *RR* 3's allegory of Roman politics. Some of these metaphorical similarities are patent, while others are less transparent and may only be, in a sense, authorized by the presence of metaphor or other figures of speech elsewhere in the text.[59] For example, we have already seen how the initial backdrop of the Ovilia figures the voting denizens of Roman Italy as sheep and follows up this image with the birdcage of citizen-birdmen in the setting's central conceit of Villa Publica-as-aviary. Or consider the case of snails, which Appius nearly personifies as servile humans by attributing to them "children" (*liberi*) in a way that simultaneously puns on the "freedom" of runaways from a poorly enclosed breeding ground and anticipates the appearance of the slave-catcher (*fugitivarius*; 3.14.1) tasked with recapturing them.[60] And it is the departure of Mr. Peacock that initiates the discussion of peafowl, for his absence, so Axius observes, precludes any defense he might have otherwise mounted against potentially untoward remarks regarding his own *gentilitas* (3.6.1).

At other times, hints of allegory seem to lie tantalizingly just below the text's surface. The case of geese and their apparent penchant for breaking their necks through excessive struggling to tear up entrenched roots "on account of their desire" (*propter cupiditatem*; 3.10.5) provides a suggestive case study. On the one hand, the attribution of *cupiditas* to the detriment—in this case, death—of the goose smacks of some kind of moralistic, almost Aesopic,

---

59. For my treatment of metaphor and allegory, see pp. 215–16 and 228 in chapter 7.
60. For discussion, see Green (1997) 438–39.

lesson either to be applied as a warning to contemporary Romans or perhaps modeled on the behavior of the excessively avaricious.[61] On the other hand, the danger is also mentioned by Pliny (*HN* 10.163), whose account tends to be anything but allegorical, and Columella (*Rust.* 8.14.8), whose expertise as agronomist far exceeds that of his counterparts,[62] so this comment may simply be a literal and sensible injunction of purely technical instruction. Or perhaps within the hybridized text of *De Re Rustica,* this passage accomplishes both ends at once, proffering literal advice to the technically inclined reader and allegorical moralizing to the litterateur in the know.

In part, the impetus to tease out metaphorical and allegorical dimensions where there may in fact be none stems from the fact that the most transparent and sustained instances of allegory are found in the longest and most elaborate discussions of *RR* 3: Merula's and Varro's accounts of the three types of aviaries (3.4.1–5.18) and Appius's treatment of apiaries (3.16.1–38).[63] I begin with the former. In response to Axius's eager desire to hear about the profitable peacock and its contemporary brethren (3.4.1), Merula first provides a general overview of aviaries, observing that there are in fact two different types (*duo genera*): one for the sake of profit (*fructus causa*), the other for the sake of pleasure (*delectationis causa*; 3.4.2). Examples of the former are found here in the city (*in urbe*) and in the Sabine countryside, whereas the prime specimen of the latter type is Varro's own aviary near Casinum. Merula then notes that there is actually a third type (*tertium genus*), which Lucullus developed as a "composite" (*coniunctum*) of the other two at his Tusculan estate, but which was ultimately found to be wanting in both utility (*inutile*) and delight (cf. *offendit,* 3.4.3). For the first (and only) time in *De Re Rustica,* Varro provides a detailed glimpse into what is presented as his own rustic practice, but one that is almost fantastical in its description. More crucially, however, for a work that is obsessed with schemes of systematization, Varro now confronts the reader with a typology that (a) solidly bifurcates the twin ends of *res rusticae* and, in fact, (b) denies the viability of the profit-pleasure

---

61. Kronenberg (2009) 124 understands this passage as an example of how some citizen-birds "are not without complicity" in the greed of a politically minded bird keeper. Note, however, that the attribution of *cupiditas* is unsecure evidence for personification, for various strands of philosophy considered desire to be some sort of base, nonrational, and motivating instinct common to both humans and animals; see, for example, Lorenz (2006).

62. See Flach (2002) 253. His observation that such cases do not seem to be acknowledged as possible dangers within the contemporary scientific literature only complicates the matter further.

63. Note that the discussion of the three types of aviaries (3.4.2–17) is to be distinguished from the ensuing treatments of specific birds (i.e., *pavones,* 3.6.1–6; *columbae,* 3.7.1–11; *turtures,* 3.8.1–3; *gallinae,* 3.9.1–21; *anseres,* 3.10.1–7; and *anates,* 3.11.1–4).

amalgam. The result is that the discussion of the aviaries feels simultaneously more organic and more incongruous than perhaps any other portion
of the dialogue. For these reasons, the aviaries have played paramount roles
in previous attempts to interpret *RR* 3 holistically, and each type will thus be
considered in turn.

In Merula's for-profit aviary, the birds generally have decent facilities and
resources for food, drink, bathing, protection, and perching (3.5.1–4).[64] In
this respect, the birds' comfort and contentment is actually to be a priority for the caretaker. Yet, the care taken for these birds is motivated *not* by
altruism nor by concern for birds *qua* birds nor by any other noble ideal, but
rather, by the cold, hard fact that well-fed, cared-for, and seemingly content
birds ultimately return greater profits in the marketplace to the owner. Thus,
food is always to be accessible for the birds (3.5.3), but in the lead-up to
market time, it ought to be *more* readily accessible, of a *greater* quantity, and
of a *quality* that renders them plumper (3.5.4). Moreover, while they always
ought to have enough light to see within the aviary, the birds should never
be able to view the external world of trees and other birds, "because the sight
of these things and longing for them emaciates the caged ones" (3.5.3). In a
similar vein, the birds that have become suitable for sale ought to be removed
to a separate coop, the *seclusorium,* so that the "segregated and secret" (*in
secluso clam*) slaughter of these birds might not cause their surviving counterparts to "lose their will to live and die at an inopportune time for the
seller" (3.5.6). Thus, in his for-profit aviary, Merula holds out a temporary
physical comfort and, as it would seem, mental repose in exchange for the
eventual finality of death.

Varro's aviary, on the other hand, is a decidedly different structure. Built
in Casinum alongside a river that runs up to his private *museum* (3.5.9),
the aviary is decorously shaped like a "writing-tablet"; has multiple walking paths; gardens of miniature trees (3.5.10–11); a plethora of colonnades;
a *tholos*; a couple of well-stocked fishponds (3.5.12); a small bird theater; a
panoply of perches; plentiful sight of the outside world through the enclosing nets (3.5.13); docks for the ducks (3.5.14); a sort of "lazy mary" serving
wheel for the convivial fowls (3.5.15–16); views of both the morning and
evening stars; and even a *horologium* (3.5.17). Pampered with food, water,
entertainment, and repose, the birds of this for-pleasure aviary enjoy what
would appear to be a thoroughly delightful physical and mental existence:

---

64. Others have provided thorough descriptions of each aviary, so I shall refrain from
repeating them *ad nauseam* and instead focus on the relevant qualities and characteristics
for my discussion. For descriptions of Varro's aviary, see n. 6, and for Varro's and Merula's,
see Kronenberg (2009) 120–24.

one that is completely free from the specter of slaughter and the boneyard of the marketplace.

In terms of its lavish ornamentation and elaborate structure of buildings, Varro's aviary is not out of place with other such edifices that began to arise in the late second century BC and that are well attested in the literary and material record.[65] Yet, scholars have rightly discerned various literary dimensions to this lavish aviary. In Green's view, Varro's aviary is a "small city-like structure for bird-citizens" that allegorizes Rome as currently "owned" by Octavian: its residents have all their needs met and enjoy other pleasurable comforts in this captive existence, yet have lost their Republican liberty and ultimately remain beholden to the *dominatio* of Octavian and his supporters.[66] To the extent that Varro's aviary is a domicile for bird-citizens, Kronenberg (2009: 122–24) follows suit. But unlike Green, who collapses the distinction between Merula's and Varro's aviaries, Kronenberg rightly emphasizes the fundamental difference in intent between the two structures. Whereas the "care" of the birds in Merula's aviary is ruthlessly managed to the advantage of the owner,[67] Varro's aviary-for-pleasure metapoetically allegorizes the life of the mind (cf. Varro's own description of the aviary as *animi causa,* 3.5.8) through its various allusions to literature and philosophy. Kronenberg thus interprets the profit-driven and pleasure-driven aviaries as allegories of, respectively, the political life of *negotium* and the contemplative life of *otium.* On her view, then, Varro's aviary ultimately symbolizes his rejection of the former course of life for the assumption of the latter's pleasures, thereby putting paid to the ethical viability of *pastio villatica* and, for that matter, of Varronian *res rusticae* as profit-driven—and, by allegory, political—enterprises.

In distinguishing between the allegorical intents of Merula's and Varro's aviaries (as well as in its learned explication of the latter), Kronenberg's reading has much to commend it, but it goes too far in its nearly unqualified validation of the moral purpose of Varro's aviary. In addition to the fact that

---

65. For recent discussions of the late Republic's ostentatious building practices, see (among others) Dyson (2003) 19–23 and Adams (2008).

66. See especially p. 443: "In other words, surrounded as it is by the sight of woodland and of free birds settled in the trees, the Varronian aviary is a study of—shall we say?—physically comfortable but spiritually tormenting confinement. There is a theater, as in Rome; basic food and water are supplied in abundance, as in Rome; but there is no way out. The birds are in a *huis clos.* Readers could draw their own conclusions." From the vantage of 37 BC, one might wish to extend Green's point about Octavian to include Antony, and possibly Lepidus as well, but her interpretation nonetheless remains an intriguing and persuasive one.

67. Here, knowledge of Cornelius Merula as a historical individual might be useful for ascertaining whether the attribution of this ruthless for-profit aviary has a specifically political dimension to it.

its bird-citizens still remain captive within their confines,[68] the lavish expenditure on Varro's extravagant, pleasure-obsessed aviary breaches the *RR*'s ethics of production and ultimately renders it suspect within the parameters of joint *fructus* and *delectatio* so consistently espoused elsewhere in *De Re Rustica*. For these reasons, it is better to view the aviaries as allegories of two imperfect *extremes* of Roman life: in the case of Merula's, the overweening obsession with private profit made at the public's expense and unbridled ambition in the political arena, and an existence thoroughly saturated in private *delectatio* and a wholesale withdrawal from public life in the case of Varro's aviary.[69] Thus, if Merula's aviary overindulges in agronomical calculus and political exploitation, Varro's aviary errs on the side of sterility and pleasure.

Yet, the potential for the for-profit and for-pleasure aviaries to coalesce into an ideal amalgamation of *fructus* and *delectatio* remains unfulfilled in *RR* 3 as well. It is worth considering Lucullus's "composite" for insight into this allegorical failure of aviary-as-lifestyle (3.4.3):

> Ex iis tertii generis voluit esse Lucullus coniunctum aviarium, quod fecit in Tusculano, ut in eodem tecto ornithonis inclusum triclinium haberet, ubi delicate cenitaret et alios videret in mazonomo positos coctos, alios volitare circum fenestras captos. Quod inutile invenerunt. Nam non tantum in eo oculos delectant intra fenestras aves volitantes, quantum offendit, quod alienus odor opplet nares.

> From these [two kinds] Lucullus wanted there to be a composite aviary of a third kind, which he built in Tusculum, so that he might have a dining table enclosed in the same structure of the aviary, where he might sup daintily (*delicate cenitaret*) and see some birds cooked and placed on the tren-

---

68. Cf. Green's observation at n. 66 that the sight of the unfettered world outside of Varro's aviary would frustrate the birds' otherwise happy existence. Kronenberg does implicitly attempt to answer this potential objection by observing that "at least [the birds] are not killed for profit" (123) and, by way of Plato's famous cave analogy in the *Republic* (514a–520a), that "these birds may not be able to leave the cave, but at least they can see the light" (124), but the connections that Green draws between Varro's aviary, the city of Rome, and the ultimately "spiritually tormenting" existence of the birds remain, in my opinion, compelling.

69. While it *may* be the case that Varro's aviary captures the state of his own personal existence in 37 BC, it is yet another thing to say that that existence constitutes an idealized result of a proper mode of life. In this last respect, I would contend Varro's aviary is self-parodic—much in the way that the interlocutors will both knowingly and unknowingly poke fun at their systematizing and sometimes pedantic ways. Cf. chapter 1 and Nelsestuen (2011) 333–37. In any case, the withdrawal of an eighty-year old man at the end of a life as intellectually *and* politically remarkable as Varro's was (cf. 1.1.1) is perhaps more than understandable.

cher, and other birds captive and flying around the windows. They found it not useful (*inutile*). For there the birds flying within the windows did not delight (*delectant*) the eyes as much as the foreign odor that filled the nostrils caused offense (*offendit*).

Lucullus's aviary for profit and pleasure would seem to be a nonstarter from the get-go; after all, the sight and smell—let alone any contact with—the birds' droppings would presumably give pause to even the most resolute gourmand. Yet, in the context of the *RR*'s other spectacular and seemingly successful dining settings—not only Hortensius's game preserve (3.13.2–3), but also Scrofa's *oporotheca* ("fruit-gallery") in *RR* 1 (1.2.10; cf. 1.59.1–3)[70]—Lucullus's failed attempt to mix pleasure with business does not seem so farfetched. Nonetheless, it still fails on both counts: not just *delectatio,* but also *utilitas.*

Reading Lucullus's failed experiment on the allegorical terms set by Merula's and Varro's aviaries allows us to view his *exemplum* as offering up a third mode of existence, which seeks to balance both *fructus* and *delectatio* in a perfect synthesis, but which instead ends up replicating the excesses of each extreme. For Lucullus is an appropriate example of a politician who pursued both lives and whose, so to speak, "excellence" in each sphere finally imploded in a multiplicity of ways.[71] A highly successful military and political leader, Lucullus was nearly unmatched in the *cursus honorum* in his heyday with but the sole exception of his rival, Pompey.[72] In wealth, he approached the proverbially rich M. Crassus.[73] In learning, he received an education that approximated that of Varro and Cicero, and he was on intimate terms with

---

70. In future work, I hope to explore the multivalent and programmatic uses of *oporothecae* in the *RR*.

71. Perhaps the best expression of this bipartite divison of Lucullus's life is found in Plutarch's *Lucullus* (39.1): "One then can discern in the life of Lucullus, just like in ancient comedy, a first part of political acts and military commands, and a second part of drinking-bouts and suppers, all-night parties, torch-races, and every mirth" (Ἔστι δ' οὖν τοῦ Λευκόλλου βίου καθάπερ ἀρχαίας κωμῳδίας ἀναγνῶναι τὰ μὲν πρῶτα πολιτείας καὶ στρατηγίας, τὰ δ' ὕστερα πότους καὶ δεῖπνα καὶ μονονουχὶ κώμους καὶ λαμπάδας καὶ παιδιὰν ἅπασαν). Keaveney (1992) 129–42 provides a reasoned corrective to the all-too-neat symmetry that sees the loss of his command against Mithradates and Tigranes and subsequent return to Rome in 66 as the decisive break between the "two lives" of Lucullus.

72. *Idem* 15–128 provides a solid narrative of Lucullus's political and military achievements (and shortcomings), which provides the basis for my brief summary of the multifaceted Lucullus.

73. Lucullus's wealth consisted of a not inconsiderable patrimony substantially augmented by his exploits in the First and Third Mithradatic Wars and occasional lending; see *idem* 144. Whether true or not, his taste for gold was a common refrain even in his own time, and such rumors undoubtedly contributed to the loss of command (*idem* 112–14).

one of their teachers, Antiochus of Ascalon.[74] Most infamous, however, was the reputation that he developed as a libertine for his extravagant estates, lavish dinner parties, and gourmandizing, all of which provided plenty of fodder for contemporaries (like Varro) and future biographers, moralists, and satirists.[75] Yet, for all his achievements in the spheres of profit and pleasure, Lucullus also proffered a negative *exemplum* of the overweening pursuit of each. In the first place, he infamously lost control of his troops during the Mithridatic War in 67 BC, thereby allowing Pompey to swoop in and receive the lion's share of credit for work that he himself had mostly done. His subsequent semi-retirement to enjoy the wealth procured on that campaign also proved unfulfilling, and his final concerted efforts in public life to oppose the First Triumvirate ended in failure and only reinforced the ignominy of his current station. And the last years of his life were spent in a state of self-relegation to his estates and, for however much they were consumed in dissolute pleasure, ultimately gave way to madness, by some accounts. Thus, the "composite aviary" of Lucullus emblematizes the life of one who supremely distinguished himself in both modes of life, yet succumbed to the excesses of each in the end.

Beyond offering a third allegory of a failed mode of life in contemporary Rome, the image of Lucullus's dining room amidst the birds evokes the opening one of Appius and his bird-clients in the Villa Publica's aviary. Like Lucullus, the eructating augur pleasures himself with cooked birds in the presence of living ones. But the comparison goes beyond each image's culinary taboo: both Lucullus and Appius were consular in status, enriched themselves in the course of discharging the duties connected to their offices (perhaps even on the same campaign), and were former brothers-in-law by virtue of Lucullus's eventually unsuccessful marriage to Appius's sister.[76] The invocation of Lucullus's unprofitable and unpleasant aviary may even tellingly hint at the state of Appius's existence in 50 BC and allude to his impending fate; roughly similar

---

74. *Idem* 11–12 calls Antiochus his "spiritual advisor." Cf. Rawson (1985) 81. Of course, this relationship was the inspiration for Cicero's initial casting of Lucullus in the aborted version of the *Academica* (2.10–12)

75. Keaveney (1992) 143–65 rightly views Cicero and Plutarch as the paramount culprits in the generally negative interpretation and reception of Lucullus's later life and provides an astute and reasoned reassessment of this retirement in extravagance.

76. For the irony lurking behind Appius's claims of *parsimonia* in his earlier life (3.16.1–2), which prompted the supposed dowerless marriage of Clodia Luculli to Lucullus and which was subsequently rectified by Lucullus's efforts, see Tatum (1992) 190–200. To the best of my knowledge, no ancient sources explicitly assert that Appius profited from his time on campaign with Lucullus, yet it would seem to be a natural inference given Lucullus's own enrichment and Appius's unwavering service as legate throughout. For Appius's exploitation of his proconsulship over Cilicia, see n. 12.

to the brother-in-law's experiences over the last decade of his life, Appius is fresh off a foreign command, about to join a failed political opposition, and will die rather ignominiously in a state of quasi-exile.[77] It would seem, then, that there are simply no heroes in *RR* 3.

## BEES AND THE SUCCESS OF THE BROTHERS VEIANII

In using the discussion of aviaries to allegorize two extremes of living and a third, hybridized, and perhaps even more deeply flawed mode, *RR* 3 would seem to present a profoundly pessimistic vision of life in contemporary Rome. There is, however, one instance of successful *pastio villatica* that, when read allegorically, proffers a positive *exemplum*: the case of the Veianii brothers, who practice a productive, elegant, and moderately profitable form of apiculture. To consider this case, we must first briefly recount Appius's and Merula's treatments of bees, for their lengthy accounts provide the necessary context for interpreting the interlude of the Veianii Brothers' successful enterprise.

Structurally, *RR* 3's account of the bees admits division into two major parts: Appius on the *ingenium* and *ars* of bees (3.16.4–9), and Merula on their housing, feeding, and production of *fructus* (3.16.12–38).[78] In keeping with *RR* 3's focus on profitable *pastio villatica,* Merula's account is much longer than that of Appius, but the most jarring difference between the two lies in their markedly different tenors. For Appius, bees resemble humans (*ut homines*) and enjoy a "partnership (*societas*) of work and buildings" (3.16.4). They have a civic state (*civitas*) consisting of king and *imperium,* and their *societas* also encompasses the common ideals of pursuing "all things pure" (*omnia pura*) and (unlike flies) of shunning all things foul and immoderately sweet (3.16.6).[79] They are neither cowardly nor foolhardy (3.16.7). They are loyal to their king and bravely defend against common enemies (3.16.8). And they live in a uniform and ordered manner with military-like efficiency and with

---

77. For Appius's death in Euboea, see the vivid account (in oracular form) of Lucan 5.64–236.

78. Note also that Appius himself claims a particular right to know (cf. *praeterea meum erat, non tuum, eas novisse volucres*) and to articulate the *ars* and *ingenium* on the basis of an implied etymological relationship between *appius* and *apis* (3.16.3)

79. In their commitment to shared ideals and the pursuit of a common *utilitas,* the bees would appear to fulfill the criteria for a *populus* as specified by Cicero in his famous definition of a *res publica* as a *res populi* in *De Re Publica* (1.39): "a gathering of many allied by a consensus of *ius* and a sharing in *utilitas*" (*coetus multitudinis iuris consensu et utilitatis communione sociatus*). Cf. pp. 227–28 in chapter 7. Note that, by avoiding both the foul and the excessively sweet, the bees would also seem to have a shared commitment to moderation.

clear "signs of peace and war among themselves" (*inter se signa pacis ac belli*; 3.16.9).[80] In terms of its harmonized *societas,* observance of moderation, and idealized military efficiency,[81] the *civitas* of the bees readily stands for an idealized version of Roman *res publica*—one that is simply not found in any of *RR* 3's microcosmic aviaries.

Merula's account paints a decidedly different picture and admits the following analysis: types of hives (3.16.12–17); types of bee kings and bees (18–19); the purchase of bees (20); methods of transferring the bees between hives (21–22); feeding (22–28); swarming time (29–31); principles for the extraction of *fructus* (32–34); and the beekeeper's duties for care (35–38).[82] In the course of this overview, various details progressively reveal that the bees' *societas* is anything but the idealized society Appius sketched. After the eminently practical treatment of the types of hives and preferred locations for them, the discussion takes an allegorical turn with its consideration of the types of bee kings and bees. In particular, it emerges that the possibility of multiple kings and the presence of drones and wasps disrupt the vitality and orderly function of the hive: the former instigating *seditiones* (3.16.18), the latter broaching the *societas* of shared work and common purpose (3.16.19). The occasional need to transfer the bees to a new hive also presents a series of threats to the bees' unity, and utmost care must be taken throughout (3.16.21–22). Moreover, the provision of the necessary raw materials for the hive turns out to be a complex affair, with sundry plants and flowers needing to be within the hive's range at the seasonally appropriate times lest the production of wax, honey, and food breaks down (3.16.22–28). The hive's periodic process of swarming to send out a new colony also offers a plethora of new dangers to both the old and new hive (3.16.29–31). The extraction of honeycomb is likewise fraught with danger, and rational calculation of the amount to be removed and of seasonal factors must be undertaken lest the long-term yield be adversely affected or the bees "grow despondent" (*ne deficiant animum*; 3.16.32–34). Finally, the balance of the bees' *societas* and *civitas* turns out to be a delicate one, consistently requiring the intervention of the beekeeper (3.16.35–38). Among other things, disparity between the bees and the seasonal travails of heat and cold "quite frequently" (*crebrius*) lead to fights in

---

80. In this last point, Appius perhaps alludes to the Optimates' contentions concerning the illegality of Caesar's Gallic Wars and thus one of the precipitating causes of the impending civil war between Caesar and Pompey.

81. One may wish to compare the *maiores'* supposed agricultural policies mentioned by Varro in 3.1.4, for discussion of which, see below.

82. The text at 3.16.22 may be marred by a brief lacuna, for discussion of which, see Flach (2002) 279.

the hive. It is thus the task of the beekeeper to maintain a semblance of order in the hive through a variety of means, including sequestration and the meting of inducements like honey or mead (3.16.35). Even rain presents a deadly challenge to the hive, which apparently requires the beekeeper to intervene with a series of actions that also befit the nursing of flies back from a moribund state (3.16.37–38). In this last respect, the bees of Merula's apiary have at last come to resemble that foul creature to which Appius initially denied any similarity.

Whereas Appius's bees emerge "as an ideal political society," Merula presents a hive founded on "self-interest and survival of the fittest," which is "constantly riven by conflicts of interest within the group."[83] But instead of the latter account deconstructing the former one,[84] the dual accounts of bee *societas* present the reader with another pair of allegorical alternatives: the fantasy of the apiary *qua* Republic as sublime political society and its present reality as a tenuous and conflict-ridden commonwealth. One is unreal and the other unfortunate, but each is ultimately untenable.

What are we to make of this set of imperfect alternatives? The answer may be found in the *exemplum* of the Veianii (3.16.10–11). Set off between the two competing accounts as a sort of brief interlude, the description of the brothers' apiary provides a modestly successful case of profitable and pleasurable apiculture.[85] In a neat twist on the interplay between the interlocutors and their author, the *auctor* for the *exemplum* of the Veianii is, according to Merula, Varro himself, who became acquainted with the brothers when they served under him in Spain in the campaign against Sertorius in the 70s BC.[86] Inheriting a small villa and a "tiny plot" (*agellum*) of a single *iugerum* in the region of Faleria, the brothers "built beehives (*alvaria*) around the entire villa, had a garden (*hortus*), and planted the rest with thyme, *cytisus*,

---

83. So Kronenberg (2009) 125–26 frames the difference between the two accounts.

84. *Idem.* Her further suggestion that Appius's account may be a riff off a bee analogy in Cicero's *De Re Publica* is intriguing, but unable to be substantiated on the basis of the extant portions of that text. Still, it would be interesting to compare the paramount role that Merula's beekeeper plays with Cicero's *rector rei publicae,* for recent discussions of whom, see J. G. F. Powell (1994) 19–29 and (2012) 14–42; Atkins (2013) 64–79; Nelsestuen (2014) 130–73; and Zarecki (2014) 77–104.

85. The Veianii are not infrequently found in the scholarship as exemplars of Italian honey production (e.g., Forbes [1966] 96; Brothwell and Brothwell [1969] 79); of the astute use of a minimal amount of land for maximal returns (e.g., Marzano [2007] 90); or of the sort of anecdotal evidence of which Vergil may have been aware in his composition of the *Georgics* (e.g., Spurr [1986b] 173–74; cf. Kronenberg [2009] 174).

86. So Flach (2002) 272 rightly infers. Of course, the possible evocation of Varro's short-lived opposition against Caesar about one year after the conversation's date is tantalizing.

and *apiastrum*."[87] By converting their meager plot into an apiary filled out by a bee garden, the Veianii have transformed their pittance of land—too small for even subsistent *agri cultura*—into a delightful spectacle of production. In so doing, they also reaped the modest, but consistent (*peraeque*), profit of 10K sesterces a year: precisely half of the previously lowest amount cited by the interlocutors elsewhere in *RR* 3 (cf. p. 186). The lesson to be drawn from this *exemplum* is left unstated, but the emphasis on the brothers' prudent management of their meager estate towards profitable *and* pleasurable ends suggests that Varro has given us an example that adheres to the ethics of production we have discerned elsewhere. Moreover, the Veianii's operation even remains insulated from the crapshoot (*alea*) of the marketplace (cf. p. 188); after all, they sell their produce to the *mercator* but do so on their own time (*suo tempore*)—and *not* that of others (*alieno*). In this respect, the Veianii's apiary would seem to be a self-determined and largely self-sufficient utopia of bee *civitas* and gives us a glimpse of a viable form of *pastio villatica,* which produces *moderated* profit and pleasure seemingly without risk in the late Republic. In their modest ambitions and by virtue of their status as humble practitioners of the otherwise elite form of *pastio villatica,* then, the Brothers Veianius serve as the antithetical counterparts to Merula, Varro, and Lucullus; stand as spiritual forebears to the virtue of moderation that is soon to become so prevalent in Augustan poetry and ideology;[88] and offer a subtle, but powerful, corrective to the unbridled excesses—material, political, and moral—of late Republican political life and culture.

## EPILOGUE

In the preface to *RR* 3, Varro provides a brief anthropology of human existence that is crucial to understanding the intent behind his account of *pastio villatica.* Distinguishing in time and space between two modes of living (*duae vitae . . . hominum*; 3.1.1), he argues that, because humans originally received the gift of *agri* from *natura* but only developed the *ars* of build-

---

87. Note that the garden (*hortus*) presumably doubles as both a source of pollen for the bees' production and for the growing of table vegetables as a nod to self-sufficiency.

88. The most famous expression of "moderation" and the pursuit of a "middle course" in Augustan poetry is found in Horace's *aurea mediocritas* ("golden mean"; *Carm.* 2.10). Cf. Hor. *Carm.* 2.3; *Sat.*1.1.106. For "moderation" as an important strand of the public image that Augustus sought to project, see Yavetz (1990) 21–41; cf. (1984) 1–36. Needless to say, the projection of a public image is not the same as actual character and, moreover, the position and program of Octavian's self-fashioning in 37 BC was a long way off from his later "rebirth" as Augustus; see, for example, Zanker (1988) 33–100 and Galinsky (1996) 80–140.

ing cities within the previous millennium (3.1.4), the older mode of life, the
*vita rustica,* was maintained in the countryside (*rus*) and predates the more
recent *vita urbana,* which, as its name would suggest, was located in the city
(3.1.1–3). Perhaps unsurprisingly, this older mode of living turns out to be the
"better" (*melior*) one, which the *maiores* in their infinite wisdom recognized:
"our ancestors kept leading their fellow-citizens from the city back to the
fields, because they were nourished by rustic Romans in peacetime and in
war they were aided by them" (*itaque non sine causa maiores nostri ex urbe
in agros redigebant suos cives, quod et in pace a rusticis Romanis alebantur
et in bello ab his allevabantur;* 3.1.4). Despite these efforts, however, the *vita
urbana* became increasingly entrenched for the Romans. At the same time,
the amount of wealth concomitant with this urbanization of life increased as
well (3.1.7), which gave rise to the historical differentiation of *res rusticae*: first
between *agri cultura* and *pastio,* and then the eventual emergence of *pastio
villatica* as a third sphere as well. In delineating *pastio villatica* as a discrete
practice (3.1.8), Varro's contribution to *res rusticae* is thus not only intellectual, but also didactic and remedial, providing a viable model of farming
production for the profit- and pleasure-minded Roman aristocrat of the late
Republic. And his agronomical efforts resemble the agricultural policies of
the *maiores* in that each seeks to buttress the rustic foundations of the city.
But unlike the *maiores,* he brings the *rus* into the *urbs* and, in so doing, provides a way to reconcile the present—with its changed material conditions as
a result of empire and its fashionable pleasures of *luxuria*—with the venerable
pursuit of profit through private farming. In these respects, *pastio villatica*
offers not just a new form of rustic enterprise, but even a renovated paradigm
of productivity for the modern *agricola.*

But if *pastio villatica* represents a new avenue of economic activity and
ideological posturing for the Roman elite, it does not come without its own
set of problems. For this new form of animal husbandry at the villa trades in
and perpetuates morally questionable practices associated with greater wealth
and increasingly fastidious tastes, thereby rendering it complicit in the pitfalls
of contemporary *luxuria* as well. Moreover, the dividends of *pastio villatica*
depend on the marketplace of a city that, for Varro's entire life, was increasingly racked with political crises, which both threaten the stability of villa
husbandry as a productive enterprise and, in a sense, vex its allegorical application to the city's politics. As we have seen, it can be difficult to determine
in *RR* 3 whether it is the agronomical "facts" or political conditions that drive
the terms of its sporadic allegorizing. Yet, it is this indeterminacy that also
makes *pastio villatica* an especially fitting subject for the metaphorization of
Rome as a villa; more patently exploitative of animals that admit greater com-

parison to Roman citizens and motivated by the lure of astoundingly lucrative payouts, *pastio villatica* may be good farming practice, but it implicates elite Romans in the exploitation of their fellow citizens: be it in the perpetuation of *luxuria* or the internecine slaughter of civil war. After all, the conversation takes place in the presence of an augur belching up fowl amongst his fellow bird-citizens and bird-clients and on the eve of seemingly interminable civil war between Caesar, Pompey, and their successors.[89] The result is that *RR* 3 offers a fundamentally conflicted account of *pastio villatica*: one that is profoundly pessimistic about the analogy of the practice to political life, yet still fashions Rome as a villa and acknowledges that the production of profit and pleasure must go on.

At the conclusion of Merula's discourse on the conflict-ridden world of bees, Pavo returns to reveal that the votes have been cast and the tribes' picks are about to be announced. Appius "speedily" (*confestim*; 3.17.1) departs to congratulate his candidate and return home thereafter. Merula quickly follows suit, but not before promising to give Axius the "third act" (*tertium actum*) on a later occasion. Alone again, Varro and Axius now await their own candidate's impending return. In the meantime, Axius reveals that the omission of *piscinae* is no matter, "for the rest is pretty much known to me" (3.17.2). Of all of *De Re Rustica*'s accounts, his ensuing one is perhaps the least technical and most anecdotal. At first, he provides a cursory overview of the two types of *piscinae*: freshwater ones (*dulces*) found "amongst the plebs and not without profit" (*apud plebem et non sine fructu*) and saltwater ones (*salsae*) that "pertain more to the eyes than to the wallet" (*magis ad oculos pertinent quam ad vesicam*) because they are built, stocked, and maintained "at great cost" (*magno*; 3.17.2). Then follow progressively lengthier descriptions of the *piscinae* of Hirrus,[90] Hortensius, and Lucullus (3.17.3–9). In driving a hard distinction between types of and ends for *piscinae,* Axius would seem to replicate the earlier allegory of aviaries one last time in piscine form:

---

89. In its cannibalistic figuration of the cycle of civil war in late Republican Rome, Varro may be seen to anticipate such prominent themes in Neronian literature, especially Lucan's *Bellum Civile.*

90. In addition to being the owner of a villa worth 4 *million* sesterces at the time of its sale due to its number of fish, Hirrus is said to have loaned Caeser some two thousand lampreys "at one time" (*uno tempore*). This loan is usually dated to 46 BC on the basis of Pliny's mention (*HN* 9.171) of a similar loan (by a Hirrius for six thousand fish on the occasion of one of Caesar's triumphs); see Flach (2002) 291–92 for a discussion of the problems with Pliny's text, the discrepancies, and possible solutions. If it is this loan to which Axius refers, Varro may have "slipped up" and had his interlocutor make an anachronistic reference, though one wonders whether the "discrepancy" derives from Pliny—by, for example, mistakenly inferring the loan to be from Caesar's dictatorship—or, in fact, is another oblique allusion to that impending dictatorship.

the for-profit freshwater ones of the *plebs* versus the for-pleasure saltwater ones of Hirrus and Hortensius. And, indeed, Lucullus also reappears—again as the would-be reconciler of the two ends. Once again, however, that man's attempted synthesis of profit and pleasure fails in its transgressive pursuit of both ends, for the Xerxean Lucullus, in seeking to connect his *piscinae* at the notoriously pleasure-laden Baiae with the salt water of the Mediterranean, "burned with such desire that he allowed the architect even to exhaust his money" (*tanta ardebat cura, ut architecto permiserit vel ut suam pecuniam consumeret*; 3.16.9). Perhaps it is the sight of the returning candidate or simply the length of the *sermo,* but Axius abruptly breaks off at this point, leaving the lesson of three imperfect *piscinae* for the reader to ponder. Having traversed air, land, and water, he—and the dialogue, as it would seem—have simply run out of space.

At last, the long-awaited candidate enters the Villa Publica as aedile-elect and receives his congratulations (3.17.10). Escorting their man to the Capitoline for the taking of the auspices,[91] Varro and Axius depart thereafter—not for any festal dinner party, as in *RR* 2, but simply to return home. Like the conclusion to that dialogue, the participants' day concludes without incident. But unlike *RR* 2, where we know that Varro, Pompey, and company triumphantly put an end to the pirate menace, the events subsequent to the final dialogue are in no way as felicitous. For, from the perspective of 37 BC, the specter of civil war would have loomed large, and any profit or pleasure derived from their candidate's successful bid for political office proved short-lived.

---

91. The taking of the auspices is the natural inference for why they went to Capitoline; see Mommsen (1887–88) 3.608ff. For the Capitoline's centrality in Roman politico-religious life, see L. Richardson (1992) 31–32; 68–70.

# CHAPTER 7

# Varro's Imperial Estate and Its Intellectual Contexts

Modo nobis stet illud, una vivere in studiis nostris, a quibus antea delectationem modo petebamus, nunc vero etiam salutem; non deesse si quis adhibere volet, non modo ut architectos verum etiam ut fabros, ad aedificandam rem publicam, et potius libenter accurrere; si nemo utetur opera, tamen et scribere et legere πολιτείας, et, si minus in curia atque in foro, at in litteris et libris, ut doctissimi veteres fecerunt, gnavare rem publicam et de moribus ac legibus quaerere.

Only let us agree on this one thing: to live together in our literary studies. From them, we previously sought only delight (*delectatio*), but now we seek even safety. And let us be present, should anyone wish to employ us, as not only architects, but even workers, for rebuilding *res publica,* and let us willingly supply our aid. But if no one should make use of our help, let us nonetheless read and write *Politeias* and—if not in the Senate and Forum, then, as the most learned men of antiquity did, in our letters and books—serve *res publica* and search out its customs and laws.

—Cicero, *Fam.* 177.5 [= 9.2.5]

IN A 2012 ARTICLE on Aristotle, Mary Dietz challenges the traditional narrative of the history of ancient political philosophy, which maintains that the Greek *polis* conceptually dominated and fundamentally structured the political thought of Plato, Aristotle, and their scions. By shifting the "perceptual field" through which the *Politics* is usually read from *polis* to "between *polis* and empire," Dietz argues that Aristotle is actually cognizant of the Greek city-state's transitory nature as the political unit *par excellence* and positions himself as an innovative proto-theorist of empire in response to the new form of polity incipient in Alexander the Great's *pambasileia*. If, as she says, "'Empire' is an idea whose time has come in political theory," for ancient political thought that time came in the form of Aristotle's *Politics*. Regardless of her argument's validity, this book has sought to show that Varro's *De Re Rustica* also contains a rudimentary theory of empire, in which the agricultural estate (*praedium*) provides a model for Roman *imperium* over Italia and the broader Mediterranean world. And this final chapter will also make a similar case for the priority of Varro as, if not the first, then certainly one of the earliest, Romans to theorize the nature of their political, military, and economic ascendancy over what they called the *orbis terrarum*.

For Cicero, quite a different time had arrived in late April of 46. Writing to Varro shortly after news of Caesar's victory over the Pompeiani in North Africa had reached Italy, Cicero has little specific advice to offer his former comrade-in-arms about their present situations other than that they are to keep lying low and "to live together in [their] literary studies."[1] No longer simply offering private "delight" (*delectatio*), these *studia* may now prove to be their own personal salvation (cf. *salutem*) and even put them in a position to contribute to the public good of "rebuilding *res publica*": be it in the Forum and Senate *or* in letters and books.[2] To be sure, the events of the next decade would prove to be perhaps even more tumultuous than either of them

---

1. For the historical circumstances of this letter, see Shackleton-Bailey (1977) 2.312 and Wiseman (2009) 108–9. Cicero's and Varro's common intellectual ground is a recurring theme of the preserved correspondence (e.g., *Fam.* 176 [= 9.3], 181 [= 9.6], and 254 [= 9.8]; cf. *Acad.* 1.1). For the time that they spent together in Pompey's camp at Dyrrhacium, see Cic. *De Div.* 1.68; 2.114; Plut. *Caes.* 36; and Wiseman (2009) 124–25.

2. For Cicero, the "*politeiai*" and investigations into "laws and customs" would refer to not only his political-philosophical works of the 50s BC (i.e., *De Oratore*, *De Re Publica*, and the possibly unpublished [or unfinished] *De Legibus*), but also his present scholarly endeavors (including *Academica*), which were soon to become a way for Cicero to practice politics outside the Senate and the Forum (for which, see especially Baraz [2012] and Zarecki [2014] 122–62). As for Varro's scholarly endeavors, Cicero most likely had *Antiquitates* in mind (most likely published in the 50s BC), but a number of other works (e.g., *Eisagogikos* for Pompey's use in consulting with the Senate in 70; Aul. Gell. *NA* 14.7.2) could be adduced as well. Note also that the purposes of their *studia*—private *delectatio* in the past, but also public utility in the present—is suggestively "Varronian" (but cf. Cic. *De Or.* 1.249) in its framing and speaks to the need for future scholarship to investigate the intertextual and, possibly, allusive relationship between Cicero's letters and *De Re Rustica*.

envisioned, and their respective fortunes could not have turned out any more differently.[3] And Varro's project of allegorizing empire through agronomy was almost certainly not what Cicero had in mind when he enjoined his counterpart to continue to "read and write *Politeias*" and to "serve *res publica*" by investigating "its customs and laws." Yet, this mutually incumbent injunction attests to the way that Cicero saw both himself and Varro as engaged political and cultural actors in the production of their ever-burgeoning oeuvres.[4] The view of Varro as an innately "apolitical" spirit is—and always was—a thoroughly modern one;[5] even in a work on agronomy addressed to his wife at the ripe old age of eighty (1.1.1–2), Varro's concern for the political life of Rome, its culture and its morality, and the nature of its *imperium* shines through.

This concluding chapter explores the historical context, intellectual antecedents, and theoretical implications of Varro's representation of the Roman empire as an agricultural estate, or *praedium,* in *De Re Rustica.* After a brief

---

3. Both men were eventually proscribed, but whereas Cicero's brief resurgence as statesman upon the death of Caesar ended in an ignominious death at the hands of Antony, Varro survived with the help of his friends (Aul. Gell. *NA* 3.10.17; App. *B. Civ.* 4.6.47), seems to have recovered his standing, and was even honored in Asinius Pollio's renovation of the Atrium Libertatis (Suet. *Aug.* 29.5) with a bust among its library's statues of famous writers in the 30s BC (Pliny *HN* 7.115).

4. Cicero's famous (and not undeserved) laudation of Varro should be brought to bear here as well (*Acad.* 1.9): "When we were strangers abroad and lost in our own city, your books led us back home, so to speak, so that at last we were able to recognize who and where we were. You revealed the age of our native land, its divisions of time, the rules of sacrifices and priesthoods; discipline at home and at war; the location of regions and places; and the names, types, functions and causes of all matters human and divine" (*Nam nos in nostra urbe peregrinantis errantisque tamquam hospites tui libri quasi domum deduxerunt, ut possemus aliquando qui et ubi essemus agnoscere. Tu aetatem patriae, tu descriptiones temporum, tu sacrorum iura tu sacerdotum, tu domesticam tu bellicam disciplinam, tu sedum regionum locorum tu omnium divinarum humanarumque rerum nomina genera officia causas aperuisti;* transl. by Wallace-Hadrill [2005] 66).

5. So Dahlmann (1935) 1176–77, who, perhaps more than any other modern scholar, is responsible for perpetuating this ultimately reductive view of the Reatinian: "[Varro] fundamentally had a thoroughly apolitical nature—entirely unlike Cicero—and for years had placed his efforts at the disposal of *res publica* not out of any joy in the business, but rather because he, as a follower of Pompey, believed that he was fulfilling his obligation as a Roman to the state" (*Er war im Grunde eine durchaus unpolitische Natur, ganz anders als Cicero, hatte jahrelang seine Kraft der res publica zur Vergügung gestellt, nicht aus Freude an der Sache, sondern weil er als Gefolgsmann des Pompeius seine Pflicht als Römer dem Staate gegenüber zu erfüllen glaubte*). Compare Appian's estimation of Varro as "a philosopher and historian, a fine soldier and fine general (φιλόσοφός τε καὶ ἱστορίας συγγραφεύς, ἐστρατευμένος τε καλῶς καὶ ἐστρατηγηκώς, καὶ ἴσως διὰ ταῦτα ὡς ἐχθρὸς μοναρχίας προυγράφη, *B. Civ.* 4.6.47). Cf. Wiseman (2009) 113–15, who follows Gabba (1956) 229–49 in attributing this estimation ultimately to Asinius Pollio, likewise a statesman and general, and a partisan of Caesar and Antony no less!

overview of the previous chapters' arguments, in which some broader and more synthetic conclusions about the model are tentatively drawn, the present discussion will survey earlier and roughly contemporary efforts to conceptualize the Roman empire. By showing how his fellow Romans' expressions demonstrate a distinct lack of nuance, are largely undifferentiated in terms of the individual parts and their relationship to the whole, and remain beholden to agent-oriented and *polis*-centric modes of thinking, I thus hope to highlight Varro's contributions to the intellectual project of conceptualizing empire. So as to better frame these achievements, I then briefly survey a variety of intellectual antecedents, including Greek philosophical treatments of household relations, Roman exemplary thought on the farmer as ideal statesman, Cicero's *De Re Publica,* and Stoic cosmopolitanism. By drawing variously on these different strands, Varro creates an original and innovative, yet also "*re*novative," vision of the Roman empire as an agricultural estate. The result is a conceptualization of the Roman state that is both traditional and novel: seeking to reconcile the agrarian and pastoral roots of the city-state with its contemporary status as a Mediterranean empire, providing a new blueprint of the farming metaphor for Roman politics, and anticipating future administrative and political developments under Augustus, the first *princeps.*

## VARRO, HIS *DE RE RUSTICA,* AND ROME IN 37 BC

Any intermediate student of Roman history worth her salt knows that Rome had an empire long before it was *the* Empire, but the point is worth restating for clarity and emphasis. In fact, if we understand empire simply as "rule over very large territory and many peoples without consent,"[6] then we can certainly speak of Roman *res publica* as possessing an empire in the mid-third century BC with the acquisition of Sicily following the First Punic War (264–41 BC), if not earlier.[7] But for as much as the steady acquisition of impe-

---

6. Such is the simple, yet effective, formulation of Mattingly (2011) 75, which is indebted to Doyle's classic 1986 work.

7. It is outside the present discussion's scope to consider whether Rome's gradual domination of the Italian peninsula over the prior century or two constituted an "empire" or, perhaps, some other form of lesser control (e.g., "hegemony"). The nature of Rome's military and "imperial" activities from the fourth to the first centuries BC is an extraordinarily complex matter, often dependent on highly specific historical, cultural, and geographical considerations, and has proved a point of considerable debate amongst modern historians; for some classic and representative discussions, see Brunt (1965b) 267–88 [= (1990) 110–33]; Brunt (1971); Badian (1968); Toynbee (1965); Harris (1978); Gruen (1984); Sherwin-White (1984); Ferrary (1988); Lintott (1993); and Kallet-Marx (1995).

rial holdings characterizes the middle and late Republics, it is the combination of this impressive expansion with, somewhat paradoxically, extended periods of internecine strife that imbues the latter period with its frenetic, almost schizophrenic, qualities. Framing these countervailing movements appositionally (i.e., external expansion vs. internal stasis), however, fails to capture another consequence of this period: the geographical and territorial conundrum of "Rome." Still beholden to the city-state in terms of its form of government and administration, "Rome" had nonetheless become the collective *patria* of an entire peninsula and, furthermore, the imperial power—sometimes formally, at other times informally—over most of the Mediterranean.[8] In the 40s and 30s BC, the marshaling of troops, seizure of lands, and slaughter of citizens in Italia, as well as the presence of significant expatriate communities in the provinces, must have exacerbated this question of identity, which the specter of Alexandria as a rival capital and Mark Antony's rumored transfer of Rome's seat of government thereto would have compounded.[9] And amidst this spatial disarray and towards the tail end of this tumultuous century sits the elderly Varro: formerly an active participant in political and military affairs, mostly sidelined now, occasionally subject to harassment depending on the prevailing political winds, and writing three books on how to farm. Why?

Perhaps the agrarian turn did offer some form of repose in retirement or even escapism, wherein writing about rustication allowed Varro to dwell upon a yesteryear of simpler times: when honorable work offered modest, but peaceable, returns. Or perhaps it really was the case that his wife, Fundania, had purchased a farm (1.1.2) and he simply wanted her to have the necessary agronomical know-how after his eventual death. Yet, as chapter 1 argued, *De Re Rustica* is not a simple technical treatise, but is written in a way that simultaneously evokes the formal and generic features of the philosophical dialogue and satire. An uneasy hybrid of three genres, the *RR* is thus characterized by a constructive tension, which prompts the reader to search for additional ways to interpret the text and ultimately allows for a reading on at least two levels: in a "sincere" manner (i.e., as an actual technical treatise on how to actually

---

8. I am indebted for the terminology of "informal" and "formal" empires to Doyle (1986). For the relationship between Rome and Italia, see pp. 74–75 in chapter 3. For the challenge that "Rome" and "Italia" presented to Greek historians, who tended to have recourse to the model of the classical *polis,* see Ando (1999) 5–34.

9. For, respectively, the confiscations of land in Italia during the civil wars and expatriate communities in the provinces, see pp. 155–56 in chapter 5 and pp. 129–30 in chapter 4. For Romans' perception of the threat posed by Alexandria as a rival capital, see Dio Cass. 50.4.1, 5.4; Nicolet (1991) 122–24; and Osgood (2006) 354. Cf. Octavian's war of propaganda against the "eastern" Antony, for which Zanker (1988) 44–77 remains important.

own a farm) and symbolically or metaphorically (i.e., in ways that somehow transcend the literal signification of the text and that collectively render it an *allegory*).[10] And the primary strand of allegorical interpretation that I have pursued in this book is a political one, wherein the farm provides both a way of talking about contemporary political issues and a model for the contemporary Roman state.

But this allegory ultimately depends on the historical configuration of Roman farm *owning* in the late Republic, and in this regard, the text functions as an agricultural treatise, albeit a primarily theoretical one. Chapter 2 considered the *RR*'s analytical, definitional, and theoretical approaches to the three spheres of rustic enterprise: *agri cultura* (*RR* 1), *pastio agrestis* (*RR* 2), and *pastio villatica* (*RR* 3). In addition to delineating these three spheres in systematic and rationalized schemes, all three books of the *RR* collectively contribute to the treatise's larger intellectual project: the creation of a newly disembedded and theoretically nuanced field of *res rusticae,* which seeks to redress contemporary anxieties over the *mos maiorum* and to establish agronomy as a subject worthy of philosophical inquiry. This process of conceptualization entails a degree of abstraction as well; whereas previous agronomists would write (or speak) with a focus on farmers and the various sorts of things that they may do, Varro revises the discourse of Roman *res rusticae* from this agent-centric preoccupation with the *agricola* to the more robust, abstract, and "scientific" concept of *agri cultura*. As we shall see, this paradigmatic shift in agronomy as an intellectual discipline also pertains to the text's political allegory.

The following four chapters developed readings of the three dialogues. By considering the "literary" material in conjunction with the "technical" content, I argued that the former sporadically invests the latter with various political meanings. For example, *RR* 1, the subject of chapter 3, devotes a fair amount of space to types of soil and the effects that each has on *agri cultura*. All fields obviously have soil, but, as it turns out, each particular field (*ager*) will have its own individual type of soil (*terra*), the particular qualities of which the farmer must account for in his choice of crops (1.9.1–7). So goes the technical discussion. But through a variety of verbal cues, symbols, and other literary devices, it emerges that Varro is also using soils and fields to talk about the relationship between "Italia" as a collective *terra* and its individual "regions," or *agri*—a point that is of central relevance to a text grappling with

---

10. By "allegory," I mean the sense in which ancient rhetoricians employ the term: as an extended metaphor (e.g., Cic. *Orat.* 94). See also the definition of *permutatio* at *Rhet. Her.* 4.46 as "speech that says one thing in its words, another thing in its thought" (*oratio aliud verbis aliud sententia demonstrans*). Cf. Boys-Stones (2003) and Kronenberg (2009) 20–23.

the spaces of empire. Varro thus exploits the semantic overlap between political and agricultural language for two ends: (1) to "reconcile" the overall qualitative superiority of Italian agriculture with the variation found amongst the specific regions therein and (2) to construct a vision of an overarching political category of "Italia": composed of individual "regions"/"fields," (*agri*), but unified by, and as, one common *terra*. In so doing, Varro presents an organic conception of Italia, reifies it as a coherent and "natural" political unit, and fashions it as the farm (*fundus*) of the Roman state.

In the course of its account of animal husbandry (*pastio agrestis*), the second dialogue (treated in chapters 4 and 5) presents two paradigms for Romans as contemporary herdsmen abroad: a more literal one, in which Romans own large-scale cattle operations in provincial lands outside Italy, and a more figurative one, in which Romans "shepherd" non-Italian peoples as military commanders and as political leaders. By taking a practice intimately connected with the foundation of Rome—after all, the city was founded by Romulus and Remus, who are of shepherd's stock—and renovating it for the contemporary Roman experience, Varro figures the provinces as literal and metaphorical pasturage to be exploited in various ways by Romans and for the Roman estate.

In *RR* 3, the focus of chapter 6, Varro articulates what he considers to be a *new* practice of rustic enterprise: *pastio villatica,* or the raising of smaller animals (such as birds, bees, and fish) at or near the villa. Because this "new" practice focuses on luxury produce and has the potential for massive financial returns (as well as great risk), it depends on the influx of wealth into the city—wealth that ultimately stems from Rome's imperial conquests. But the dialogue also associates this new practice of luxury with the rise of private luxury villas and, through its setting in the Villa Publica in Rome, with the city itself. In so doing, Varro fashions the city of Rome—the center of an empire before Rome had an "Emperor"—as the new "villa" of Roman *imperium.*

In sum, the *RR*'s three individual dialogues associate three distinct spheres of *res rusticae*—field cultivation, large animal husbandry, and small animal husbandry—with three different areas of an agricultural estate (*praedium*): the fields, pastures, and villa, respectively. In turn, each location of this estate corresponds to a different area under Roman *imperium*: with the farmland corresponding to Italy, the pastures to the provinces, and the villa to Rome. The result is that the Varronian estate provides a model *of,* and *for,* the contemporary Roman state, which prescriptively structures the relationships between, and ordering of, its constituent parts. On this reading, *De Re Rustica*'s presentation of a substantially revised agronomical vision systematizes and articulates the new agricultural opportunities available to elite owners of large-scale estates; traces the historical development of these new types of farming from the putative subsistent practices of the forefathers and presents them as viable rustic enterprises within the contemporary world; metaphorizes this updated scheme as a model for Roman *imperium* over the ancient Mediterranean; and, consequently, renovates traditional agrarian ideology for the Roman state and its citizens.

## PRIOR ROMAN CONCEPTIONS OF EMPIRE

Yet, we may wish to ask: what is the broader significance of this model? Why does the text's representation of the Roman empire as a farm *matter*? Historical praxis is not the answer, for there is no evidence that any Roman—from the future Princeps, Augustus himself, to the lowliest of the burgeoning class of bureaucrats—drew upon this model for the subsequent administration of the empire, nor even that the treatise was read in Rome for any reason other than its farming content. Nonetheless, Varro's model constitutes an important moment in intellectual history, for it represents an early—perhaps even the earliest—example of a Roman thinking in a relatively nuanced and systematic fashion about the nature of the Roman state as something *more than* a city-state and *less than* complete world domination. More specifically, Varro's model of empire-as-farm presents a differentiated account of Roman *imperium,* wherein a nexus of geographical spaces, ethnic considerations, and political and social factors demarcates and rationalizes the different parts and assigns disparate values to each in a scheme that resembles what modern theorists of empire describe as a "core" and a "periphery."[11] In this respect, Varro should be regarded as an important Roman thinker on the nature of the Roman state, and while *De Re Rustica* may not be an overt work of political philosophy, it nonetheless provides a rudimentary model for, and theory of, Roman empire. On this estimation as well, the *RR* anticipates subsequent developments under the first emperor, Augustus, whose actions and policies

---

11. The analysis of an empire into a "core" (or metropole) as the ruling state and "periphery" as the subject state(s) has been a part of the theoretical discourse since at least Doyle's 1986 work (e.g., p. 11; 19). At times, this terminology may be applied more narrowly, as e.g., Subrahmanyam (2006) 220 applies it to "colonial empires," which he observes are "usually schematized as a particular type of empire that is fundamentally characterized by exploitative economic relations between an imperial core and a subject periphery." Whether or not the Roman empire was historically speaking a "colonial empire" remains a matter of some debate for students of Roman imperialism (cf. n. 7); instead, that Varro is depicting it as such is my current contention.

are fundamental to the creation of a coherent "territorial empire": a political entity in which space is a rationalized factor regularly taken into careful consideration in its administration, or, to put it another way, where geographical boundaries and administrative activities largely coincide.[12]

So as to begin to substantiate these claims, I will survey some prior and contemporaneous Roman ways of construing the extent of the empire before the Empire. My evidence is primarily textual and I am particularly indebted to the thorough survey of Richardson (2008), whose exhaustive philological analysis of *imperium* and *provincia* demonstrates, among other things, the perils of using their English cognates to construe their Late Republican usages as well as of assuming a spatial sense to them.[13] For these reasons, I retain the Latin words throughout. It should also be noted that the visual and material ways in which space was construed in the Roman world fundamentally differed from those of modernity. For example, the use of maps is infrequently attested and, even if an elite citizen had access to them, there is no guarantee that the map would resemble anything we might recognize as being "accurate" or was informed by "cartographic" sensibilities.[14] For these technological reasons alone, it is perhaps unsurprising that spatial conceptions of the vast extent of Roman control over the Mediterranean remain remarkably vague, imprecise, and underdeveloped. As a preliminary example, let us consider a formulation found in *Rhetorica ad Herennium,* a rhetorical treatise usually dated to the early first century BC. In this case, an unidentified, but almost certainly Roman, speaker is apparently deliberating over some policy or action of the Italian allies related to the Social War (4.13):

> Nedum illi imperium orbis terrae, cui imperio omnes gentes, reges, nationes partim vi, partim voluntate consenserunt, cum aut armis aut liberalitate a populo Romano superati essent, ad se transferre tantulis viribus conarentur.

> Still less would [the Italians] attempt with such trifling resources to transfer to themselves the *imperium* of the whole world (*orbis terrae*), to the very *imperium* which all peoples, kings, and nations have consented—some by force, others voluntarily—when they were overcome by either the arms or the generosity of the Roman people.

---

12. I owe this term and its definition to the discussion of Nicolet (1991) 187–207.

13. Richardson's 2008 monograph builds off the work presented in his 1991 article (pp. 1–9). For Varro's use of these terms, see Richardson (2008) 101. Within the *RR, imperium* appears once in Appius's treatment of bees (3.16.6; cf. p. 204) and *provincia* is found only in Scrofa's account of his grandfather's military service in Macedonia (2.4.1; cf. pp. 148–49).

14. For further discussion and bibliography, see n. 30 in chapter 3.

Whether by arms or by liberality, Roman *imperium* is here extended to the *orbis terrae,* a phrase that often serves as the Latin gloss of the Greek *oikoumene* and literally means something like "the sphere of the earth," but which admits looser rendering as "the whole world." To be sure, one might wish to chalk up this particular formulation simply to forensic hyperbole and, if we knew more about the context of this quote,[15] we might actually be able to solidify such a claim. Still, the fact remains that this expansive and wholly undifferentiated conception of the Roman empire is commonplace in the Late Republic.[16]

Another frequent formulation involves framing the extent of Roman power in terms of "land and sea" (*terra et mari*). In his speech "On Behalf of the Manilian Law" (*Pro Lege Manilia*),[17] Cicero invokes the results of the previous year's Lex Gabinia (67 BC), which charged Pompey with his unprecedented command over the entire Mediterranean and "made it so that once again you [i.e., the Roman people] seemed to have command over all peoples and nations on land and on sea (*terra marique*)" (*effecit ut aliquando vere videremini omnibus gentibus ac nationibus terra marique imperare*; 56).[18] Just as the previous example emphasized the subjugation of "all peoples, kings, and nations" (*omnes gentes, reges, nationes*), so Cicero insists on the Romans' *imperium* over "all peoples and nations" (*omnibus gentibus ac nationibus*). But in place of the wholly undifferentiated *orbis terrae,* the orator splits the spatial extent of Roman rule into the only slightly more discriminated parts of land and sea (*terra marique*). Another variation of this large-scale division of the *orbis terrae* is found in the triple triumph Pompey celebrated in 61 BC (Plut. *Pomp.* 45). The extent of his imperial achievement, which Plutarch presents as the conquest of the entire known world (*oikoumene*), was divided along the canonical three continents found in Greek geographical thinking: Europe, Asia, and Libya (i.e., Africa). Whether it be framed in terms of the *orbis terrae, mari et terra,* or three continents, such formulations of the areas of the world subject to Rome—what modern scholars easily call the "Roman empire"—remain expansive, but imprecise, without nuance, and only marginally differentiated.

---

15. Caplan (1954) 260–61 offers the tribune of 90, Q. Varius Severus Hybrida, as a possible candidate for the speech's source, but the example could also be a creation of the unknown rhetorician's own making.

16. So Richardson (2008) 56 shows.

17. This law transferred Lucullus's command against Mithridates to Pompey in 66; cf. pp. 202–3 in chapter 6.

18. Varro owes his service as Pompey's legate in the Pirate Wars to the passage of this law in 67; cf. p. 119 in chapter 4.

If spatial conceptions of Roman *imperium* are decidedly deficient in the Roman world of the first century BC, it may not be surprising to find that the relationships between the various parts are conceptually underdeveloped as well. Let us consider the list of resources which Cicero claims the Roman people enjoy, but which Catiline, their supposed enemy in 63 BC, does not (*Cat.* 2.25):[19] "a Senate, the Roman equestrian class, a city, a treasury, taxes, the rest of Italy, all provinces, and the outside peoples" (*senatu, equitibus Romanis, urbe, aerario, vectigalibus, cuncta Italia, provinciis omnibus, exteris nationibus*). On the one hand, Cicero provides a more differentiated view of Roman *imperium* than was found in the previous examples and divides up some of the resources along the lines seen in Varro's *RR*: there is the city, there is Italy as a whole (*cuncta Italia*), and there are "all the provinces" (*provinciae omnes*). By ordering the list in terms of size (i.e., from "smallest" entity to "largest") and in roughly expanding concentric circles from the perspective of the city of Rome, Cicero seems also to acknowledge a distinction between the elements as spaces: the city of Rome is distinct from the rest of Italy, and Italy is somehow distinct from the provinces. The inclusion of the last element, the "outside peoples" (*exterae nationes*), might even suggest that Cicero is expressing a view of the Roman empire as a bounded territorial state by virtue of the potential geographical sense of *exterae* ("outside" or "foreign") and its possible demarcation from *provinciae*. On the other hand, for every such example of an "outside people" as referring to a nation spatially *beyond* the sphere of Roman *imperium,* there are just as many that illustrate that the *exterae nationes* can be found *within* the provinces and, in that respect, simply denote peoples who either have not yet submitted to Roman rule or, in fact, are "provincial" subjects already.[20] Moreover, it is crucial that not all the elements of Cicero's list admit spatial construal. Instead, what the list offers is a view of different aspects of the Roman state, many of which happen to be spatial in nature and are arranged in a roughly expanding fashion, but all of which are, more fundamentally, things over which the Roman people have control.[21] And it is that power—not the space—that is the organizing principle for the list: hence, the inclusion of entities like the equestrians, the

---

19. The bibliography on Catiline, the so-called Catilinarian Conspiracy, and its sources is vast; see, for example, Hardy (1924), Yavetz (1963) 485–99, and Wiseman (1994) 346–66. Whether or not Catiline was the "enemy" Cicero made him out to be is outside the scope of the present discussion.

20. See Richardson (2008) 86–89 for an overview of the late Republican evidence.

21. In the case of the *exterae nationes,* the "control" that the Roman people enjoy is relative, of course; Cicero would seem to be implying that they would at least respect Roman *imperium* probably in the form of noninterference (e.g., by refusing to provide Catiline with aid) or perhaps even by providing limited support of some kind.

treasury, and tax revenues. Thus, while this passage may not evince a coherent territorial conception of the Roman state[22]—let alone a nuanced geographical understanding—the seeds for the conception of it as such have certainly been sown. But even if we grant that this passage offers a more robust view of Roman *imperium* than found in the previous examples, it still connotes little sense of the relationships *between* and *among* the various parts.

Once again, the objection might be raised that this evidence is drawn from "other" contexts (e.g., forensic), in which "other" priorities (e.g., persuasion) simply precluded more explicit articulation. And, again, it is true that accurate or precise representations of the Roman state and the areas subject to its control are not the primary focuses of any of those contexts. But even this last observation partly reinforces the point that, in the late Republic, there is a decided lack of concern for conceiving the Roman state and the extent of its imperial possessions in anything more than the most expansive and imprecise of terms. Nor is this to say that there was a complete disregard for geography and other spatial concerns, for there is plenty of discussion of Rome's conquest of a specific tribe, city, or region as well as of individual relationships between Roman *res publica* (or one of its representatives) and its subject peoples.[23] But the ways in which those discussions are conducted are mostly framed in terms of specific actors and particular cases. In a sense, then, thinking about the "empire" in the Late Republic is agent-centric and case-based, and these discussions are rarely undertaken from a theoretical, institutional, or systemic perspective. For example, consider what is perhaps Cicero's most abstract and theoretical discussion of "empire" (*De Officiis* 2.26–27):

> Verum tamen quam diu imperium populi Romani beneficiis tenebatur, non iniuriis, bella aut pro sociis aut de imperio gerebantur, exitus erant bellorum aut mites aut necessarii, regum, populorum, nationum portus erat et refugium senatus, nostri autem magistratus imperatoresque ex hac una re maximam laudem capere studebant, si provincias, si socios aequitate et fide defendissent. Itaque illud patrocinium orbis terrae verius quam imperium poterat nominari.

> But still, as long as the *imperium* of the Roman people was maintained through kindly deeds, and not by injuries, wars were waged either on behalf of allies or that *imperium*; the ends of wars were either mild or only what

---

22. Cf. Richardson (2008) 89, who takes an even more skeptical line.

23. For examples of Cicero's and Caesar's discussion of space within the context of concerns related to empire, see Riggsby (2006) 21–45.

was necessary; the senate was a safe haven and refuge for kings, peoples, and nations; and, furthermore, our magistrates and commanders eagerly sought to seize the greatest praise from this one thing: if they defended the *provinciae* and our allies with fairness and good faith. And so was it more truly able to be called a patronage (*patrocinium*) of the world than *imperium.*

In the course of presenting his (apologetic) claim that, historically, Roman military actions vis-à-vis allies and other nations are better understood as actions befitting a patron's *beneficia* for his clients, Cicero uses two terms that merit special consideration: *provincia* and *imperium.* As Richardson's exhaustive survey (2008: 10–116) demonstrates, late Republican usage of these terms does not strongly or consistently attest to the territorial senses found in later periods. In the case of *provinciae,* while there is a clear spatial sense to it, it would be a mistake to assume that the term also connotes fixed and regularized administrative units within the larger Roman empire. In fact, a *provincia* in the sense of a defined administrative unit of space is never attested in Cicero or, for that matter, any Republican writer with the sole exception of Julius Caesar, who is the single extant source most closely engaged in the practicalities of building and administering an empire.[24] As for *imperium,* there seems to be no geographical or territorial conception underlying its usage in this particular instance; instead, it denotes "power." So much is also implied in Cicero's recasting of *imperium* as *patrocinium,* that is, as a patron-client relationship.[25] In this last respect, it is not insignificant that the nature of "empire" is framed in terms of a social relationship between individual actors and that imperial actions are evaluated from the perspective of personal conduct, responsibility, and morality: hence, an agent-centric view of empire.

   It is possible that this agent-centric view of Rome and the world subject to its *imperium* derives from the political structures of the city itself, in which magistrates would as a matter of course negotiate extensively with the Senate over all sorts of matters of state on an often *ad hoc* basis. What

---

24. So Richardson (2008) 85–86.

25. The most basic dynamic of a patron-client relationship is where the patron bestows *beneficia* on the client, who in turn now has an informal, though still socially meaningful and powerful, obligation (*officia*) to his benefactor. Cf. Dyck (1998b) 401–2. For an excellent discussion of this passage, see Steel (2001) 192–94, who astutely notes that the casting of empire as *patrocinium orbis terrae* "is barely . . . metaphorical, since individual Romans had set themselves up as patrons of provincial communities from the beginning of Rome's overseas expansion" (194). One consistent theme in Steel's work is the persistence of Cicero's view of empire' within his speeches in personal terms, which she considers to be partly determined by genre and the performative context.

*is* clear, however, is that Roman conceptions of the world and their administration of it were in a state of considerable flux during the first century BC. As Nicolet has so masterfully discussed, the institutions and mechanisms by which Rome determined citizenship and administered its territory in the late Republic remained fundamentally tied to its city-state roots. For example, the use of tribes, a fluid, easily manipulated, outdated, and *de facto* nongeographical affiliation, remained the basis for citizenship.[26] In terms of administration, he observes that "the empire . . . still constituted until the end of the Republic a series of complex and entangled institutions where no basic principle existed, and in which territoriality was but a badly coordinated component."[27] The multiplicity of individual alliances, the sheer variation of the terms therein, and the continuing *ad hoc* nature and conception of *provinciae* all attest to the empire's pervasive lack of rationality.[28] By revising the basis of Roman citizenship and solidifying control of Rome's extensive Mediterranean holdings through significant administrative changes, Augustus fundamentally transformed the juridical and administrative foundations of Rome into a territorial state.[29] As monumental a role as Augustus did play, these actions could not have occurred without the tentative beginning to many of these processes in the late Republic, including the consideration of the place of Rome and Italy in relation to the rest of the world and a greater geographical awareness in general.[30] And some aspects of those emerging trends can be discerned in the passages just discussed. Still, Nicolet's overall contention that Augustus and his Principate were the primary catalysts for this massive shift in the administration and ideological conception of the Roman state remains crucial to understanding the problems that Rome faced when it came to its empire.

Varro, whose life spanned almost the entirety of the late Republic and who may have lived just long enough to see Octavian become "Augustus" in 27 BC, stands on the cusp of this monumental transition. In this respect, his vision of Roman *imperium* as that of a *praedium*—of an estate, composed of three distinct areas unified under and structured by the metaphor of one property—represents in 37 BC an inchoate conception of the Roman state as a territorial one. Moreover, just as his reconstitution of the field of *res rusti-*

---

26. Nicolet (1991) 197–99, which is the English version of his 1988 work.

27. *Idem* 190.

28. *Idem* 191–92.

29. *Idem* 189–207.

30. Interestingly enough, he adduces Varro (in a lost work, *De Ora Maritima*) as an important contributor to Roman geographical knowledge, as well as Posidonius, the Stoic philosopher who had personal ties with Pompey and Cicero (65–68).

*cae* involved the abstraction and theorization of *agri cultura* from the figure of the *agricola,* so his conceptualization of Roman *imperium-*as-*praedium* represents a shift from agent-centric thinking about the empire to a more abstract and systemic perspective. Consequently, the *RR* should be understood as an intellectual precursor to the sorts of innovations introduced by Augustus as well as a watershed in Roman efforts to theorize the nature of its political control. And it is in this last respect that Varro's work is a rudimentary political philosophy that attempts to account for the imperial realities of the Roman state.

## GREEK AND ROMAN INTELLECTUAL ANTECEDENTS

If Varro's work constitutes a "watershed" in Roman political theory, we might be curious about its intellectual heritage. This section briefly explores four different antecedents for this model: Greek philosophical treatments of household relations, Roman exemplary thought on the farmer as an ideal statesman, Cicero's *De Re Publica,* and the Stoic theory of cosmopolitanism. As we shall see, Varro's intellectual contribution lies in not only the unique and innovative synthesis, but also the learned extrapolation of these various precursors.

Among extant Greek philosophical texts (and, presumably, scores of lost ones as well[31]), a long tradition conceptually links management of the household with the management of the state by focusing on the similarity—usually on epistemological grounds—between the *oikonomos,* the household manager, and the statesman. For example, the *Memorabilia* (3.4) of Xenophon, a man whose work seems to have had some purchase at Rome and whose *Oeconomicus* served as an important precedent for Varro's *RR,*[32] recounts an exchange between Socrates and a certain Nicomachides. Upset that the Athenians appointed as general a renowned *oikonomos* with no prior experience in commanding soldiers, Nicomachides rejects Socrates' contention that a good household manager would in fact make for a good general. Socrates then explains why Nicomachides ought not "despise household-managing men" (μὴ καταφρόνει . . . τῶν οἰκονομικῶν ἀνδρῶν; *Mem.* 3.4.12), for the difference between "management of private matters" (ἡ τῶν ἰδίων ἐπιμέλεια) and "public ones" (τῶν κοινῶν) is only a matter of "scale" (πλήθος), and

---

31. For a useful overview of the extensive "economic" tradition in antiquity, see Natali (1995) 95–128.

32. Cf. n. 10 in chapter 1. For further discussion of this example and others, see Nelsestuen (2014) 148–151.

judicious knowledge (cf. ἐπιστάμενοι) of one sphere translates into prudent action in the other. Assuming the text's lack of irony,[33] Xenophon's Socrates advocates for an epistemological correlation between the *oikonomos* and the manager of political affairs. A similar argument is found in Plato (*Resp.* 258e4–259d5), while Aristotle (*Pol.* 1252a7–16) vehemently denies the similarity, but even the denial attests to the strength of the conceptual affinity between the household manager, the *oikonomos,* and the statesman. Three points emerge from this brief survey: first, there is a philosophical tradition of analogizing the management of a household with that of a city-state; second, this conceptual affinity is agent-centric, that is, it focuses on individuals within, not the institutions or principles of, the polity; and third, this tradition presumes that the polity in which this individual is to act is a *polis,* that is, a city-state.

In addition to the Greek philosophical tradition, Varro could also draw upon a more indigenous one, which likewise correlated the ideal statesman with the head of a household, and more specifically, with farmers. The most famous instantiation of this tradition is Cincinnatus, who came from the plow to be "the only hope of the *imperium* of the Roman people" (Livy 3.26.7–10). The details of his appointment to the dictatorship in the field, saving of the state, and subsequent resignation of his emergency post in the span of fourteen days need not concern us here.[34] Only slightly less well known is Atilius Serranus (falsely etymologized as "the Sower"[35]), who likewise was out sowing his fields when summoned to save the Roman state.[36] Cicero's praise of this figure in his youthful defense speech, *Pro Roscio Amerino,* leaves no doubt about the relationship between farming and exemplary citizenship, for Serranus (and farmers like him) "increased the *res publica* and this *imperium* and the reputation of the Roman people by these properties and fields, by cities and peoples" (50). Deriving *not* from any material or economic calculus, these farmers' exemplary statuses as ideal citizens and statesmen instead stem from the tradition's valorization of the ethics and morality for which

---

33. For the emergence of an "ironic" reading of Xenophon in the twentieth century, see Kronenberg (2009) 8–11, who rightly notes that this approach is "strongly associated with the polarizing figure of Leo Strauss." For other examples of the *oikonomos-politikos* analogy, see *idem* 21 n. 78.

34. For Cincinnatus, see Cic. *Dom.* 86; *Sen.* 56.4–5; Dion. Hal. *Ant. Rom.* 10.17.3; and Val. Max. 4.4.7.

35. For the derivation of "Serranus" from *sero* ("to sow"), see Serv. *ad Aen.* 6.844. Cf. *MRR* 1.208 n. 1.

36. For Atilius Serranus, see Cic. *Rosc. Am.* 50; *Sest.* 72; Val. Max. 4.4.5; and Pliny *HN* 18.20.

they stand in their unrelenting efforts on fields of trifling sizes.[37] Unlike the Greek philosophical tradition, this one is—or, at least from a Roman vantage, appears to be—"native" and, moreover, is "ideological" in the sense that it both constructs the farmer as a moral and political subject and commends the representation of this profession to its audience as a normative, laudable, and desirable one to engage in. In these last respects, the Roman tradition goes beyond the Greek philosophical one's analogical emphasis to equate farming with politics and idealize that connection, but likewise remains agent-centric in its focus on the figure of the *agricola*.

If these two intellectual strands generally underlie *De Re Rustica*'s exposition of the farm as a model for the Roman empire, what (if anything) prompts the shift in perspective from agent (farmer/statesman) to system (farm/state) remains to be discerned. Two additional precursors may go some way in informing the cause of this shift. The first comes from what is basically the first avowed work of political philosophy in the Roman tradition, Cicero's *De Re Publica* (ca. 56–51 BC). In that work, which posits the ideal form of government in terms of a mixed constitution (1.69) and locates its closest historical instantiation in the city of Rome (2.2–3), Cicero provides a formal definition of *res publica,* which is fairly important in the history of Western political philosophy, but which is also presumably the first attempt to do such a thing in Rome (1.39):

> "Est igitur," inquit Africanus, "res publica res populi, populus autem non omnis hominum coetus quoquo modo congregatus, sed coetus multitudinis iuris consensu et utilitatis communione sociatus."

> "So a *res publica*," says Africanus, " is a property (*res*) belonging to a *populus,* but a *populus* is not every gathering of humans herded together (*congregatus*) in some way, but an assemblage of many allied by a consensus with respect to justice and by an association for advantage (*utilitas*)."

As Schofield (1995: 63–83) has shown,[38] Cicero's definition of *res publica* as a *res populi* uses a property metaphor to attribute ownership of this *res* ("its affairs and interests"; 73) to the *populus,* thereby rendering the people "sovereign." The implications of this definition are substantial, but what is of

---

37. For further discussion of this tradition, see Nelsestuen (2014) 152–57. Note also that this tradition is what Kronenberg (2009) 74 presumably means by "the cultural myth of the virtuous farmer," which, on her reading, Varro's *RR* ultimately explodes. Cf. the discussion of her approach on pp. 22–23 of chapter 1.

38. Cf. Nelsestuen (2014) 162–63.

particular relevance to the present discussion is the repeated and marked use of metaphors to create this definition and to explicate some of its claims. As just mentioned, *res* quite clearly means "property," thereby metaphorically reifying the otherwise abstract concept of *res publica* (literally, "a public thing"). Thus, we could basically translate *res populi* as the "people's estate." Moreover, in *congregatus,* we also see the bold use of a metaphor from the animal world, specifically, of pack or herd animals, like those that are kept and raised on an estate's pastures. *De Re Publica* has countless other metaphors,[39] and metaphor is not only a common philosophical tactic for construing abstract concepts, but also a fundamental aspect of human cognition in general.[40] But for various reasons that cannot be explored fully here,[41] farming metaphors are of particular importance to Cicero's *De Re Publica.* Moreover, in figuring *res publica* as the "people's estate," Cicero also lays the foundation for Varro's subsequent construction of *imperium-as-praedium.* Yet, where the metaphors in Cicero's work are but momentary figures meant to render concrete and intelligible the otherwise abstract political concept of *res publica,* Varro reverses the terms of transference and has the *praedium* explicate *imperium.*

Though we see the beginnings of a shift away from an agent-centric metaphorization of the farmer in Cicero's *De Re Publica*—after all, *res publica* is figured as the people's *estate*—the metaphor is not really elaborated any further and, in any case, remains tied to a thoroughly polis-centric discussion of types of government (1.42–70). So what prompts the paradigm shift in Varro's thinking? Notwithstanding the slim possibility that Varro both had access to Aristotle's *Politics*[42] and read that work with an eye attuned to its theoretical implications "between city and empire,"[43] I suggest that Stoic notions of citizenship and, in particular, "cosmopolitanism"—the idea that we, as humans and by virtue of our status as rational animals, belong to a common and universal polity, that is, the *cosmos*—may provide the impetus in two different

---

39. See the handy (though not complete) list in Zetzel (1995) 266 s.v. "imagery and metaphor."

40. The 1980 work of Lakoff and Johnson remains essential for this still-burgeoning area of scholarly inquiry.

41. See Nelsestuen (2014) 130–73, where I argue that the lacunose Book 5 uses the figure of the farm overseer—a slave bailiff—to refashion the ideal statesman from a farmer of the state into a *public servant* of the people's estate. Note also that *De Re Publica* 1.39 continues to use metaphors from the world of farming: *congregatio* (1.40) and, even after the lacuna, *semina* (1.41). For the suggestion that Cicero used a bee analogy in *De Re Publica,* which the *RR* may subvert, see Kronenberg (2009) 125–26. Cf. n. 84 in chapter 6.

42. The transmission of Aristotle to Rome is complex and tenuous; even Cicero, for example, likely did not know the *Politics* directly. For discussion, see Barnes (1997) 1–69.

43. See Dietz (2012) 175–93 and the opening remarks of this chapter.

ways.[44] In the first place, Stoic treatments of citizenship and cosmopolitanism often entail some degree of repudiation of the normative conception of a city and encourage forms of identification that (to varying degrees) eschew traditional emphasis on *polis*-oriented affiliation. For example, even if to speak of a "cosmopolitan" thread or, for that matter, a "cosmic city" in Zeno's *Republic* is anachronistic or incorrect, his antinomian injunctions *not* to build temples, law courts, and gymnasia in cities (Diog. Laert. 7.32–33) would have seriously challenged traditional Greek conceptions of the *polis,* while Seneca, the later Roman Stoic of the first century AD, could assert the primacy of the cosmic city over the local *patria* in which one happened to be born (*De Otio* 4.1). At the root of at least this latter position lies the belief that membership in the world community depends on, at a minimum, the faculty of reason, which renders contingencies such as spatial proximity, familial relations, or ethnicity of secondary import at best.[45] Thus, by destabilizing the centrality of the *polis* and its authority as both a juridical and an affective entity, the Stoics provide an opening for a political philosophy that is not tied so strongly to the individuals, form, and institutions of the classical *polis* per se. And it is this paradigm shift that may generally provide the impetus behind the one detected in Varro's politico-agricultural thought.

Second, there may be a more specific Stoic thread on which Varro draws for his depiction of the Roman empire. In a famous (and controversial) piece of testimony from *On the Fortune of Alexander,* Plutarch recounts how Zeno's *Republic* provided some sort of theoretical blueprint for Alexander's attempted practical implementation of a universal community (329A–B):

Καὶ μὴν ἡ πολὺ θαυμαζομένη πολιτεία τοῦ . . . Ζήνωνος εἰς ἓν τοῦτο
συντείνει κεφάλαιον, ἵνα μὴ κατὰ πόλεις μηδὲ δήμους οἰκῶμεν ἰδίοις ἕκα-

44. Here, my discussion is complicated by the fact that there is serious disagreement about the presence of later, firmly attested Stoic ideas (like cosmopolitanism and its ethical mechanic, *oikeiosis*) in the works of the early Stoics, Zeno, the third-century BC founder, as well as his successor, Chrysippus. In the case of Zeno, for example, while it is clear that he is concerned with the criteria for inclusion in his polity and, thus, in citizenship, it remains contentious whether or not this polity is "cosmopolitan." For two standard positions in the debate, see Schofield (1991) and Vogt (2008), the former of whom sees cosmopolitanism as a development of later Stoicism and retrospectively attributed to Zeno, the latter of whom views it as a crucial and fundamental element in the founder's work from the beginning. For this reason, I am framing my discussion in general terms of "Stoic notions of citizenship" and "cosmopolitanism."

45. For this last point, see Schofield (1991) 101–3. Cf. Vogt (2008) 72: "If the cosmic perspective in some sense encompasses *all human beings,* it seems that the Stoics leave behind the limitations of political theories that focus on one state, unrelated to others, in favor of a worldwide perspective." In the ethical terminology of Stoicism, considerations like one's place of birth or physical proximity would fall under the class of "indifferents" or "intermediates" (cf. Diog. Laert. 7.101–3).

στοι διωρισμένοι δικαίοις, ἀλλὰ πάντας ἀνθρώπους ἡγώμεθα δημότας καὶ πολίτας, εἷς δὲ βίος ᾖ καὶ κόσμος, ὥσπερ ἀγέλης συννόμου νόμῳ κοινῷ συντρεφομένης. τοῦτο Ζήνων μὲν ἔγραψεν ὥσπερ ὄναρ ἢ εἴδωλον εὐνομίας φιλοσόφου καὶ πολιτείας ἀνατυπωσάμενος.

The much admired *Republic* of Zeno . . . is aimed at this one main point, that our household arrangements should not be based on cities or parishes, each one marked out by its own legal system, but we should regard all men as our fellow-citizens and local residents, and there should be one way of life and order, like that of a herd grazing together and nurtured by a common law[/pasture] (νόμῳ κοινῷ). Zeno wrote this, picturing as it were a dream or image of a philosopher's well-regulated society.[46]

The cosmopolitan imperative to regard "all men as . . . fellow-citizens" and their figuration as a "herd grazing together and nurtured by a common law/pasture" render this passage fertile with interpretative possibilities for the scholar of pastoral metaphors for politics. In particular, the pun on law (νόμος; *nom*os) and pasture (νομός; no*mos*) wittily unites the citizen-herd by means of the shared bond of a "common law" (νόμος) and sustenance of a "common pasture" (νομός). Implicitly, it conjoins the *cosmos* with *nomos*—a particularly Stoic idea—and thus also figures the *cosmos* as a universal pastureland, which could, as discussed further below, have important implications for the representation of the provinces as pastures in Varro's own work. Yet, this passage is fraught with a number of difficulties, which have wrought disparate estimations of its validity as a source for Zenonian Stoicism and which render this direct connection tenuous at best.[47] For now, let me simply observe that this passage provides evidence for the use of rustic analogies in

---

46. I have adopted the standard scholarly translation of Long and Sedley (1987) 429.

47. For the various uses of this evidence in scholarship over the past two centuries, see Richter (2011) 11–16. On the one hand, Schofield (1991) 104–11 subjects each component of the testimonium to extensive critique only to conclude that "the one incontrovertibly [early] Stoic idea and expression not just in the latter part of the text but in the entire passage is *nomos koinos*: common law" (110). Otherwise, everything else constitutes, in his view, Plutarchean elaboration on the basis of later Stoic thought and by means of generalized Greek philosophical vocabulary. In the latter case, he holds up the herd simile, its "most questionable feature" (107), as one such example of elaboration that draws particularly on Platonic imagery and vocabulary. Schofield's philological analysis is so trenchant that even an ardent defender of this passage's overall fidelity to Zeno's *Republic* like Vogt (2008: 87) concedes the "taint[ing] by Platonic vocabulary," by which she would seem to refer especially to the herd simile. This is not the place to make a case for a specifically Zenonian or Stoic use of the herd simile, though I do think there are grounds for such a case. For example, as Schofield acknowledges (108 n. 8), the herd simile does appear in later Stoics (e.g., Hierocles col. XI 14 von Arnim).

Stoic thought. In addition, the possibility remains that Varro, a man widely conversant in the Greek philosophical tradition and whose penchant for such plays on words is (as we have seen in previous chapters) notoriously prevalent elsewhere, drew inspiration for his own work from this punning simile: whether it be found in Zeno's original work, the subsequent Stoic tradition, or in the works of another philosophical sect. On this view, then, Varro appropriates, extends, and develops this metaphor in *De Re Rustica* so as to model the contemporary Roman empire as a new kind of Roman farm with provinces for pastures.

## VARRO'S CONCEPTION OF *IMPERIUM-AS-PRAEDIUM*

The previous section suggested that Stoic political philosophy served as an important intellectual precursor for Varro's *RR*. The question thus arises: does Varro's text evince a cosmopolitan view of empire, wherein all those who inhabit the bounds of lands subject to Roman *imperium*—Romans, Italians, and provincials alike—are citizen-cattle of the same pastures? Notwithstanding the fact that later Stoics (especially those in a Roman context) do not adhere to a radical cosmopolitan view of the world and instead allow for priorities in commitments (especially to one's *patria*),[48] there are good reasons to think otherwise. While it may not be readily apparent, the implications of Varro's allegory are not merely spatial, but also quasi-juridical and perhaps even ethical; in particular, the model assigns different values to the different parts composing the whole of Varro's imperial estate, and it is this disparity in treatment that provides insight into the dynamics of empire implicit in the treatise's theory.

At a first glance, however, this disparity is not entirely evident. Recall that on this model, the provinces are the pastures, Italy is the farmstead and fields, and Rome the villa. While each space is distinguished in terms of function, the ends remain the same for the respective farming practice; be he farmer (1.4.1), shepherd (2.pref.6; 2.8.5), or *dominus* (3.3.1), the practitioner of *res rusticae* is to aim at (1) utility (*utilitas*) for the pursuit of produce/profit (*fructus*) and at (2) pleasure (*voluptas*) for the pursuit of delight (*delectatio*). As I discussed in chapters 2 and 6, the *RR* consistently conjoins these two ends as the twin goals of *res rusticae*, though the latter ought to remain subordinate to the primary pursuit of produce/profit through utility (1.4.1). Notwithstanding the

---

48. See Richter (2011) 80–86, who rightly observes that "for Cato's Stoic sage" in Cic. *De Fin.* 3.62ff., "the natural affinity for all of humanity provides the basis of local and specific political allegiance" (82).

important critique that *RR* 3 presents to this system's applicability to the city of Rome itself through *pastio villatica* and the particularly noteworthy case of the aviaries,[49] the *RR* provides a panoply of examples where the delightful is congruent with or actually enhances the profitable (e.g., the spatial arrangement of crops, 1.7.2; the physical appearance of cattle, 2.5.6–10). The twin goals of profit and pleasure would thus appear to be uniform throughout all spheres of Roman *imperium* as an agricultural *praedium*. Thus, understanding the twofold pursuit of profit and pleasure as the "ethical system" of *res rusticae* might lead to the conclusion that the avowed ethical treatment is the same for each area of the estate (fields, pastures, and the villa) and, consequently, for their respective territorial analogues (Italy, provinces, and Rome) as well.

Nonetheless, there is a "prioritization" in terms of the function, valuation, and, consequently, ethical treatment of each agricultural space. By "prioritization," I mean the following: that there is an implicit hierarchy of the respective spaces; that this hierarchy hinges on the status accorded to each space as determined by its rustic function and the social value assigned to that function; and that this functional and qualitative hierarchy determines in part the way in which each respective space is demarcated, categorized (in a quasi-juridical fashion), and treated (i.e., ethically). Furthermore, this ethico-spatial framework for the estate in turn maps onto the political space adumbrated within the treatise's allegory. I begin with *agri cultura*, field cultivation, which is the practice associated with Italy and which is also the central, core term of Varro's reconstitution of *res rusticae*. As Varro makes clear, the management of fields entails active and conscientious care, requiring diligent attention to location, nature of the soil, prior and prospective methods of fertilization, regional factors, and usage patterns (e.g., 1.6.1–7.10; 1.9.1–7; 1.16.1–6; 1.23.1–26, etc.). In fact, the tending (*cultura*) of a field (*ager*) might even necessitate its periodic lack of use in accordance with the prevailing Roman methods of fallowing (e.g., 1.44.2–3) and crop rotation.[50] As for pasturage, however, Varro pays virtually no attention to its quality or condition, let alone its maintenance. Instead, reckoning of it occurs only incidentally— as, for example, in the mention of meadows (*prata*) dedicated solely to animal husbandry in Cato's lists of preferred types of land (1.7.9) or in respect to the preferred terrain or ecosystem for the maintenance of a particular animal (e.g., wooded lands for goats, 2.3.6)—or in otherwise extrinsic contexts, as in the repeated references to the practice of bringing animals onto recently harvested lands so as to feed the animals, but more importantly, to clear the

---

49. See pp. 197–210 in chapter 6.

50. For Roman practices in fallowing and crop rotation, see White (1970) 110–24.

stubble and to fertilize the land through the animals' droppings (e.g., 1.19.3, 2.2.12). In sum, pasturage rarely constitutes the focus of the treatise; instead, it seems to be taken as a given and assumed to be available for the more pertinent concern of procuring returns from animals.

This last practice—the bringing of animals onto a field for the purpose of the herd's sustenance and the land's renewal—merits further consideration, for it potentially confuses the treatise's strict demarcation of space. Repeatedly mentioned in Books 1 and 2, and even upheld as an example of the close "alliance" (*societas,* 2.pref.5; cf. *adfinis* in 1.2.15) between *agri cultura* and animal husbandry, this practice is nonetheless highly qualified in terms of the animals. For one thing, the treatise consistently maintains that it is only sheep that are to be brought onto the field, while it explicitly and vehemently denies any place to goats (1.2.17, 2.3.7). The present lines of inclusion and exclusion may simply reflect the reality that sheep are quite mild, docile, and gentle, which makes their presence on a field less potentially invasive— especially when compared to the rapacious, unruly, and riotous mob that a herd of goats constitutes (2.3.8–9).[51] But it is difficult not to read more deeply into the allegorical implications here when we acknowledge that the treatise's sporadic anthropomorphizing tends to figure Roman citizens as sheep and non-Romans as goats.[52] Are we to understand that the treatise is seeking to deny a place in Italy to non-Italians, in what amounts to a quasi-xenophobic, exclusionary injunction? It is not outside the realm of possibility, but we run the (ever-present) risk of pushing the metaphorical implications too far. Instead, the metaphors reinforce the treatise's larger program of articulating a coherent, systematically defined discourse of *res rusticae,* which associates three distinct spheres with three discrete areas of the estate. On this view, the inclusion of sheep and exclusion of goats underscores the distinction implicitly being drawn between Italy and the provinces. Additional support for this position may be found in Varro's deprecatory lament of contemporary Romans' subversion of farmland for pastureland—and *not* vice versa (2.pref.4).[53] Or in de-allegorized terms, when Varro rues the misuse of fields as pastures, he is deploring the treatment of Italy as just another province,

---

51. Cf. pp. 139–45 in chapter 4.

52. Compare the anthropomorphic characterizations of sheep as orderly Roman legionaries (2.2.9) and citizen voters as sheep (3.2.10) with the repeated characterization of goats as hostile enemies (e.g., *inimicae,* 1.2.20), whose *sanitas* is fundamentally suspect (e.g., *sanae,* 2.3.5; 2.3.8) and whose unsociability issues forth in constant infighting and requires the forceful intervention of the *pastor* (2.3.8).

53. Cf. pp. 159–60 in chapter 5, where the transference of pastoralism to provincial pastures seeks to exclude both the economic exploitation of "Faustulean" shepherd-owners and the bellicose activities of "Romulean" shepherd-generals from the bounds of Italy.

which has both personal import for Varro and historical resonance for the peninsula, seeing how each was at various times a victim of the civil wars and proscriptions that ravaged and exploited Roman citizens and Italians alike over the prior century.

There may also be prior social mores and values lurking beneath this asymmetrical concern, for the figuration of Italy as farmland and non-Italian Mediterranean holdings as pastures taps into the social superiority and greater respectability of the practitioner of *agri cultura* (i.e., the *agricola*) over the practitioner of *pastio* (i.e., the *pastor*). As discussed in chapters 2 and 4,[54] this implicit hierarchy stems from juridical and material bases; the term *agricola,* "farmer," regularly denotes one who is a free citizen and an owner of land used for any farming practice (including animal husbandry), whereas the term *pastor,* "shepherd," tends to refer to one who engages specifically in animal husbandry, often does not own the animals she or he tends, and was not infrequently servile. In turn, the greater social valuation of the *agricola* renders *agri cultura* as the culturally superior activity over animal husbandry. Thus, the mere ascriptions of *agri cultura* to Italia and of *pastio* to the provinces implicitly buttress the superior status of the Italian peninsula vis-à-vis the other Mediterranean lands subject to Rome's *imperium.*

Finally, if we accept a Stoic inspiration or basis for the representation of the provinces as pastures, this cosmopolitan underpinning may appear to present a challenge to this last conclusion. Were it not for the fact that at least one contemporary Roman was already working out a way to accommodate a form of cosmopolitanism with the commitments of local political allegiance,[55] such an assessment might stand. But even without that particular recalibration of Stoic cosmopolitanism, the seeds of subversion for this view may, for Varro, already be sown within Stoic psychology and ethics. As the defining characteristic of humans (as well as of gods), rationality is what renders them citizens of the cosmic city. Yet, rationality is also *exclusive* to humans, according to the Stoics, and is thus simply not found in other animals: hence, the human as *zoon logikon.*[56] One consequence of this lack of rationality is that obligations of justice do not pertain to human-animal interactions (Diog. Laert. 7.129); consequently, humans "have no obligation to refrain from using them in any matter that benefits humans."[57] Thus, if cosmopolitan pastures do

---

54. See pp. 70–71 in chapter 2 and p. 136 in chapter 4.

55. See n. 48.

56. Such is the reworking of Aristotle's famous formulation of the human as *zoon politikon* that Sextus Empiricus attributes to Chrysippus in *Against the Professors* 2.8–11. See Richter (2011) 67–74 for discussion.

57. So Newmyer (2011) 73 rightly puts it.

stand in for the provinces and if provincials dwell therein as Stoicized animals (cf. the text's emphasis on the goat's lack of *sanitas,* 2.3.5–8), then it may be the case that cosmopolitan bonds, the dictates of *oikeiosis,* and obligations of justice and ethical treatment simply (at least for Varro) do not extend to the subject denizens of these provinces.

But even if we reject this last point, it remains that the ethical implications of the disparate treatments of farmland and pastureland for the treatise's allegory indicate that the long-term condition and treatment of Italy matters in a way in which that of the provincial pastures simply does not. In place of concern for the enduring care for and vitality of the pastures, we find a greater imperative to secure profits derived from animals. Thus, whether consciously or not, Varro's vision of Roman *imperium* as an agricultural estate takes a more benevolent view of Italy and a more exploitative view of the provinces, one in which provincial pastures are subordinate to and ultimately serve the needs of Italian fields.

There is, however, another nexus of factors to consider in this treatise's tripartite treatment of *res rusticae.* In Book 3, Varro identifies *pastio villatica,* "animal husbandry of the villa," as a new and recent type of rustic practice, which occurs at the villa of the estate and through discussion of which he metaphorizes the city of Rome as the villa of Roman *imperium.* In the first place, the relationship between Rome and the provinces as modeled by the treatise is easy to infer; as one city within Italy, it would clearly share in the privileged position enjoyed by the peninsula within this model and at the expense of the provinces. Yet, Rome is not merely "one city within Italy," but *the* city, that is, the political epicenter of the peninsula as well as the metropole of Roman *imperium* in general. Thus, it is not so much the relationship between the provinces and the city of Rome that is at the heart of the issue in the latter's representation as a villa, but rather, the relationship between the city and the peninsula. From a modern perspective, the notion of "*tota Italia*" as a singular unified entity can be, so to speak, "natural," and, as discussed in chapter 3 (pp. 74–75), it is easy to forget how recent the political unification of the area from the Straits of Messina to the Alpine foothills was. Given that the relationship between Rome and the rest of the peninsula was rife with political and ideological pitfalls, figuration of Italia as the farmland and Rome as the villa provides an elegant conceptual solution for Varro. On the one hand, as one *terra* ("soil"/"land") comprising numerous *agri* ("fields"/"regions"), Italia serves as a unifying concept that subsumes Latium and, by implication, Rome within its bounds. In this respect, Varro anticipates the emphasis placed on *tota Italia* in the Augustan period. On the other hand, by representing Rome as the villa of this *fundus,* Varro distinguishes this city from the rest of Italy in a way that both preserves its status as political hegemon and still complements the unity of these two, potentially separate entities, which are now united by the common spatial area implicit in *fundus*. Moreover, by isolating and articulating the emergence of villa husbandry as a new rustic practice (3.1.8), which is distinct from *agri cultura* and *pastio* and both realized through and continually dependent on the recent influx of wealth (cf. pp. 208–9 in chapter 6), Varro centrally locates the city within the model in a way that connects that centrality with the historical and material conditions of its *imperium*. Given that Varro is a Roman citizen writing in Latin, this last observation may seem unsurprising, but it is worth recalling that recent political and military events in the 40s and 30s BC had suggested that the geographical and political centrality of the city of Rome was not unassailable.[58] Thus, as the villa of the imperial estate, Rome is afforded the opportunity to produce and enjoy luxury foodstuffs at home, while retaining its preeminent status as political *dominus* and imperial domicile of Italian fields and Mediterranean pastures.

## CONCLUSION: SOME FINAL THOUGHTS ON VARRO AND MODERN POLITICAL THEORY

This book has argued that Varro's *De Re Rustica* allegorizes Roman *imperium* on the model of a contemporary agricultural estate (*praedium*). By figuring Italy as the farm, the provinces as pastures, and the city of Rome as the villa, Varro anticipates Augustus's subsequent transformation of Rome into a territorial state and provides a theory of empire for Roman *imperium*. And in this theory, the city of Rome and, to a lesser extent, Italy constitute the "core" of this *imperium*, while the provinces correspond to the "periphery" which that core exploits. In this final section, I conclude by provisionally offering two ways in which Varro's theory of empire might be introduced to current discussions in political theory.

First, contemporary political theory on imperialism has paid increasing attention to the role that modern liberalism has played—whether explicitly or implicitly—in the creation and perpetuation of early-modern and modern empires.[59] While this nexus of ideas was once believed to be inherently anti-imperial in its tenets, more recent scholarship has explored the various ways in which the liberal tradition and thinkers associated with it have been

---

58. See my earlier discussion on p. 205.
59. The present discussion owes much to the overview of Pitts (2012) 351–87.

complicit with imperial or imperialistic structures, agencies, sentiments, or actions. For example, scholars have explored the potential role that his day job as an official with the East India Company played in John Stuart Mill's political thought,[60] while fundamental tenets associated with liberalism (such as "equality"), which were once viewed uncritically as morally empowering or individually liberating, have come under greater scrutiny for their forcible universalization of particular, culturally specific values; tacit support of imperial actions; or outright cooption by imperial agents.[61] While modern liberalism is obviously not an intellectual tradition on which Varro could draw, we might still observe that his model of empire is likewise intimately connected with his own personal experiences with Roman imperialism as well as with ideologies, values, and philosophies that, at least from the perspective of the metropole, were generally understood to be empowering or emancipatory in some respect. For example, he, like many of the other elites of his day, partly grounded his *libertas* and concomitant economic and social status through the "farming" of multiple slave-run estates as absentee owner,[62] while the agrarian underpinnings (in both an economic sense and an ideological sense) of Roman society and culture tended to idealize the independent yeoman. Moreover, in its revision of traditional ideology (e.g., Roman thought on the farmer) in conjunction with other, more clearly progressive, and essentially emancipatory intellectual currents (e.g., Stoic cosmopolitanism), Varro's *RR* suggests that imperialism may contain within it a propensity to coopt liberatory intellectual movements. Indeed, one could even ask if his goal of production of *fructus* and framework of utility constitutes, like some instantiations of modern liberal thought, an attempt to universalize and to project as unassailable what is otherwise a fundamentally differentiated, hierarchical, and unequal ethical system for the disparate parts of empire.

The second direction returns to Dietz, the opening line of whose article in turn opened this chapter, and relates to her discussion of postnational citizenship: what she has described as the "imperative to question the relationship between the construction of the alien, the foreigner, and the stranger" vis-à-vis the status of a citizen (2012: 289). Like Aristotle's *Politics*, Varro's *RR* endeavors to define citizens and noncitizens—those who "belong" (to put it loosely) and mere inhabitants—in the face of changing geographical horizons and spatial categories, increasing ethnic variegation, and the present crisis in the prevailing political order. Unlike Dietz's Aristotle, however,

60. *Idem* 359.

61. *Idem* 357–61, 364–66.

62. See Rawson (1976) 85–102.

Varro attempts to buttress those categories through the multivalent representation of Italy as the farm and the provinces as pastures. To be sure, his conception of empire enhances (or, at least, reaffirms) the status of one historically disenfranchised group (Italians) at the expense of another, more recently disenfranchised group ("provincials"). In so doing, Varro gives previously marginalized groups a new centrality, while perpetuating the marginalization of others on the periphery. By virtue of this relegation of many and elevation of fewer, Varro's model may suggest that imperial dynamics of inclusion and exclusion tend to be more complex than sometimes assumed. Moreover, while the representation of the provinces as pastures may assign a distinct function (i.e., "land subject to grazing/exploitation") and define a place for them within the *praedium* of empire, it also renders that space a loosely demarcated, somewhat nebulous, and certainly underdefined entity (or is it entities?[63]) and potentially dehumanizes the subjects of that space as nonrational animals, thereby cultivating insurmountable difference between Italians and "provincials." Thus, we may wish to consider further whether Varro's model anticipates the predilection for contemporary imperialism in a globalized world to seek to incorporate subaltern or nonenfranchised groups through new juridical configurations—equally founded upon, and indeed embracing, the poetics of ambiguity.

---

63. For the creation of ambiguities as a deliberate strategy by architects of empire, see Pitts (2012) 372.

# Cicero's and Varro's Dialogues

# CICERO

| WORK/BOOK | YEAR | SETTING | | |
|---|---|---|---|---|
| | | Place | Date | Occasion |
| De Oratore | 56/5 | Crassus's villa at Tusculum | 91 | Roman games |
| De Re Publica | 54–51 | Scipio's villa | 129 | Feriae Latinae |
| De Legibus | 52/1–46 (?) | Cicero's villa at Arpinum | 50s (?) | Visit |
| De Partitione Oratoria | 46/5 | ? | 46/5 | ? |
| Orator | 46 | ? | 46 | ? |
| Brutus | 46 | Cicero's home (*domi*) | 46 | Visit |
| Academica v. 1 | 46/5 | Catulus's villa at Cumae (1)<br>Hortensius's villa at Bauli (2) | 63/0 | Visit |
| Academica v. 2 | 46/5 | Varro's villa near Puteoli | 45 | Visit |
| De Finibus 1–2 | 46/5 | Cicero's villa at Cumae | 50 | Visit |
| De Finibus 3–4 | 46/5 | Lucullus's villa at Tusculum | 52 | Use of library |
| De Finibus 5 | 46/5 | Athens; Garden of Academy | 79 | Lecture of Antiochus |
| Tusculanae Disputationes | 45 | Cicero's villa at Tusculum | 45 | Visit |
| De Natura Deorum | 45 | Cotta's villa | 77/6 | Feriae Latinae |
| De Divinatione | 45/4 | Cicero's villa at Tusculum | 45/4 | Visit |
| De Fato | 44 | Cicero's villa at Puteoli | 44/3 | Visit |
| De Senectute<br>(Cato Maior) | 44 | Cato's villa (?) | 150 | Visit |
| De Amicitia<br>(Laelius) | 44 | Laelius's villa | 129 | Visit |

| MAJOR CHARACTERS | MINOR CHARACTERS | DEDICATEE | MULTIPLE PREFACES? |
|---|---|---|---|
| M. Antonius<br>L. Licinius Crassus<br>C. Julius Caesar Strabo<br>    Vopiscus | P. Sulpicius Rufus<br>C. Aurelius Cotta<br>Q. Mucius Q. F. Scaevola<br>Q. Lutatius Catulus | Q. Tullius Cicero | Yes |
| Scipio Aemilianus<br>C. Laelius Sapiens<br>L. Furius Philus<br>M. Manilius<br>Sp. Mummius | Q. Aelius Tubero<br>P. Rutilius Rufus<br>Q. Mucius Q. F. Scaevola<br>C. Fannius M. F. | Q. Tullius Cicero | Yes |
| Cicero<br>Atticus<br>Q. Tullius Cicero | N/A | None (?) | N/A |
| Cicero Sr.<br>Cicero Jr. | N/A | None<br>(Son?) | N/A |
| Cicero | N/A<br>(Brutus) | Brutus | N/A |
| Cicero | Atticus<br>Brutus | Brutus | N/A |
| Catulus | [Atticus?] | ? | ? |
| Cicero<br>Varro | Atticus | Varro | ? |
| L. Manlius Torquatus<br>Cicero | C. Valerius Triarius | Brutus | Yes |
| Cato the Younger<br>Cicero | N/A | Brutus | Yes |
| M. Pupius Piso Calpurnius | Cicero<br>Q. Tullius Cicero<br>L. Tullius Cicero<br>Atticus | Brutus | Yes |
| M.<br>A. | N/A | Brutus | Yes |
| C. Velleius<br>Q. Lucilius Balbus<br>C. Cotta | Cicero | Brutus | No |
| Cicero<br>Q. Tullius Cicero | N/A | ? | ? |
| A. Hirtius<br>Cicero | N/A | ? | ? |
| Cato Maior | Scipio Aemilianus<br>C. Laelius Sapiens | Atticus | N/A |
| C. Laelius Sapiens | Q. Mucius Q. F. Scaevola<br>C. Fannius | Atticus | N/A |

# VARRO

| WORK/BOOK | YEAR | SETTING | | |
|---|---|---|---|---|
| | | Place | Date | Occasion |
| De Re Rustica 1 | 37 | Temple of Tellus in Rome | 45–37 | Sementivalia |
| De Re Rustica 2 | 37 | Epirus | 67 | Pompey's Pirate War |
| De Re Rustica 3 | 37 | Villa Publica in Rome | 50 | Election of aediles |

| MAJOR CHARACTERS | MINOR CHARACTERS | DEDICATEE | MULTIPLE PREFACES? |
|---|---|---|---|
| Cn. Tremelius Scrofa<br>C. Licinius Stolo | Varro<br>C. Fundanius<br>P. Agrasius<br>C. Agrius<br>L. Fundilius<br>Fundilius's freedman | Fundania | Yes |
| Cn. Tremelius Scrofa<br>Varro<br>Atticus<br>Cossinius<br>Murrius<br>Q. Lucienus<br>Vaccius | Menates (?)<br>Vitulus's freedman | Turranius Niger | Yes |
| Q. Axius<br>Appius Claudius Pulcher<br>Cornelius Merula<br>Varro | Fircellius Pavo<br>Minucius Pica<br>M. Petronius Passer<br>Pantuleius Parra<br>Unnamed candidate | Pinnius | Yes |

# Sources, Citations, and Other Authorities

# BOOK I

| PASSAGE | DIRECT QUOTATIONS | INDIRECT CITATIONS | APPEALS TO TRADITION OR UNNAMED AUTHORITY |
|---------|-------------------|--------------------|--------------------------------------------|
| 1.1 | | | |
| 1.7 | | | *sermones* |
| 1.11 | | | Sources for contents of *De Re Rustica* |
| 2.2 | | | |
| 2.3 | | Geographical division of world | |
| 2.5 | | Need for day and night | |
| 2.7 | Vines in Phrygia | | |
| | Corn in Argos | | |
| | Wine in Ager Gallicus | | |
| | | Wine in Faventia | |
| 2.10 | | | General esteem for expertise of Scofa/Stolo |
| 2.13 | | Greek, Latin, and Carthaginian writers | |
| 2.16 | | Relationship between shepherds and farmers | |
| 2.17–18 | Grazing of goats | | |
| 2.20 | | | Origin of olive tree |
| 2.22 | | Clay pits | |
| 2.25 | Killing of bedbugs | | |
| 2.26 | Depilatory | | |
| 2.27 | Remedy for foot pain | | |
| 2.28 | | Recipes in ag. works | |
| | Cabbage | | |
| 4.1 | Elements | | |
| 4.5 | | Importance of location | |
| 5.1 | | Theophrastus's works | |

| TRADITIONAL ROMAN SAYINGS | ATTRIBUTION OF SOURCE | SPEAKER | GREEK, ROMAN, CARTHAGINIAN, OR NOT AVAILABLE |
|---|---|---|---|
| *est homo bulla . . .* | *ut dicitur* | VARRO (author) | N/A |
| | *ego*/autopsy | VARRO (author) | R |
| | autopsy | VARRO (author) | R |
| | Reading | VARRO (author) | R |
| | Hearing | VARRO (author) | R |
| *Romanus sedendo . . .* | *vetus proverbium* | Varro (character) | R |
| *longissimam esse . . .* | *dici* | Agrius | R |
| | Eratosthenes | Agrius | G |
| | Pacuvius | Fundanius | R |
| | Homer | Fundanius | G |
| | Homer | Fundanius | G |
| | Cato | Fundanius | R |
| | Marcius Libo | Fundanius | R |
| | *dicunt* | Agrius | R |
| | *alii scripserunt* | Scrofa | G/R/C |
| | Dicaearchus | Varro (character) | G |
| | *leges colonicas* | Agrius | R |
| | *leges colonicas* | Fundanius | R |
| | *dicitur* | Fundanius | G |
| | Sasernae | Scrofa | R |
| | Sasernae | Stolo | R |
| | Sasernae | Scrofa (?) | R |
| | Sasernae | Stolo | R |
| | Cato | Varro (?) | R |
| | Cato | Agrius | R |
| | Ennius | Scrofa | R |
| | Hippocrates | Scrofa | G |
| | Varro | Scrofa | R |
| | Theophrastus | Agrius/Stolo | G |

# BOOK I *(continued)*

| PASSAGE | DIRECT QUOTATIONS | INDIRECT CITATIONS | APPEALS TO TRADITION OR UNNAMED AUTHORITY |
|---------|-------------------|--------------------|-------------------------------------------|
| 7.1 | Importance of location | | |
| | | | Value of *quincunces* |
| 7.6–7 | Effect of soil on crops | | |
| 7.8 | | | Crops and soil |
| 7.9 | Types of land | | |
| | | | Types of land |
| 7.10 | | Types of land | |
| | | | Types of land |
| | | Types of land | |
| 8.1 | | | Vineyards |
| 9.7 | | Soil | |
| 10.2 | | | 2 *iugera = haeredium* |
| 16.5 | | Overseer and *familia* | |
| 17.3 | | Hired workers | |
| 18.1 | Number of slaves | | |
| 18.2 | | Number of slaves | |
| 19.1 | | Inarticulate equipment | |
| 22.3 | Equipment | | |
| 22.4 | | | Equipment |
| 22.5 | | | Equipment |
| 24.1 | Planting | | |
| 24.4 | Planting | | |
| 37.1 | | | |
| | | Lunar dating | |
| 37.3 | | | |
| 37.5 | Plane tree in Athens | | |
| 38.1 | | Manuring | |
| 38.2 | | Manuring | |
| 38.3 | | | Manuring |

| TRADITIONAL ROMAN SAYINGS | ATTRIBUTION OF SOURCE | SPEAKER | GREEK, ROMAN, CARTHAGINIAN, OR NOT AVAILABLE |
|---|---|---|---|
| | Cato | Stolo | R |
| | *maiores* | Scrofa | R |
| | Theophrastus (twice) | Scrofa | G |
| | | Scrofa | G |
| | Autopsy | Scrofa | R |
| | Cato | Stolo | R |
| | *alii* | Scrofa | N/A |
| | *ego*/autopsy | Scrofa | R |
| | *maiores* | Scrofa | R |
| | Caesar Vopiscus | Scrofa | R |
| | *qui putent* | Scrofa | N/A |
| | Diophanes | Stolo | G |
| | *dicitur* | Scrofa | R |
| | Sasernae | Scrofa | R |
| | Cassius Dionysius | Scrofa | G |
| | Cato | Scrofa | R |
| | Saserna | Scrofa | R |
| | Cato | Scrofa | R |
| | Saserna | Scrofa | R |
| | Cato | Stolo | R |
| | *alii* | Stolo | N/A |
| | Cato | Stolo | R |
| | Cato | Stolo | R |
| | Cato | Scrofa | R |
| Lunar dating | *dicitur* | Scrofa | R |
| | Athenians and *alii* | Scrofa | G |
| *octavo Ianam . . .* | Country saying | Scrofa | R |
| | Theophrastus | Stolo | G |
| | Cassius Dionysius | Stolo | G |
| | Cassius Dionysius | Stolo | G |
| | *negant* | Stolo | N/A |

## **BOOK I** *(continued)*

| PASSAGE | DIRECT QUOTATIONS | INDIRECT CITATIONS | APPEALS TO TRADITION OR UNNAMED AUTHORITY |
|---------|-------------------|--------------------|-------------------------------------------|
| 40.1 | | Seeds in air | |
| | Seed in water | | |
| 40.3 | Proper time for seed | | |
| | | | Proper time for seed |
| 40.5 | | | Proper grafting |
| 42 | | | Alfalfa |
| 44.2–3 | | Sowing | |
| 46 | | | Summer solstice |
| 48.2 | | *gluma* as a word | |
| 50.3 | | | Etymologies for straw |
| | | | Cutting of grain |
| 58 | Grapes | | |
| 60 | Olives | | |

| TRADITIONAL ROMAN SAYINGS | ATTRIBUTION OF SOURCE | SPEAKER | GREEK, ROMAN, CARTHAGINIAN, OR NOT AVAILABLE |
|---|---|---|---|
| | Anaxagoras | Stolo | G |
| | Theophrastus | Stolo | G |
| | Theophrastus | Stolo | G |
| | *quidam* | Stolo | N/A |
| | Haruspices | Stolo | R |
| | *scribunt* | Stolo | N/A |
| | [Theophrastus] | Stolo | G |
| | | Agrius | G |
| | *dicitur* | Stolo | N/A |
| | Ennius | Stolo | R |
| | *alii* | Stolo | R |
| | *dicatur* | Stolo | N/A |
| | Cato | Stolo | R |
| | Cato | Stolo | R |

# BOOK II

| PASSAGE | DIRECT QUOTATIONS | INDIRECT CITATIONS | APPEALS TO TRADITION OR UNNAMED AUTHORITY |
|---|---|---|---|
| 1.2 | Expertise of Scrofa | | |
| 1.3 | | *principium generandi* | |
| | | No *principium generandi* | |
| 1.3–5 | | Stages of humans | |
| 1.6 | | Primacy of shepherds | |
| 1.7–9 | | | Value of flocks/names |
| 1.9 | | Name of Italia | |
| 1.20 | Sacred pigs | | |
| 1.27 | | | Births from mules |
| | | Births from mules | |
| 2.5–6 | Selling pigs | | |
| 3.3 | Goats | | |
| 3.5 | Selling goats | | |
| | | Goats breathe from ears | |
| 3.10 | | Size of flocks | |
| 4.7 | | | Pig pregnancies |
| 4.11 | Size of Gallic sows | | |
| | | Size of Lusitanian sows | |
| 4.16 | Sacred pigs | | |
| 4.18 | | Aeneas and sows | |
| 4.20 | | | Pigs and horns |
| 5.1 | *poimena laon* | | |
| 5.3 | | "Italia" from *taurus* | |
| | | | Etymology of Italia |
| 5.5 | | Speaking ox | |
| 5.6 | | | Stages of life for cattle |

| TRADITIONAL ROMAN SAYINGS | ATTRIBUTION OF SOURCE | SPEAKER | GREEK, ROMAN, CARTHAGINIAN, OR NOT AVAILABLE |
|---|---|---|---|
| | Homer | Varro (character) | G |
| | Thales | Varro (character) | G |
| | Zeno | Varro (character) | G |
| | Pythagoras | Varro (character) | G |
| | Aristotle | Varro (character) | G |
| | Dicearchus | Varro (character) | G |
| | Greek and Roman writers | Varro (character) | G/R |
| | | Varro (character) | G/R |
| | *maiores* | Varro (character) | R |
| | Piso | Varro (character) | R |
| | Plautus | Scrofa | R |
| | *dicatur* | Vaccius | N/A |
| | Mago | Varro (character) | C |
| | Cassius Dionysius | Varro (character) | G |
| | Legal formula | Atticus | R |
| | Cato | Cossinius | R |
| | *actio Manilia* | Cossinius | R |
| | Archelaus | Cossinius | G |
| | Gaberius | Cossinius | R |
| | Menas | Cossinius | G (?) |
| | Murrius | Cossinius | R |
| | *dicuntur* | Scrofa | N/A |
| | Cato | Scrofa | R |
| | Atilius of Spain | Scrofa | R |
| | Plautus | Scrofa | R |
| | Priests | Scrofa | R |
| | *dicuntur* | Scrofa | N/A |
| | Homer | Lucienus | G |
| | Timaeus | Varro (character) | G |
| | *alii* | Varro (character) | N/A |
| | Senatorial records | Vaccius | R |
| | *dicuntur* | Vaccius | N/A |

# BOOK II *(continued)*

| PASSAGE | DIRECT QUOTATIONS | INDIRECT CITATIONS | APPEALS TO TRADITION OR UNNAMED AUTHORITY |
|---|---|---|---|
| 5.11 | Selling oxen | | |
| 5.13 | | Oxen dismounting cows | |
| 5.18 | | Health of cows | |
| 7.1 | | Value of mares | |
| 7.9 | | | Horse that kills mare |
| 8.3 | | | Quality of Arcadian jacks |
| 8.6 | | Keeping of mules | |
| 9.6 | | | Wayfinding of dogs |
| | Dogs and boiled frogs | | |
| 9.9 | | | |
| 10.9 | | Illyrican slavewomen | |
| 11.10 | | | Advent of barbers |
| 11.11 | | Goat skins as clothes | |
| 11.12 | | | Goat skins as clothes |

| TRADITIONAL ROMAN SAYINGS | ATTRIBUTION OF SOURCE | SPEAKER | GREEK, ROMAN, CARTHAGINIAN, OR NOT AVAILABLE |
|---|---|---|---|
|  | Lex Manilia | Vaccius | R |
|  | Aristotle | Vaccius | G |
|  | Mago | Vaccius | C |
|  | Q. Modius Equiculus | Lucienus | R |
|  | *memoria* | Lucienus | R |
|  | *maiores* | Murrius | R |
|  | Autopsy | Murrius | R |
|  | Varro (character) | Murrius | R |
|  | P. Aufidius Pontianus | Atticus | R |
|  | Saserna | Atticus | R |
| The loyalty of dogs | Proverb | Atticus | N/A |
|  | Autopsy | Varro (character) | R |
|  | *dicuntur* | Atticus | N/A |
|  | Caecilius | Cossinius | R |
|  | Terence | Cossinius | R |
|  | *dicunt* | Atticus (?) | N/A |

# BOOK III

| PASSAGE | DIRECT QUOTATIONS | INDIRECT CITATIONS | APPEALS TO TRADITION OR UNNAMED AUTHORITY |
|---|---|---|---|
| 1.1 | | | Two modes of human life |
| 1.2 | | | Oldest cities |
| | Age of Rome | | |
| 1.3 | | | Age of Thebes |
| 1.4 | | | Origin of human arts |
| | | | Return of Romans to *rus* |
| | | | Terra = Mater and Ceres |
| 2.1 | | | |
| 2.3 | | | Nature of villa |
| 2.7–8 | | Seian house | |
| 2.12 | | Axius's husbandry | |
| 2.13 | | Villa husbandry | |
| | | Villa husbandry | |
| | | | Villa husbandry |
| 2.14 | | Seius's profit | |
| 2.15 | | Profit from aviary | |
| 2.17 | | Profit from villa | |
| | | Profit from *piscina* | |
| 3.2 | | | *leporaria* |
| 3.5 | | Raising of chickens | |
| | | | Raising of peafowl |
| 3.6 | | | Aviaries |
| 3.8 | | *leporaria* | |
| 3.9–10 | | *piscinae* | |
| | | | *piscinae* |
| | | *piscinae* | |

| TRADITIONAL ROMAN SAYINGS | ATTRIBUTION OF SOURCE | SPEAKER | GREEK, ROMAN, CARTHAGINIAN, OR NOT AVAILABLE |
|---|---|---|---|
| | *traditae sunt* | VARRO (author) | N/A |
| | *traditum sit* | VARRO (author) | N/A |
| | Ennius | VARRO (author) | R |
| | *dicuntur* | VARRO (author) | N/A |
| | *dicantur* | VARRO (author) | N/A |
| | *maiores* | VARRO (author) | R |
| | *appellabant* | VARRO (author) | R |
| *malum consilium . . .* | *dicitur* | Varro (character) | R |
| | *maiores* | Appius | R |
| | Marcus Seius | Appius | R |
| | Lucius Merula | Appius | R |
| | Lucius Merula | Appius | R |
| | Autopsy | Appius | R |
| | Mago | Appius | C |
| | Cassius Dionysius | Appius | G |
| | *alii* | Appius | N/A |
| | Seius's *libertus* | Merula | R |
| | Varro's aunt | Varro (character) | R |
| | Lucius Abuccius | Merula | R |
| | Cato the Younger | Merula | R |
| | *maiores* | Merula | R |
| | *augurs* | Merula | R |
| | *patresfamiliae* | Merula | R |
| | *Maiores* | Merula | R |
| | Axius's father | Merula | R |
| | Varro | Merula | R |
| | Philippus/Ummidius | Merula | R |
| | *nostra aetas* | Merula | R |
| | Sergius Orata | Merula | R |
| | Licinius Murena | Merula | R |
| | Philippus | Merula | R |
| | Hortensius | Merula | R |
| | Luculli | Merula | R |

# BOOK III *(continued)*

| PASSAGE | DIRECT QUOTATIONS | INDIRECT CITATIONS | APPEALS TO TRADITION OR UNNAMED AUTHORITY |
|---|---|---|---|
| 4.2 | | Aviary for delight | |
| 4.3 | | Aviary for delight/profit | |
| 4.8 | | First aviary in peristyle | |
| 6.1 | | Raising of peafowl | |
| 6.2 | | | Raising of peafowl |
| | | Raising of peafowl | |
| 6.3 | | Raising of peafowl | |
| 6.6 | | Raising of peafowl | |
| 7.5 | | | Use of pigeon droppings |
| 7.10 | | Price of pigeons | |
| 9.11 | | | Proper care of eggs |
| 9.17 | | | Islands named from hens |
| 10.1 | | Raising of geese | |
| 11.4 | | Conception by voice | |
| 12.1 | | Hunting preserves | |
| 12.4 | | Hares | |
| 12.5 | | | Italian hares |
| 12.6 | | Etymology of *lepus* | |
| 13.1–2 | | Animals and horn | |
| 16.4 | | Bougonia | |
| | | Wasps from horses | |
| 16.5 | | Properties of hexagon | |
| 16.7 | | | Bees = *volucres Musarum* |

| TRADITIONAL ROMAN SAYINGS | ATTRIBUTION OF SOURCE | SPEAKER | GREEK, ROMAN, CARTHAGINIAN, OR NOT AVAILABLE |
|---|---|---|---|
| | Varro | Merula | R |
| | Lucullus | Merula | R |
| | M. Laenius Strabo | Appius | R |
| | M. Aufidius Lurco | Merula | R |
| | *dicantur* | Merula | N/A |
| | M. Piso | Merula | R |
| | M. Seius | Merula | R |
| | Q. Hortensius | Merula | R |
| | Abuccius | Merula | R |
| | *scripserint* | Merula | N/A |
| | L. Axius | Merula | R |
| | *aiunt* | Merula | N/A |
| | *dicitur* | Merula | N/A |
| | Scipio Metellus | Axius | R |
| | M. Seius | Axius | R |
| | | Merula | R |
| | Archelaus | Merula | G |
| | Q. Fulvius Lipinnus | Appius | R |
| | Titus Pompeius | Appius | R |
| | Archelaus | Appius | G |
| | *dicitur* | Appius | R |
| | L. Aelius | Appius | R |
| | *ego* | Appius | R |
| | Varro/M. Pupius Piso | Appius | R |
| | Q. Hortensius/*ego* | Axius | R |
| | Archelaus | Appius | G |
| | | Appius | G |
| | *geometrae* | Appius | G |
| | *dicuntur* | Appius | N/A |

# BOOK III *(continued)*

| PASSAGE | DIRECT QUOTATIONS | INDIRECT CITATIONS | APPEALS TO TRADITION OR UNNAMED AUTHORITY |
|---------|-------------------|---------------------|-------------------------------------------|
| 16.10 | | Profit from bees | |
| 16.18 | | | Three kinds of bees |
| | | Three kinds of bees | |
| | | Two kinds of bees | |
| 16.22 | | Health of bees | |
| 16.24 | | | Sources for bees' work |
| 16.33 | | | Amounts of honey |
| 16.34 | | | Times for honey |
| 17.3 | | *Piscinae* | |
| 17.4 | | Painting analogy | |
| | | Lydian fish | |
| 17.5 | | Buying fish from Puteoli | |
| 17.8 | | M. Lucullus's carelessness | |
| 17.9 | | L. Lucullus's extravance | |

| TRADITIONAL ROMAN SAYINGS | ATTRIBUTION OF SOURCE | SPEAKER | GREEK, ROMAN, CARTHAGINIAN, OR NOT AVAILABLE |
|---|---|---|---|
| | Seius | Merula | R |
| | Varro | Merula | R |
| | Veianii/Varro | Merula | R |
| | *alii* | Merula | N/A |
| | [Aristotle] | Merula | G |
| | Menecrates | Merula | G |
| | [Menecrates] | Merula | G |
| | *dicunt* | Merula | N/A |
| | *alii dicunt* | Merula | N/A |
| | *putant* | Merula | N/A |
| | Hirrus | Axius | R |
| | Pausias | Axius | G |
| | Varro | Axius | R |
| | Q. Hortensius | Axius | R |
| | Q. Hortensius | Axius | R |
| | Q. Hortensius | Axius | R |

**TOTAL NUMBER OF APPEALS TO SOURCES BY ETHNICITY:**

128 Roman
45 Greek
4 Carthaginian
30 Unspecified

# APPENDIX 3

# Spatial Terminology in
# *De Re Rustica* 1

~

## Ager

In the sense of "field" (i.e., the place of agricultural activity) (55 instances): 1.2.9, 1.2.12, 1.2.17, 1.2.20, 1.2.21, 1.2.21, 1.2.21, 1.2.21, 1.2.22, 1.2.23, 1.2.23, 1.2.23, 1.3.1, 1.4.2, 1.4.3, 1.4.3, 1.4.4, 1.6.1, 1.6.2, 1.7.5, 1.7.8, 1.7.9(C [= quotation from Cato]), 1.10.2, 1.10.2, 1.12.1, 1.13.4, 1.13.6, 1.14.3, 1.15.1, 1.16.1, 1.16.3, 1.16.6, 1.18.1, 1.18.1(C), 1.18.4, 1.19.1, 1.22.2, 1.24.1(C), 1.24.1(C), 1.25.1(C), 1.25.1(C), 1.36.1, 1.36.1, 1.37.1, 1.38.1, 1.38.1, 1.38.2, 1.40.1, 1.44.3, 1.50.3, 1.51.1, 1.55.7, 1.55.7, 1.57.3.

In the sense of "soil" (i.e., *terra*) (6 instances): 1.9.6, 1.23.3, 1.23.3, 1.24.1(C), 1.24.1(C), 1.35.1.

In the sense of "place" or "position" (i.e., *locus*) (2 instances): 1.24.1(C), 1.24.2(C).

In the sense of "farm" (8 instances): 1.4.5, 1.7.1(C), 1.11.2, 1.11.2, 1.16.4, 1.18.6, 1.23.4, 1.51.1.

In the sense of "region" (16 instances): 1.2.7(C), 1.2.7(C), 1.2.7(C), 1.2.7, 1.2.10, 1.7.6, 1.8.2, 1.10.1, 1.14.3, 1.14.3, 1.14.4, 1.14.4, 1.14.4, 1.14.4, 1.18.6, 1.57.2.

## Terra

In the sense of "soil" (73 instances)

Referring to quality (21 instances): 1.6.1, 1.7.5, 1.8.7, 1.9.1, 1.9.3, 1.9.5, 1.9.6, 1.9.7, 1.9.7, 1.20.2, 1.20.4, 1.23.2, 1.23.2, 1.23.3, 1.27.2, 1.32.1, 1.36.1, 1.40.3, 1.44.1, 1.44.2, 1.55.7.

Referring to the material (38 instances): 1.2.16, 1.8.4, 1.8.6, 1.9.2, 1.9.3, 1.9.5, 1.14.2, 1.14.4, 1.23.2, 1.27.3, 1.29.1, 1.29.1, 1.29.3, 1.31.2, 1.32.1, 1.35.1, 1.37.5, 1.38.1, 1.39.3, 1.40.3, 1.40.4, 1.44.3,

1.45.1, 1.45.3, 1.45.3, 1.45.3, 1.45.3, 1.45.3, 1.50.1, 1.50.1, 1.50.2, 1.51.1, 1.52.2, 1.55.1, 1.57.2, 1.57.3, 1.59.3, 1.63.1.

Referring to the element (14 instances): 1.1.5, 1.1.5, 1.9.1, 1.2.20, 1.2.23, 1.2.27, 1.3.1, 1.4.1, 1.4.4, 1.4.4, 1.5.4, 1.9.3, 1.13.4, 1.15.1.

In the sense of "field" (i.e., *ager*) (6 instances): 1.2.16, 1.8.5, 1.19.2, 1.29.2, 1.30.1, 1.43.1.

In the sense of "place" or "position" (i.e., *locus*) (2 instances): 1.42.1, 1.42.1.

In the sense of "country" or "land" (6 instances): 1.2.3, 1.2.3, 1.2.5, 1.2.7, 1.9.1, 1.9.1.

## Locus

In the sense of "place" or "position" (53 instances)

Without any qualities derived from environment (29 instances): 1.2.8, 1.2.23, 1.4.4, 1.6.2, 1.7.2, 1.7.2, 1.7.7, 1.8.5, 1.11.2, 1.12.4, 1.13.1, 1.14.3, 1.17.3, 1.22.6, 1.23.1, 1.23.1, 1.23.4, 1.23.5, 1.23.6, 1.31.4, 1.38.1, 1.39.3, 1.40.3, 1.40.6, 1.44.1, 1.44.1, 1.44.4, 1.50.2, 1.52.1.

With qualities derived from environment (24 instances): 1.6.3, 1.6.5, 1.6.6, 1.7.7, 1.9.4, 1.12.2, 1.12.3, 1.12.4, 1.17.3, 1.20.2, 1.20.2, 1.23.5, 1.23.5, 1.23.5, 1.24.4(C), 1.39.1, 1.40.3, 1.41.1, 1.45.2, 1.50.3, 1.51.1, 1.51.2, 1.57.1, 1.59.1.

In the sense of "field" (i.e., *ager*) (no instances)

In the sense of "soil" (i.e., *terra*) (4 instances): 1.24.1(C), 1.24.1(C), 1.24.2(C), 1.25.1(C).

# SPATIAL TERMINOLOGY IN CATO'S *DE AGRI CULTURA*

## Ager

In the sense of "field" (i.e., the place of agricultural activity) (17 instances): 1.4, 1.7, 3.1, 6.1, 6.1, 6.4, 6.4, 10.1, 61.1, 105.1, 141.1, 141.2, 141.3, 136.1, 137.1, 141.1, 155.1.

In the sense of "soil" (i.e., *terra*) (6 instances): 1.7, 6.1, 6.1, 6.2, 34.2, 61.2.

In the sense of "place" or "position" (i.e., *locus*) (6 instances): 6.1, 6.1, 6.2, 6.2, 34.2, 61.2.

In the sense of "farm" (2 instances): 1.4, 6.1.

In the sense of "region" (no instances)

## Terra

In the sense of "soil" (49 instances)

Referring to quality (8 instances): 5.6, 34.1, 34.2, 37.1, 128.1, 135.2, 135.2, 151.3.

Referring to the material (41 instances): 14.3, 14.4, 28.1, 29.1, 28.2, 28.2, 32.2, 41.4, 41.4, 41.4, 45.1, 45.3, 46.1, 46.2, 48.2, 48.2, 51.1, 51.1, 52.1, 61.2, 65.1, 94.1, 114.1, 114.1, 115.2, 129.1, 129.1, 133.1, 133.1, 133.3, 133.4, 141.1, 141.2, 141.3, 143.3, 151.2, 151.2, 151.3, 151.3, 151.4, 161.1.

Referring to the element (no instances)

In the sense of "field" (i.e., *ager*) (3 instances): 3.4, 64.1, 64.1.

In the sense of "place" or "position" (i.e., *locus*) (no instances)

In the sense of "country" or "land" (no instances)

## Locus

In the sense of "place" or "position" (44 instances)

Without any qualities derived from environment (26 instances): 1.5, 1.7, 5.5, 6.1, 6.1, 18.2, 26.1, 35.2, 35.2, 35.2, 40.1, 42.1, 45.1, 46.1, 49.1, 67.2, 68.1, 91.1, 136.1, 147.1, 148.2, 151.2, 151.2, 157.11, 161.1, 161.3.

With qualities derived from environment (18 instances): 6.3, 6.3, 6.4, 6.4, 8.1, 9.1, 14.5, 27.1, 34.1, 34.1, 34.2, 35.1, 35.1, 35.1, 43.1, 46.1, 50.2, 131.2.

In the sense of "field" (i.e., *ager*) (no instances)

In the sense of "soil" (i.e., *terra*) (14 instances): 1.3, 6.2, 6.4, 8.1, 8.1, 14.5, 35.1, 35.1, 35.2, 35.2, 40.1, 44.1, 44.1, 161.1.

# Geographical References in
# *De Re Rustica* 1

| PASSAGE | ITALIAN REGION | ITALIA | "OTHER" REGIONS | SUBJECT | CITATION |
|---------|----------------|--------|-----------------|---------|----------|
| 1.2.1 | | Italia | | *Italia picta* | |
| 1.2.3–4 | | Italia | | | |
| | | Italia | | "Scientific" *laus Italiae* | Eratosthenes |
| | | | Asia | | |
| | | | Europa | | |
| 1.2.6–8 | | Italia | | | |
| | Campania | | | | |
| | Falernia | | | | |
| | Apulia | | | | |
| | Venafrum | | | | |
| | | Italia | | | |
| | | | Phrygia | | Homer |
| | | | Argos | "Rhetorical" *laus Italiae* | |
| | | Italia | | | |
| | Ariminium | | | | |
| | Picenum | | | | Cato |
| | Ager Gallicus | | | | |
| | Faventia | | | | |
| | Faventia | | | | Libo Marcius |
| | | Italia | | | |

| PASSAGE | ITALIAN REGION | ITALIA | "OTHER" REGIONS | SUBJECT | CITATION |
|---|---|---|---|---|---|
| 1.2.20 | | | Athens | Origin of olive tree | Athenians |
| 1.4.5 | | | Corcyra | Varro's service | |
| 1.6.3 | Apulia | | | Importance of climate | |
| | Vesuvius | | | | |
| 1.7.6–7 | | | Cortynia/Crete | | Theophrastus |
| | Sybaris/Thurii | | | Importance of soil quality | |
| | | | Elephantine | | |
| | | | Smyrna | | |
| | Consentia | | | | |
| | Reate | | | | |
| | | | Epirus | | Theophrastus |
| | | | Transalpine Gaul | | |
| 1.7.10 | Rosea | | | Meadows | Caesar Vopiscus |
| | | Italia | | | |
| 1.8.1–2 | | | Hispania | Vineyards without props | |
| | | Italia | | | |
| | Falernia | | | | |
| | Arpi | | | | |
| | Brundisium | | | | |
| | Mediolanum | | | Vineyards with props | |
| | Canusium | | | | |
| | | Italia | | | |
| | Mediolanum | | | | |
| | Canusium | | | | |
| 1.8.6 | | | Asia | | |
| | | | Pandateria | Methods for training vines | |
| | | Italia | | | |
| | Reate | | | | |
| 1.9.1 | | Italia | | Example of *terra communis* | |
| 1.9.5–6 | Pupinia | | | Types of soil | |
| | Etruria | | | | |
| | Tiber | | | | |

| PASSAGE | ITALIAN REGION | ITALIA | "OTHER" REGIONS | SUBJECT | CITATION |
|---|---|---|---|---|---|
| 1.10.1 | | | Hispania ulterior | | |
| | Campania | | | Systems of measurement | |
| | Ager Romanus | | | | |
| | Ager Latinus | | | | |
| 1.13.6 | | | Hispania | Kinds of wine jars | |
| | | Italia | | | |
| 1.14.3–4 | Crustumeria | | | | |
| | Reate | | | | |
| | Tusculum | | | | |
| | Ager Gallicus | | | Types of enclosures | |
| | Ager Sabinus | | | | |
| | | | Hispania | | |
| | Tarentum | | | | |
| 1.15 | Sabine | | | | |
| | Vesuvius | | | Trees used as enclosures | |
| | Crustumeria | | | | |
| 1.16.2 | | | Sardinia/Oeliem | Brigandage | |
| | | | Hispania/Lusitania | | |
| 1.17.2 | | | Asia | | |
| | | | Egypt | Use of day laborers | |
| | | | Illyricum | | |
| 1.17.5 | | | Epirus | Excellence of slaves | |
| 1.18.6 | | | Gaul | Slaves per land | |
| | Liguria | | | | |
| 1.20.4 | Campania | | | Plowing with cows, donkeys | |
| 1.24 | Sallentine | | | | |
| | Sergia (?) | | | Varieties of olives | Cato |
| | Colminia (?) | | | | |
| | Licinia (?) | | | | |
| 1.25 | Aminnia | | | | |
| | Aminnia | | | | |
| | Murgentia (Sic.) | | | Varieties of grapes | Cato |
| | Apicia (?) | | | | |
| | Lucania | | | | |

| PASSAGE | ITALIAN REGION | ITALIA | "OTHER" REGIONS | SUBJECT | CITATION |
|---|---|---|---|---|---|
| 1.29.2 | Apulia | | | Plowing techniques | |
| 1.32.2 | | | [Transalpine?] Gaul | Etymology for beans | |
| 1.37.1 | | | Athens | Lunar dating | |
| 1.37.5 | | | Athens | Nature of tree roots | Theophrastus |
| 1.41.6 | | | Chios | Varieties of figs | |
| | | | Chalcidia | | |
| | | | Lydia | | |
| | | | Africa | | |
| | | Italia | | | |
| 1.44.1–2 | Etruria | | | Considerations for sowing and planting | Theophrastus |
| | Sybaris | | | | |
| | | Italia | | | |
| | | | Gadara/Syria | | |
| | | | Byzacium/Africa | | |
| | | | Olynthia | | |
| 1.50.1–2 | Umbria | | | Harvesting | |
| | Picenum | | | | |
| | Roma | | | | |
| 1.51.2 | Bagienni [= Liguria?] | | | Use of a threshing floor | |
| 1.52.2 | | | Hispania citerior | Method of threshing | |
| 1.57.2–3 | | | Cappadocia | Methods of grain storage | |
| | | | Thrace | | |
| | | | Hispania citerior | | |
| | Apulia | | | | |
| | | | Hispania citerior | | |
| 1.58.3 | Aminnia | | | Grapes | Cato |
| | Apicia (?) | | | | |
| | Aminnia | | | | |
| 1.59.2 | Roma | | | Fruit galleries (*oporothecae*) | |
| 1.69.3 | Roma | | | Announcement of mistaken assassination of Fundilius | |

| | ITALIAN REGIONS | ITALIA | "OTHER" REGIONS |
|---|---|---|---|
| Total number of references by category | 62 | 15 | 39 |
| Number of references excluding citations of other authorities | 42 | 14 | 26 |

# APPENDIX 5

# Geographical References in *De Re Rustica* 2

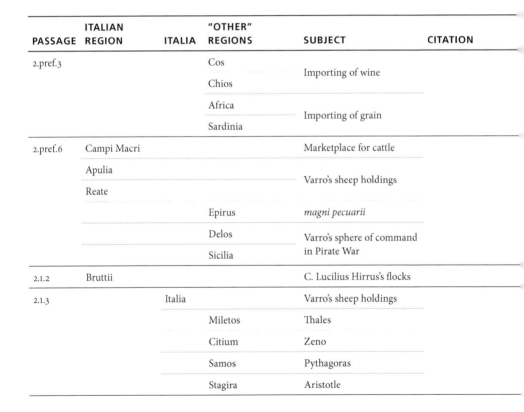

| PASSAGE | ITALIAN REGION | ITALIA | "OTHER" REGIONS | SUBJECT | CITATION |
|---|---|---|---|---|---|
| 2.pref.3 | | | Cos | Importing of wine | |
| | | | Chios | | |
| | | | Africa | Importing of grain | |
| | | | Sardinia | | |
| 2.pref.6 | Campi Macri | | | Marketplace for cattle | |
| | Apulia | | | Varro's sheep holdings | |
| | Reate | | | | |
| | | | Epirus | *magni pecuarii* | |
| | | | Delos | Varro's sphere of command in Pirate War | |
| | | | Sicilia | | |
| 2.1.2 | Bruttii | | | C. Lucilius Hirrus's flocks | |
| 2.1.3 | | Italia | | Varro's sheep holdings | |
| | | | Miletos | Thales | |
| | | | Citium | Zeno | |
| | | | Samos | Pythagoras | |
| | | | Stagira | Aristotle | |

| PASSAGE | ITALIAN REGION | ITALIA | "OTHER" REGIONS | SUBJECT | CITATION |
|---|---|---|---|---|---|
| 2.1.5 | | | Phrygia | Wild sheep | |
| | | | Samothrace | | |
| | | Italia | | Wild goats | |
| | Fiscellum | | | | |
| | Tetrica | | | | |
| | | | Dardania | | |
| | | | Maedica | Wild cattle | |
| | | | Thrace | | |
| | | | Phrygia | Wild asses | |
| | | | Lycaonia | | |
| | | | Hispania Citerior | Wild horses | |
| 2.1.6 | | | Argos | Golden fleece | |
| | | | Colchis | | |
| | | | Libya | | |
| | | | Africa | Golden sheep | |
| | | | Graecia | | |
| 2.1.8–9 | Mt. Cantherius | | | | |
| | | | Aegean | | |
| | | | Thracian Bosphorus | | |
| | | | Cimmerian Bosphorus | Place names derived from animals | |
| | | | Mt. Taurus/Syria | | |
| | | | Graecia | | |
| | | | Argos | | |
| | | Italia | | | |
| 2.1.14 | | | Arcadia | | |
| | | | Greece | Asses | |
| | | Italia | | | |
| | Reate | | | | |
| 2.1.16 | Apulia | | | Sheep | |
| | Samnium | | | | |
| 2.1.17 | Rosea | | | Mules | |
| | Burbur | | | | |

| PASSAGE | ITALIAN REGION | ITALIA | "OTHER" REGIONS | SUBJECT | CITATION |
|---|---|---|---|---|---|
| 2.1.19 | | | Hispania | | |
| | | | Lusitania | "Wind-eggs" | |
| | | | Olisipo | | |
| | | | Mt. Tagrus | | |
| 2.1.26 | | | Troy | 1,000 ships in Trojan War | |
| | Rome | | | Centumviral court | |
| 2.1.27 | Rome | | | Mule giving birth | |
| | | Italia | | | |
| | | Italia | | Swallows'/storks' birth | |
| | | | Syria | | |
| | | | Judaea | Date palms | |
| | | Italia | | | |
| 2.2.1 | | | Epirus | | |
| | | | Pergamis | "Home" of speakers | |
| | | | Maledos | | |
| 2.2.3 | | Italia | | Long-tailed sheep | |
| | | | Syria | Short-tailed sheep | |
| 2.2.9 | Apulia | | | Transhumance of sheep | |
| | Reate | | | | |
| 2.2.18 | Tarentum | | | Jacketing of sheep | |
| | | | Attica | | |
| 2.2.20 | | | Epirus | Shepherd-to-sheep ratio | |
| 2.3.3 | Soracte | | | | Cato |
| | Fiscellum | | | Wild goats | |
| | | Italia | | | |
| | Caprasia | | | | |
| 2.3.4 | | | Melia | *caprae* | |
| 2.3.9 | Ager Gallicus | | | Numbers/size of goat herds | |
| 2.3.10 | Sallentini | | | Size of goat herds | |
| | Casinum | | | Size of goat herds | |
| 2.4.1 | | Italia | | Homeland of Scrofa | |
| | | | Macedonia | Grandfather's service | |

| PASSAGE | ITALIAN REGION | ITALIA | "OTHER" REGIONS | SUBJECT | CITATION |
|---------|----------------|--------|-----------------|---------|----------|
| 2.4.9–10 | Etruria | | | Marriage rites | |
| | Latium | | | Marriage rites | |
| | Magna Graecia | | | Marriage rites | |
| 2.4.10–11 | | | Gaul | | |
| | | | Gaul | | |
| | Rome | | | | |
| | | | Comacini | Bacon | |
| | | | Cavari | | |
| | Insubrians/Italia | | | | Cato |
| | | | Lusitania/ Hispania Citerior | | Atilius Hispaniensis |
| 2.4.12 | | | Arcadia | Wondrously fat sow | |
| | Venetia | | | | |
| 2.4.16 | | | Epidamnus | Sacred pigs | Plautus |
| 2.4.18 | Lavinium | | | Portent of sow and 30 piglets | |
| | Alba | | | | |
| 2.5.1 | | | Epirus | "Home" of speakers | |
| 2.5.3 | | Italia | | | Timaeus |
| | | | Graecia | Etymology of Italia | |
| | | | Sicilia | | *alii* |
| 2.5.4–5 | | | Attica | | |
| | | | Peloponnesus | | |
| | | | Athens | | |
| | | | Argos | Respect for cattle | |
| | | | Phoenicia | | |
| | Rome | | | | Senatorial records |
| 2.5.9–10 | | Italia | | | |
| | | | Gaul | | |
| | Liguria | | | | |
| | | | Epirus | | |
| | | | Graecia | | |
| | | Italia | | Importance of cattle's breed | |
| | | Italia | | | |
| | | Italia | | | |
| | | | Thracia | | |

| PASSAGE | ITALIAN REGION | ITALIA | "OTHER" REGIONS | SUBJECT | CITATION |
|---|---|---|---|---|---|
| 2.6.1–2 | Reate | | | | |
| | | | Arcadia | | |
| | | | Peloponnesus | | |
| | | | Arcadia | Asses | |
| | | Italia | | | |
| | Reate | | | | |
| 2.6.2 | | | Sicilia | Fish | |
| | | | Rhodes | | |
| 2.6.3 | | | Phrygia | Wild asses | |
| | | | Lycaonia | | |
| 2.6.3 | | Italia | | Domesticated asses | |
| 2.6.5 | Campania | | | | |
| | Brundisium | | | Herds of asses | |
| | Apulia | | | | |
| 2.7.1 | | | Peloponnesus | Horses | |
| | Apulia | | | | |
| 2.7.6 | | | Graecia | | |
| | | | Thessalia | | |
| | | Italia | | Importance of horses' breed | |
| | Apulia | | | | |
| | Rosea | | | | |
| 2.7.16 | | | Graecia | Etymology of *hippiatroi* | |
| 2.8.3 | Reate | | | Mules | |
| | | | Arcadia | | |
| 2.8.5 | Reate | | | Mules with hard hoofs | |
| 2.8.6 | Reate | | | Homeland of Murrius | |
| 2.9.5 | | | Laconia | | |
| | | | Epirus | Importance of dogs' breed | |
| | Sallentini | | | | |
| 2.9.6 | Amiternum | | | | |
| | Umbria | | | | |
| | Metaponto | | | Anecdote regarding loyalty of dogs | P. Aufidius Pontianus |
| | Heraclea | | | | |
| | Umbria | | | | |

| PASSAGE | ITALIAN REGION | ITALIA | "OTHER" REGIONS | SUBJECT | CITATION |
|---|---|---|---|---|---|
| 2.10.4 | | | Bastuli | | |
| | | | Turduli | Slaves | |
| | | | Gaul | | |
| 2.10.7–9 | | | Illyricum | | |
| | | | Liburnia | Slaves | |
| | | | Illyricum | | |
| 2.10.11 | Apulia | | | Slave-to-mare ratio | |
| | Lucania | | | | |
| 2.11.8 | | | Hispania Citerior | Sheepshearing twice a year | |
| 2.11.10 | | Italia | | Barbers | |
| | | | Sicilia | Barbers | |
| | Ardea | | | Barbers | |
| 2.11.11 | | | Gaetulia | Use of sheep skins as clothing | |
| | | | Sardinia | | |
| | | | Graecia | | |
| 2.1.12 | | | Phrygia | Shearing of goats | |
| | | | Cilicia | | |

| | ITALIAN REGIONS | ITALIA | "OTHER" REGIONS |
|---|---|---|---|
| Total number of references by category | 53 | 19 | 92 |
| Number of references excluding citations of other authorities | 43 | 18 | 88 |

# APPENDIX 6

# Varro at Corcyra in 67 or 48 BC

AS WE HAVE SEEN, *RR* 3 never explicitly refers to the impending war between Pompey and Caesar, yet the dialogue does allude to it in a variety of ways. There may, however, be one direct mention of that conflict in *RR* 1. Shortly after Scrofa lays out the twin pursuits of *utilitas* and *voluptas* for *res rusticae* (1.4.1–2), he asserts the importance of rational knowledge (*scientia*) of placement and arrangement for alleviating a farm's unhealthy and, consequently, unprofitable and undesirable situation, which would otherwise make *agri cultura* nothing less than a "crapshoot (*alea*) for the owner's life and property" (*alea domini vitae ac rei familiaris*; 1.4.3). Pointedly, the two examples he uses to illustrate these claims come from medical and nonagricultural settings. In the first, he states (by way of rhetorical question) that Hippocrates "saved not just one field, but many towns by his knowledge during a great pestilence" (*in magna pestilentia non unum agrum, sed multa oppida scientia servavit*, 1.4.5; cf. Pliny *HN* 7.123). The second example he adduces is Varro at "the time when the army and fleet were at Corcyra, and all the houses were stuffed with the sick and dead" (*cum Corcyrae esset exercitus ac classis et omnes domus repletae essent aegrotis ac funeribus*). Scrofa would seem to be alluding to one of two occasions in which Varro was in the vicinity of Corcyra: either to his stint of service as legate in Pompey's pirate war in 67 BC,[1] or to the time Varro spent in Pompey's camp in 48 BC after he

---

1. Cf. p. 119 in chapter 4. For a review of the arguments in favor of this dating, see Heurgon (1978) 121. Perhaps Varro's act of salvation is what earned him the *corona rostrata* (cf. n. 17 in chapter 5)?

surrendered to Caesar and shortly before Pompey was to suffer defeat at Pharsalus.[2] Given the paucity of evidence, the precise dating remains an insoluble question. But if we accept the latter dating, this passage would be the only explicit reference to the civil strife that continued to afflict the Roman state in various ways at the time of the work's composition in 37 BC. Scrofa proceeds to relate that Varro modified windows and doors for the purpose of blocking out pestilential winds and letting in salubrious ones and "led back his comrades and staff unharmed by his diligence" (*diligentia suos comites ac familiam incolumes reduxit*). In using examples from nonagricultural contexts, Varro's Scrofa would seem to be encouraging the transferability and applicability of agronomical precepts to nonagricultural contexts. In this respect, one wonders whether there is a programmatic element to this passage, which encourages a metaphorical understanding of the otherwise unattested "restoration" (*reduxit*) of his fellow comrades (*comites*) in the context of this *pestilentia*.[3] Or perhaps Scrofa is suggesting that, by the diligent use of agronomy to mitigate (but not remove) this particular instance of *pestilentia,* one can thereby escape (but not necessarily overcome) political strife. But regardless of its precise date and even if this anecdote is strictly a historical one and does not illustrate the allegorical applicability of agronomical *scientia* to dire political or military situations, it still reinforces the *RR*'s more general tendency to suggest connections between *res rusticae* and politics.

---

2. For this view, see Flach (1996) 246–47. For Varro's time in Dyrrhacium, see pp. 5–6 and n. 10 in the introduction.

3. Note that *incolumes* can refer to bodily or physical integrity (*TLL* s.v. *incolumis* I; *OLD* s.v. *incolumis* 1) as well as to integrity in terms of "power, wealth, position, or sim." (*OLD* s.v. 2; cf. *TLL* II. A.1; II.C).

# BIBLIOGRAPHY

Adams, G. W. (2008). *Rome and the Social Role of Elite Villas in Its Suburbs*. Oxford: Oxford University Press.

Agache, S. (1987). "L'actualité de la *Villa Publica* en 55–54 av. J.-C." In *L'urbs: Espace urbain et histoire (Ier s. ap. J. C.)*. *Actes du colloque international organisé par la Centre national de la recherche scientifique et l'École française de Rome (Rome, 8–12 mai 1985)*. Pp. 211–34. Paris: de Boccard.

Albers, J. (2009). "Die römische Saepta in republikanischer Zeit." *Hefte des Archäologischen Seminars der Universität Bern*. 21: 7–22.

Alföldy, G. (1986). "Die Rolle des Einzelnen in der Gesellschaft des römischen Kaiserreiches." In *Die römische Gesellschaft*. Pp. 334–77. Stuttgart: F. Steiner Verlag Wiesbaden.

Alfonsi, L. (1961–4). "La tradizione ciceroniana dell' 'Economico' di Senofonte." *Ciceroniana* 3–6: 7–17.

Alpers, P. (1997). *What Is Pastoral?* Chicago: University of Chicago Press.

Ampolo, C. (1988). "Rome archaïque: Une societé pastorale?" In *Pastoral Economies in Classical Antiquity*. Ed. by C. R. Whittaker. Pp. 120–33. Cambridge: Cambridge Philological Society.

Anderson, W. S. (1982). *Essays on Roman Satire*. Princeton: Princeton University Press.

Ando, C. (2001). "Vergil's Italy: Ethnography and Politics in First-Century Rome." *Clio and the Poets*. Leiden: Brill.

———. (1999). "Was Rome a Polis?" *Classical Antiquity* 18: 5–34.

Ash, H. B. (1941). *Columella: On Agriculture*. Cambridge, MA: Harvard University Press.

Ash, H. B., and W. D. Hooper. (1934). *Marcus Porcius Cato: On Agriculture. Marcus Terentius Varro: On Agriculture*. Cambridge, MA: Harvard University Press.

Astbury, R. (2002). *M. Terentius Varro. Saturarum Menippearum Fragmenta.* Monachii: K. G. Saur.

Astin, A. E. (1988). "*Regimen Morum.*" *Journal of Roman Studies*: 14–34.

———. (1978). *Cato the Censor.* Oxford: Oxford University Press.

Atkins, J. (2013). *Cicero on Politics and the Limits of Reason.* Cambridge: Cambridge University Press.

Aujac, G. (1998). "Ératosthène et la géographie physique." *Sciences exactes et sciences appliquées à Alexandrie.* Ed. by Gilbert Argoudet Jean-Yves Guillaumin. Pp. 247–62. Saint-Etienne: Publications de l'Université de Saint-Etienne.

Badian, E. (1970/71). "Roman Politics and the Italians 131–91 BC." *Dialoghi di Archeologia* 4/5: 373–421.

———. (1970). "Additional Notes on Roman Magistrates." *Athenaeum* 48: 3–14.

———. (1968). *Roman Imperialism in the Late Republic.* Oxford: Clarendon Press.

Bakhtin, M. M. (1986). *Speech Genres and Other Late Essays.* Transl. by V. W. McGee. Austin: University of Texas Press.

———. (1981). *The Dialogic Imagination.* Transl. by C. Emerson and M. Holquist. Austin: University of Texas Press.

Baraz, Y. (2012). *A Written Republic: Cicero's Philosophical Politics.* Princeton, NJ: Princeton University Press.

Barnes, J. (1997). "Roman Aristotle." In *Philosophia Togata II: Plato and Aristotle at Rome.* Ed. by J. Barnes. Pp. 1–69. Oxford: Oxford University Press.

Baslez, M. (2002). "Mobilité et ouverture de la communauté 'romaine' de Délos." In *Les Italiens dans le monde grec: IIe siècle av. J.-C.—Ier siècle ap. J.-C.: Circulation, activités, integration.* Ed. by C. Hasenohr and C. Müller. Pp. 55–65. Athènes: École française d'Athènes.

Beard, M. (1987). "A Complex of Times. No More Sheep on Romulus' Birthday." *Proceedings of the Cambridge Philological Society* 33: 1–15.

———. (1986). "Cicero and Divination: The Formation of a Latin Discourse." *Journal of Roman Studies* 76: 33–46.

Beard, M., J. North, and S. Price. (1998). *Religions of Rome.* 2 vols. Cambridge: Cambridge University Press.

Bertrandy, F. (1995). "Les relations entre l'Afrique du nord et l'Italie: l'exemple des Seii à la fin de la République et au début de l'Empire." *Epigraphica* 57: 61–85.

Blank, D. (2012). "Varro and Antiochus." In *The Philosophy of Antiochus.* Ed. by D. Sedley. Pp. 250–89. Cambridge: Cambridge University Press.

Blösel. (2000). "Die Geschichte des Begriffes mos maiorum von den Anfängen bis zu Cicero." In *Mos maiorum: Untersuchungen zu den Formen der Identitätsstiftung und Stabilisierung in der römischen Republik.* Ed. by B. Linke and M. Stemmler. Pp. 25–97. Stuttgart: Steiner.

Bodel, J. (2012). "Villaculture." In *Roman Republican Villas: Architecture, Context, and Ideology.* Ed. by J. A. Becker and N. Terrenato. Pp. 45–60. Ann Arbor: University of Michigan Press.

Boissier, Gaston. (1861). *Etude sur la vie et les ouvrages de M. T. Varron.* Paris: L. Hachette.

Boscherini, S. (1993). "La medicina in Catone e Varrone." *Aufstieg und Niedergang der römischen Welt: Geschichte und Kultur Roms im Spiegel der neueren Forschung.* 37.1: 729–55.

Bowersock, G. W. (1971). "A Date in the Eighth *Eclogue.*" *Harvard Studies in Classical Philology* 75: 73–80.

Boyce, B. (1991). *The Language of the Freedmen in Petronius'* Cena Trimalchionis. Leiden: Brill.

Boys-Stones, G. R. (Ed.). (2003). *Metaphor, Allegory, and the Classical Tradition: Ancient Thought and Modern Revisions.* Oxford: Oxford University Press.

Branham, R. B. (2009). "Satire." In *The Oxford Handbook of Philosophy and Literature.* Ed. By R. Eldrige. Pp. 139–61. Oxford: Oxford University Press.

Bresson, A. (2002). "Italiens et Romains à Rhodes et à Caunos." In *Les Italiens dans le monde grec: IIe siècle av. J.-C.—Ier siècle ap. J.-C.: Circulation, activités, integration.* Ed. by C. Hasenohr and C. Müller. Pp. 147–62. Athènes: École française d'Athènes.

Brodersen, K. (1997). *Terra cognita: Studien zur römischen Raumerfassung.* Hildesheim: G. Olms Verlag.

Brothwell, D. R., and P. Brothwell. (1969). *Food in Antiquity: A Survey of the Diet of Early Peoples.* Baltimore: Johns Hopkins University Press.

Broughton, T. (1952). *The Magistrates of the Roman Republic.* New York: American Philological Association.

Brunt, P. A. (1990). *Roman Imperial Themes.* Oxford: Oxford University Press.

———. (1988). *The Fall of the Roman Republic and Related Essays.* Oxford: Clarendon Press.

———. (1975). "Two Great Roman Landowners." *Latomus* 34: 619–35.

———. (1973). "Corrigendum: Cn. Tremellius Scrofa the Agronomist." *Classical Review* 23: 195.

———. (1972). "Cn. Tremellius Scrofa the Agronomist." *Classical Review* 22: 304–8.

———. (1971). *Italian Manpower 225 BC–AD 14.* Oxford: Oxford University Press.

———. (1965a). "Italian Aims at the Time of the Social War." *Journal of Roman Studies* 55: 90–109.

———. (1965b). "British and Roman Imperialism." *Comparative Studies in Society and History.* 7: 267–88.

Brunt, P. A., and J. M. Moore. (1967). *Res Gestae Divi Augusti: The Achievements of the Divine Augustus.* Oxford: Oxford University Press.

Burkert, W. (1961). "Hellenistische Pseudopythagorica." *Philologus* 105: 226–46.

Burkhalter, F. (1999). "La mosaïque nilotique de Palestrina et les 'pharaonica' d'Alexandrie." *Topoi* 9.1: 230–60.

Cairns, F. (1972). *Generic Composition in Greek and Roman Poetry.* Edinburgh: Edinburgh University Press.

Campbell, J. B. (2000). *The Writings of the Roman Land Surveyors: Introduction, Text, Translation and Commentary.* London: Society for the Promotion of Roman Studies.

Caplan, H. (1954). *Ad C. Herennium de ratione dicendi.* Cambridge, MA: Harvard University Press.

Cardauns, B. (2001). *Marcus Terentius Varro: Einführung in sein Werk.* Heidelberg: Winter.

Cary, E. (1937). *Dionysius of Halicarnassus. Roman Antiquities.* Cambridge: Loeb Classical Library.

Cavazza, F. (1995). "Il significato di *aeditu(m)us,* e dei suo i presunti sinonimi, e le relative mansioni." *Latomus* 54: 58–61.

Cèbe, J. (1990). *Varron.* Satires ménippées: *Édition, traduction et commentaire.* Rome: Ecole française de Rome.

Chassignet, M. (1986). *Les origines: Caton.* Paris: Belles Lettres.

Chevallier, R. (1976). *Roman Roads.* Berkeley: The University of California Press.

Christol, M. (2002). "Narbonne." In *Les Italiens dans le monde grec: IIe siècle av. J.-C.—Ier siècle ap. J.-C.: Circulation, activités, integration.* Ed. by C. Hasenohr and C. Müller. Pp. 41–54. Athènes: École française d'Athènes.

Cichorius, C. (1922). *Römische Studien.* Leipzig: Teubner.

Claridge, A. (2009). *Rome: An Oxford Archaeological Guide.* Oxford: Oxford University Press.

Clark, K. (1999). *Between Geography and History.* Oxford: Oxford University Press.

Clausen (1994). *A Commentary on Virgil,* Eclogues. New York: Oxford University Press.

———. (1972). "On the Date of the First *Eclogue.*" *Harvard Studies in Classical Philology* 76: 201–6.

Coarelli, F. (2007). *Rome and Environs.* Transl. by J. J. Clauss and D. P. Harmon. Berkeley: University of California Press.

———. (2001). "Les 'Saepta' et la technique du vote à Rome de la fin de la République à Auguste." *Pallas* 55: 37–51.

———. (1996). *Revixit ars: arte e ideologia a Roma: dai modelli ellenistici alla tradizione repubblicana.* Rome: Quasar.

———. (1990). "La pompe di Tolomeo Filadelfo e il mosaic nilotico di Palestrina." *Ktema:* 225–51.

Coleman, R. (1977). *Vergil: Eclogues.* Cambridge: Cambridge University Press.

———. (1975). "Vergil's Pastoral Modes." *Ramus* 4: 140–62.

Connolly, J. (2007). *The State of Speech: Rhetoric and Political Thought in Ancient Rome.* Princeton, NJ: Princeton University Press.

———. (2001). "Picture Arcadia: The Politics of Representation in Vergil's *Eclogues.*" *Vergilius* 47: 89–116.

Connors, C. (1997). "Field and Forum: Culture and Agriculture in Roman Rhetoric." In *Roman Eloquence: Rhetoric in Society and Literature.* Ed. by W. J. Dominik. Pp. 71–89. New York: Routledge.

Constans, L. A. (1921). *Un correspondant de Ciceron, Ap. Claudius Pulcher.* Paris: E. DeBoccard.

Conte, G. B. (1996). *The Hidden Author: An Interpretation of Petronius's Satyricon.* Berkeley: University of California Press.

———. (1994a). *Latin Literature: A History.* Baltimore: Johns Hopkins University Press.

———. (1994b). *Genres and Readers.* Baltimore: Johns Hopkins University Press.

———. (1986). *The Rhetoric of Imitation: Genre and Poetic Memory in Virgil and Other Latin Poets.* Transl., ed. and with a foreword by C. Segal. Ithaca, NY: Cornell University Press.

Cornell, T. J. (2014). *The Fragments of the Roman Historians.* 3 vols. Oxford: Oxford University Press.

Crawford, J. W. (1984). *M. Tullius Cicero: The Lost and Unpublished Orations.* Goettingen: Vandenhoeck und Ruprecht.

Cucchiarelli, A. (2006). "Speaking from Silence: The Stoic Paradoxes of Persius." In *The Cambridge Companion to Roman Satire.* Ed. by K. Freudenburg. Cambridge: Cambridge University Press.

Currie, H. M. (1976). "The Third *Eclogue* and the Roman Comic Spirit." *Mnemosyne* 29: 411–20.

Dahlmann, H. (1935). "M. Terentius Varro." *Paulys Real-encyclopadie der classischen Altertumswissenschaft.* Supplb. 6: 1172–1277. Stuttgart: J. B. Metzler.

Daly, L. (1967). *Contributions to a History of Alphabetization in Antiquity and the Middle Ages.* Bruxelles: Latomus.

D'Arms, J. (1970). *Romans on the Bay of Naples: A Social and Cultural Study of the Villas and Their Owners from 150 BC to AD 400.* Cambridge, MA: Harvard University Press.

David, J. (1996). *The Roman Conquest of Italy.* Transl. by Antonia Nevill. Oxford: Blackwell.

Della Corte, F. (1965). *Varrone, il terzo gran lume romano.* Genova: Pubblicazioni dell'Istituto universitario di magistero.

Dench, E. (2005). *Romulus' Asylum: Roman Identities from the Age of Alexander to the Age of Hadrian.* Oxford: Oxford University Press.

———. (1995). *From Barbarians to New Men: Greek, Roman, and Modern Perceptions of Peoples of the Central Apennines.* Oxford: Clarendon Press.

Deniaux, E. (2002). "Les 'gentes' de Délos et la mobilité sociale à Rome au Ier siècle av. J.-C." In *Les Italiens dans le monde grec: IIe siècle av. J.-C.—Ier siècle ap. J.-C.: Circulation, activités, integration.* Ed. by C. Hasenohr and C. Müller. Pp. 29–39. Athènes: École française d'Athènes.

De Souza, P. (1999). *Piracy in the Graeco-Roman World.* Cambridge: Cambridge University Press.

Diederich, S. (2007). *Römische Agrarhandbücher zwischen Fachwissenschaft, Literatur und Ideologie.* Berlin: Walter de Gruyter.

Dietz, M. G. (2012). "Between Polis and Empire: Aristotle's *Politics.*" *American Political Science Review* 106.2: 275–93.

Dilke, O. A. W. (1985). *Greek and Roman Maps.* Ithaca, NY: Cornell University Press.

———. (1971). *The Roman Land Surveyors: An Introduction to the agrimensores.* Newton Abbot: David and Charles.

Doyle, M. W. (1986). *Empires*. Ithaca, NY: Cornell University Press.

Dueck, D. (2000). *Strabo of Amasia: Greek Man of Letters in Augustan Rome*. London: Routledge.

Dugan, J. (2005). *Making a New Man: Ciceronian Self-fashioning in the Rhetorical Works*. New York: Oxford University Press.

DuQuesnay, I. (1984). "Horace and Maecenas. The Propaganda Value of *Sermones* I." In *Poetry and Politics in the Age of Augustus*. Ed. by T. Woodman and D. West. Pp. 19–58. Cambridge: Cambridge University Press.

———. (1981). "Vergil's First Eclogue." *Papers of the Liverpool Latin Seminar* 3: 29–182.

———. (1979). "From Polyphemus to Corydon: Vergil, *Eclogue* 2 and the *Idylls* of Theocritus." In *Creative Imitation and Latin Literature*. Ed. by T. Woodman and D. West. Pp. 35–69. Cambridge: Cambridge University Press.

Dyck, A. (2004). *A Commentary on Cicero*, De legibus. Ann Arbor: University of Michigan Press.

———. (1998a). "Cicero the Dramaturge: Verisimilitude and Consistency of Characterization in Some of His Dialogues." In *Essays for P. MacKendrick*. Ed. by Gareth L. Schmeling and Jon D. Mikalson. Pp. 151–64. Wauconda, IL: Bolchazy-Carducci.

———. (1998b). *A Commentary on Cicero*, De Officiis. Ann Arbor: University of Michigan Press.

Dyson, S. L. (2003). *The Roman Countryside*. London: Duckworth.

———. (1992). *Community and Society in Roman Italy*. Baltimore: Johns Hopkins University Press.

Edwards, C. (1993). *The Politics of Immorality in Ancient Rome*. Cambridge: Cambridge University Press.

Eldrige, R. (2009). *The Oxford Handbook of Philosophy and Literature*. Oxford: Oxford University Press.

Fantham, E. (2004). *The Roman World of Cicero's* De Oratore. Oxford: Oxford University Press.

Fear, A. T. (1996). *Rome and Baetica: Urbanization in Southern Spain c.50 BC–AD 150*. Oxford: Oxford University Press.

Fehling, D. (1957). "Varro und die grammatische Lehre von der Analogie und der Flexion." *Glotta* 36: 48–100.

Ferrari, G. (1999). "The Geography of Time: The Nile Mosaic and the Library at Praeneste." *Rivista di Antichita* 8.2: 359–86.

Ferrary, J. L. (2002). "La création de la province d'Asie et la présence italienne en Asie Mineure." In *Les Italiens dans le monde grec: IIe siècle av. J.-C.—Ier siècle ap. J.-C.: Circulation, activités, integration*. Ed. by C. Hasenohr and C. Müller. Pp. 133–46. Athènes: École française d'Athènes.

———. (1988). *Philhellénisme et impérialisme*. Paris: de Boccard.

Fish, S. (1980). *Is There a Text in This Class? The Authority of Interpretive Communities*. Cambridge, MA: Harvard University Press.

Flach, D. (2006). *Marcus Terentius Varro: Über die Landwirtschaft*. Darmstadt: Wissenschaftliche Buchgesellschaft.

———. (2002). *Marcus Terentius Varro: Gespräche über die Landwirtschaft. Buch 3*. Darmstadt: Wissenschaftliche Buchgesellschaft.

———. (1997). *Marcus Terentius Varro: Gespräche über die Landwirtschaft. Buch 2*. Darmstadt: Wissenschaftliche Buchgesellschaft.

———. (1996). *Marcus Terentius Varro: Gespräche über die Landwirtschaft. Buch 1*. Darmstadt: Wissenschaftliche Buchgesellschaft.

Follet, S. (2002). "Les Italiens à Athènes (IIe siècle av. J.-C.—Ier siècle ap. J.-C.)." In *Les Italiens dans le monde grec: IIe siècle av. J.-C.—Ier siècle ap. J.-C.: Circulation, activités, integration*. Ed. by C. Hasenohr and C. Müller. Pp. 79–88. Athènes: École française d'Athènes.

Forbes, R. J. (1966). *Studies in Ancient Technology, Volume 6*. Leiden: E. J. Brill.

Fortenbaugh, W., and E. Pender. (2009). *Heraclides of Pontus: Discussion*. New Brunswick, NJ: Transaction Publishers.

Foucault, M. (1972). *The Archaeology of Knowledge*. Transl. by A. M. Sheridan Smith. London: Tavistock.

Fowler, A. (1982). *Kinds of Literature: An Introduction to the Theory of Genres and Modes*. Cambridge, MA: Harvard University Press.

Fox, M. (2007). *Cicero's Philosophy of History*. Oxford: Oxford University Press.

Frayn, J. M. (1984). *Sheep-rearing and the Wool Trade in Italy during the Roman Period*. Liverpool: Francis Cairns.

Freudenburg, K. (2005). *Cambridge Companion to Roman Satire*. Cambridge: Cambridge University Press.

———. (2001). *Satires of Rome: Threatening Poses from Lucilius to Juvenal*. Cambridge: Cambridge University Press.

———. (1993). *The Walking Muse: Horace on the Theory of Satire*. Princeton: Princeton University Press.

Frier, B. (1985). *The Rise of the Roman Jurists: Studies in Cicero's* Pro Caecina. Princeton: Princeton University Press.

Frischer, B. (1991). *Shifting Paradigms: New Approaches to Horace's* Ars poetica. Atlanta: Scholars Press.

Frye, N. (1957). *Anatomy of Criticism*. Princeton, NJ: Princeton University Press.

Fuchs, G. (1962). "Varros Vogelhaus Bei Casinum." *Mitteilungen des Deutschen Archäologischen Instituts (Röm. Abt.)* 69: 96–105.

Fuhrmann, M. (1960). *Das systematische Lehrbuch: Ein Beitrag zur Geschichte der Wissenschaft in der Antike*. Goettingen: Vandenhoek and Ruprecht.

Gabba, E. (1988). "La pastorizia nell'età tardo-imperiale in Italia." In *Pastoral Economies in Classical Antiquity*. Ed. by C. R. Whittaker. Pp. 134–42. Cambridge: Cambridge Philological Society.

———. (1985). "La transumanza nell'Italia romana, evidenza e problemi: qualche prospettiva per l'eta altomedioevale." *Studi sardi* 31: 373–89.

———. (1979). "Sulle strutture agrarie dell'Italia romana fra III e I sec. a.C." In *Strutture agrarie e allevamento trasnumante nell'Italia Romana (III-I sec. a.C.).* Ed. by M. Pasquinucci and E. Gabba. Pp. 15–73. Pisa: Giardini.

———. (1978). "Il problema dell'unità dell'Italia romana." In *La Cultura Italica: Atti del Convegno della Società Italiana di Glottologia.* Ed. by E. Campanile. Pp. 11–27. Pisa: Giardini. (Reprinted in Gabba, E. (1994). *Italia Romana.* Como: Edizioni New Press.)

———. (1976). *Republican Rome, the Army, and the Allies.* Transl. by P. J. Cuff. Berkeley: University of California Press.

———. (1956). *Appiano e la storia delle guerre civili.* Florence: La nuova Italia.

Galinsky, Karl. (2005). *The Cambridge Companion to the Age of Augustus.* Cambridge: Cambridge University Press.

———. (1996). *Augustan Culture: An Interpretative Introduction.* Princeton, NJ: Princeton University Press.

Gallagher, R. L. (2001). "Metaphor in Cicero's *De Re Publica.*" *Classical Quarterly.* 51.2: 509–19.

Gargola, D. J. (1995). *Lands, Laws, & Gods: Magistrates & Ceremony in the Regulation of Public Lands in Republican Rome.* Chapel Hill: University of North Carolina Press.

Garnsey, P. (1988). "Mountain Economies in Southern Europe: Thoughts on the Early History, Continuity, and Individuality of Mediterranean Upland Pastoralism." In *Pastoral Economies in Classical Antiquity.* Ed. by C. R. Whittaker. Pp. 196–209. Cambridge: Cambridge Philological Society.

Gelzer, M. (1969). *The Roman Nobility.* Transl. by R. Seager. Oxford: Blackwell.

Giardina, A. (1994). "L'identità incompiuta dell'Italia Romana." In *L'Italie d'Auguste à Dioclétien.* Pp. 1–89. Rome: Collection de l'école française de Rome.

Gildenhard, I. (2007). *Paideia Romana. Cicero's* Tusculan Disputations. Cambridge: Cambridge Philological Society.

Goetz, G. (1929). *M. Terenti Varronis Rerum Rusticarum libri tres.* Leipzig: Teubner.

Goody, J. (1977). *The Domestication of the Savage Mind.* Cambridge: Cambridge University Press.

Gottschalk, H. B. (1980). *Heraclides of Pontus.* Oxford: Clarendon Press.

Gowers, E. (2005). "The Restless Companion: Horace, *Satires* 1 and 2." In *The Cambridge Companion to Roman Satire.* Ed. by K. Freudenburg. Pp. 48–61. Cambridge: Cambridge University Press.

———. (1993a). "Horace, *Satires* 1.5: An Inconsequential Journey." *Proceedings of the Cambridge Philological Society* 39: 48–66.

———. (1993b). *The Loaded Table: Representations of Food in Roman Literature.* Oxford: Oxford University Press.

Gowing, A. (1992). *The Triumviral Narratives of Appian and Cassius Dio.* Ann Arbor: University of Michigan Press.

Green, C. M. C. (2012). "The Shepherd of the People: Varro on Herding for the Villa Publica in *De Re Rustica*." In *Roman Republican Villas: Architecture, Context, and Ideology*. Ed. by J. A. Becker and N. Terrenato. Pp. 32–41. Ann Arbor: University of Michigan Press.

———. (1997). "Free as a Bird: Varro *De Re Rustica* 3." *American Journal of Philology* 118: 427–48.

Griffin, M. (1998). "Cynicism and the Romans: Attraction and Repulsion." In *The Cynics: The Cynic Movement in Antiquity and its Legacy*. Ed. by R. B. Branham and M. Goulet-Cazé. Pp. 190–201. Berkeley: University of California Press.

———. (1995). "Philosophical Badinage in Cicero's Letters to His Friends." In *Cicero the Philosopher*. Ed. by J. G. F. Powell. Pp. 325–46. Oxford: Oxford University Press.

Gros, P. (1992). *Vitruvius. De l'architecture, Livre IV. Texte établi, trad. et commenté*. Paris: Les Belles Lettres.

Gruen, E. S. (1984). *The Hellenistic World and the Coming of Rome*. Berkeley and Los Angeles: University of California Press.

Gutzwiller, K. (1991). *Theocritus' Pastoral Analogies: The Formation of a Genre*. Madison: University of Wisconsin Press.

Habicht, C. (1989). "The Seleucids and Their Rivals." In *Cambridge Ancient History*, 2nd ed., Vol. 8. Ed. by F. W. Walbank, A. E. Astin, M. W. Frederiksen, and R. M. Ogilvie. Pp. 324–87. Cambridge: Cambridge University Press.

Habinek, T. N. (2005). "Satire as Aristocratic Play." In *Cambridge Companion to Roman Satire*. Ed. by K. Freudenburg. 177–91. Cambridge: Cambridge University Press.

———. (1998). *The Politics of Latin Literature: Writing, Identity, and Empire in Ancient Rome*. Princeton, NJ: Princeton University Press.

———. (1997). "The Invention of Sexuality in the World-City of Rome." In *The Roman Cultural Revolution*. Ed. by Thomas Habinek and Alessandro Schiesaro. Pp. 23–43. Cambridge: Cambridge University Press.

———. (1994). "Ideology for an Empire in the Prefaces to Cicero's Dialogues." *Ramus* 23: 55–67.

Halperin, D. (1990). "Pastoral Violence in the Georgics: Commentary on Ross." *Arethusa* 1990 23: 77–93.

———. (1983). *Before Pastoral: Theocritus and the Ancient Tradition of Bucolic Poetry*. New Haven, CT: Yale University Press.

Hamilton, J. R. (1955). "Didius and the *Villa publica*." *Numismatic Chronicle* 15: 224–28.

Hardie, P. (2002). *Ovid's Poetics of Illusion*. Cambridge: Cambridge University Press.

———. (1998). *Virgil*. Oxford: Oxford University Press.

Hardy, E. G. (1924). *Some Problems in Roman History*. Oxford: Clarendon Press.

Harries, J. (2006). *Cicero and the Jurists: From Citizens' Law to the Lawful State*. London: Duckworth.

Harris, W. V. (1978). *War and Imperialism in Republican Rome 320–70 BC*. Oxford: Clarendon Press.

Harvey, P. (1979). "Catullus 114–115: Mentula, *bonus agricola.*" *Historia* 28: 329–55.

Hasenohr, C. (2002). "Les collèges de magistri et la communauté italienne de Délos." In *Les Italiens dans le monde grec: IIe siècle av. J.-C.—Ier siècle ap. J.-C.: Circulation, activités, integration.* Ed. by C. Hasenohr and C. Müller. Pp. 67–76. Athènes: École française d'Athènes.

Hasenohr, C., and C. Müller (2002). *Les Italiens dans le monde grec: IIe siècle av. J.-C.—Ier siècle ap. J.-C.: Circulation, activités, integration.* Athènes: École française d'Athènes.

Heisterhagen, R. (1952). *Die literarische Form der Rerum rusticarum libri Varros.* Unpublished dissertation: Philipps-Universität Marburg.

Henderson, J. (2004). *Morals and Villas in Seneca's Letters: Places to Dwell.* Cambridge: Cambridge University Press.

———. (2002). "Columella's Living Hedge: The Roman Gardening Book." *Journal of Roman Studies* 92: 110–33.

———. (1998a). "Virgil's Third *Eclogue*: How Do You Keep an Idiot in Suspense?" *Classical Quarterly* 48: 213–28.

———. (1998b). "Virgil, *Eclogue* 9: Valleydiction." *Proceedings of the Virgil Society* 23: 149–76.

Heurgon, J. (1978). *Economie rurale. Varron; texte etabli, traduit et commente par Jacques Heurgon.* Paris: Belles Lettres.

———. (1950). "L'effort de style de Varron dans les *Res Rusticae.*" *Revue de philologie, de littérature et d'histoire anciennes* 1950: 57–71.

Highet, G. (1949). "The Philosophy of Juvenal." *Transactions of the American Philological Association* 80: 254–70.

Hinard, F. (1985). *Les proscriptions de la Rome républicaine.* Rome: Ecole française de Rome.

Hirzel, R. (1895). *Der Dialog: Ein literarhistorischer Versuch.* Leipzig: S. Hirzel.

Hogan, P. C. (2003). *Cognitive Science, Literature, and the Arts.* New York: Routledge.

Holliday, P. J. (2002). *The Origins of Roman Historical Commemoration in the Visual Arts.* Cambridge: Cambridge University Press.

Hooper, W. D., and H. B. Ash. (1934). *Cato: On Agriculture. Varro: On Agriculture.* Cambridge, MA: Harvard University Press.

Horden, P., and Purcell, N. (2000). *The Corrupting Sea.* Oxford: Blackwell.

Hubbard, T. K. (1998). *The Pipes of Pan: Intertextuality and Literary Filiation in the Pastoral Tradition from Theocritus to Milton.* Ann Arbor: University of Michigan Press.

Huby, P. M. (2001). "The *Controversia* between Dicaearchus and Theophrastus about the Best Life." In *Dicaearchus of Messana: Text, Translation, and Discussion.* Ed. by W. Fortenbaugh and E. Schütrumpf. Pp. 311–28. New Brunswick, NJ: Transaction Publishers.

Huffman, C. (2005). *Archytas of Tarentum: Pythagorean, Philosopher and Mathematician King.* Cambridge: Cambridge University Press.

Hunter, R. L. (1985). *The New Comedy of Greece and Rome.* Cambridge: Cambridge University Press.

Hutchinson, G. (2006). *Propertius: Elegies. Book IV.* Cambridge: Cambridge University Press.

Janni, P. (1984). *La mappa e il periplo: Cartografia antica e spazio odologico.* Rome: Bretschneider.

Jauss, H. J. (1982). *Toward an Aesthetic of Reception.* Transl. by Timothy Bahti. Minneapolis: University of Minnesota Press.

Jones, C. P. (1999). "Atticus in Ephesus." *Zeitschrift fur Papyrologie und Epigraphik* 124: 89–94.

Jones, F. (2011). *Virgil's Garden: The Nature of Bucolic Space.* London: Bristol Classical Press.

Jones, J. H. (1935). "The Dramatic Date of Varro *Res Rusticae,* Book II." *Classical Review* 49.6: 214–15.

Jones, R. E. (1939). "Cicero's Accuracy of Characterization in his Dialogues." *American Journal of Philology* 69: 307–25.

Kallet-Marx, R. (1995). *Hegemony to Empire: The Development of Roman Imperium from 148 to 62 BC.* Berkeley: University of California Press.

Keane, C. (2004). *Figuring Genre in Roman Satire.* Oxford: Oxford University Press.

Keaveney, Arthur. (1992). *Lucullus: A Life.* London: Routledge.

———. (1987). *Rome and the Unification of Italy.* London: Croom Helm.

Keil, H. (1889). *M. Terenti Varronis rerum rusticarum libri tres.* Lipsiae: Teubner.

Keil, H., and G. Goetz. (1929). *M. Terenti Varronis rerum rusticarum libri tres.* Lipsiae: Teubner.

Kelly, G. P. (2006). *A History of Exile in the Roman Republic.* Cambridge: Cambridge University Press.

Kenney, E. J. (1983). "Virgil and the Elegiac Sensibility." *Illinois Classical Studies* 8: 44–59.

———. (1971). *Lucretius: De Rerum Natura. Book III.* Cambridge: Cambridge University Press.

Knoche, U. (1975). *Roman Satire.* Bloomington: Indiana University Press.

Kolendo, J. (1994). "Praedia suburban e la loro redditivita." In *Land Use in the Roman Empire.* Ed. by J. Carlsen and J. E. Skydsgaard. Pp. 59–72. Rome: L'Erma di Bretschneider.

Kronenberg, L. (2009). *Allegories of Farming from Greece and Rome: Philosophical Satire in Xenophon, Varro, and Virgil.* Cambridge: Cambridge University Press.

Krostenko, B. (2001). *Cicero, Catullus, and the Language of Social Performance.* Chicago: University of Chicago Press.

Lakoff, G., and M. Johnson. (1980). *Metaphors We Live By.* Chicago: University of Chicago Press.

Laurence, R. (1999). *The Roads of Roman Italy: Mobility and Cultural Change.* London: Routledge.

Lausberg, H. (1998). *Handbook of Literary Rhetoric: A Foundation for Literary Study.* Transl. by M. T. Bliss, A. Jansen, and D. E. Orton. Ed. by D. E. Orton and R. D. Anderson. Leiden: E. J. Brill.

Leach, E. W. (2004). *The Social Life of Painting in Ancient Rome and the Bay of Naples.* Cambridge: Cambridge University Press.

———. (1999). "Ciceronian '*Bi-Marcus*': Correspondence with M. Terentius Varro and L. Papirius Paetus in 46 BC." *Transactions of the American Philological Association:* 139–80.

———. (1974). *Vergil's Eclogues. Landscapes of Experience.* Ithaca, NY: Cornell University Press.

Leo, F. (1903). "Vergils erste und neunte Ekloge." *Hermes* 38: 1–18.

Linderski, J. (1989). "Garden Parlors: Nobles and Birds." In *Studia Pompeiana et Classica in Honor of Wilhelmina F. Jashemski, vol. II, Classica.* Ed. by R. I. Curtis. Pp. 105–28. New Rochelle, NY: Orpheus.

———. (1985.) "The Dramatic Date of Varro, *De Re Rustica,* Book III and the Elections in 54." *Historia* 34.2: 248–54.

———. (1980). "De villa Appio Pulchro falso attributa." *La Parola de Passola* 35: 272–73.

Ling, R. (1991). *Roman Painting.* Cambridge: Cambridge University Press.

Lintott, A. (1993). *Imperium Romanum: Politics and Administration.* London: Routledge.

———. (1992). *Judicial Reform and Land Reform in the Roman Republic.* Cambridge: Cambridge University Press.

Lipka, M. (2002). "Notes on *fagus* in Vergil's *Eclogues*." *Philologus* 146: 133–38.

Lloyd, G. E. (1984). "Hellenistic Science." In *Cambridge Ancient History,* 2nd ed., Vol. 7, Part 1. Ed. by F. W. Walbank, A. E. Astin, M. W. Frederiksen, and R. M. Ogilvie. Pp. 321–52. Cambridge: Cambridge University Press.

Long, A. A. (1997). "Stoic Philosophers on Persons, Property-Ownership, and Community." In *Aristotle and After.* Ed. by R. Sorabji. 68: 11–31. London: Bulletin of the Institute of Classical Studies of the University of London.

Long, A. A., and D. N. Sedley. (1987). *The Hellenistic Philosophers. Volume 1. Translations of the Principal Sources, with Philosophical Commentary.* Cambridge: Cambridge University Press.

Lorenz, H. (2006). *The Brute Within: Appetitive Desire in Plato and Aristotle.* Oxford: Clarendon Press.

Magno, P. (2006). "Ennio del *De re rustica* di Varrone." *Latomus* 65.1: 75–82.

Mahaffy, J. P. (1890). "The Work of Mago on Agriculture." *Hermathena* 7: 29–35.

Martin, R. (1995). "*Ars an quid aliud?* La conception Varronienne de l'agriculture." *Revue des études latines* 73: 80–91.

———. (1971). *Recherches sur les agronomes latins et leurs conceptions économiques et sociales.* Paris: Belles Lettres.

Martindale, C. (1997). "Green Politics: The *Eclogues*." In *The Cambridge Companion to Virgil.* Ed. by C. Martindale. Pp. 107–24. Cambridge: Cambridge University Press.

Marzano, A. (2007). *Roman Villas in Central Italy: A Social and Economic History.* Leiden: Brill.

Mattingly, D. J. (2011). *Imperialism, Power, and Identity.* Princeton, NJ: Princeton University Press.

Maxfield, V. (1981). *The Military Decorations of the Roman Army.* Berkeley: The University of California Press.

Mayer, R. (2005). "Sleeping with the Enemy: Satire and Philosophy." In *Cambridge Companion to Roman Satire*. Ed.by K. Freudenburg. Pp. 146–59. Cambridge: Cambridge University Press.

———. (1991). *Tacitus: Dialogus de Oratoribus*. Cambridge: Cambridge University Press.

Mayer, R. G. (2005). "Creating a Literature of Information in Rome." In *Wissensvermittlung in dichterischer Gestalt*. Ed. by M. Horster and C. Reitz. Pp. 227–41. Stuttgart: Steiner.

McAlhany, J. (2003). *Language, Truth, and Illogic in the Writings of Varro*. Unpublished Ph.D. dissertation: Columbia University.

McCall, M. H. Jr. (1969). *Ancient Rhetorical Theories of Simile and Comparison*. Cambridge, MA: Harvard University Press.

McEwen, I. K. (2003). *Vitruvius: Writing the Body of Architecture*. Cambridge, MA: MIT Press.

Meyboom, P. G. P. (1995). *The Nile Mosaic of Palestrina: Early Evidence of Egyptian Religion in Italy*. Leiden: Brill.

Michel, J. H. (1979). "Le meridien de Skodra et le partage du monde. . . ." In *Atti Conv. Intern. Accad. Rom. Constantiniana* 4.1: 181–91.

Moatti, C. (1997). *La raison de Rome: Naissance de l'esprit critique à la fin de la République (IIe-Ier siècle avant Jésus-Christ)*. Paris: Seuil.

———. (1991). "La crise de la tradition à la fin de la République romaine à travers la littérature juridique et la science des antiquaires." In *Continuità et trasformazioni fra Repubblica e Principato*. Ed. by M. Pani. Pp. 31–46. Bari: Edipuglia.

Mommsen, T. (1887–88). *Römisches Staatsrecht*. Leipzig: S. Hirzel.

Morgan, M. G. (1974). "Three Notes on Varro's *Logistorici*." *Museum Helveticum* 31: 117–28.

———. (1973). "Villa Publica and Magna Mater: Two Notes on Manubial Building at the Close of the Second Century BC." *Klio* 55: 213–45.

Müller, C. (2002). "Les Italiens en Béotie du IIe siècle av. J.-C. au Ier siècle ap. J.-C." In *Les Italiens dans le monde grec: IIe siècle av. J.-C.—Ier siècle ap. J.-C.: Circulation, activités, integration*. Ed. by C. Hasenohr and C. Müller. Pp. 89–100. Athènes: École française d'Athènes.

Musti, D., G. A. Mansuelli, and A. Bernardi. (1990). "Italia." *Enciclopedia Virgiliana* 3: 34–50.

Natali, C. (1995). "*Oikonomia* in Hellenistic Political Thought." In *Justice and Generosity*. Ed. By A. Laks and M. Schofield. Pp. 95–128. Cambridge: Cambridge University Press.

Nelsestuen, G. (2014). "Overseeing *res publica*: The *Rector* as *Vilicus* in *De Re Publica* 5." *Classical Antiquity* 33: 130–73.

———. (2011). "Polishing Scrofa's Agronomical *Eloquentia*: Representation and Critique in Varro's *De Re Rustica*." *Phoenix* 65: 315–51.

Newmyer, S. T. (2011). *Animals in Greek and Roman Thought: A Sourcebook*. London: Routledge.

Nicolet, C. (1994). "Economy and Society, 133–43 BC." In *Cambridge Ancient History*, 2nd ed., Vol. 9. Ed. by J. A. Crook, A. Lintott, and E. Rawson. Pp. 599–643. Cambridge: Cambridge University Press.

———. (1991). *Space, Geography, and Politics in the Early Roman Empire*. Ann Arbor: University of Michigan Press.

———. (1984). "Augustus, Government, and the Propertied Classes." In *Caesar Augustus: Seven Aspects*. Ed. by F. Millar and E. Segal. Pp. 89–128. Oxford: Oxford University Press.

———. (1974). *L'ordre équestre à l'époque républicaine (312–43 avant J. C.), II: Prosopographie des chevaliers romains. réimpr. conforme à la 1ᵉʳ éd. de 1966*. Paris: de Boccard.

———. (1970). "Le libre III des 'Res rusticae' de Varron et les allusions au déroulement des comices tributes." *Revue des études anciennes* 72.2: 113–37.

———. (1966). *L'ordre équestre à l'époque républicaine (312–43 av. J. C.), I: Définitions juridiques et structures sociales*. Paris: de Boccard.

Nightingale, A. (2004). *Spectacles of Truth in Classical Greek Philosophy: Theoria in Its Cultural Context*. Cambridge: Cambridge University Press.

North, J. A. (1996). "Religion and Rusticity." In *Urban Society in Roman Italy*. Ed. by T. Cornell and K. Lomas. Pp. 144–55. New York: St. Martin's Press.

Ogilvie, R. M. (1965). *A Commentary on Livy, Books 1–5*. Oxford: Clarendon Press.

O'Gorman, E. (2005). "Citation and Authority in Seneca's *Apocolocyntosis*." In *Cambridge Companion to Roman Satire*. Ed. by K. Freudenburg. Pp. 95–108. Cambridge: Cambridge University Press.

Orlin, E. M. (2007). "Augustan Religion and the Reshaping of Roman Memory." *Arethusa* 40.1: 73–92.

Osgood, J. (2006). *Caesar's Legacy: Civil War and the Emergence of the Roman Empire*. Cambridge: Cambridge University Press.

O'Sullivan, T. (2011). *Walking in Roman Culture*. Cambridge: Cambridge University Press.

Pasquinnuci, M. (1979). "La transumante nell'Italia romana." In *Strutture agrarie e allevamento transumante nell'Italia Romana (III-I sec. a.C.)*. Ed. by M. Pasquinucci and E. Gabba. Pp. 79–182. Pisa: Giardini.

Pasquinucci, M., and E. Gabba (Eds.). (1979). *Strutture agrarie e allevamento trasnumante nell'Italia Romana (III-I sec. a.C.)*. Pisa: Giardini.

Payne, M. (2007). *Theocritus and the Invention of Fiction*. Cambridge: Cambridge University Press.

Percival, J. (1976). *The Roman Villa: An Historical Introduction*. Berkeley: The University of California Press.

Perkell, C. (1990). "On *Eclogue* 1.79–83." *Transactions of the American Philological Association* 120: 171–81.

Perkins, D. (1992). *Is Literary History Possible?* Baltimore: Johns Hopkins University Press.

Perl, G. (1980). "Cn. Tremelius Scrofa in Gallia Transalpina: Zu Varro, *RR* I." *American Journal of Ancient History* 5: 97–109.

Perret, J. (1961). *Les Bucoliques*. Paris: Presses Universitaires.

Phillips, K. M. (1962). *The Barberini Mosaic*. Unpublished PhD dissertation: Princeton.

Pitts, J. (2012). "Political Theory of Empire and Imperialism: An Appendix." In *Empire and Modern Political Thought*. Ed. by S. Muthu. Pp. 351–87. Cambridge: Cambridge University Press.

Polanyi, K. (1957). *The Great Transformation*. New York: Rinehart.

Pomeroy, S. B. (1995). *Xenophon Oeconomicus: A Social and Historical Commentary*. Oxford: Oxford University Press.

Powell, A. (2002). "'An island amid the flame': The Strategy and Imagery of Sextus Pompeius, 43–36 BC." In *Sextus Pompeius*. Ed. by A. Powell and K. Welch. Pp.103–33. Wales: Classical Press of Wales.

Powell, J. G. F. (2012). "Cicero's *De Re Publica* and the Virtues of the Statesman." In *Cicero's Practical Philosophy*. Ed. by W. Nicgorski. Pp. 14–42. Notre Dame, IN: University of Notre Dame Press.

———. (2006). *M. Tullius Ciceronis. De Re Publica, De Legibus, Cato Maior de Senectute, Laelius de Amicitia*. Oxford: Oxford University Press.

———. (1998). *Cicero the Philosopher*. Oxford: Oxford University Press.

———. (1994). "The *rector rei publicae* of Cicero's *De Republica*." *Scripta classica Israelica* 13: 19–29.

———. (1988). *Cicero: Cato Maior de Senectute*. Cambridge: Cambridge University Press.

Putnam, M. (1970). *Virgil's Pastoral Art: Studies in the* Eclogues. Princeton, NJ: Princeton University Press.

Purcell, N. (2003). "The Way We Used to Eat: Diet, Community, and History at Rome." *American Journal of Philology* 124: 329–58.

———. (1995). "The Roman Villa and the Landscape of Production." In *Urban Society in Roman Italy*. Ed. by T. J. Cornell and K. Lomas. Pp. 151–79. London: UCL Press.

Radke, G. (1967). "*Italia*: Beobachtungen zu der Geschichte eines Landenames." *Romanitas* 8: 35–51.

Ramsey, J. T. (2003). *Cicero: Philippics I-II*. Cambridge: Cambridge University Press.

Rawson, E. (1985). *Intellectual Life in the Late Roman Republic*. London: Duckworth Press.

———. (1983). *Cicero: A Portrait*. Ithaca, NY: Cornell University Press.

———. (1976). "The Ciceronian Aristocracy and Its Properties." In *Studies in Roman Property*. Ed. by M. I. Finley. Pp. 85–102. Cambridge: Cambridge University Press.

Reay, B. (2005). "Agriculture, Writing, and Cato's Aristocratic Self-Fashioning." *Classical Antiquity* 24.2: 331–61.

Reitzenstein, R. (1893). *Epigramm und Skolion.: Ein Beitrag zur Geschichte der alexandrinischen Dichtung*. Giessen: J. Ricker.

Relihan, J. C. (1993). *Ancient Menippean Satire*. Baltimore: Johns Hopkins University Press.

———. (1984). "On the Origin of Menippean Satire as the Name of a Literary Genre." *Classical Philology* 79: 226–29.

Reynolds, L. D. (1983). *Texts and Transmission*. Oxford: Clarendon Press.

Richardson, J. S. (2008). *The Language of Empire*. Cambridge: Cambridge University Press.

———. (1991). "*Imperium Romanum*: Empire and the Language of Power." *Journal of Roman Studies* 81: 1–9.

———. (1986). *Hispaniae: Spain and the Development of Roman Imperialism*. Cambridge: Cambridge University Press.

———. (1983). "The Triumph of Metellus Scipio and the Dramatic Date of Varro *RR* 3." *Classical Quarterly* 23: 456–63.

Richardson, L. (1992). *A New Topographical Dictionary of Ancient Rome*. Baltimore: Johns Hopkins University Press.

Richter, D. (2011). *Cosmopolis: Imagining Community in Late Classical Athens and the Early Roman Empire*. Oxford: Oxford University Press.

Riggsby, A. M. (2006). *War in Words*. Austin: University of Texas Press.

———. (2003). "Pliny in Space (and Time)." *Arethusa* 36: 167–86.

Rinkewitz, W. (1981). *Pastio villatica: Untersuchungen zur intensiven Hoftierhaltung in der römischen Landwirtschaft*. Frankfurt: Peter Lang.

Rizakis, A. D. (2002). "L'émigration romaine en Macédoine et la communauté marchande de Thessalonique." In *Les Italiens dans le monde grec: IIe siècle av. J.-C.—Ier siècle ap. J.-C.: Circulation, activités, integration*. Ed. by C. Hasenohr and C. Müller. Pp. 109–32. Athènes: École française d'Athènes.

Rodgers, R. H. (2010). *L. Iuni Moderati Columellae Res Rustica: Incerti Auctoris Liber de arboribus*. Oxford: Oxford University Press.

Roller, M. (2010). "Demolished Houses, Monumentality, and Memory in Roman Culture." *Classical Antiquity* 29: 117–80.

———. (2009). "The Exemplary Past in Roman Historiography and Culture." In *The Cambridge Companion to the Roman Historians*. Ed. by A. Feldherr. Pp. 214–30. Cambridge: Cambridge University Press.

———. (2001). *Constructing Autocracy: Aristocrats and Emperors in Julio-Claudian Rome*. Princeton, NJ: Princeton University Press.

Rösche-Binde, C. (1998). *Vom "deinos aner" zum "diligentissimus investigator antiquitatis": Zur komplexen Beziehungzwischen M. Tullius Cicero und M. Terentius Varro*. Munich: Urtz.

Roselaar, S. T. (2010). *Public Land in the Roman Republic*. Oxford: Oxford University Press.

Rosenmeyer, T. (1973). *The Green Cabinet: Theocritus and the European Pastoral Lyric*. Berkeley: University of California Press.

Ross, D. O. Jr. (1990). "The Pastoral in the *Georgics: si numquam fallit imago*." *Arethusa* 1990 23: 59–75.

———. (1979). "Two Rustic Notes." *Classical Philology* 74: 52–56.

———. (1975). *Backgrounds to Augustan poetry. Gallus, Elegy and Rome*. Cambridge: Cambridge University Press.

Roth, R. (2007). "Varro's *picta Italia* (*RR* I. 2. 1) and the Odology of Roman Italy." *Hermes* 135.3: 286–300.

Rudd, N. (1989). *Epistles Book II; and Epistle to the Pisones (Ars Poetica)*. Cambridge: Cambridge University Press.

Rumpf, L. (2008). "Bucolic *nomina* in Virgil and Theocritus: On the Poetic Technique of Virgil's *Eclogues*." In *Vergil's Eclogues*. Ed. by K. Volk. Pp. 54–78. Oxford: Oxford University Press.

Saddington, D. B. (2007). "*Classes*: The Evolution of the Roman Imperial Fleets." In *A Companion to the Roman Army*. Ed. by P. Erdkamp. Pp. Oxford: Blackwell.

Sakellariou, M. B. (1997). *Epirus: 4000 years of Greek History and Civilization*. Athens: Ekdotike Athenon.

Salmon, E. T. (1982). *The Making of Roman Italy*. London: Thames and Hudson.

———. (1969). *Roman Colonization under the Republic*. London: Thames & Hudson.

Salvatore, A. (1978). *Scienza e poesia in Roma: Varrone e Virgilio*. Naples: Guida Editori.

Salway, B. (2005). "The Nature and Genesis of the Peutinger Map." *Imago Mundi* 57.2: 119–35.

Saunders, T. (2001). "Dicaearchus' Historical Anthropology." In *Dicaearchus of Messana: Text, Translation, and Discussion*. Ed. by W. Fortenbaugh and E. Schütrumpf. Pp. 237–54. New Brunswick, NJ: Transaction Publishers.

Schiappa, E. (1999). *The Beginnings of Rhetorical Theory in Classical Greece*. New Haven, CT: Yale University Press.

———. (1990). "Did Plato Coin *rhetorike?*" *American Journal of Philology* 111: 457–70.

Schmidt, E. A. (2008). "Arcadia: Modern Occident and Classical Antiquity." In *Vergil's Eclogues*. Ed. by K. Volk. Pp. 16–47. Oxford: Oxford University Press.

———. (1987). *Bukolische Leidenschaft oder über antike Hirtenpoesie*. Frankfurt: Lang.

Schofield, M. (1995). "Cicero's Definition of *Res Publica*." In *Cicero the Philosopher*. Ed. by J. Powell. Pp. 63–83. Oxford: Oxford University Press.

———. (1991). *The Stoic Idea of the City*. Cambridge: Cambridge University Press.

Schütrumpf, E. (2008). *Heraclides of Pontus: Texts and Translation*. New Brunswick, NJ: Transaction Publishers.

———. (2001). "Dikaiarchs *Bios Hellados* und die Philosophie des vierten Jahrhunderts." In *Dicaearchus of Messana: Text, Translation, and Discussion*. Ed. by W. Fortenbaugh and E. Schütrumpf. Pp. 237–254. New Brunswick, NJ: Transaction Publishers.

Scullard, H. H. (1989). "Rome and Carthage." In *Cambridge Ancient History*, 2nd ed., Vol. 7, Part 2. Ed. by A. Drummond, F. W. Walbank, A. E. Astin, M. W. Frederiksen, and R. M. Ogilvie. Pp. 486–569. Cambridge: Cambridge University Press.

Seager, R. (1979). *Pompey: A Political Biography*. Berkeley: University of California Press.

Shackleton-Bailey, D. R. (1977). *Cicero: Epistulae ad Familiares*. Cambridge: Cambridge University Press.

———. (1965). *Cicero: Letters to Atticus*. Cambridge: Cambridge University Press.

Shatzman, I. (1975). *Senatorial Wealth and Roman Politics*. Bruxelles: Latomus.

———. (1968). "Four Notes on Roman Magistrates." *Athenaeum* 46: 345–54.

Sherwin-White, A. N. (1984). *Roman Foreign Policy in the East, 168 BC to AD 1*. London: Duckworth.

————. (1973). *The Roman Citizenship*. Oxford: Oxford University Press.

Skutsch, O. (1985). *The Annals of Q. Ennius*. Oxford: Clarendon Press.

Skydsgaard, J. E. (1978). "Transhumance in Ancient Italy." *Analecta Romana Instituti Danici* 7: 7–36.

————. (1968). *Varro the Scholar: Studies in the First Book of Varro's De Re Rustica*. Köbenhavn: Munksgaard.

Slater, N. W. (1990). *Reading Petronius*. Baltimore: Johns Hopkins University Press.

Smith, J. T. (1997). *Roman Villas: A Study in Social Structure*. London: Routledge.

Smith, M. S. (1975). *Cena Trimalchionis*. Oxford: Oxford University Press.

Snell, B. (1953). *The Discovery of the Mind: The Greek Origins of European Thought*. Cambridge, MA: Harvard University Press.

Spencer, D. (2010). *Roman Landscape: Culture and Identity*. Cambridge: Cambridge University Press.

Spurr, M. S. (1986a). *Arable Cultivation in Roman Italy, c. 200 BC –c. AD 100*. London: Society for the Promotion of Roman Studies.

————. (1986b). "Agriculture and the *Georgics*." *Greece and Rome* 33: 164–86.

Steel, C. E. W. (2001). *Cicero, Rhetoric, and Empire*. Oxford: Oxford University Press.

Steinmeyer-Schareika, A. (1978). *Das Nilmosaik von Palestrina und eine ptolemaeische Expedition nach Aethiopien*. Bonn: Habelt.

Stobbe, H. F. (1868). "Die candidati Caesaris." *Philologus*: 88–112.

Strauss, L. (1972). *Xenophon's Socrates*. Ithaca, NY: Cornell University Press.

Subrahmanyam, S. (2006). "Imperial and Colonial Encounters: Some Comparative Reflections." In *Lessons of Empire: Imperial Histories and American Power*. Ed. By C. Calhoun, F. Cooper, and K. W. Moore. Pp. 217–28. New York: The New Press.

Svarlien, J. (1994). "Lucilianus Character." *American Journal of Philology* 115: 253–67.

Syme, R. (1939). *The Roman Revolution*. Oxford: Oxford University Press.

————. (1937). "Who Was Decidius Saxa?" *Journal of Roman Studies*: 127–37.

Talbert, R. (2010). *Rome's World: The Peutinger Map Reconsidered*. Cambridge: Cambridge University Press.

————. (2004). "Cartography and Taste in Peutinger's Roman Map." In *Space in the Roman World: Its Perception and Presentation*. Ed. by K. Brodersen and R. Talbert. Pp. 113–31. Münster: Antike Kultur und Geschichte 5.

Tarver, T. (1997). "Varro and the Antiquarianism of Philosophy." In *Philosophia Togata II*. Ed. by J. Barnes and M. Griffin. Pp. 130–64. Oxford: Oxford University Press.

Tatum, W. J. (1999). *The Patrician Tribune*. Chapel Hill: University of North Carolina Press.

————. (1992). "The Poverty of the Claudii Pulchri: Varro, *De Re Rustica* 3.16.1–2." *Classical Quarterly* 42.1: 190–200.

———. (1990). "The *lex Clodia de censoria notione.*" *Classical Philology* 85: 34–43.

Taylor, L. R. (1966). *Roman Voting Assemblies from the Hannibalic War to the Dictatorship of Caesar.* Ann Arbor: University of Michigan Press.

———. (1960). *The Voting Districts of the Roman Republic: The Thirty-Five Urban and Rural Tribes.* Rome: American Academy.

Terrenato, N. (2001). "The Auditorium Site and the Origins of the Roman Villa." *Journal of Roman Archaeology* 14: 5–32.

Thibodeau, P. (2011). *Playing the Farmer: Representations of Rural Life in Vergil's* Georgics. Berkeley: University of California Press.

———. (2006). "The Addressee of Vergil's Eighth *Eclogue.*" *Classical Quarterly* 56.2: 618–23.

Thomas, R. F. (1982). *Lands and Peoples in Roman Poetry: The Ethnographical Tradition.* Cambridge: Cambridge Philological Society.

Thompson, D. J. (1984). "Agriculture." In *Cambridge Ancient History,* 2nd ed., Vol. 7, Part 1. Ed. by F. W. Walbank, A. E. Astin, M. W. Frederiksen, and R. M. Ogilvie. Pp. 363–70. Cambridge: Cambridge University Press.

Thompson, J. (1988). "Pastoralism and Transhumance in Roman Italy." In *Pastoral Economies in Classical Antiquity.* Ed. by C. R. Whittaker. Pp. 213–15. Cambridge: Cambridge Philological Society.

Timmerman, D. M., and E. Schiappa. (2010). *Classical Greek Rhetorical Theory and the Disciplining of Discourse.* Cambridge: Cambridge University Press.

Toll, K. (1991). "The *Aeneid* as an Epic of National Identity: *Italiam laeto socii clamore salutant.*" *Helios* 18: 3–14.

———. (1997). "Making Roman-ness and the *Aeneid.*" *Classical Antiquity* 16.1: 34–56.

Toynbee, A. J. (1965). *Hannibal's Legacy: The Hannibalic War's Effects on Roman Life.* London: Oxford University Press.

Tuan, Y. (1977). *Space and Place: The Perspective of Experience.* Minneapolis: University of Minnesota Press.

van Buren, A. W., and R. M. Kennedy. (1919). "Varro's Aviary at Casinum." *Journal of Roman Studies* 9: 59–66.

Van Nuffelen, P. (2010). "Varro's Divine Antiquities: Roman Religion as an Image of Truth." *Classical Philology* 105.2: 162–88.

Van Ooteghem, J. (1966). "La Villa Publica de Rome." *Les Études Classiques* 34: 340–45.

———. (1954). *Pompee le Grand: Batisseur d'Empire.* Brussel: Paleis der Academien.

Van Sickle, J. (2010). *Virgil's Book of Bucolics, the Ten Eclogues Translated into English Verse.* Baltimore: The Johns Hopkins University Press.

Vasaly, A. (1993). *Representations: Images of the World in Ciceronian Oratory.* Berkeley: University of California Press.

Vlastos, G. (1991). *Socrates, Ironist and Moral Philosopher.* Ithaca, NY: Cornell University Press.

Vogt, K. M. (2008). *Law, Reason, and the Cosmic City.* Oxford: Oxford University Press.

Volk, K. (2008). *Vergil's Eclogues*. Oxford: Oxford University Press.

Von Albrecht, M. (1997). *A History of Roman Literature: From Livius Andronicus to Boethius*. New York: Brill.

———. (1989). *Masters of Roman Prose from Cato to Apuleius: Interpretative Studies*. Leeds: Cairns Publications.

Wallace-Hadrill, A. (2008). *Rome's Cultural Revolution*. Cambridge: Cambridge University Press.

———. (2005). "*Mutatas formas*: The Augustan Transformation of Roman Knowledge." In *The Cambridge Companion to the Age of Augustus*. Ed. by K. Galinsky. Pp. 55–84. Cambridge: Cambridge University Press.

———. (1997). "*Mutatio Morum*: The Idea of a Cultural Revolution." In *The Roman Cultural Revolution*. Ed. by T. N. Habinek and A. Schiesaro. Pp. 3–22. Cambridge: Cambridge University Press.

Watson, A. (1995). *The Spirit of Roman Law*. Athens: University of Georgia Press.

White, K. D. (1973). "Roman Agricultural Writers I: Varro and his Predecessors." *Aufstieg und Niedergang der römischen Welt: Geschichte und Kultur Roms im Spiegel der neueren Forschung* 1.4: 439–97.

———. (1970). *Roman Farming*. Ithaca, NY: Cornell University Press.

Whittaker, C. R. (1988). *Pastoral Economies in Classical Antiquity*. Cambridge: Cambridge Philological Society.

Williams, G. (1980). *Figures of Thought in Roman Poetry*. New Haven, CT: Yale University Press.

———. (1968). *Tradition and Originality in Roman Poetry*. Oxford: Oxford University Press.

Williamson, C. (2005). *The Laws of the Roman People: Public Law in the Expansion and Decline of the Roman Republic*. Ann Arbor: University of Michigan Press.

———. (1990). "The Roman Aristocracy and Positive Law." *Classical Philology* 85: 267–76.

Wiseman, T. P. (2009). *Remembering the Roman People: Essays on Late-Republican Politics and Literature*. Oxford: Oxford University Press.

———. (1994). "The Senate and the *populares*, 69–60 BC." In *Cambridge Ancient History*. 2nd Ed. Vol. 9. Ed. by J. A. Crook, A. Lintott, and E. Rawson. Pp. 327–66. Cambridge: Cambridge University Press.

———. (1974). *Cinna the Poet, and Other Roman Essays*. Leicester: Leicester University Press.

———. (1971). *New Men in the Roman Senate, 139 BC–AD 14*. Oxford: Oxford University Press.

Woodman, A. J. (1988). *Rhetoric in Classical Historiography: Four Studies*. London: Croom Helm.

Yavetz, Z. (1990). "The Personality of Augustus: Reflections on Syme's *Roman Revolution*." In *Between Republic and Empire: Interpretations of Augustus and His Principate*. Ed. by K. A. Raaflaub and M. Tohar. Pp. 21–41. Berkeley: University of California Press.

———. (1984). "The *Res Gestae* and Augustus' Public Image." In *Caesar Augustus: Seven Aspects*. Ed. by F. Millar and E. Segal. Pp. 1–36. Oxford: Clarendon Press.

———. (1963). "The Failure of Catiline's Conspiracy." *Historia* 12: 485–99.

Zanker, P. (1988). *The Power of Images in the Age of Augustus.* Ann Arbor: The University of Michigan Press.

Zarecki, J. (2014). *Cicero's Ideal Statesman in Theory and Practice.* London: Bloomsbury.

Zetzel, J. E. G. (1999). *Cicero. On the Commonwealth and On the Laws.* Cambridge: Cambridge University Press.

———. (1995). *Cicero: De Re Publica.* Cambridge: Cambridge University Press.

———. (1972). "Cicero and the Scipionic Circle." *Harvard Studies in Classical Philology* 76: 173–80.

Ziolkowski, A. (1992). *The Temples of Mid-Republican Rome and Their Historical and Topographical Context.* Roma: "L'Erma" di Bretschneider.

# INDEX LOCORUM

Made in the USA
Monee, IL
02 August 2022